Muslims! the Holy Bible is Telling us the Truth; Not the quran!

Introduction

I want to say to muslims and EVERYONE, I LOVE YOU WITH ALL MY HEART, I really want you ALL to be saved and to go to HEAVEN. I write this saying, I LOVE YOU muslims, but I absolutely detest your cult. Anything that gets you to imagine you are so much better than other people, that you want to hate them and murder them is of the devil. I hate the lies of the devil, islam is one of the worst of them. We cannot be afraid to tell the Truth, because the Truth sets and keep us free! If we cannot speak critically of worldviews that have caused slavery, oppression, death and destruction, like islam, (not just in the past but before our eyes even today) then we all are already enslaved by the evil devil. We are no longer a free nation of free people.

This is my conclusion after researching the history, doctrines and practices of islam and after conversing with muslims online over this past decade. I have left this book mostly as answers to their questions. It seems to me that most muslims do not realize they are deceptively handling the Holy Scriptures but others do it intentionally lying to themselves and the rest of the world. They do not understand the implications for their own souls or they wouldn't do it. I have tried to leave behind here something you can tell anyone from islam. (all liars will be cast into the lake of fire when our Lord Jesus Christ judges their wicked soul – Rev 21:8) Some of my answers are redundant because muslims tend to DENY THE DIVINITY OF THE ONE TRUE GOD, Jesus Christ, and so they look for anyway they can do it REPETIVELY. So, I answered them over the years in writing this book, REPETIVELY. I included them as such to get people to understand the common objections of islam to Christianity. May they find Grace to trust in the Lord Jesus Christ with all their heart and soul, before they take their last breath and find them before the God, they have actively denied their entire life.

I think that allowing muslims into our nations is an act of betrayal to all law-abiding citizens and their children (risking not only our lives in our nations, but for all non-islamic citizens worldwide) and is not allowing muslims to deal with their cult prior to coming into free and law-abiding nations an extremely serious risk. I hope this will educate most people about how dangerous letting this group of people with diametrically opposed positions to our own laws and culture. Muslims tend to migrate into other nations and when their numbers suffice, violence ensues, burning churches, destroying museums, libraries and musical instruments and replacing that civilization with enslaving the people under islam. It is a standard of practice historically with islam. In islamic nations, everyone is required to be a muslim. People don't have any equal rights; it is oppressive and barbaric. Read the book **"I am n"** *by the Voice of Martyrs* for just how barbaric islam really is, it doesn't describe islam just as distant history, it describes islam today.

As long as we buy oil from oil rich OPEC, the Saudi Arabia government, our nation is and all other nations doing so, are enriching islam, countries that ban the Holy Bible and severely persecute people who are not muslims. (oppress, enslave, maltreat and murder) Some might consider these acts of treason; especially when we let muslims invest in or bribe media personalities, politicians, and American businesses to infiltrate and spread the cause of islam. We should have DEMANDED that they leave behind their false god, before we do business with them. Buying into an oppressive regime made the arm of allah that much stronger. We must cease to do business with them or oil rich Saudis are increasingly bribing their way into our society. It's true that for this betrayal we are suffering. Already, there is censorship of free speech among book publishers, media, social media and internet search engines. Loyalty to the dollar, is causing corruption to spread, as loyalty to the One True God, diminishes in our once Christian nations. If they want our business, they need to convert to the same kind of freedom we all champion. The freedom that only the One True God can give us. Freedom to do RIGHTEOUSLY is directly opposed to people who want to do wickedly. And is why departure from Our Lord Jesus Christ, and His Righteous Commandments in the Holy Bible, automatically causes suffering, death and destruction for all people who do so. (Deuteronomy 28, Blessed for listening to and obeying our Eternal Creator, cursed for departing from Him and following the evil devil instead.

The devil deceives people, makes people think they know better than our Eternal Creator, and such deceived persons, controlled by their base desires, end up destroying each other in violence, because the evil devil rules their hearts and minds and makes them evil like unto himself. If you do not know our Eternal Creator, who is the Truth, you are still being deceived by the devil. 1Jn 5:20, Jn 14:6-9, Jn 8:32-36)

What I am witnessing would have me using hydrogen fuel-based motors for all transit and a virtual end on the outrageous dependency on fossil fuels. At least until the Saudis formerly renounced their evil allah, and his gang of organized criminals of islam. Any islamic nation banning the Holy Bible is showing that they are under the influence of the spirit of antichrist, the devil. I would feel much better about doing business with any other nations, as long as they had the freedom to let their people study the Words of Almighty God in the Holy Bible; as He commands all of us to do. Especially if those nations made their Peace with God, by openly acknowledging our Lord Jesus Christ as the Lord of All that He is, so that we all could live together peacefully. Acts 4:12, Acts 10:34-43

The construction of the ground zero mosque could be perceived as acquiescence to islam! It was an insult to every American that gave their lives and a code of submission to the demonic cult of islam. It should have NEVER been allowed to be constructed. I don't know who gave into the cult of islam, but it certainly wasn't with my permission! As far as I can tell our American Christian Heritage is under attack and it's due to the corruption of our leaders and people of influence in our nation. Many of those in power want to corrupt our nation so they can they do whatever they want to, sexually. Yes, I know the conspiracies theories of 911 and how it had to have been an inside job; false flag operation, but that doesn't change the fact that the islamic world CHEERED over the deaths of Americans. The last time Christian nations faced islam was during the dark ages and it took brave crusaders to repel the islamic invaders. Back then, muslims had raped and murdered their way all up into Europe and so crusaders had to repel them back into the middle east; our nations would have never been the same had they fallen to islam. In my own opinion, every nation of Western Christendom that has allowed islamic immigration is committing treason and is endangering all law-abiding citizens in our nations as a result. The two worldviews are the antithesis of each other. Under islam: NO FREEDOM; under Western Christendom: FREEDOM! The two do not belong together. I hope this book settles that account.

It takes LOVE to tell someone they're wrong about the things that matter most! I am loving muslims by telling them their cult is not anything trustworthy or commendable. Mankind must love them all enough not to rationalize their cult within the framework of extremism! Trying to legitimize what is inherently illegitimate; trying to legalize what is inherently unlawful. The entire cult of islam is not anything that can be practiced under lawful nations because it has the propensity to defend their cult through violence and terrorism, that the quran endorses. It is essential to recognize islam is a violent criminal organization in doctrine and practice! It cannot be allowed under any LAWFUL society! Patronizing muslims with the acceptable notion that it is lawful to practice has only enabled the violent terrorist organizations to continue to proliferate around the world, burning men, women and children alive in churches, beheading innocent people, or otherwise reducing any non-muslims to oppressed, second class citizens; in persecutions and maltreatment that are in fact, crimes against humanity. IT IS PAST TIME THAT THE ILLEGAL ORGANIZATION OF islam WAS DECLARED UNIVERSALLY AS SUCH BY THE REST OF THE WORLD! And it's past time to universally deprogram them from their cult. Whenever ANY muslim wishes to immigrate into our lawful nations of Western Christendom, THEY MUST RENOUNCE the cult of islam PERPETUALLY, because the dogmas, doctrines and practices of islam are inherently criminal, and violently so. Otherwise, leave all muslims in their evil islamic nations and stop buying anything from them. Muslims will see soon enough that the One True God does not favor them by how much they starve! We must tell muslims to stop worshipping their false god, allah, which is just another name of satanil, the father of all lies. This book exposes that islam is founded on lies; the devil is the father of lies (Jn 8:43-45) and so islam is demonic.

Most of this book is in question-and-answer format to show muslims how their cult of islam has universally brainwashed them to the point where they are denying obvious answers. When it is SO FULL of LIES it is DEFINITELY FROM THE DEVIL! And is why the many hundreds of non-abrogated verses on violence fills the more thoroughly brainwashed among them.

https://www.thereligionofpeace.com/pages/quran/violence.aspx These many non-abrogated verses of violence MEANS THAT islam is a criminal organization in doctrine and practice. And is why islam has had non-stop battles with other people ever since it was founded. It cannot be practiced anywhere because murder is not allowed, and islam teaches muslims to murder!

When we take the life of Jesus Christ and try to portray it on the screen, it is something so Good that even little kids can watch it, up until they took the Most Innocent and Holy and then Crucified Him. But if we were to take the real muhammad based on islamic trusted sources in the quran, hadiths, and other historic sources and put it into film, it would be a horror film of violent brutality, sexual immorality, pedophilia, slavery and robbery that would be almost too terrible to watch at any age. The truth is that islam was founded by criminals and it remains a criminal organization to this day.

http://www.annaqed.com/en/muslims-under-themicroscope/muhammad-and-his-crimes-against-humanity

QUOTE FROM THERELIGIONOFPEACE.COM - "

Quran

Quran (2:244) - "*Then fight in the cause of Allah, and know that Allah Heareth and knoweth all things.*" (See also: Response to Apologists)

Quran (2:216) - "**Fighting is prescribed for you**, *and ye dislike it. But it is possible that ye dislike a thing which is good for you, and that ye love a thing which is bad for you. But Allah knoweth, and ye know not.*" Not only does this verse establish that violence can be virtuous, but it also contradicts the myth that fighting is intended only in self-defense, since the audience was obviously not under attack at the time. From the Hadith, we know that this verse was narrated at a time that Muhammad was actually trying to motivate his people into raiding merchant caravans for loot. (See also: Response to Apologists)

Quran (3:56) - "*As to those who reject faith, I will punish them with terrible agony in this world and in the Hereafter, nor will they have anyone to help.*" (See also: Response to Apologists)

Quran (3:151) - *"Soon shall We cast terror into the hearts of the Unbelievers, for that they joined companions with Allah, for which He had sent no authority"*. This speaks directly of polytheists, yet it also includes Christians, since they believe in the Trinity (ie. what Muhammad incorrectly believed to be 'joining companions to Allah'). (See also: Response to Apologists)

Quran (4:74) - *"Let those fight in the way of Allah who sell the life of this world for the other. Whoso fighteth in the way of Allah, be he slain or be he victorious, on him We shall bestow a vast reward."* The martyrs of Islam are unlike the early Christians, who were led meekly to the slaughter. These Muslims are killed in battle as they attempt to inflict death and destruction for the cause of Allah. This is the theological basis for today's suicide bombers. (See also: Response to Apologists)

Quran (4:76) - *"Those who believe fight in the cause of Allah, and those who disbelieve, fight in the cause of Taghut (Satan, etc.). So fight you against the friends of Shaitan (Satan)"* The Arabic for the word "fight" is from *qital*, meaning physical combat.

Quran (4:89) - *"They but wish that ye should reject Faith, as they do, and thus be on the same footing (as they): But take not friends from their ranks until they flee in the way of Allah (From what is forbidden). But if they turn renegades, seize them and slay them wherever ye find them; and (in any case) take no friends or helpers from their ranks."* (See also: Response to Apologists)

Quran (4:95) - *"Not equal are those of the believers who sit (at home), except those who are disabled (by injury or are blind or lame, etc.), and those who strive hard and fight in the Cause of Allah with their wealth and their lives. Allah has preferred in grades those who strive hard and fight with their wealth and their lives above those who sit (at home).Unto each, Allah has promised good (Paradise), but Allah has preferred those who strive hard and fight, above those who sit (at home) by a huge reward "* This passage criticizes "peaceful" Muslims who do not join in the violence, letting them know that they are less worthy in Allah's eyes. It also demolishes the modern myth that "Jihad" doesn't mean holy war in the Quran, but rather a spiritual struggle. Not only is this Arabic word (mujahiduna) used in this passage, but it is clearly *not* referring to anything spiritual, since the physically disabled are given exemption. (The Hadith reveals the context of the passage to be in response to a blind man's protest that he is unable to engage in Jihad, which would not make sense if it meant an internal struggle). (See also: Response to Apologists)

Quran (4:101) - *"And when you (Muslims) travel in the land, there is no sin on you if you shorten your Salat (prayer) if you fear that the disbelievers may attack you, verily, **the disbelievers are ever unto you open enemies.**"* Mere disbelief makes one an "open" enemy of Muslims.

Quran (4:104) - *"And be not weak hearted in pursuit of the enemy; if you suffer pain, then surely they (too) suffer pain as you suffer pain..."* Is pursuing an injured and retreating enemy really an act of self-defense? (See also: Response to Apologists)

Quran (5:33) - *"The punishment of those who wage war against Allah and His messenger and strive to make mischief in the land is only this, that they should be murdered or crucified or their hands and their feet should be cut off on opposite sides or they should be imprisoned; this shall be as a disgrace for them in this world, and in the hereafter they shall have a grievous chastisement"* (See also: Response to Apologists)

Quran (8:12) - *"(Remember) when your Lord inspired the angels... "I will cast terror into the hearts of those who disbelieve. Therefore strike off their heads and strike off every fingertip of them"* No reasonable person would interpret this to mean a spiritual struggle, given that it both followed and preceded confrontations in which non-Muslims were killed by Muslims. The targets of violence are "*those who disbelieve*" - further defined in the next verse (13) as those who "*defy and disobey Allah.*" Nothing is said about self-defense. In fact, the verses in sura 8 were narrated shortly after a battle provoked by Muhammad, who had been trying to attack a lightly-armed caravan to steal goods belonging to other people. (See also: Response to Apologists)

Quran (8:15) - *"O ye who believe! When ye meet those who disbelieve in battle, turn not your backs to them. (16)Whoso on that day turneth his back to them, unless maneuvering for battle or intent to join a company, he truly hath incurred wrath from Allah, and his habitation will be hell, a hapless journey's end."*

Quran (8:39) - *"And fight with them until there is no more fitna (disorder, unbelief) and religion is all for Allah"* Some translations interpret "fitna" as "persecution", but the traditional understanding of this word is not supported by the historical context (See notes for 2:193). The Meccans were simply refusing Muhammad access to their city during the pilgrimage. Other Muslims were allowed to travel there - but not as an armed group, since Muhammad had declared war on Mecca prior to his eviction. The Meccans were also acting in defense of their religion, as it was Muhammad's intention to destroy their idols and establish Islam by force (which he later did). Hence the critical part of this verse is to fight until *"religion is only for Allah"*, meaning that the true justification of violence was the unbelief of the opposition. According to the Sira (Ibn Ishaq/Hisham 324) Muhammad further explains that *"Allah must have no rivals."* (See also: Response to Apologists)

Quran (8:57) - *"If thou comest on them in the war, deal with them so as to strike fear in those who are behind them, that haply they may remember."*

Quran (8:67) - *"It is not for a Prophet that he should have prisoners of war until he had made a great slaughter in the land..."*

Quran (8:59-60) - *"And let not those who disbelieve suppose that they can outstrip (Allah's Purpose). Lo! they cannot escape. Make ready for them all thou canst of (armed) force and of horses tethered, that thereby ye may dismay the enemy of Allah and your enemy."* As Ibn Kathir puts it in his tafsir on this passage, "Allah commands Muslims to prepare for war against disbelievers, as much as possible, according to affordability and availability." (See also: Response to Apologists)

Quran (8:65) - *"O Prophet, exhort the believers to fight..."*

Quran (9:5) - *"So when the sacred months have passed away, then slay the idolaters wherever you find them, and take them captive and besiege them and lie in wait for them in every ambush, then if they repent and keep up prayer and pay the poor-rate, leave their way free to them."* According to this verse, the best way of staying safe from Muslim violence at the time of Muhammad was to convert to Islam: prayer (*salat*) and the poor tax (*zakat*) are among the religion's Five Pillars. The popular claim that the Quran only inspires violence within the context of self-defense is seriously challenged by this passage as well, since the Muslims to whom it was written were obviously not under attack. Had they been, then there would have been no waiting period (earlier verses make it a duty for Muslims to fight in self-defense, even during the sacred months). The historical context is Mecca *after* the idolaters were subjugated by Muhammad and posed no threat. Once the Muslims had power, they violently evicted those unbelievers who would not convert. (See also: Response to Apologists)

[Note: The verse says to fight unbelievers "*wherever you find them*". Even if the context is a time of battle (which it was not) the reading appears to sanction attacks against those "unbelievers" who are not on the battlefield. In 2016, the Islamic State referred to this verse in urging the faithful to commit terror attacks: *Allah did not only command the 'fighting' of disbelievers, as if to say He only wants us to conduct frontline operations against them. Rather, He has also ordered that they be slain wherever they may be – on or off the battlefield.* (source)]

Quran (9:14) - "*Fight against them so that Allah will punish them by your hands and disgrace them and give you victory over them and heal the breasts of a believing people.*" Humiliating and hurting non-believers not only has the blessing of Allah, but it is ordered as a means of carrying out his punishment and even "heals" the hearts of Muslims.

Quran (9:20) - "*Those who believe, and have left their homes and striven with their wealth and their lives in Allah's way are of much greater worth in Allah's sight. These are they who are triumphant.*" The Arabic word interpreted as "striving" in this verse is the same root as "Jihad". The context is obviously holy war.

Quran (9:29) - "*Fight those who believe not in Allah nor the Last Day, nor hold that forbidden which hath been forbidden by Allah and His Messenger, nor acknowledge the religion of Truth, (even if they are) of the People of the Book, until they pay the Jizya with willing submission, and feel themselves subdued.*" "People of the Book" refers to Christians and Jews. According to this verse, they are to be violently subjugated, with the sole justification being their religious status. Verse 9:33 tells Muslims that Allah has instructed them to make Islam "superior over all religions." This chapter was one of the final "revelations" from Allah and it set in motion the tenacious military expansion, in which Muhammad's companions managed to conquer two-thirds of the Christian world in the next 100 years. Islam is intended to dominate all other people and faiths. (See also: Response to Apologists)

Quran (9:30) - *"And the Jews say: Ezra is the son of Allah; and the Christians say: The Messiah is the son of Allah; these are the words of their mouths; they imitate the saying of those who disbelieved before; may Allah destroy them; how they are turned away!"* (See also: Response to Apologists)

Quran (9:38-39) - *"O ye who believe! what is the matter with you, that, when ye are asked to go forth in the cause of Allah, ye cling heavily to the earth? Do ye prefer the life of this world to the Hereafter? But little is the comfort of this life, as compared with the Hereafter. Unless ye go forth, He will punish you with a grievous penalty, and put others in your place."* This is a warning to those who refuse to fight, that they will be punished with Hell. The verse also links physical fighting to the "cause of Allah" (or "way of Allah"). (See also: Response to Apologists)

Quran (9:41) - *"Go forth, light or heavy* (some translations read "armed") *and strive with your wealth and your lives in the way of Allah! That is best for you if ye but knew."* See also the verse that follows (9:42) - *"If there had been immediate gain (in sight), and the journey easy, they would (all) without doubt have followed thee, but the distance was long, (and weighed) on them"* This contradicts the myth that Muslims are to fight only in self-defense, since the wording implies that battle will be waged a long distance from home (in another country and - in this case - on Christian soil, according to the historians). (See also: Response to Apologists)

Quran (9:73) - *"O Prophet! strive hard against the unbelievers and the hypocrites and be unyielding to them; and their abode is hell, and evil is the destination."* Dehumanizing those who reject Islam, by reminding Muslims that unbelievers are merely firewood for Hell, makes it easier to justify slaughter. It explains why today's devout Muslims generally have little regard for those outside the faith. The inclusion of "hypocrites" (non-practicing) within the verse also contradicts the apologist's defense that the targets of hate and hostility are wartime foes, since there was never an opposing army made up of non-religious Muslims in Muhammad's time. (See also Games Muslims Play: Terrorists Can't Be Muslim Because They

Kill Muslims for the role this verse plays in Islam's perpetual internal conflicts). (See also: Response to Apologists)

Quran (9:88) - *"But the Messenger, and those who believe with him, strive and fight with their wealth and their persons: for them are (all) good things: and it is they who will prosper."* (See also: Response to Apologists)

Quran (9:111) - *"Allah hath purchased of the* believers *their persons and their goods; for theirs (in return) is the garden (of Paradise): they* fight in His cause, and slay and are slain*: a promise binding on Him in truth, through the Law, the Gospel, and the Quran: and who is more faithful to his covenant than Allah? then rejoice in the bargain which ye have concluded: that is the achievement supreme."* How does the Quran define a true believer? (See also: Response to Apologists)

Quran (9:123) - *"O you who believe! fight those of the unbelievers who are near to you and let them find in you hardness."* (See also: Response to Apologists)

Quran (17:16) - *"And when We wish to destroy a town, We send Our commandment to the people of it who lead easy lives, but they transgress therein; thus the word proves true against it, so We destroy it with utter destruction."* Note that the crime is moral transgression, and the punishment is "utter destruction." (Before ordering the 9/11 attacks, Osama bin Laden first issued Americans an invitation to Islam).

Quran (18:65-81) - This parable lays the theological groundwork for honor killings, in which a family member is murdered because they brought shame to the family, either through apostasy or perceived moral indiscretion. The story (which is not found in any Jewish or Christian source) tells of Moses encountering a man with "special knowledge" who does things which don't seem to make sense on the surface, but are then justified according to later explanation. One such action is to murder a youth for no apparent reason (v.74). However, the wise man later explains that it was feared that the boy would "grieve" his parents by "disobedience and ingratitude." He was killed so that Allah could provide them a 'better' son. [Note: This parable along with verse 58:22 is a major reason that honor killing is sanctioned by Sharia. Reliance of the Traveler (Umdat al-Saliq) says that punishment for murder is not applicable when a parent or grandparent kills their offspring (o.1.12).] (See also: Response to

Apologists)

Quran (21:44) - "...See they not that We gradually reduce the land (in their control) from its outlying borders? Is it then they who will win?"

Quran (25:52) - "Therefore listen not to the Unbelievers, but strive against them with the utmost strenuousness with it." - The root for Jihad is used twice in this verse - although it may not have been referring to Holy War when narrated, since it was prior to the hijra at Mecca. The "it" at the end is thought to mean the Quran. Thus the verse may have originally meant a non-violent resistance to the 'unbelievers.' Obviously, this changed with the hijra. 'Jihad' after this is almost exclusively within a violent context. The enemy is always defined as people, rather than ideas.

Quran (33:60-62) - "If the hypocrites, and those in whose hearts is a disease (evil desire for adultery, etc.), and those who spread false news among the people in Al-Madinah, cease not, We shall certainly let you overpower them, then they will not be able to stay in it as your neighbors but a little while Accursed, wherever found, they shall be seized and killed with a (terrible) slaughter." This passage sanctions slaughter (rendered as "merciless" and "horrible murder" in other translations) against three groups: hypocrites (Muslims who refuse to "fight in the way of Allah" (3:167) and hence don't act as Muslims should), those with "diseased hearts" (which include Jews and Christians 5:51-52), and "alarmists" or "agitators - those who speak out against Islam. It is worth noting that the victims are to be *sought out,* which is what today's terrorists do.

Quran (47:3-4) - "Those who disbelieve follow falsehood, while those who believe follow the truth from their Lord... So, when you meet (fighting Jihad in Allah's Cause), those who disbelieve smite at their necks till when you have killed and wounded many of them, then bind a bond firmly (on them, i.e. take them as captives)... If it had been Allah's Will, He Himself could certainly have punished them (without you). But (He lets you fight), in order to test you, some with others. But those who are killed in the Way of Allah, He will never let their deeds be lost." Holy war is to be pursued against those who reject Allah. The unbelievers are to be killed and wounded. Survivors are to be held captive for ransom. The only reason Allah doesn't do the dirty work himself is to to test the faithfulness of Muslims. Those who kill pass the test. (See also: 47:4 for more context) (See also: Response to Apologists)

Quran (47:35) - *"Be not weary and faint-hearted, crying for peace, when ye should be uppermost* (Shakir: "have the upper hand") *for Allah is with you,"* (See also: Response to Apologists)

Quran (48:17) - *"There is no blame for the blind, nor is there blame for the lame, nor is there blame for the sick (that they go not forth to war). And whoso obeyeth Allah and His messenger, He will make him enter Gardens underneath which rivers flow; and whoso turneth back, him will He punish with a painful doom."* Contemporary apologists sometimes claim that Jihad means 'spiritual struggle.' If so, then why are the blind, lame and sick exempted? This verse also says that those who do not fight will suffer torment in hell.

Quran (48:29) - *"Muhammad is the messenger of Allah. And those with him are hard (ruthless) against the disbelievers and merciful among themselves"* Islam is **not** about treating everyone equally. This verse tells Muslims that two very distinct standards are applied based on religious status. Also the word used for 'hard' or 'ruthless' in this verse shares the same root as the word translated as 'painful' or severe' to describe Hell in over 25 other verses including 65:10, 40:46 and 50:26..

Quran (61:4) - *"Surely Allah loves those who fight in His cause"* Religion of Peace, indeed! The verse explicitly refers to "rows" or "battle array," meaning that it is speaking of physical conflict. This is followed by (61:9), which defines the "cause": *"He it is who has sent His Messenger (Mohammed) with guidance and the religion of truth (Islam) to make it* **victorious over all religions even though the infidels may resist.***"* (See next verse, below). Infidels who resist Islamic rule are to be fought. (See also: Response to Apologists)

Quran (61:10-12) - *"O You who believe! Shall I guide you to a commerce that will save you from a painful torment. That you believe in Allah and His Messenger (Muhammad), and that you strive hard and fight in the Cause of Allah with your wealth and your lives, that will be better for you, if you but know! (If you do so) He will forgive you your sins, and admit you into Gardens under which rivers flow, and pleasant dwelling in Gardens of 'Adn-Eternity ['Adn(Edn) Paradise], that is indeed the great success."* This verse refers to physical battle waged to make Islam victorious over other religions (see verse 9). It uses the Arabic root for the word Jihad.

Quran (66:9) - *"O Prophet! Strive against the disbelievers and the hypocrites, and be stern with them. Hell will be their home, a hapless journey's end."* The root word of "Jihad" is used again here. The context is clearly holy war, and the scope of violence is broadened to include "hypocrites" - those who call themselves Muslims but do not act as such. (See also: Response to Apologists)

Quran (2:191-193) - *"And kill them wherever you find them, and turn them out from where they have turned you out. And Al-Fitnah* [disbelief or unrest] *is worse than killing... but if they desist, then lo! Allah is forgiving and merciful. And fight them until there is no more Fitnah* [disbelief and worshipping of others along with Allah] *and worship is for Allah alone. But if they cease, let there be no transgression except against Az-Zalimun(the polytheists, and wrong-doers, etc.)"* (Translation is from the Noble Quran) The verse prior to this (190) refers to *"fighting for the cause of Allah those who fight you"* leading some to claim that the entire passage refers to a defensive war in which Muslims are defending their homes and families. The historical context of this passage is **not** defensive warfare, however, since Muhammad and his Muslims had just relocated to Medina and were *not* under attack by their Meccan adversaries. In fact, the verses urge *offensive* warfare, in that Muslims are to drive Meccans out of their own city (which they later did). Verse 190 thus means to fight those who offer resistance to Allah's rule (ie. Muslim conquest). The use of the word "persecution" by some Muslim translators is disingenuous - the actual Arabic words for persecution (*idtihad*) - and oppression are not used instead of *fitna*. Fitna can mean disbelief, or the disorder that results from unbelief or temptation. A strict translation is 'sedition,' meaning rebellion against authority (the authority being Allah). This is certainly what is meant in this context since the violence is explicitly commissioned *"until religion is for Allah"* - ie. unbelievers desist in their unbelief. [Editor's note: these notes have been modified slightly after a critic misinterpreted our language. Verse 193 plainly says that 'fighting' is sanctioned even if the *fitna* 'ceases'. This is about religious order, not real persecution.] (See also: Response to Apologists)

Other verses calling Muslims to Jihad can be found here at AnsweringIslam.org

Hadith and Sira

Sahih Bukhari (52:177) - *Allah's Apostle said, "The Hour will not be established until you fight with the Jews, and the stone behind which a Jew will be hiding will say. "O Muslim! There is a Jew hiding behind me, so kill him."*

Sahih Bukhari (52:256) - *The Prophet... was asked whether it was permissible to attack the pagan warriors at night with the probability of exposing their women and children to danger. The Prophet replied, "They (i.e. women and children) are from them (i.e. pagans)."* In this command, Muhammad establishes that it is permissible to kill non-combatants in the process of killing a perceived enemy. This provides justification for the many Islamic terror bombings.

Sahih Bukhari (52:65) - *The Prophet said, 'He who fights that Allah's Word (Islam) should be superior, fights in Allah's Cause.* Muhammad's words are the basis for offensive Jihad - spreading Islam by force. This is how it was understood by his companions, and by the terrorists of today. (See also Sahih Bukhari 3:125)

Sahih Bukhari (52:220) - *Allah's Apostle said... 'I have been made victorious with terror'*

Sahih Bukhari (52:44) - *A man came to Allah's Apostle and said, "Instruct me as to such a deed as equals Jihad (in reward)." He replied, "I do not find such a deed."*

Abu Dawud (14:2526) (considered daif) - *The Prophet said, Three things are the roots of faith: to refrain from (killing) a person who utters, "There is no god but Allah" and not to declare him unbeliever whatever sin he commits, and not to excommunicate him from Islam for his any action; and jihad will be performed continuously since the day Allah sent me as a prophet...*

Abu Dawud (14:2527) (considered daif) - *The Prophet said: Striving in the path of Allah (jihad) is incumbent on you along with every ruler, whether he is pious or impious*

Sahih Muslim (1:33) - *the Messenger of Allah said: I have been commanded to fight against people till they testify that there is no god but Allah, that Muhammad is the messenger of Allah*

Sahih Bukhari (8:387) - *Allah's Apostle said, "I have been ordered to fight the people till they say: 'None has the right to be worshipped but Allah'. And if they say so, pray like our prayers, face our Qibla and slaughter as we slaughter, then their blood and property will be sacred to us and we will not interfere with them except legally."*

Sahih Muslim (1:30) - *"The Messenger of Allah said: I have been commanded to fight against people so long as they do not declare that there is no god but Allah."*

Sahih Bukhari (52:73) - *"Allah's Apostle said, 'Know that Paradise is under the shades of swords'."*

Sahih Bukhari (11:626) - *[Muhammad said:] "I decided to order a man to lead the prayer and then take a flame to burn all those, who had not left their houses for the prayer, burning them alive inside their homes."*

Sahih Muslim (1:149) - *"Abu Dharr reported: I said: Messenger of Allah, which of the deeds is the best? He (the Holy Prophet) replied: Belief in Allah and Jihad in His cause..."*

Sahih Muslim (20:4645) - *"...He (the Messenger of Allah) did that and said: There is another act which elevates the position of a man in Paradise to a grade one hundred (higher), and the elevation between one grade and the other is equal to the height of the heaven from the earth. He (Abu Sa'id) said: What is that act? He replied: Jihad in the way of Allah! Jihad in the way of Allah!"*

Sahih Muslim (20:4696) - *"the Messenger of Allah (may peace be upon him) said: 'One who died but did not fight in the way of Allah nor did he express any desire (or determination) for Jihad died the death of a hypocrite.'"*

Sahih Muslim (19:4321-4323) - Three hadith verses in which Muhammad shrugs over the news that innocent children were killed in a raid by his men against unbelievers. His response: "*They are of them* (meaning the enemy)."

Sahih Muslim (19:4294) - "*Fight against those who disbelieve in Allah. Make a holy war... When you meet your enemies who are polytheists, invite them to three courses of action. If they respond to any one of these, you also accept it and withhold yourself from doing them any harm. Invite them to (accept) Islam; if they respond to you, accept it from them and desist from fighting against them... If they refuse to accept Islam, demand from them the Jizya. If they agree to pay, accept it from them and hold off your hands. If they refuse to pay the tax, seek Allah's help and fight them.*"

Sahih Muslim (31:5917) - "*Ali went a bit and then halted and did not look about and then said in a loud voice: 'Allah's Messenger, on what issue should I fight with the people?' Thereupon he (the Prophet) said: 'Fight with them until they bear testimony to the fact that there is no god but Allah and Muhammad is his Messenger'.*" The pretext for attacking the peaceful farming community of Khaybar was not obvious to the Muslims. Muhammad's son-in-law Ali asked the prophet of Islam to clarify the reason for their mission to kill, loot and enslave. Muhammad's reply was straightforward. The people should be fought because they are not Muslim.

Sahih Muslim (31:5918) - "*I will fight them until they are like us.*" Ali's reply to Muhammad, after receiving clarification that the pretext for attacking Khaybar was to convert the people (see above verse).

Sahih Bukhari 2:35 "*The person who participates in (Holy Battles) in Allah's cause and nothing compels him do so except belief in Allah and His Apostle, will be recompensed by Allah either with a reward, or booty (if he survives) or will be admitted to Paradise (if he is killed).*"

Sunan an-Nasa'i (Sahih) "*Whoever dies without having fought or thought of fighting, he dies on one of the branches of hypocrisy*"

Sunan Ibn Majah 24:2794 (Sahih) - "*I came to the Prophet and said: 'O Messenger of Allah, which Jihad is best?' He said: '(That of a man) whose blood is shed and his horse is wounded.'*" Unlike the oft-quoted "Greater/Lesser" verse pertaining to Jihad, this is judged to be authentic, and clearly establishes that the 'best' Jihad involves physical violence.

Tabari 7:97 *The morning after the murder of Ashraf, the Prophet declared, "Kill any Jew who falls under your power."* Ashraf was a poet, killed by Muhammad's men because he insulted Islam. Here, Muhammad widens the scope of his orders to kill. An innocent Jewish businessman was then slain by his Muslim partner, merely for being non-Muslim.

Tabari 9:69 *"Killing Unbelievers is a small matter to us"* The words of Muhammad, prophet of Islam.

Tabari 17:187 *"'By God, our religion (din) from which we have departed is better and more correct than that which these people follow. Their religion does not stop them from shedding blood, terrifying the roads, and seizing properties.' And they returned to their former religion."* The words of a group of Christians who had converted to Islam, but realized their error after being shocked by the violence and looting committed in the name of Allah. The price of their decision to return to a religion of peace was that the men were beheaded and the woman and children enslaved by the caliph Ali.

Ibn Ishaq/Hisham 484: - *"Allah said, 'A prophet must slaughter before collecting captives. A slaughtered enemy is driven from the land. Muhammad, you craved the desires of this world, its goods and the ransom captives would bring. But Allah desires killing them to manifest the religion.'"*

Ibn Ishaq/Hisham 990: Cutting off someone's head while shouting 'Allahu Akbar' is not a 'perversion of Islam', but a tradition of Islam that began with Muhammad. In this passage, a companion recounts an episode in which he staged a surprise ambush on a settlement: *"I leapt upon him and cut off his head and ran in the direction of the camp shouting 'Allah akbar' and my two companions did likewise".*

Ibn Ishaq/Hisham 992: - *"Fight everyone in the way of Allah and kill those who disbelieve in Allah."* Muhammad's instructions to his men prior to a military raid.

Ibn Kathir (Commentary on verses 2:190-193 - *Since Jihad involves killing and shedding the blood of men, Allah indicated that these men are committing disbelief in Allah, associating with Him (in the worship) and hindering from His path, and this is a much greater evil and more disastrous than killing.* One of Islam's most respected scholars clearly believed that Jihad means physical warfare.

Saifur Rahman, The Sealed Nectar p.227-228 - *"Embrace Islam... If you two accept Islam, you will remain in command of your country; but if your refuse my Call, you've got to remember that all of your possessions are perishable. My horsemen will appropriate your land, and my Prophethood will assume preponderance over your kingship."* One of several letters from Muhammad to rulers of other countries. The significance is that the recipients were not making war or threatening Muslims. Their subsequent defeat and subjugation by Muhammad's armies was justified merely on the basis of their unbelief.

See also: Classical Islamic Scholars on Jihad from WikiIslam

Notes

Other than the fact that Muslims haven't killed every non-Muslim under their domain, there is very little else that they can point to as proof that theirs is a peaceful, tolerant religion. Where Islam is dominant (as in the Middle East and Pakistan) religious minorities suffer brutal persecution with scant introspection. Where Islam is in the minority (as in Thailand, the Philippines and Europe) there is the threat of violence if Muslim demands are not met. Either situation seems to provide a justification for religious terrorism, which is persistent and endemic to Islamic fundamentalism.

This begins with the Quran. Few verses of Islam's most sacred text can be construed to fit the contemporary virtues of religious tolerance and universal brotherhood. Those that do are earlier "Meccan" verses which are abrogated by later ones. The example of Muhammad is that Islam is a religion of peace when Muslims do not have the power and numbers on their side. Once they do, things change.

Many Muslims are peaceful and do not want to believe what the Quran really says. They prefer a more narrow interpretation that is closer to the Judeo-Christian ethic. Some just ignore harsher passages. Others reach for "textual context" across different suras to subjectively mitigate these verses with others so that the message fits their personal moral preference. Although the Quran itself claims to be clear and complete, these apologists speak of the "risks" of trying to interpret verses without their "assistance."

The violent verses of the Quran have played a key role in massacre and genocide. This includes the brutal slaughter of tens of millions of Hindus for five centuries beginning around 1000 AD with Mahmud of Ghazni's bloody conquest. Both he and the later Tamerlane (Islam's Genghis Khan) slaughtered an untold number merely for defending their temples from destruction. Buddhism was nearly wiped off the Indian subcontinent. Judaism and Christianity met the same fate (albeit more slowly) in areas conquered by Muslim armies, including the Middle East, North Africa and parts of Europe, including today's Turkey. Zoroastrianism, the ancient religion of a proud Persian people is despised by Muslims and barely survives in modern Iran.

Violence is so ingrained in Islam that it has never really stopped being at war, either with other religions or with itself.

Muhammad was a military leader, laying siege to towns, massacring the men, raping their women, enslaving their children, and taking the property of others as his own. On several occasions he rejected offers of surrender from the besieged inhabitants and even butchered captives. He inspired his followers to battle when they did not feel it was right to fight, promising them slaves and booty if they did and threatening them with Hell if they did not. Muhammad allowed his men to rape traumatized women captured in battle, usually on the very day their husbands and family members were slaughtered.

The popular apologist argument that many verses of violence apply to war is shaded by the fact that war was started by Muslims, both in Muhammad's time and since. For the most part, Islamic armies waged *aggressive* campaigns, and the religion's most dramatic military conquests were made by actual companions of Muhammad in the decades following his death.

The early Islamic principle of warfare was that the civilian population of a town was to be destroyed (ie. men executed, women and children taken as slaves) if they defended themselves and resisted Islamic hegemony. Although modern apologists claim that Muslims are only supposed to "attack in self-defense", this oxymoron is flatly contradicted by the accounts of Islamic historians and others that go back to the time of Muhammad.

Some modern-day scholars are more candid than others. One of the most respected Sunni theologians is al-Qaradawi, who justifies terror attacks against Western targets by noting that there is no such thing as a civilian population in a time of war:

"It has been determined by Islamic law that the blood and property of people of Dar al-Harb *[ie. non-Muslim people who resist Islamic conquest]* is not protected... In modern war, all of society, with all its classes and ethnic groups, is mobilized to participate in the war, to aid its continuation, and to provide it with the material and human fuel required for it to assure the victory of the state fighting its enemies. Every citizen in society must take upon himself a role in the effort to provide for the battle. The entire domestic front, including professionals, laborers, and industrialists, stands behind the fighting army, even if it does not bear arms."

Sheikh Muhammad Bin Abdul Lateef, a favorite of ISIS, has admitted:

'Jihad is a part of Islam without which Islam cannot be established and without which it is not possible to uphold the laws of sharia'.

Consider the example of the Qurayza Jews, who were completely obliterated only five years after Muhammad arrived in Medina. Their leader opted to stay neutral when their town was besieged by a Meccan army that was sent to take revenge for Muhammad's deadly caravan raids. The tribe killed no one from either side and even surrendered peacefully to Muhammad after the Meccans had been turned back. Yet the prophet of Islam had every male member of the Qurayza beheaded, and every woman and child enslaved, even raping one of the captives himself (what Muslim apologists might refer to as "same day marriage").

One of Islam's most revered modern scholars, Sheikh Yusuf al-Qaradawi, openly sanctions offensive Jihad: *"In the Jihad which you are seeking, you look for the enemy and invade him. This type of Jihad takes place only* when the Islamic state is invading other [countries] **in order to spread the word of Islam** *and to remove obstacles standing in its way."*

Qutb wrote: *"Islam has the right to take the initiative...this is God's religion and it is for the whole world. It has the right to destroy all obstacles in the form of institutions and traditions ... it attacks institutions and traditions to release human beings from their poisonous influences, which distort human nature and curtail human freedom. Those who say that Islamic Jihad was merely for the defense of the 'homeland of Islam' diminish the greatness of the Islamic way of life."*

The widely respected [Dictionary of Islam](#) defines Jihad as *"A religious war with those who are unbelievers in the mission of Muhammad. It is an incumbent religious duty, established in the Quran and in the Traditions as a divine institution, and enjoined specially for the purpose of advancing Islam and of repelling evil from Muslims...[Quoting from the Hanafi school, Hedaya, 2:140, 141.],* **"The destruction of the sword is incurred by infidels, although they be not the first aggressors,** *as appears from various passages in the traditions which are generally received to this effect."*

Dr. Salah al-Sawy, the chief member of the Assembly of Muslim Jurists in America, stated in 2009 that *"the Islamic community does not possess the strength to engage in* offensive jihad at this time," tacitly affirming the legitimacy of violence for the cause of Islamic rule - bound only by the capacity for success. ([source](#))

Muhammad's failure to leave a clear line of succession resulted in perpetual internal war following his death. Those who knew him best first fought afterwards to keep remote tribes from leaving Islam and reverting to their preferred religion (the Ridda or 'Apostasy wars'). Then the violence turned within. Early Meccan converts battled later ones as hostility developed between those immigrants who had traveled with Muhammad to Mecca and the Ansar at Medina who had helped them settle in. Finally there was a violent struggle within Muhammad's own family between his favorite wife and favorite daughter - a jagged schism that has left Shias and Sunnis at each others' throats to this day.

The strangest and most untrue thing that can be said about Islam is that it is a religion of peace. If every standard by which the West is judged and condemned (slavery, imperialism, intolerance, misogyny, sexual repression, warfare...) were applied equally to Islam, the verdict would be devastating. Islam never gives up what it conquers, be it religion, culture, language or life. Neither does it make apologies or any real effort at moral progress. It is the least open to dialogue and the most self-absorbed. It is convinced of its own perfection, yet brutally shuns self-examination and represses criticism.

This is what makes the Quran's verses of violence so dangerous. They are given the weight of divine command. While Muslim terrorists take them literally, and understand that Islam is incomplete without Jihad, moderates offer little to contradict them - outside of personal opinion. Indeed, what do they have? Speaking of peace and love may win over the ignorant, but when every twelfth verse of Islam's holiest book either speaks to Allah's hatred for non-Muslims or calls for their death, forced conversion, or subjugation, it is little wonder that sympathy for terrorism runs as deeply as it does in the broader community - even if most Muslims prefer not to interpret their personal viewpoint of Islam in this way.

Although scholars like Ibn Khaldun, one of Islam's most respected philosophers, understood that *"the holy war is a religious duty, because of the universalism of the Muslim mission and (the obligation to) convert everybody to Islam either by persuasion or by force"*, many other Muslims are either unaware or willfully ignorant of the Quran's near absence of verses that preach universal non-violence. Their understanding of Islam comes from what they are taught by others. Believers in the West are often led to think that their religion is like Christianity - preaching the New Testament virtues of peace, love, and tolerance. They are somewhat surprised and embarrassed to find that the Quran and the bloody history of Islam's genesis say otherwise.

Others simply accept the violence. In 1991, a Palestinian couple in America was convicted of stabbing their daughter to death for being too Westernized. A family friend came to their defense, excoriating the jury for not understanding the "culture", claiming that the father was merely following "the religion" and saying that the couple had to "discipline their daughter or lose respect." (source). In 2011, unrepentant Palestinian terrorists, responsible for the brutal murders of civilians, women and children explicitly in the name of Allah were treated to a luxurious "holy pilgrimage" to Mecca by the Saudi king - without a single Muslim voice raised in protest.

The most prestigious Islamic university in the world today is Cairo's alAzhar. While the university is very quick to condemn secular Muslims who critique the religion, it has never condemned ISIS as a group of infidels despite horrific carnage in the name of Allah. When asked why, the university's Grand Imam, Ahmed al-Tayeb explained: " *Al Azhar cannot accuse any [Muslim] of being a kafir [infidel], as long as he believes in Allah and the Last Day—even if he commits every atrocity.*"

For their part, Western liberals would do well not to sacrifice critical thinking to the god of political correctness, or look for reasons to bring other religion down to the level of Islam merely to avoid the existential truth that it is both different and dangerous.

There are just too many Muslims who take the Quran literally... and too many others who couldn't care less about the violence done in the name of Islam.

See also Cruelty in the Quran from the Skeptic's Annotated Quran"

END QUOTE

And it's not just these verses of violence from the quran, but the quran encourages many other crimes against humanity as you can read in the topical index:
https://www.thereligionofpeace.com/pages/quran/index.aspx

These verses mean islam in doctrine is at non-stop jihad/WAR with the rest of the world! It never ends, it's just a perpetually evil, criminal organization! Which is why islam has founded the greatest number of violent terrorist organizations in the history of the world.
https://www.google.com/search?client=opera&q=list+of+islamic+terrorist+groups&sourceid=opera&ie=UTF-8&oe=UTF-8

Comprehend this about islam, whenever anyone commits murder, they do so IN VIOLATION OF GOD's Commandments in the Holy Bible! THOU SHALT NOT MURDER! but when committing homicide or murder in the name of allah, murder is praiseworthy! allah, of the quran and islam, is in fact another name of the devil!

People, including muslims, NEED TO UNDERSTAND that the HOLY BIBLE is about GOD REVEALING HIMSELF TO MANKIND and our relationship with Him as our ETERNAL CREATOR. It's why people should begin reading the New Testament, because that is when God showed Himself and explained what His Words in the Old Testament meant, so people would stop using them in deceitful ways. He explained that all His Commandments are built upon LOVING HIM AND EACH OTHER, so anyone determining that the scriptures encourage evil of any kind are mistaken. HE ALSO TOLD US HIS MERCY AND FORGIVENESS TRIUMPHS OVER HIS JUDGEMENT/JUSTICE. Which is why Christians have accepted martyrdom, hoping and praying all persons come into forgiveness and peace with God. Now Christians will defend themselves when war is declared upon them, (islam has been at war with the rest of humanity ever since it began) So all Christians worldwide need to pray to God and ask Him to end all the devil's deceptions, and end wickedness in this world permanently, our God is MIGHTY in Battle. Ask Him for Wisdom and Strategies to defend yourselves against this last rise of the antichrist. Our Lord Jesus Christ loves His People, He knows what is best. It's also why the Law of God is tempered by Mercy in Christians nations, only the most heinous offenders can merit the death penalty. Just as the crusaders bravely fought against the raiding muslims during the dark ages. We each have to decide with our own God given conscience how to live a life pleasing to Jesus Christ as we read His Commandments in the scriptures. It would seem that for the most part in this life we are to practice forgiveness even unto death, but God assures us that for all who DO NOT REPENT of their wicked ways, HE TELLS US HE IS DECLARING VENGEANCE, with all the martyred saints, all the persecuted Christians, to come back with HIM and cause such evil persons to cease. So, people everywhere need to REPENT and LEARN TO LIVE RIGHTEOUSLY, BY HIS GRACE AND HIS HOLY SPIRIT. (2Cor 10:6, Isaiah 13:5-7, Isaiah 34:1-2, 2Thes 1:8-9 and many other locations that talk about the Vengeance of the Lord for all who do not REPENT and LEARN to Live Righteously.)

FROM THE VERY FIRST WORDS A MUSLIM IS TAUGHT TO UTTER THEY TELL THE WORLD THEY NEITHER KNOW GOD or even his characteristics, their propensity from knowing Him is curtailed by their outspoken beliefs about him!

Whenever muslims tell the world their god has no children and no partners they are telling the world their god is not the REAL GOD! The Real God, Jesus Christ, created and made a world full of children who all belong to him! (Mt 19:14) And the REAL GOD includes mankind in his Plans and Purposes. So muslims shouldn't do anything their god tells them to do or they are partnering with him by definition! Muslims you are not serving the REAL GOD, Jesus Christ! And your foundational declaration of faith, shows you do not understand even what you are saying and are lying against REALITY before your own eyes.

This book serves in part to answer them redundantly about anything I've ever heard one of them try to ask about the Holy Bible. Most all of their nonsense is just that: nonsense! They rip words out of context in order to show themselves to be LIARS, just like the scriptures record! 1Jn 2:21-23 All muslims must repent if they do not want to be cast into the lake of fire!

The reason the Son says He does NOTHING without the Father, speaks ONLY what the Father says, Does ONLY what the Father wills, is because "the Son" refers to His Visible Image, and "the Father" refers to His Invisible, Pervasive and Transcendent, Eternal Existence (Ephesians 4:6). You can no more separate "the Father" and "the Son" than you can separate your own spirit and body. (They are one and yet the spirit is greater, because the flesh is made up of the dust of the earth, while the spirit is the breath of life from God. Your own body does nothing without your spirit - James 2:26)

God tells us hundreds of times in the Prophets He would come in the flesh as the Messiah:
https://www.accordingtothescriptures.org/prophecy/353prophecies.html

So, Jesus Christ is God and is why He plainly says so throughout the entire Holy Bible. To look at Him is to look at God.

John 14:6-9
New King James Version
6 Jesus said to him, "I am the way, the truth, and the life. No one comes to the Father except through Me.

The Father Revealed
7 "If you had known Me, you would have known My Father also; and from now on you know Him and have seen Him."

8 Philip said to Him, "Lord, show us the Father, and it is sufficient for us."

9 Jesus said to him, "Have I been with you so long, and yet you have not known Me, Philip? He who has seen Me has seen the Father; so how can you say, 'Show us the Father'?

read verse 9 as many times as it takes.

Colossians 1:15-19
The Supremacy of the Son of God
15 The Son is the image of the invisible God, the firstborn over all creation. 16 For in him all things were created: things in heaven and on earth, visible and invisible, whether thrones or powers or rulers or authorities; all things have been created through him and for him. 17 He is before all things, and in him all things hold together. 18 And he is the head of the body, the church; he is the beginning and the firstborn from among the

dead, so that in everything he might have the supremacy. 19 For God was pleased to have all his fullness dwell in him,

Jesus Christ plainly states He is God and proved He is God like no one else in the entire history of the world.

So, when the scriptures teach that Jesus Christ is God and He is SUPREME in EVERYTHING that means He is the: God of gods, Man of men, Father of fathers, Son of sons, Servant of servants, Prophet of prophets, First and Last, Beginning and End, Angel of angels, Spirit of spirits, King of kings, Lord of lords, Star of stars, etc. etc. etc. which is why the contents of the Holy Bible refers to Him in all these ways and more. So, Christians are not the ones who are not honoring God in the Holy Bible, muslims are the ones calling God, the Prophets, the Apostles, including Paul, all liars.

13You call Me Teacher and Lord, and rightly so, because I am. https://biblehub.com/john/13-13.htm

Jesus Appears to Thomas
…27Then Jesus said to Thomas, "Put your finger here and look at My hands. Reach out your hand and put it into My side. Stop doubting and believe." 28Thomas replied, "My Lord and my God!" 29Jesus said to him, "Because you have seen Me, you have believed; blessed are those who have not seen and yet have believed."… https://biblehub.com/john/20-28.htm

The scriptures are crystal clear that Jesus Christ is God.

20And we know that the Son of God has come and has given us understanding, so that we may know Him who is true; and we are in Him who is true— in His Son Jesus Christ. He is the TRUE God and eternal life. 21Little children, keep yourselves from idols....
https://biblehub.com/1_john/5-20.htm

God's Grace Brings Salvation
...12It instructs us to renounce ungodliness and worldly passions, and to live sensible, upright, and godly lives in the present age, 13as we await the blessed hope and glorious appearance of our great God and Savior Jesus Christ. 14He gave Himself for us to redeem us from all lawlessness and to purify for Himself a people for His own possession, zealous for good deeds.... https://biblehub.com/titus/2-13.htm

and is so emphatic about the fact Jesus Christ is the One True God, that He tells us anyone denying He is God who came in the flesh is an antichrist!

1 John 4:1-6
Test the Spirits
4 Beloved, do not believe every spirit, but test the spirits to see whether they are from God, for many false prophets have gone out into the world. 2 By this you know the Spirit of God: every spirit that confesses that Jesus Christ has come in the flesh is from God, 3 and every spirit that does not confess Jesus is not from God. This is the spirit of the antichrist, which you heard was coming and now is in the world already. 4 Little children, you are from God and have overcome them, for he who is in you is greater than he who is in the world. 5 They are from the world; therefore they speak from the world, and the world listens to them. 6 We are from God. Whoever knows God listens to us; whoever is not from God does not listen to us. By this we know the Spirit of truth and the spirit of error.

allah is NOT the God of the Holy Bible. allah is more like the devil than JESUS CHRIST, the God of the Holy Bible!

https://www.thereligionofpeace.com/pages/articles/jesusmuhammad.aspx it has come to my attention that the Holy Bible in the Arabic language refers to God as "allah" - ANY AND ALL HOLY BIBLES referring to God as "allah" NEED TO BE RECALLED! they are NOT the same!
https://www.bible.ca/islam/islam-allahs-daughters.htm - not historically, not doctrinally, and not empirically. allah in the quran DIRECTLY CONTRADICTS Jesus Christ in the Holy Bible, they are NOT the same! Which is why muslims attacked and murdered Christians, Jews and anyone not loyal to their cult! allah is most definitely NOT the same God as the God who declares Himself to us all in the Holy Bible! Jesus Christ is THE ONE TRUE GOD, allah was a pagan idol that muhammad adopted to begin the cult of islam and as such IS A LIE. (Like I said, allah is much more like the devil, than he is like God.)

Not one muslim sees, hears or knows God and that's because islam has taught them all to deny Him instead! REPENT! muslims and obey His Commandment to Be Baptized in His Name! be filled with His Holy Spirit of Truth and then tell everyone you can that they must KNOW THE LORD! Yes, there are muslims that have Visions and Dreams of Jesus Christ, because God wants to reveal Himself to them since some muslims are nearly impervious to the rest of us PREACHING HIS GOSPEL. Christians are praying for you muslims! We know how oppressive your cult is and how difficult it is to leave it in islamic nations. We NEVER want people to be afraid of DEATH or PERSECUTION just for accepting Jesus Christ, but ACCEPT HIM no matter what other people are doing, your everlasting destiny depends on it!

The Great Commission
...18Then Jesus came to them and said, "All authority in heaven and on earth has been given to Me. 19Therefore go and make disciples of all nations, baptizing them in the name of the Father, and of the Son, and of the Holy Spirit, 20and teaching them to obey all that I have commanded you. And surely I am with you always, even to the end of the age."...
https://biblehub.com/matthew/28-19.htm

"Brothers, what shall we do?" 38 Peter replied, "Repent and be baptized, every one of you, in the name of Jesus Christ for the forgiveness of your sins, and you will receive the gift of the Holy Spirit. 39This promise belongs to you and your children and to all who are far off—to all whom the Lord our God will call to Himself."... https://biblehub.com/acts/2-38.htm

Peter and John Before the Council
...11This Jesus is 'the stone you builders rejected, which has become the cornerstone.' 12 Salvation exists in no one else, for there is no other name under heaven given to men by which we must be saved." 13When they saw the boldness of Peter and John and realized that they were unschooled, ordinary men, they marveled and took note that these men had been with Jesus.... https://biblehub.com/acts/4-12.htm

Far too many muslims try in vain to demote or denigrate Jesus the Christ (Messiah=God in the flesh) to just another prophet like David, but their false assertions are not true.

David needed help from JESUS CHRIST, WHO IS GOD.

I have shown all mankind (including muslims) repeatedly that Jesus Christ is GOD and yet you continue to try in vain to DENY Him, which means you are exceedingly wicked and need to repent. So, this is my attempt to try and bring you to your senses.

https://www.gotquestions.org/Lord-said-to-my-Lord.html - David states plainly that Jesus Christ is LORD! David states Jesus CHRIST is his Lord!

When the scriptures state LORD in all capitals that is the English version of YHWH. YHWH IS GOD and is the Hebrew Name for JESUS CHRIST.

https://www.youtube.com/watch?v=0p2ZqRCipX4 - YHWH not only means "I AM THAT I AM" but the letters tell us about the fact He would come and be crucified in our behalf.

WHEN YHWH CAME IN THE FLESH AS THE MESSIAH (https://www.accordingtothescriptures.org/prophecy/353prophecies.html) HE FULFILLED HIS OWN PROPHECIES THAT PROVES HE IS GOD! Including the words He uttered on the cross!

The Psalm of the Cross
1For the choirmaster. To the tune of "The Doe of the Dawn." A Psalm of David. My God, my God, why have You forsaken me? Why are You so far from saving me, so far from my words of groaning?

Everything in the Holy Bible from Genesis to Revelation is JESUS CHRIST speaking as the ONE TRUE GOD and so He knew His Law and Prophecies and is the ONLY ONE WHO CAN FULFILL THEM ALL!

The Fulfillment of the Law
16In the same way, let your light shine before men, that they may see your good deeds and glorify your Father in heaven. 17Do not think that I have come to abolish the Law or the Prophets. I have not come to abolish them, but to fulfill them. 18For I tell you truly, until heaven and earth pass away, not a single jot, not a stroke of a pen, will disappear from the Law until everything is accomplished.... https://biblehub.com/matthew/5-17.htm

ONLY GOD CAN FULFILL ALL HIS LAW AND PROPHECIES! NO ONE ELSE!

And so, God tells us WHEN HE CAME IN THE FLESH AS THE MESSIAH that He emptied Himself and walked among us humbly (https://biblehub.com/philippians/2-7.htm)! And that is why if you ONLY focus on His humanity, you are blind to His Divinity! In other words, every time He spoke of "the Father" He was speaking about HIMSELF! not anyone else! BUT He was referring to His Eternal, Transcendent, Pervasive, Invisible Existence (https://biblehub.com/ephesians/4-6.htm), and every time He spoke about "the Son" He was referring to His Visible Image that ALWAYS does the will of the FATHER and ALWAYS speaks the words of the FATHER EXACTLY AS THE FATHER WANTS THEM SPOKEN because that is who He is! THE FATHER, THE SON, and THE HOLY SPIRIT are all describing ONE GOD but is distinguishing various aspects of THE ONE GOD so that no one can wrongly assume, like you are doing, that He is something less than He really is!

In other words, to see Jesus Christ, is to see God, but He wants us to know He is MUCH MORE than JUST His Visible Image!

John 14:6-9
New King James Version
6 Jesus said to him, "I am the way, the truth, and the life. No one comes to the Father except through Me.

The Father Revealed
7 "If you had known Me, you would have known My Father also; and from now on you know Him and have seen Him."

8 Philip said to Him, "Lord, show us the Father, and it is sufficient for us."

9 Jesus said to him, "Have I been with you so long, and yet you have not known Me, Philip? He who has seen Me has seen the Father; so how can you say, 'Show us the Father'?

Colossians 1:15-19

The Supremacy of the Son of God

15 The Son is the image of the invisible God, the firstborn over all creation. 16 For in him all things were created: things in heaven and on earth, visible and invisible, whether thrones or powers or rulers or authorities; all things have been created through him and for him. 17 He is before all things, and in him all things hold together. 18 And he is the head of the body, the church; he is the beginning and the firstborn from among the dead, so that in everything he might have the supremacy. 19 For God was pleased to have all his fullness dwell in him,

If you continue to deny the One True God, and twist the meaning of His Words in the Holy Bible, then there is no hope whatsoever for you and you will end up in the lake of fire for being so evil. (Rev. 21:8)

A New Heaven and a New Earth

…7The one who overcomes will inherit all things, and I will be his God, and he will be My son. 8But to the cowardly and unbelieving and abominable and murderers and sexually immoral and sorcerers and idolaters and all liars, their place will be in the lake that burns with fire and sulfur. This is the second death." https://biblehub.com/revelation/21-8.htm

The ONLY WAY to escape the lake of fire is to acknowledge Jesus, the Christ, as the Lord and Savior that He is, the One True God who came in the flesh, and receive Him personally as such!

12But to all who did receive Him, to those who believed in His name, He gave the right to become children of God— 13children born not of blood, nor of the desire or will of man, but born of God….
https://biblehub.com/john/1-12.htm

Peter and John Before the Council

...11This Jesus is 'the stone you builders rejected, which has become the cornerstone.' 12 Salvation exists in no one else, for there is no other name under heaven given to men by which we must be saved." 13When they saw the boldness of Peter and John and realized that they were unschooled, ordinary men, they marveled and took note that these men had been with Jesus.... https://biblehub.com/acts/4-12.htm

24That is why I told you that you would die in your sins. For unless you believe that I am He, you will die in your sins." 25"Who are You?" they asked. "Just what I have been telling you from the beginning," Jesus replied.... https://biblehub.com/john/8-24.htm

ONLY GOD HAS BEEN SPEAKING WITH MANKIND FROM THE BEGINNING AND ONLY GOD CAN TELL US THAT WE WILL DIE IN OUR SINS FOR DENYING HIM!

36Whoever believes in the Son has eternal life. Whoever rejects the Son will not see life. Instead, the wrath of God remains on him."
https://biblehub.com/john/3-36.htm

muslims, you have never heard or seen God. you do not know God and yet you argue with those of us who do. you, like all muslims, are following the lying criminal muhammad who came along CENTURIES AFTER Jesus Christ and His EYEWITNESS APOSTLES who ALL tell us PLAINLY that Jesus Christ is GOD. so, you and all muslims are the ones twisting His Words and denying EVERY LOCATION IN THE ENTIRE HOLY BIBLE THAT PLAINLY STATES JESUS CHRIST IS GOD!

For example! JESUS CHRIST SAYS that the entire Holy Bible is all about Him as the One who has Eternal Life and that we all must come to Him to have that life!

John 5:39-40
English Standard Version
39 You search the Scriptures because you think that in them you have eternal life; and it is they that bear witness about me, 40 yet you refuse to come to me that you may have life.

He furthermore states REPEATEDLY that HE IS GOD!

13 You call Me Teacher and Lord, and rightly so, because I am.
https://biblehub.com/john/13-13.htm

Jesus Appears to Thomas
…27 Then Jesus said to Thomas, "Put your finger here and look at My hands. Reach out your hand and put it into My side. Stop doubting and believe." 28 Thomas replied, "My Lord and my God!" 29 Jesus said to him, "Because you have seen Me, you have believed; blessed are those who have not seen and yet have believed."… https://biblehub.com/john/20-28.htm

THAT TO LOOK AT HIM IS TO SEE GOD!

John 14:6-9
New King James Version
6 Jesus said to him, "I am the way, the truth, and the life. No one comes to the Father except through Me.

The Father Revealed
7 "If you had known Me, you would have known My Father also; and from now on you know Him and have seen Him."

8 Philip said to Him, "Lord, show us the Father, and it is sufficient for us."

9 Jesus said to him, "Have I been with you so long, and yet you have not known Me, Philip? He who has seen Me has seen the Father; so how can you say, 'Show us the Father'?

Jn 17:3 doesn't say what muslims THINK it says. Instead, the words "...only true God" are CONNECTED with "Jesus Christ" by the single word "kai". "kai" means "AND, EVEN, ALSO, NAMELY" so "only true God" is NOT SEPARATE from "JESUS CHRIST"! Just like He tells us!

The Unbelief of the Jews
...29My Father who has given them to Me is greater than all. No one can snatch them out of My Father's hand. **30I and the Father are one."** 31At this, the Jews again picked up stones to stone Him....
https://biblehub.com/john/10-30.htm

The reason why you and all unbelievers have never seen or heard God is because you are all still in your sins and are all still dead to Him! YOU ALL MUST REPENT AND OBEY HIM AND RECEIVE HIS HOLY SPIRIT OF TRUTH!

The Great Commission
...18Then Jesus came to them and said, "All authority in heaven and on earth has been given to Me. 19Therefore go and make disciples of all nations, baptizing them in the name of the Father, and of the Son, and of the Holy Spirit, 20and teaching them to obey all that I have commanded you. And surely I am with you always, even to the end of the age."...
https://biblehub.com/matthew/28-19.htm

37When the people heard this, they were cut to the heart and asked Peter and the other apostles, "Brothers, what shall we do?" 38 Peter replied, "Repent and be baptized, every one of you, in the name of Jesus Christ for the forgiveness of your sins, and you will receive the gift of the Holy Spirit. 39This promise belongs to you and your children and to all who are far

off—to all whom the Lord our God will call to Himself."...
https://biblehub.com/acts/2-38.htm

Peter and John Before the Council
...11This Jesus is 'the stone you builders rejected, which has become the cornerstone.' 12 Salvation exists in no one else, for there is no other name under heaven given to men by which we must be saved." 13When they saw the boldness of Peter and John and realized that they were unschooled, ordinary men, they marveled and took note that these men had been with Jesus.... https://biblehub.com/acts/4-12.htm

So, it's not just the Apostle Paul who plainly says Jesus Christ is God. Jesus Christ says He is God. All the Prophets say He is God and ALL His Disciples say He is God. (Acts 10: 34-43)

God's Grace Brings Salvation
...12It instructs us to renounce ungodliness and worldly passions, and to live sensible, upright, and godly lives in the present age, 13as we await the blessed hope and glorious appearance of our great God and Savior Jesus Christ. 14He gave Himself for us to redeem us from all lawlessness and to purify for Himself a people for His own possession, zealous for good deeds.... https://biblehub.com/titus/2-13.htm

20And we know that the Son of God has come and has given us understanding, so that we may know Him who is true; and we are in Him who is true— in His Son Jesus Christ. He is the TRUE God and eternal life. 21Little children, keep yourselves from idols....
https://biblehub.com/1_john/5-20.htm

Jesus Christ never tried to save Himself from the crucifixion. He states repeatedly that was His Divine Mission. 1)He told the Prophets He would come as the Messiah
https://www.accordingtothescriptures.org/prophecy/353prophecies.html

2) He told the Prophets He is our Redeemer - https://bible.knowingjesus.com/topics/God,-As-Redeemer - Redeemer means God paid the price to Save us - https://www.preceptaustin.org/tetelestai-paid_in_full 3) Even when God came in the flesh He knew He was going to be crucified before it happened:

Jesus the Good Shepherd

...17The reason the Father loves Me is that I lay down My life in order to take it up again. 18No one takes it from Me, but I lay it down of My own accord. I have authority to lay it down and authority to take it up again. This charge I have received from My Father." 19Again there was division among the Jews because of Jesus' message.... https://biblehub.com/john/10-18.htm

John 2:19

Jesus answered, "Destroy this temple, and in three days I will raise it up again."

John 5:26

For as the Father has life in Himself, so also He has granted the Son to have life in Himself.

John 10:11

I am the good shepherd. The good shepherd lays down His life for the sheep.

John 10:15

just as the Father knows Me and I know the Father. And I lay down My life for the sheep.

The Second Prediction of the Passion

30Going on from there, they passed through Galilee. But Jesus did not want anyone to know, 31because He was teaching His disciples. He told them, " The Son of Man will be delivered into the hands of men. They will kill Him, and after three days He will rise." 32But they did not understand this statement, and they were afraid to ask Him about it....
https://biblehub.com/mark/9-31.htm

Matthew 16:21

From that time on Jesus began to show His disciples that He must go to Jerusalem and suffer many things at the hands of the elders, chief priests, and scribes, and that He must be killed and on the third day be raised to life.

Matthew 27:63

"Sir," they said, "we remember that while He was alive that deceiver said, 'After three days I will rise again.'

Mark 8:31

Then He began to teach them that the Son of Man must suffer many things and be rejected by the elders, chief priests, and scribes, and that He must be killed and after three days rise again.

Mark 9:12

He replied, "Elijah does indeed come first, and he restores all things. Why then is it written that the Son of Man must suffer many things and be rejected?

Mark 10:34

who will mock Him and spit on Him and flog Him and kill Him. And after three days He will rise again."

So God, Jesus Christ, NEVER tried to "save himself" from the cross, it was the very reason He came into this world to suffer and die for us, to redeem and save us! (When He prayed in the Garden of Gethsemane, sweating drops of blood, was due to the fact as GOD, HE KNEW, He was about to REALLY SUFFER! and our flesh, even His Flesh, HATES suffering! So He showed us when we go through trials in this life WE HAVE TO PRAY INTENSELY for STRENGTH to FACE IT AND GO THROUGH IT! only when we follow, worship and love God not just when things are roses and good for us, but also when they are hard and difficult, even unto death, do we show we REALLY love Him and are true Disciples of Christ.) Many worship Jesus Christ/God when their life is going smoothly but as soon as hardship comes, some grow bitter and angry, and blame God; so their religion was in vain. They didn't know Him and really didn't love Him. The ones that gave their lives as He gave His, are the ones that showed Him and us all that they were TRUE DISCIPLES of Christ, TRUE Christians who worshiped Him in Spirit and Truth, hating the flesh, these bodies of sin and death. (Rev 12:7-11) In other words, True Christians, go through suffering and even death, still loving and worshiping and obeying our Lord and Savior Jesus Christ, the One True God.

Jesus Christ CLAIMED to be GOD! He CLAIMED to have ETERNAL LIFE! He CLAIMED to be THE RESURRECTION AND THE LIFE!

John 5:39-40
English Standard Version

39 You search the Scriptures because you think that in them you have eternal life; and it is they that bear witness about me, 40 yet you refuse to come to me that you may have life.

28I give them eternal life, and they will never perish. No one can snatch them out of My hand. 29My Father who has given them to Me is greater than all. No one can snatch them out of My Father's hand....
https://biblehub.com/john/10-28.htm

Jesus Comforts Martha and Mary

...24Martha replied, "I know that he will rise again in the resurrection at the last day." 25 Jesus said to her, "I am the resurrection and the life. Whoever believes in Me will live, even though he dies. 26And everyone who lives and believes in Me will never die. Do you believe this?"...
https://biblehub.com/john/11-25.htm

Then HE PROVED IT by dying publicly and raising up His Own Body from the Grave and appearing to His Disciples afterward! That's why they bowed at His feet and worshiped Him because then they fully knew He was indeed the God, the Messiah, the One who has and gives Eternal Life!

Jesus Appears to Thomas

...27Then Jesus said to Thomas, "Put your finger here and look at My hands. Reach out your hand and put it into My side. Stop doubting and believe." 28Thomas replied, "My Lord and my God!" 29Jesus said to him, "Because you have seen Me, you have believed; blessed are those who have not seen and yet have believed."... https://biblehub.com/john/20-28.htm

And before He left this world He Created and Made to return to Heaven, Reigning over His Creation, He commanded them to wait until they received Power from Him by Pouring out His Holy Spirit upon them.

The Ascension

...7Jesus replied, "It is not for you to know times or seasons that the Father has fixed by His own authority. 8But you will receive power when the Holy Spirit comes upon you, and you will be My witnesses in Jerusalem, and in all Judea and Samaria, and to the ends of the earth." 9After He had said this, they watched as He was taken up, and a cloud hid Him from their sight.... https://biblehub.com/acts/1-8.htm

And so that's why the Holy Bible exists and is why the Apostles gave their lives testifying to the whole world that Jesus Christ is LORD and SAVIOR, the ONE TRUE GOD! (that's how Christianity began)

The Great Commission

...18Then Jesus came to them and said, "All authority in heaven and on earth has been given to Me. 19Therefore go and make disciples of all nations, baptizing them in the name of the Father, and of the Son, and of the Holy Spirit, 20and teaching them to obey all that I have commanded you. And surely I am with you always, even to the end of the age."...
https://biblehub.com/matthew/28-19.htm

37When the people heard this, they were cut to the heart and asked Peter and the other apostles, "Brothers, what shall we do?" 38 Peter replied, "Repent and be baptized, every one of you, in the name of Jesus Christ for the forgiveness of your sins, and you will receive the gift of the Holy Spirit. 39This promise belongs to you and your children and to all who are far off—to all whom the Lord our God will call to Himself."...
https://biblehub.com/acts/2-38.htm
Peter and John Before the Council

...11This Jesus is 'the stone you builders rejected, which has become the cornerstone.' 12 Salvation exists in no one else, for there is no other name under heaven given to men by which we must be saved." 13When they saw the boldness of Peter and John and realized that they were unschooled, ordinary men, they marveled and took note that these men had been with Jesus.... https://biblehub.com/acts/4-12.htm

The Holy Bible doesn't say "God can never be a man" in fact it says HUNDREDS of times that God would come in the flesh as the Messiah.

https://www.accordingtothescriptures.org/prophecy/353prophecies.html
That fact is said so strongly that anyone who denies God came in the flesh, God calls an antichrist (1Jn 4:1-6).

Muslims! the Holy Bible is Telling us the Truth; Not the quran!

I repeat!

The reason the Son says He does NOTHING without the Father, speaks ONLY what the Father says, Does ONLY what the Father wills, is because "the Son" refers to His Visible Image, and "the Father" refers to His Invisible, Pervasive and Transcendent, Eternal Existence (Ephesians 4:6). You can no more separate "the Father" and "the Son" than you can separate your own spirit and body. (they are one and yet the spirit is greater, because the flesh is made up of the dust of the earth, while the spirit is the breath of life from God. Your own body does nothing without your spirit - James 2:26)

God tells us hundreds of times in the Prophets He would come in the flesh as the Messiah:
https://www.accordingtothescriptures.org/prophecy/353prophecies.html

So Jesus Christ is God and is why He plainly says so throughout the entire Holy Bible. To look at Him is to look at God. WE KNOW GOD BY KNOWING JESUS CHRIST!

John 14:6-9

New King James Version

6 Jesus said to him, "I am the way, the truth, and the life. No one comes to the Father except through Me.

The Father Revealed

7 "If you had known Me, you would have known My Father also; and from now on you know Him and have seen Him."

8 Philip said to Him, "Lord, show us the Father, and it is sufficient for us."

9 Jesus said to him, "Have I been with you so long, and yet you have not known Me, Philip? He who has seen Me has seen the Father; so how can you say, 'Show us the Father'?

read verse 9 as many times as it takes.

Colossians 1:15-19

The Supremacy of the Son of God

15 The Son is the image of the invisible God, the firstborn over all creation. 16 For in him all things were created: things in heaven and on earth, visible and invisible, whether thrones or powers or rulers or authorities; all things have been created through him and for him. 17 He is before all things, and in him all things hold together. 18 And he is the head of the body, the church; he is the beginning and the firstborn from among the dead, so that in everything he might have the supremacy. 19 For God was pleased to have all his fullness dwell in him,

This SUPREMACY IN ALL THINGS means JESUS CHRIST is the: God of gods, Man of men, Spirit of spirits, Angel of angels, Lord of lords, King of kings, Teacher of teacher, Star of stars, Heaven of heavens, Holy of holies, Servant of servants, Prophets of prophets, Apostle of apostles, First and Last, Beginning and End, Father of fathers, Son of sons, etc. etc. which is WHY THE SCRIPTURES REFER TO HIM IN ALL THESE WAYS AND MORE!

Jesus Christ plainly states He is God and proved He is God like no one else in the entire history of the world.

13You call Me Teacher and Lord, and rightly so, because I am.
https://biblehub.com/john/13-13.htm

Jesus Appears to Thomas
…27Then Jesus said to Thomas, "Put your finger here and look at My hands. Reach out your hand and put it into My side. Stop doubting and believe." 28Thomas replied, "My Lord and my God!" 29Jesus said to him, "Because you have seen Me, you have believed; blessed are those who have not seen and yet have believed."… https://biblehub.com/john/20-28.htm

The scriptures are crystal clear that Jesus Christ is God.

20And we know that the Son of God has come and has given us understanding, so that we may know Him who is true; and we are in Him who is true— in His Son Jesus Christ. He is the TRUE God and eternal life. 21Little children, keep yourselves from idols.…
https://biblehub.com/1_john/5-20.htm
God's Grace Brings Salvation
…12It instructs us to renounce ungodliness and worldly passions, and to live sensible, upright, and godly lives in the present age, 13as we await the blessed hope and glorious appearance of our great God and Savior Jesus Christ. 14He gave Himself for us to redeem us from all lawlessness and to purify for Himself a people for His own possession, zealous for good deeds.… https://biblehub.com/titus/2-13.htm

and is so emphatic about the fact Jesus Christ is the One True God, that He tells us anyone denying He is God who came in the flesh is an antichrist!

1 John 4:1-6
English Standard Version
Test the Spirits
4 Beloved, do not believe every spirit, but test the spirits to see whether they are from God, for many false prophets have gone out into the world. 2 By this you know the Spirit of God: every spirit that confesses that Jesus Christ has come in the flesh is from God, 3 and every spirit that does not confess Jesus is not from God. This is the spirit of the antichrist, which you heard was coming and now is in the world already. 4 Little children, you are from God and have overcome them, for he who is in you is greater than he who is in the world. 5 They are from the world; therefore they speak from the world, and the world listens to them. 6 We are from God. Whoever knows God listens to us; whoever is not from God does not listen to us. By this we know the Spirit of truth and the spirit of error.

Not one muslim sees, hears or knows God and that's because islam has taught them to deny Him instead! REPENT! muslims and obey His Commandment to Be Baptized in His Name! be filled with His Holy Spirit of Truth and then tell everyone you can that they must KNOW THE LORD!
The Great Commission
...18Then Jesus came to them and said, "All authority in heaven and on earth has been given to Me. 19Therefore go and make disciples of all nations, baptizing them in the name of the Father, and of the Son, and of the Holy Spirit, 20and teaching them to obey all that I have commanded you. And surely I am with you always, even to the end of the age."...
https://biblehub.com/matthew/28-19.htm

ONE NAME for the Father, the Son and the Holy Spirit because those are just ways of REFERRING TO JESUS CHRIST.

"Brothers, what shall we do?" 38 Peter replied, "Repent and be baptized, every one of you, in the name of Jesus Christ for the forgiveness of your sins, and you will receive the gift of the Holy Spirit. 39This promise belongs to you and your children and to all who are far off—to all whom the Lord our God will call to Himself."... https://biblehub.com/acts/2-38.htm

Peter and John Before the Council
...11This Jesus is 'the stone you builders rejected, which has become the cornerstone.' 12 Salvation exists in no one else, for there is no other name under heaven given to men by which we must be saved." 13When they saw the boldness of Peter and John and realized that they were unschooled, ordinary men, they marveled and took note that these men had been with Jesus.... https://biblehub.com/acts/4-12.htm

islam is teaching muslims things that just aren't true.

They are taught to say things like "allah has no sons" "allah has no partners" etc. etc. but that's RIDICULOUS! so much so that we instantly know "allah" is a false god.

The whole world is full of sons and daughters that the One True God, Jesus Christ, Created and Made! And the One True God COMMANDS us to tell others about Him, live righteously, feed the hungry, clothe the naked, etc. etc. etc. So just obeying God creates "partners" by definition. So islam isn't just teaching lies BUT OBVIOUS ones that make muslims all look as if they've not just been deceived but brainwashed!

For example, when they quote Numbers 23:19 and wrongly claim that it says God can NEVER be a man. That's not what the verse says at all! From the very first chapter in the Holy Bible we know GOD IS A MAN! So nowhere in the Holy Bible does God ever say He isn't one!

The Sixth Day
...26Then God said, "Let Us make man in Our image, after Our likeness, to rule over the fish of the sea and the birds of the air, over the livestock, and over all the earth itself and every creature that crawls upon it." 27So God created man in His own image; in the image of God He created him; male and female He created them. 28God blessed them and said to them, "Be fruitful and multiply, and fill the earth and subdue it; rule over the fish of the sea and the birds of the air and every creature that crawls upon the earth."... https://biblehub.com/genesis/1-27.htm

so what Numbers 23:19 actually says in the original language is that God doesn't tell lies like sinful men do and God doesn't change His Mind whimsically like sinful men do.

God has no need to repent because He is Righteous and Holy, Perfect in all His Ways. "ish" in the Hebrew refers to sinful mankind; whereas "adama or adam" refers to righteous mankind. So when God says He is not a lying "ish", He is denying that He is evil and denying that He is a liar; not that He is a Righteous, Holy Man.

https://biblehub.com/interlinear/genesis/1-27.htm - in the original language "image" means also "likeness" In other words, from the very first chapter God tells us that mankind are made to be like Him! so God is a Man and men are gods! In fact, God says so plainly!

The Unbelief of the Jews
...32But Jesus responded, "I have shown you many good works from the Father. For which of these do you stone Me?" 33" We are not stoning You for any good work," said the Jews, "but for blasphemy, because You, who are a man, declare Yourself to be God." 34Jesus replied, "Is it not written in your Law: 'I have said you are gods'?35If he called them gods to whom the word of God came— and the Scripture cannot be broken— 36then what about the One whom the Father sanctified and sent into the world? How then can you accuse Me of blasphemy for stating that I am the Son of

God?... https://biblehub.com/john/10-34.htm

So islam and the quran are teaching muslims things that just aren't true, because the deceiver, satanil, doesn't want people to recognize the One True God, Jesus Christ, because He is the ONLY ONE who can SAVE them! (in other words, deliver them from being slaves of the devil and cast into the lake of fire with that wicked one.)

Peter and John Before the Council
...11This Jesus is 'the stone you builders rejected, which has become the cornerstone.' 12 Salvation exists in no one else, for there is no other name under heaven given to men by which we must be saved." 13When they saw the boldness of Peter and John and realized that they were unschooled, ordinary men, they marveled and took note that these men had been with Jesus.... https://biblehub.com/acts/4-12.htm

God tells us in the Holy Bible that He intended to come as the Messiah centuries before He actually did so.
https://www.accordingtothescriptures.org/prophecy/353prophecies.html
- Jesus Christ, the One True God, told the prophets since the Beginning that He would come as the Messiah, in the flesh.

Courtesy of
https://www.accordingtothescriptures.org/prophecy/353prophecies.html
it has these in many languages, it's an excellent resource!

Scripture	Prophecy	Fulfillment
1. Gen. 3:15	Seed of a woman (virgin birth)	Galatians 4:4-5, Matthew 1:18

2.	Gen. 3:15	He will bruise Satan's head	Hebrews 2:14, 1John 3:8
3.	Gen. 3:15	Christ's heel would be bruised with nails on the cross	Matthew 27:35, Luke 24:3940
4.	Gen. 5:24	The bodily ascension to heaven illustrated	Mark 16:19, Rev. 12:5
5.	Gen. 9:26, 27	The God of Shem will be the Son of Shem	Luke 3:23-36
6.	Gen. 12:3	Seed of Abraham will bless all nations	Galatians 3:8, Acts 3:25, 26
7.	Gen. 12:7	The Promise made to Abraham's Seed	Galatians 3:16
8.	Gen. 14:18	A priest after the order of Melchizedek	Hebrews 6:20
9.	Gen. 14:18	King of Peace and Righteousness	Hebrews 7:2
10.	Gen. 14:18	The Last Supper foreshadowed	Matthew 26:26-29

11. Gen. 17:19	Seed of Isaac (Gen. 21:12)	Romans 9:7
12. Gen. 22:8	The Lamb of God promised	John 1:29
13. Gen. 22:18	As Isaac's seed, will bless all nations	Galatians 3:16
14. Gen. 26:2-5	The Seed of Isaac promised as the Redeemer	Hebrews 11:18
15. Gen. 28:12	The Bridge to heaven	John 1:51
16. Gen. 28:14	The Seed of Jacob	Luke 3:34
17. Gen. 49:10	The time of His coming	Luke 2:1-7; Galatians 4:4
18. Gen. 49:10	The Seed of Judah	Luke 3:33
19. Gen. 49:10	Called Shiloh or One Sent	John 17:3
20. Gen. 49:10	Messiah to come before Judah lost identity	John 11:47-52

21. Gen. 49:10	Unto Him shall the obedience of the people be	John 10:16
22. Ex. 3:13-15	The Great "I AM"	John 4:26; 8:58
23. Ex. 12:3-6	The Lamb presented to Israel 4 days before Passover	Mark 11:7-11
24. Ex. 12:5	A Lamb without blemish	Hebrews 9:14; 1Peter 1:19
25. Ex. 12:13	The blood of the Lamb saves from wrath	Romans 5:8
26. Ex. 12:21-27	Christ is our Passover	1Corinthians 5:7
27. Ex. 12:46	Not a bone of the Lamb to be broken	John 19:31-36
28. Ex. 15:2	His exaltation predicted as Yeshua	Acts 7:55, 56
29. Ex. 15:11	His Character-Holiness	Luke 1:35; Acts 4:27
30. Ex. 17:6	The Spiritual Rock of Israel	1Corinthians 10:4

31. Ex. 33:19	His Character-Merciful	Luke 1:72
32. Lev. 1:2-9	His sacrifice a sweet smelling savor unto God	Ephesians 5:2
33. Lev. 14:11	The leper cleansed-Sign to priesthood	Luke 5:12-14; Acts 6:7
34. Lev. 16:15-17	Prefigures Christ's oncefor-all death	Hebrews 9:7-14
35. Lev. 16:27	Suffering outside the Camp	Matthew 27:33; Heb. 13:11, 12
36. Lev. 17:11	The Blood-the life of the flesh	Matthew 26:28; Mark 10:45
37. Lev. 17:11	It is the blood that makes atonement	Rom. 3:23-24; 1John 1:7
38. Lev. 23:36-37	The Drink-offering: "If any man thirst"	John 7:37
39. Num. 9:12	Not a bone of Him broken	John 19:31-36
40. Num. 21:9	The serpent on a pole-Christ lifted up	John 3:14-18; 12:32

41. Num. 24:17	Time: "I shall see him, but not now."	John 1:14; Galatians 4:4
42. Deut. 18:15	"This is of a truth that prophet."	John 6:14
43. Deut. 18:15-16	"Had ye believed Moses, ye would believe me."	John 5:45-47
44. Deut. 18:18	Sent by the Father to speak His word	John 8:28, 29
45. Deut. 18:19	Whoever will not hear must bear his sin	Acts 3:22-23
46. Deut. 21:23	Cursed is he that hangs on a tree	Galatians 3:10-13
47. Joshua 5:14-15	The Captain of our salvation	Hebrews 2:10
48. Ruth 4:4-10	Christ, our kinsman, has redeemed us	Ephesians 1:3-7
49. 1 Sam. 2:35	A Faithful Priest	Heb. 2:17; 3:1-3, 6; 7:24-25
50. 1 Sam. 2:10	Shall be an anointed King to the Lord	Mt. 28:18, John 12:15

#	Reference	Prophecy	Fulfillment
51.	2 Sam. 7:12	David's Seed	Matthew 1:1
52.	2 Sam. 7:13	His Kingdom is everlasting	2Peter 1:11
53.	2 Sam. 7:14	The Son of God	Luke 1:32, Romans 1:3-4
54.	2 Sam. 7:16	David's house established forever	Luke 3:31; Rev. 22:16
55.	2 Ki. 2:11	The bodily ascension to heaven illustrated	Luke 24:51
56.	1 Chr. 17:11	David's Seed	Matthew 1:1; 9:27
57.	1 Chr. 17:12-13	To reign on David's throne forever	Luke 1:32, 33
58.	1 Chr. 17:13	"I will be His Father, He...my Son."	Hebrews 1:5
59.	Job 9:32-33	Mediator between man and God	1 Timothy 2:5
60.	Job 19:23-27	The Resurrection predicted	John 5:24-29

#	Reference	Description	Fulfillment
61.	Psa. 2:1-3	The enmity of kings foreordained	Acts 4:25-28
62.	Psa. 2:2	To own the title, Anointed (Christ)	John 1:41, Acts 2:36
63.	Psa. 2:6	His Character-Holiness	John 8:46; Revelation 3:7
64.	Psa. 2:6	To own the title King	Matthew 2:2
65.	Psa. 2:7	Declared the Beloved Son	Matthew 3:17, Romans 1:4
66.	Psa. 2:7, 8	The Crucifixion and Resurrection intimated	Acts 13:29-33
67.	Psa. 2:8, 9	Rule the nations with a rod of iron	Rev. 2:27; 12:5; 19:15
68.	Psa. 2:12	Life comes through faith in Him	John 20:31
69.	Psa. 8:2	The mouths of babes perfect His praise	Matthew 21:16
70.	Psa. 8:5, 6	His humiliation and exaltation	Hebrews 2:5-9

71. Psa. 9:7-10	Judge the world in righteousness	Acts 17:31
72. Psa. 16:10	Was not to see corruption	Acts 2:31; 13:35
73. Psa. 16:9-11	Was to arise from the dead	John 20:9
74. Psa. 17:15	The resurrection predicted	Luke 24:6
75. Psa. 18:2-3	The horn of salvation	Luke 1:69-71
76. Psa. 22:1	Forsaken because of sins of others	2 Corinthians 5:21
77. Psa. 22:1	"My God, my God, why hast thou forsaken me?"	Matthew 27:46
78. Psa. 22:2	Darkness upon Calvary for three hours	Matthew 27:45
79. Psa. 22:7	They shoot out the lip and shake the head	Matthew 27:39-44
80. Psa. 22:8	"He trusted in God, let Him deliver Him"	Matthew 27:43

81. Psa. 22:9-10	Born the Saviour	Luke 2:7
82. Psa. 22:12-13	They seek His death	John 19:6
83. Psa. 22:14	His blood poured out when they pierced His side	John 19:34
84. Psa. 22:14, 15	Suffered agony on Calvary	Mark 15:34-37
85. Psa. 22:15	He thirsted	John 19:28
86. Psa. 22:16	They pierced His hands and His feet	John 19:34, 37; 20:27
87. Psa. 22:17, 18	Stripped Him before the stares of men	Luke 23:34, 35
88. Psa. 22:18	They parted His garments	John 19:23, 24
89. Psa. 22:20, 21	He committed Himself to God	Luke 23:46
90. Psa. 22:20, 21	Satanic power bruising the Redeemer's heel	Hebrews 2:14

#	Reference	Description	Fulfillment
91.	Psa. 22:22	His Resurrection declared	John 20:17
92.	Psa. 22:27-28	He shall be the governor of the nations	Colossians 1:16
93.	Psa. 22:31	"It is finished"	John 19:30, Heb. 10:10, 12, 14, 18
94.	Psa. 23:1	"I am the Good Shepherd"	John 10:11, 1Peter 2:25
95.	Psa. 24:3	His exaltation predicted	Acts 1:11; Philippians 2:9
96.	Psa. 30:3	His resurrection predicted	Acts 2:32
97.	Psa. 31:5	"Into thy hands I commit my spirit"	Luke 23:46
98.	Psa. 31:11	His acquaintances fled from Him	Mark 14:50
99.	Psa. 31:13	They took counsel to put Him to death	Mt. 27:1, John 11:53
100.	Psa. 31:14, 15	"He trusted in God, let Him deliver him"	Matthew 27:43

101. Psa. 34:20	Not a bone of Him broken	John 19:31-36
102. Psa. 35:11	False witnesses rose up against Him	Matthew 26:59
103. Psa. 35:19	He was hated without a cause	John 15:25
104. Psa. 38:11	His friends stood afar off	Luke 23:49
105. Psa. 38:12	Enemies try to entangle Him by craft	Mark 14:1, Mt. 22:15
106. Psa. 38:12-13	Silent before His accusers	Matthew 27:12-14
107. Psa. 38:20	He went about doing good	Acts 10:38
108. Psa. 40:2-5	The joy of His resurrection predicted	John 20:20
109. Psa. 40:6-8	His delight-the will of the Father	John 4:34, Heb. 10:5-10

110. Psa. 40:9	He was to preach the Righteousness in Israel	Matthew 4:17
111. Psa. 40:14	Confronted by adversaries in the Garden	John 18:4-6
112. Psa. 41:9	Betrayed by a familiar friend	John 13:18
113. Psa. 45:2	Words of Grace come from His lips	John 1:17, Luke 4:22
114. Psa. 45:6	To own the title, God or Elohim	Hebrews 1:8
115. Psa. 45:7	A special anointing by the Holy Spirit	Mt. 3:16; Heb. 1:9
116. Psa. 45:7, 8	Called the Christ (Messiah or Anointed)	Luke 2:11
117. Psa. 45:17	His name remembered forever	Ephesians 1:20-21, Heb. 1:8
118. Psa. 55:12-14	Betrayed by a friend, not an enemy	John 13:18
119. Psa. 55:15	Unrepentant death of the Betrayer	Matthew 27:3-5; Acts 1:16-19

#	Reference	Description	Fulfillment
120.	Psa. 68:18	To give gifts to men	Ephesians 4:7-16
121.	Psa. 68:18	Ascended into Heaven	Luke 24:51
122.	Psa. 69:4	Hated without a cause	John 15:25
123.	Psa. 69:8	A stranger to own brethren	John 1:11; 7:5
124.	Psa. 69:9	Zealous for the Lord's House	John 2:17
125.	Psa. 69:14-20	Messiah's anguish of soul before crucifixion	Matthew 26:36-45
126.	Psa. 69:20	"My soul is exceeding sorrowful."	Matthew 26:38
127.	Psa. 69:21	Given vinegar in thirst	Matthew 27:34
128.	Psa. 69:26	The Saviour given and smitten by God	John 17:4; 18:11
129.	Psa. 72:10, 11	Great persons were to visit Him	Matthew 2:1-11

130. Psa. 72:16	The corn of wheat to fall into the Ground	John 12:24-25
131. Psa. 72:17	Belief on His name will produce offspring	John 1:12, 13
132. Psa. 72:17	All nations shall be blessed by Him	Galatians 3:8
133. Psa. 72:17	All nations shall call Him blessed	John 12:13, Rev. 5:8-12
134. Psa. 78:1-2	He would teach in parables	Matthew 13:34-35
135. Psa. 78:2	To speak the Wisdom of God with authority	Matthew 7:29
136. Psa. 80:17	The Man of God's right hand	Mark 14:61-62
137. Psa. 88	The Suffering and Reproach of Calvary	Matthew 27:26-50
138. Psa. 88:8	They stood afar off and watched	Luke 23:49
139. Psa. 89:9	He calms the wind and the sea	Matthew 8:26

140. Psa. 89:27	Firstborn	Colossians 1:15, 18
141. Psa. 89:27	Emmanuel to be higher than earthly kings	Luke 1:32, 33
142. Psa. 89:35-37	David's Seed, throne, kingdom endure forever	Luke 1:32, 33
143. Psa. 89:36-37	His character-Faithfulness	Revelation 1:5; 19:11
144. Psa. 90:2	He is from everlasting (Micah 5:2)	John 1:1
145. Psa. 91:11, 12	Identified as Messianic; used to tempt Christ	Luke 4:10, 11
146. Psa. 97:9	His exaltation predicted	Acts 1:11; Ephesians 1:20
147. Psa. 100:5	His character-Goodness	Matthew 19:16, 17
148. Psa. 102:1-11	The Suffering and Reproach of Calvary	John 19:16-30

#	Reference	Description	Fulfillment
149.	Psa. 102:25-27	Messiah is the Preexistent Son	Hebrews 1:10-12
150.	Psa. 109:25	Ridiculed	Matthew 27:39
151.	Psa. 110:1	Son of David	Matthew 22:42-43
152.	Psa. 110:1	To ascend to the righthand of the Father	Mark 16:19
153.	Psa. 110:1	David's son called Lord	Matthew 22:44, 45
154.	Psa. 110:4	A priest after Melchizedek's order	Hebrews 6:20
155.	Psa. 112:4	His character—Compassionate, Gracious, et al	Matthew 9:36
156.	Psa. 118:17, 18	Messiah's Resurrection assured	Luke 24:5-7; 1Cor. 15:20
157.	Psa. 118:22, 23	The rejected stone is Head of the corner	Matthew 21:42, 43
158.	Psa. 118:26	The Blessed One presented to Israel	Matthew 21:9

159. Psa. 118:26	To come while Temple standing	Matthew 21:12-15
160. Psa. 132:11	The Seed of David (the fruit of His Body)	Luke 1:32, Act 2:30
161. Psa. 129:3	He was scourged	Matthew 27:26
162. Psa. 138:1-6	The supremacy of David's Seed amazes kings	Matthew 2:2-6
163. Psa. 147:3, 6	The earthly ministry of Christ described	Luke 4:18
164. Prov. 1:23	He will send the Spirit of God	John 16:7
165. Prov. 8:23	Foreordained from everlasting	Rev. 13:8, 1Peter 1:19-20
166. Song. 5:16	The altogether lovely One	John 1:17
167. Isa. 2:3	He shall teach all nations	John 4:25
168. Isa. 2:4	He shall judge among the nations	John 5:22

169. Isa. 6:1	When Isaiah saw His glory	John 12:40-41
170. Isa. 6:8	The One Sent by God	John 12:38-45
171. Isa. 6:9-10	Parables fall on deaf ears	Matthew 13:13-15
172. Isa. 6:9-12	Blinded to Christ and deaf to His words	Acts 28:23-29
173. Isa. 7:14	To be born of a virgin	Luke 1:35
174. Isa. 7:14	To be Emmanuel-God with us	Matthew 1:18-23, 1Tim. 3:16
175. Isa. 8:8	Called Emmanuel	Matthew 1:23
176. Isa. 8:14	A stone of stumbling, a Rock of offense	1Peter 2:8
177. Isa. 9:1, 2	His ministry to begin in Galilee	Matthew 4:12-17
178. Isa. 9:6	A child born-Humanity	Luke 1:31
179. Isa. 9:6	A Son given-Deity	Luke 1:32, John 1:14, 1Tim. 3:16

#	Verse	Description	Reference
180.	Isa. 9:6	Declared to be the Son of God with power	Romans 1:3, 4
181.	Isa. 9:6	The Wonderful One, Peleh	Luke 4:22
182.	Isa. 9:6	The Counsellor, Yaatz	Matthew 13:54
183.	Isa. 9:6	The Mighty God, El Gibor	1Cor. 1:24, Titus 2:13
184.	Isa. 9:6	The Everlasting Father, Avi Adth	John 8:58; 10:30
185.	Isa. 9:6	The Prince of Peace, Sar Shalom	John 16:33
186.	Isa. 9:7	Inherits the throne of David	Luke 1:32
187.	Isa. 9:7	His Character-Just	John 5:30
188.	Isa. 9:7	No end to his Government, Throne, and kingdom	Luke 1:33
189.	Isa. 11:1	Called a Nazarene-the Branch, Netzer	Matthew 2:23
190.	Isa. 11:1	A rod out of Jesse-Son of Jesse	Luke 3:23, 32

#	Verse	Description	Fulfillment
191.	Isa. 11:2	Anointed One by the Spirit	Matthew 3:16, 17, Acts 10:38
192.	Isa. 11:2	His Character-Wisdom, Knowledge, et al	Colossians 2:3
193.	Isa. 11:3	He would know their thoughts	Luke 6:8, John 2:25
194.	Isa. 11:4	Judge in righteousness	Acts 17:31
195.	Isa. 11:4	Judges with the sword of His mouth	Rev. 2:16; 19:11, 15
196.	Isa. 11:5	Character: Righteous & Faithful	Rev. 19:11
197.	Isa. 11:10	The Gentiles seek Him	John 12:18-21
198.	Isa. 12:2	Called Jesus-Yeshua	Matthew 1:21
199.	Isa. 22:22	The One given all authority to govern	Revelation 3:7
200.	Isa. 25:8	The Resurrection predicted	1Corinthians 15:54

201. Isa. 26:19	His power of Resurrection predicted		Matthew 27:50-54
202. Isa. 28:16	The Messiah is the precious corner stone		Acts 4:11, 12
203. Isa. 28:16	The Sure Foundation		1Corinthians 3:11, Mt. 16:18
204. Isa. 29:13	He indicated hypocritical obedience to His Word		Matthew 15:7-9
205. Isa. 29:14	The wise are confounded by the Word		1Corinthians 1:18-31
206. Isa. 32:2	A Refuge-A man shall be a hiding place		Matthew 23:37
207. Isa. 35:4	He will come and save you		Matthew 1:21
208. Isa. 35:5-6	To have a ministry of miracles		Matthew 11:2-6
209. Isa. 40:3, 4	Preceded by forerunner		John 1:23

210. Isa. 40:9	"Behold your God."	John 1:36; 19:14
211. Isa. 40:10.	He will come to reward	Revelation 22:12
212. Isa. 40:11	A shepherd-compassionate life-giver	John 10:10-18
213. Isa. 42:1-4	The Servant-as a faithful, patient redeemer	Matthew 12:18-21
214. Isa. 42:2	Meek and lowly	Matthew 11:28-30
215. Isa. 42:3	He brings hope for the hopeless	Mt. 12:14-21; John 4:1-54
216. Isa. 42:4	The nations shall wait on His teachings	John 12:20-26
217. Isa. 42:6	The Light (salvation) of the Gentiles	Luke 2:32
218. Isa. 42:1, 6	His is a worldwide compassion	Matthew 28:19, 20
219. Isa. 42:7	Blind eyes opened.	John 9:25-38

220. Isa. 43:11	He is the only Saviour.	Acts 4:12
221. Isa. 44:3	He will send the Spirit of God	John 16:7, 13
222. Isa. 45:21-25	He is Lord and Saviour	Philippians 3:20, Titus 2:13
223. Isa. 45:23	He will be the Judge	John 5:22; Romans 14:11
224. Isa. 46:9, 10	Declares things not yet done	John 13:19
225. Isa. 48:12	The First and the Last	John 1:30, Revelation 1:8, 17
226. Isa. 48:16, 17	He came as a Teacher	John 3:2
227. Isa. 49:1	Called from the womb-His humanity	Matthew 1:18
228. Isa. 49:5	A Servant from the womb.	Luke 1:31, Philippians 2:7
229. Isa. 49:6	He will restore Israel	Acts 3:19-21; 15:16-17

230. Isa. 49:6	He is Salvation for Israel	Luke 2:29-32
231. Isa. 49:6	He is the Light of the Gentiles	John 8:12, Acts 13:47
232. Isa. 49:6	He is Salvation unto the ends of the earth	Acts 15:7-18
233. Isa. 49:7	He is despised of the Nation	John 1:11; 8:48-49; 19:14-15
234. Isa. 50:3	Heaven is clothed in black at His humiliation	Luke 23:44, 45
235. Isa. 50:4	He is a learned counselor for the weary	Matthew 7:29; 11:28, 29
236. Isa. 50:5	The Servant bound willingly to obedience	Matthew 26:39
237. Isa. 50:6	"I gave my back to the smiters."	Matthew 27:26
238. Isa. 50:6	He was smitten on the cheeks	Matthew 26:67
239. Isa. 50:6	He was spat upon	Matthew 27:30

#	Verse	Description	NT Reference
240.	Isa. 52:7	Published good tidings upon mountains	Matthew 5:12; 15:29; 28:16
241.	Isa. 52:13	The Servant exalted	Acts 1:8-11; Eph. 1:19-22, Php. 2:5-9
242.	Isa. 52:14	The Servant shockingly abused	Luke 18:31-34; Mt. 26:67, 68
243.	Isa. 52:15	Nations startled by message of the Servant	Luke 18:31-34; Mt. 26:67, 68
244.	Isa. 52:15	His blood shed sprinkles nations	Hebrews 9:13-14, Rev. 1:5
245.	Isa. 53:1	His people would not believe Him	John 12:37-38
246.	Isa. 53:2	Appearance of an ordinary man	Philippians 2:6-8
247.	Isa. 53:3	Despised	Luke 4:28-29
248.	Isa. 53:3	Rejected	Matthew 27:21-23
249.	Isa. 53:3	Great sorrow and grief	Matthew 26:37-38, Luke 19:41, Heb. 4:15

250.	Isa. 53:3	Men hide from being associated with Him	Mark 14:50-52
251.	Isa. 53:4	He would have a healing ministry	Matthew 8:16-17
252.	Isa. 53:4	Thought to be cursed by God	Matthew 26:66; 27:41-43
253.	Isa. 53:5	Bears penalty for mankind's iniquities	2Cor. 5:21, Heb. 2:9
254.	Isa. 53:5	His sacrifice provides peace between man and God	Colossians 1:20
255.	Isa. 53:5	His sacrifice would heal man of sin	1Peter 2:24
256.	Isa. 53:6	He would be the sin-bearer for all mankind	1John 2:2; 4:10
257.	Isa. 53:6	God's will that He bear sin for all mankind	Galatians 1:4
258.	Isa. 53:7	Oppressed and afflicted	Matthew 27:27-31

259. Isa. 53:7	Silent before his accusers	Matthew 27:12-14
260. Isa. 53:7	Sacrificial lamb	John 1:29, 1Peter 1:18-19
261. Isa. 53:8	Confined and persecuted	Matthew 26:47-75; 27:1-31
262. Isa. 53:8	He would be judged	John 18:13-22
263. Isa. 53:8	Killed	Matthew 27:35
264. Isa. 53:8	Dies for the sins of the world	1John 2:2
265. Isa. 53:9	Buried in a rich man's grave	Matthew 27:57
266. Isa. 53:9	Innocent and had done no violence	Luke 23:41, John 18:38
267. Isa. 53:9	No deceit in his mouth	1Peter 2:22
268. Isa. 53:10	God's will that He die for mankind	John 18:11
269. Isa. 53:10	An offering for sin	Matthew

		20:28, Galatians 3:13
270. Isa. 53:10	Resurrected and live forever	Romans 6:9
271. Isa. 53:10	He would prosper	John 17:1-5
272. Isa. 53:11	God fully satisfied with His suffering	John 12:27
273. Isa. 53:11	God's servant would justify man	Romans 5:8-9, 18-19
274. Isa. 53:11	The sin-bearer for all mankind	Hebrews 9:28
275. Isa. 53:12	Exalted by God because of his sacrifice	Matthew 28:18
276. Isa. 53:12	He would give up his life to save mankind	Luke 23:46
277. Isa. 53:12	Numbered with the transgressors	Mark 15:27-28; Luke 22:37
278. Isa. 53:12	Sin-bearer for all mankind	1Peter 2:24

279. Isa. 53:12	Intercede to God in behalf of mankind	Luke 23:34, Rom. 8:34
280. Isa. 55:3	Resurrected by God	Acts 13:34
281. Isa. 55:4	A witness	John 18:37
282. Isa. 55:4	He is a leader and commander	Hebrews 2:10
283. Isa. 55:5	God would glorify Him	Acts 3:13
284. Isa. 59:16	Intercessor between man and God	Matthew 10:32
285. Isa. 59:16	He would come to provide salvation	John 6:40
286. Isa. 59:20	He would come to Zion as their Redeemer	Luke 2:38
287. Isa. 60:1-3	He would shew light to the Gentiles	Acts 26:23
288. Isa. 61:1	The Spirit of God upon him	Matthew 3:16-17
289. Isa. 61:1	The Messiah would preach the good news	Luke 4:16-21

#	Reference	Prophecy	Fulfillment
290.	Isa. 61:1	Provide freedom from the bondage of sin	John 8:31-36
291.	Isa. 61:1-2	Proclaim a period of grace	Galatians 4:4-5
292.	Jer. 11:21	Conspiracy to kill Jesus	John 7:1, Matthew 21:38
293.	Jer. 23:5-6	Descendant of David	Luke 3:23-31
294.	Jer. 23:5-6	The Messiah would be both God and Man	John 13:13, 1Ti 3:16
295.	Jer. 31:22	Born of a virgin	Matthew 1:18-20
296.	Jer. 31:31	The Messiah would be the new covenant	Matthew 26:28
297.	Jer. 33:14-15	Descendant of David	Luke 3:23-31
298.	Eze. 34:23-24	Descendant of David	Matthew 1:1
299.	Eze. 37:24-25	Descendant of David	Luke 1:31-33
300.	Dan. 2:44-45	The Stone that shall break the kingdoms	Matthew 21:44

301. Dan. 7:13-14	He would ascend into heaven	Acts 1:9-11
302. Dan. 7:13-14	Highly exalted	Ephesians 1:20-22
303. Dan. 7:13-14	His dominion would be everlasting	Luke 1:31-33
304. Dan. 9:24	To make an end to sins	Galatians 1:3-5
305. Dan. 9:24	To make reconciliation for iniquity	Romans 5:10, 2Cor. 5:1821
306. Dan. 9:24	He would be holy	Luke 1:35
307. Dan. 9:25	His announcement	John 12:12-13
308. Dan. 9:26	Cut off	Matthew 16:21; 21:38-39
309. Dan. 9:26	Die for the sins of the world	Hebrews 2:9
310. Dan. 9:26	Killed before the destruction of the temple	Matthew 27:50-51

#	Reference	Description	Fulfillment
311.	Dan. 10:5-6	Messiah in a glorified state	Revelation 1:13-16
312.	Hos. 11:1	He would be called out of Egypt	Matthew 2:15
313.	Hos. 13:14	He would defeat death	1Corinthians 15:55-57
314.	Joel 2:32	Offer salvation to all mankind	Romans 10:9-13
315.	Jonah 1:17	Death and resurrection of Christ	Matthew 12:40; 16:4
316.	Mic. 5:2	Born in Bethlehem	Matthew 2:1-6
317.	Mic. 5:2	Ruler in Israel	Luke 1:33
318.	Mic. 5:2	From everlasting	John 8:58
319.	Hag. 2:6-9	He would visit the second Temple	Luke 2:27-32
320.	Hag. 2:23	Descendant of Zerubbabel	Luke 2:27-32
321.	Zech. 3:8	God's servant	John 17:4

322. Zech. 6:12-13	Priest and King	Hebrews 8:1
323. Zech. 9:9	Greeted with rejoicing in Jerusalem	Matthew 21:8-10
324. Zech. 9:9	Beheld as King	John 12:12-13
325. Zech. 9:9	The Messiah would be just	John 5:30
326. Zech. 9:9	The Messiah would bring salvation	Luke 19:10
327. Zech. 9:9	The Messiah would be humble	Matthew 11:29
328. Zech. 9:9	Presented to Jerusalem riding on a donkey	Matthew 21:6-9
329. Zech. 10:4	The cornerstone	Ephesians 2:20
330. Zech. 11:4-6	At His coming, Israel to have unfit leaders	Matthew 23:1-4
331. Zech. 11:4-6	Rejection causes God to remove His protection	Luke 19:41-44
332. Zech. 11:4-6	Rejected in favor of another king	John 19:13-15

#	Prophecy	Fulfillment
333. Zech. 11:7	Ministry to "poor," the believing remnant	Matthew 9:35-36
334. Zech. 11:8	Unbelief forces Messiah to reject them	Matthew 23:33
335. Zech. 11:8	Despised	Matthew 27:20
336. Zech. 11:9	Stops ministering to those who rejected Him	Matthew 13:10-11
337. Zech. 11:10-11	Rejection causes God to remove protection	Luke 19:41-44
338. Zech. 11:10-11	The Messiah would be God	John 14:7
339. Zech. 11:12-13	Betrayed for thirty pieces of silver	Matthew 26:14-15
340. Zech. 11:12-13	Rejected	Matthew 26:14-15
341. Zech. 11:12-13	Thirty pieces of silver cast in the house of the Lord	Matthew 27:3-5
342. Zech. 11:12-13	The Messiah would be God	John 12:45

343. Zech. 12:10	The Messiah's body would be pierced	John 19:34-37
344. Zech. 12:10	The Messiah would be both God and man	John 10:30
345. Zech. 12:10	The Messiah would be rejected	John 1:11
346. Zech. 13:7	God's will He die for mankind	John 18:11
347. Zech. 13:	A violent death	Mark 14:27
348. Zech. 13:7	Both God and man	John 14:9
349. Zech. 13:7	Israel scattered as a result of rejecting Him	Matthew 26:31-56
350. Zech. 14:4	He would return to the Mt. of Olives	Acts 1:11-12
351. Mal. 3:1	Messenger to prepare the way for Messiah	Mark 1:1-8
352. Mal. 3:1	Sudden appearance at the temple	Mark 11:15-16

353. Mal. 3:1	Messenger of the new covenant	Luke 4:43
354. Mal. 3:6	The God who changes not	Hebrews 13:8
355. Mal. 4:5	Forerunner in spirit of Elijah	Mt. 3:1-3; 11:10-14; 17:11-13
356. Mal. 4:6	Forerunner would turn many to righteousness	Luke 1:16-17

Again, thanks to
https://www.accordingtothescriptures.org/prophecy/353prophecies.html
who has these prophecies available in many languages!
ALL COMBINED THESE PROPHECIES ALL TELL US OVERWHELMINGLY THAT JESUS CHRIST IS THE ONE TRUE GOD!

IT SHOULD BE OBVIOUS that the god, allah, of the quran, IS NOT THE ONE TRUE GOD OF THE HOLY BIBLE! Because the god of the quran DIRECTLY CONTRADICTS the God of the Holy Bible! so, anyone saying allah and JESUS CHRIST/YHWH are the same, knows next to nothing about either and/or are lying! NEVER refer to GOD ALMIGHTY as "allah"!

muhammad was a false prophet who has nothing to do with the God of the Holy Bible and is the reason muslims have been at war with Holy Bible believers throughout history to this very day!
http://www.answeringmuslims.com/2014/04/50-reasons-muhammadwas-not-prophet.html

https://www.youtube.com/watch?v=xwqrBuC0J00 - 50 reasons muhammad was not a prophet.

https://www.youtube.com/watch?v=I_To-cV94Bo - islam has been at war with the rest of humanity ever since muhammad and his gang of rapists, robbers, slavers, and murderers began it! It has never been a lawful religion! It is a criminal organization! Even in muslims nations, you can be KILLED for trying to leave islam. (Proving islam is a cult of murderers! - https://www.google.com/search?client=opera&q=islamic+apostasy+death+penalty+nations&sourceid=opera&ie=UTF-8&oe=UTF-8)

But JESUS CHRIST IS THE ONE TRUE GOD and he is NOT named "allah".

6For unto us a child is born, unto us a son is given, and the government will be upon His shoulders. And He will be called Wonderful Counselor, Mighty God, Everlasting Father, Prince of Peace. 7Of the increase of His government and peace there will be no end. He will reign on the throne of David and over his kingdom, to establish and sustain it with justice and righteousness from that time and forevermore. The zeal of the LORD of Hosts will accomplish this.... https://biblehub.com/isaiah/9-6.htm

If you read those prophecies cited above all combined, they tell details of how God told the Prophets from the Beginning He would come as the Messiah, a Humble Servant, a Man.

So, God refers to the Messiah (Himself in the flesh) as the "Son of Man" AND as the "Son of God" because God has always taught us that we are made in His Image and Likeness. (In other words, men are more than just these fleeting bodies of flesh, that are born on earth and then die shortly later; we have spirits, the breath of life itself, given us from our Creator.) Gen 1:27 (we are NOT an evolved ape! WE ARE MADE IN HIS IMAGE FROM THE BEGINNING AND TO THIS DAY AND FOREVER!)

The Sixth Day

...26Then God said, "Let Us make man in Our image, after Our likeness, to rule over the fish of the sea and the birds of the air, over the livestock, and over all the earth itself and every creature that crawls upon it." 27So God created man in His own image; in the image of God He created him; male and female He created them. 28God blessed them and said to them, "Be fruitful and multiply, and fill the earth and subdue it; rule over the fish of the sea and the birds of the air and every creature that crawls upon the earth."... https://biblehub.com/genesis/1-27.htm

7Then the LORD God formed man from the dust of the ground and breathed the breath of life into his nostrils, and the man became a living being. https://biblehub.com/genesis/2-7.htm

So, when God came in the flesh, He identified Himself exactly as He had been teaching mankind from the Beginning.

...24That is why I told you that you would die in your sins. For unless you believe that I am He, you will die in your sins." 25"Who are You?" they asked. "Just what I have been telling you from the beginning," Jesus replied. https://biblehub.com/john/8-25.htm

Plainly stating that anyone who doesn't believe He is God who came in the flesh, the Messiah, would die in their sins. (Not be forgiven by Him because they don't even acknowledge He is the One who Created and Made them and Judges their soul!)

36Whoever believes in the Son has eternal life. Whoever rejects the Son will not see life. Instead, the wrath of God remains on him."
https://biblehub.com/john/3-36.htm

So every time Jesus Christ says, "I AM", He is saying He is YHWH in the flesh and every time He says I AM TRUTH, I AM LIFE, I AM THE GOOD SHEPHERD, I AM LIGHT, I AM THE RESURRECTION, I AM THE SON OF MAN, I AM THE SON OF GOD, these are all His Way of telling us He is the SAME GOD who spoke with Moses and All the Prophets!

AND He tells us that when He came in the flesh, He emptied Himself, taking on the form of a Man:

Attitude of Christ
...6Who, existing in the form of God, did not consider equality with God something to be grasped, 7but emptied Himself, taking the form of a servant, being made in human likeness. 8And being found in appearance as a man, He humbled Himself and became obedient to death—even death on a cross.... https://biblehub.com/philippians/2-7.htm

So not only do we KNOW who our Creator is, Jesus Christ, BUT that He understands EVERYTHING He has subjected all mankind to! Having experienced fully Himself existence as one of us, walking and living among us.

Jesus the Great High Priest
14Therefore, since we have a great high priest who has passed through the heavens, Jesus the Son of God, let us hold firmly to what we profess. 15For we do not have a high priest who is unable to sympathize with our weaknesses, but we have one who was tempted in every way that we are, yet was without sin. 16Let us then approach the throne of grace with confidence, so that we may receive mercy and find grace to help us in our time of need.... https://biblehub.com/hebrews/4-15.htm

GOD, JESUS CHRIST, IS ABLE TO COMFORT US LIKE NO ONE ELSE CAN BECAUSE HE KNOWS EVERYTHING! EVERYTHING ANY OF US WILL FACE! GO THROUGH! HE THE ONE WHO SHOWED US HE IS VICTORIOUS OVER DEATH! WE CAN TRUST HIM WITH OUR LIVES!

Jesus Christ the One True God is SUPREME IN EVERYTHING which is why the scriptures refer to Him as the: God of gods, Man of men, King of kings, Lord of lords, Prophet of prophets, Father of fathers, Son of sons, Servant of servants, First and Last, Beginning and End, Angel of angels, Spirit of spirits, Holy of holies, Heaven of heavens, Star of stars and much, much more!

Colossians 1:15-19
The Supremacy of the Son of God
15 The Son is the image of the invisible God, the firstborn over all creation. 16 For in him all things were created: things in heaven and on earth, visible and invisible, whether thrones or powers or rulers or authorities; all things have been created through him and for him. 17 He is before all things, and in him all things hold together. 18 And he is the head of the body, the church; he is the beginning and the firstborn from among the dead, so that in everything he might have the supremacy. 19 For God was pleased to have all his fullness dwell in him,

So, everything Jesus Christ said and did was God showing us by His Own Example how He wants us to live and when we face hard trials (like our own suffering and deaths) that we NEED TO PRAY! REALLY PRAY FOR STRENGTH to endure! and NEVER GIVE UP THE FAITH! That the One who Proved He is the Way to Eternal Life, will likewise give eternal life to those who love, trust and obey Him.

John 5:39-40
English Standard Version

39 You search the Scriptures because you think that in them you have eternal life; and it is they that bear witness about me, 40 yet you refuse to come to me that you may have life.

28 I give them eternal life, and they will never perish. No one can snatch them out of My hand. 29 My Father who has given them to Me is greater than all. No one can snatch them out of My Father's hand....
https://biblehub.com/john/10-28.htm

Jesus Comforts Martha and Mary
...24 Martha replied, "I know that he will rise again in the resurrection at the last day." 25 Jesus said to her, "I am the resurrection and the life. Whoever believes in Me will live, even though he dies. 26 And everyone who lives and believes in Me will never die. Do you believe this?"...
https://biblehub.com/john/11-25.htm

Jesus Christ "the Son" is the Visible Image of "the Father" so when He says the Father is greater than the Son and yet also says "I and the Father are One." that's just similar to how our own spirits are greater than our own bodies, because our bodies suffer and die and return to the dust while our spirits still exist afterward to give account to our Lord Jesus Christ, the One True God and Judge of all souls.

That's why He said to see Him is to see the Father because Jesus Christ is God, who came in the flesh.

John 14:6-9
New King James Version
6 Jesus said to him, "I am the way, the truth, and the life. No one comes to the Father except through Me.

The Father Revealed

7 "If you had known Me, you would have known My Father also; and from now on you know Him and have seen Him."

8 Philip said to Him, "Lord, show us the Father, and it is sufficient for us."

9 Jesus said to him, "Have I been with you so long, and yet you have not known Me, Philip? He who has seen Me has seen the Father; so how can you say, 'Show us the Father'?

He always received worship as God - https://www.openbible.info/topics/worshipping_jesus and even complained when some should have done so but didn't:

https://biblehub.com/luke/17-17.htm and acknowledges plainly He is God - https://biblehub.com/john/20-28.htm

Jesus and the Samaritan Woman
…24God is Spirit, and His worshipers must worship Him in spirit and in truth." 25The woman said, "I know that Messiah" (called Christ) "is coming. When He comes, He will explain everything to us." 26Jesus answered, "I who speak to you am He."… https://biblehub.com/john/4-25.htm

The Messiah is GOD in the flesh. So, Jesus Christ plainly identifies Himself as such and is why those who didn't believe Him tried repeatedly to stone Him for blasphemy.

https://hebrew4christians.com/Names_of_G-d/Messiah/messiah.html

13You call Me Teacher and Lord, and rightly so, because I am.
https://biblehub.com/john/13-13.htm

The Unbelief of the Jews
...32But Jesus responded, "I have shown you many good works from the Father. For which of these do you stone Me?" 33" We are not stoning You for any good work," said the Jews, "but for blasphemy, because You, who are a man, declare Yourself to be God." https://biblehub.com/john/10-33.htm

Jesus Appears to Thomas
...27Then Jesus said to Thomas, "Put your finger here and look at My hands. Reach out your hand and put it into My side. Stop doubting and believe." 28Thomas replied, "My Lord and my God!" 29Jesus said to him, "Because you have seen Me, you have believed; blessed are those who have not seen and yet have believed."... https://biblehub.com/john/20-28.htm

When people were shouting in worship to Him, unbelievers asked Him to tell those worshipping Him to be silent but He said if those people didn't shout His Praises, then even the rocks would!

The Triumphal Entry
...35Then they led the colt to Jesus, threw their cloaks over it, and put Jesus on it. 36 As He rode along, the people spread their cloaks on the road. 37And as He approached the descent from the Mount of Olives, the whole multitude of disciples began to praise God joyfully in a loud voice for all the miracles they had seen:38"Blessed is the King who comes in the name of the Lord!" "Peace in heaven and glory in the highest!" 39But some of the Pharisees in the crowd said to Him, "Teacher, rebuke Your disciples!" 40"I tell you," He answered, "if they remain silent, the very stones will cry out."... https://biblehub.com/luke/19-39.htm

So, Jesus Christ from Genesis to Revelation tells us He is the One True God over and over and over again.

20And we know that the Son of God has come and has given us understanding, so that we may know Him who is true; and we are in Him who is true— in His Son Jesus Christ. He is the TRUE God and eternal life. 21Little children, keep yourselves from idols....
https://biblehub.com/1_john/5-20.htm

God's Grace Brings Salvation
...12It instructs us to renounce ungodliness and worldly passions, and to live sensible, upright, and godly lives in the present age, 13as we await the blessed hope and glorious appearance of our great God and Savior Jesus Christ. 14He gave Himself for us to redeem us from all lawlessness and to purify for Himself a people for His own possession, zealous for good deeds.... https://biblehub.com/titus/2-13.htm

Jesus is Coming
...12"Behold, I am coming soon, and My reward is with Me, to give to each one according to what he has done. 13I am the Alpha and the Omega, the First and the Last, the Beginning and the End." 14Blessed are those who wash their robes, so that they may have the right to the tree of life and may enter the city by its gates.... https://biblehub.com/revelation/22-13.htm

...10"You are My witnesses," declares the LORD, "and My servant whom I have chosen, so that you may consider and believe Me and understand that I am He. Before Me no god was formed, and after Me none will come. 11I, yes I, am the LORD, and there is no Savior but Me. 12I alone decreed and saved and proclaimed—I, and not some foreign god among you. So

you are My witnesses," declares the LORD, "that I am God....
https://biblehub.com/isaiah/43-11.htm

Peter and John Before the Council
...11This Jesus is 'the stone you builders rejected, which has become the cornerstone.' 12 Salvation exists in no one else, for there is no other name under heaven given to men by which we must be saved." 13When they saw the boldness of Peter and John and realized that they were unschooled, ordinary men, they marveled and took note that these men had been with Jesus.... https://biblehub.com/acts/4-12.htm

John 8:48-59
English Standard Version
Before Abraham Was, I Am
48 The Jews answered him, "Are we not right in saying that you are a Samaritan and have a demon?" 49 Jesus answered, "I do not have a demon, but I honor my Father, and you dishonor me. 50 Yet I do not seek my own glory; there is One who seeks it, and he is the judge. 51 Truly, truly, I say to you, if anyone keeps my word, he will never see death." 52 The Jews said to him, "Now we know that you have a demon! Abraham died, as did the prophets, yet you say, 'If anyone keeps my word, he will never taste death.' 53 Are you greater than our father Abraham, who died? And the prophets died! Who do you make yourself out to be?" 54 Jesus answered, "If I glorify myself, my glory is nothing. It is my Father who glorifies me, of whom you say, 'He is our God.'[a] 55 But you have not known him. I know him. If I were to say that I do not know him, I would be a liar like you, but I do know him and I keep his word. 56 Your father Abraham rejoiced that he would see my day. He saw it and was glad." 57 So the Jews said to him, "You are not yet fifty years old, and have you seen Abraham?"[b] 58 Jesus said to them, "Truly, truly, I say to you, before Abraham was, I am." 59 So they picked up stones to throw at him, but Jesus hid himself and went out of the temple.

18"Why do you call Me good?" Jesus replied. "No one is good except God alone. https://biblehub.com/mark/10-18.htm

So here He said, no one is good except God and then He says He is Good!

https://www.biblegateway.com/passage/?search=John%2010&version=ESV

John 10
English Standard Version
I Am the Good Shepherd
10 "Truly, truly, I say to you, he who does not enter the sheepfold by the door but climbs in by another way, that man is a thief and a robber. 2 But he who enters by the door is the shepherd of the sheep. 3 To him the gatekeeper opens. The sheep hear his voice, and he calls his own sheep by name and leads them out. 4 When he has brought out all his own, he goes before them, and the sheep follow him, for they know his voice. 5 A stranger they will not follow, but they will flee from him, for they do not know the voice of strangers." 6 This figure of speech Jesus used with them, but they did not understand what he was saying to them.

7 So Jesus again said to them, "Truly, truly, I say to you, I am the door of the sheep. 8 All who came before me are thieves and robbers, but the sheep did not listen to them. 9 I am the door. If anyone enters by me, he will be saved and will go in and out and find pasture. 10 The thief comes only to steal and kill and destroy. I came that they may have life and have it abundantly. 11 I am the good shepherd. The good shepherd lays down his life for the sheep. 12 He who is a hired hand and not a shepherd, who does not own the sheep, sees the wolf coming and leaves the sheep and flees, and the wolf snatches them and scatters them. 13 He flees because he is a hired hand and cares nothing for the sheep. 14 I am the good shepherd.

So Jesus Christ tells us all plainly HUNDREDS of times in the Holy Bible that He is God and that forgiveness of sins and eternal life is only through Him! Acts 10:34-43 JESUS CHRIST IS LORD OF ALL!

https://www.facebook.com/reel/1041681090188915 - the Holy Bible is telling us the Truth. Those who passed on those facts of history gave their lives to put the Truth in your hands!

muslims and other people are always asking, "Why did God do this or that?" like today I saw another one asking, Why was it necessary for God to come and die for us on the cross?

Because sin, disobedience to the One who is Truth and Life itself, causes death automatically. God is Love, so not Loving Him, disobeying Him, separates us from Him. If we don't love God, we don't love each other, and is why people have been hating and killing each other throughout history. So sin factually causes suffering and death and God showed us all that when He suffered and died for us on the cross.

Sin Separates Us from God

1Surely the arm of the LORD is not too short to save, nor His ear too dull to hear. 2But your iniquities have built barriers between you and your God, and your sins have hidden His face from you, so that He does not hear. 3For your hands are stained with blood, and your fingers with iniquity; your lips have spoken lies, and your tongue mutters injustice....
https://biblehub.com/isaiah/59-2.htm

Ephesians 2:1-10 ESV

And you were dead in the trespasses and sins in which you once walked, following the course of this world, following the prince of the power of the air, the spirit that is now at work in the sons of disobedience— among whom we all once lived in the passions of our flesh, carrying out the desires of the body and the mind, and were by nature children of wrath, like the rest of mankind. But God, being rich in mercy, because of the great love with which he loved us, even when we were dead in our trespasses, made us alive together with Christ—by grace you have been saved— and raised us up with him and seated us with him in the heavenly places in Christ Jesus, so that in the coming ages he might show the immeasurable riches of his grace in kindness toward us in Christ Jesus. For by grace you have been saved through faith. And this is not your own doing; it is the gift of God, not a result of works, so that no one may boast.

For we are his workmanship, created in Christ Jesus for good works, which God prepared beforehand, that we should walk in them.

Peter and John Before the Council

...11This Jesus is 'the stone you builders rejected, which has become the cornerstone.' 12 Salvation exists in no one else, for there is no other name under heaven given to men by which we must be saved."
https://biblehub.com/acts/4-12.htm

A Call to Holiness

...17Since you call on a Father who judges each one's work impartially, conduct yourselves in reverent fear during your stay as foreigners. 18For you know that it was not with perishable things such as silver or gold that you were redeemed from the empty way of life you inherited from your forefathers, 19but with the precious blood of Christ, a lamb without blemish or spot.... https://biblehub.com/1_peter/1-18.htm

When God came in the flesh to suffer and die for us on the cross, He was openly showing us 1) sin is totally unacceptable to Him because it leads to suffering and death and 2) He loves us so much He was willing to suffer and die for us just to bring us back to Him (Love triumphs over hatred, Good triumphs over evil, God beat the devil and death openly!)

https://www.accordingtothescriptures.org/prophecy/353prophecies.html

https://bible.knowing-jesus.com/topics/God,-As-Redeemer - God told us centuries in advance He would Redeem us.
https://www.preceptaustin.org/tetelestai-paid_in_full - Jesus Christ is our Redeemer, the One True God, who only could pay the price in full for the sins of mankind.

John 14:6-9

New King James Version

6 Jesus said to him, "I am the way, the truth, and the life. No one comes to the Father except through Me.

The Father Revealed

7 "If you had known Me, you would have known My Father also; and from now on you know Him and have seen Him."

8 Philip said to Him, "Lord, show us the Father, and it is sufficient for us."

9 Jesus said to him, "Have I been with you so long, and yet you have not known Me, Philip? He who has seen Me has seen the Father; so how can you say, 'Show us the Father'?

John 5:39-40

English Standard Version

39 You search the Scriptures because you think that in them you have eternal life; and it is they that bear witness about me, 40 yet you refuse to come to me that you may have life.

Jesus Christ says He is God repeatedly. (many hundreds of times over in the Holy Bible, His very Name says He is God)

1) Jesus Christ ALWAYS RECEIVED WORSHIP AS GOD - https://www.openbible.info/topics/worshipping_jesus and even complains when people should have and didn't:

The Ten Lepers
...16He fell facedown at Jesus' feet in thanksgiving to Him—and he was a Samaritan. 17"Were not all ten cleansed?" Jesus asked. "Where then are the other nine? 18Was no one found except this foreigner to return and give glory to God?"... https://biblehub.com/luke/17-17.htm

2) Jesus Christ says the entire Holy Bible is all about Him, the One who has Eternal Life and that we must come to Him to have that life.

John 5:39-40
English Standard Version
39 You search the Scriptures because you think that in them you have eternal life; and it is they that bear witness about me, 40 yet you refuse to come to me that you may have life.

3) He says He is the One who has been telling us He is God from the Beginning and that if we don't believe Him, we will die in our sins!

...23Then He told them, "You are from below; I am from above. You are of this world; I am not of this world. 24That is why I told you that you would die in your sins. For unless you believe that I am He, you will die in your sins." 25"Who are You?" they asked. "Just what I have been telling you from the beginning," Jesus replied.... https://biblehub.com/john/8-24.htm

John 8:48-59

Before Abraham Was, I Am

48 The Jews answered him, "Are we not right in saying that you are a Samaritan and have a demon?" 49 Jesus answered, "I do not have a demon, but I honor my Father, and you dishonor me. 50 Yet I do not seek my own glory; there is One who seeks it, and he is the judge. 51 Truly, truly, I say to you, if anyone keeps my word, he will never see death." 52 The Jews said to him, "Now we know that you have a demon! Abraham died, as did the prophets, yet you say, 'If anyone keeps my word, he will never taste death.' 53 Are you greater than our father Abraham, who died? And the prophets died! Who do you make yourself out to be?" 54 Jesus answered, "If I glorify myself, my glory is nothing. It is my Father who glorifies me, of whom you say, 'He is our God.'[a] 55 But you have not known him. I know him. If I were to say that I do not know him, I would be a liar like you, but I do know him and I keep his word. 56 Your father Abraham rejoiced that he would see my day. He saw it and was glad." 57 So the Jews said to him, "You are not yet fifty years old, and have you seen Abraham?"[b] 58 Jesus said to them, "Truly, truly, I say to you, before Abraham was, I am." 59 So they picked up stones to throw at him, but Jesus hid himself and went out of the temple.

(the people that heard and saw Him first hand understood He was claiming to be God, it's why those who didn't believe Him picked up stones to stone Him!)

5) He plainly acknowledged He is God:

Jesus Appears to Thomas

...27Then Jesus said to Thomas, "Put your finger here and look at My hands. Reach out your hand and put it into My side. Stop doubting and believe." 28Thomas replied, "My Lord and my God!" 29Jesus said to him, "Because you have seen Me, you have believed; blessed are those who have not seen and yet have believed."... https://biblehub.com/john/20-28.htm

6) He gives us His Holy Spirit of Truth to testify to the entire world that He is God:

The Ascension
...7Jesus replied, "It is not for you to know times or seasons that the Father has fixed by His own authority. 8But you will receive power when the Holy Spirit comes upon you, and you will be My witnesses in Jerusalem, and in all Judea and Samaria, and to the ends of the earth."
https://biblehub.com/acts/1-8.htm

7) He Begins the Holy Bible with telling us He is God and tells us His Name and how to identify He is God HUNDREDS OF TIMES OVER!

https://www.youtube.com/watch?v=0p2ZqRCipX4

https://www.accordingtothescriptures.org/prophecy/353prophecies.html

8 - He Ends the Holy Bible with telling us He is God and that His Rewards (and Consequences) are with Him when He returns!

Jesus is Coming
...12"Behold, I am coming soon, and My reward is with Me, to give to each one according to what he has done. 13I am the Alpha and the Omega, the First and the Last, the Beginning and the End." 14Blessed are those who wash their robes, so that they may have the right to the tree of life and may enter the city by its gates.... https://biblehub.com/revelation/22-13.htm

9) Even the stars He Created and Made tell us Jesus Christ is God!
https://www.youtube.com/watch?v=PHCftvj_Prw

https://www.youtube.com/watch?v=EUQEMqF5dL8

10) billions on earth from all over this world are telling everyone Jesus Christ is God because He has given them His Holy Spirit of Truth and they KNOW BEYOND ALL DOUBT HE IS THE ONE TRUE GOD!

20And we know that the Son of God has come and has given us understanding, so that we may know Him who is true; and we are in Him who is true— in His Son Jesus Christ. He is the TRUE God and eternal life. 21Little children, keep yourselves from idols....
https://biblehub.com/1_john/5-20.htm

So those who DON'T KNOW GOD personally yet, should be listening to THE BILLIONS OF US WHO DO! JESUS CHRIST IS THE ONE TRUE GOD!

WE KNOW GOD PERSONALLY! JESUS CHRIST IS WHO HE IS! we don't just have a head knowledge about Him, we are in a relationship with Him, He speaks to us, tells us what to do, where to go, teaches us EVERYTHING! We are in an ongoing RELATIONSHIP WITH GOD! All true Christians, have HIS HOLY SPIRIT! WE KNOW GOD PERSONALLY!

<u>*Living in the Spirit*</u>
8Those controlled by the flesh cannot please God. **9**You, however, are controlled not by the flesh, but by the Spirit, if the Spirit of God lives in you. And if anyone does not have the Spirit of Christ, he does not belong to Christ. **10**But if Christ is in you, your body is dead because of sin, yet your spirit is alive because of righteousness.... https://biblehub.com/romans/8-9.htm

muhammad brought death and destruction, so muhammad is NOT the Comforter! The Comforter is the HOLY SPIRIT OF TRUTH, THE SPIRIT OF GOD, THE SPIRIT OF JESUS CHRIST, JUST LIKE HE PLAINLY TELLS US! Jesus Christ is the TRUTH (Jn 14:6) and HIS HOLY SPIRIT is the SPIRIT of TRUTH! (Jn 16:13)

John 14:20-26
King James Version

20 At that day ye shall know that I am in my Father, and ye in me, and I in you.

21 He that hath my commandments, and keepeth them, he it is that loveth me: and he that loveth me shall be loved of my Father, and I will love him, and will manifest myself to him.

22 Judas saith unto him, not Iscariot, Lord, how is it that thou wilt manifest thyself unto us, and not unto the world?

23 Jesus answered and said unto him, If a man love me, he will keep my words: and my Father will love him, and we will come unto him, and make our abode with him.

24 He that loveth me not keepeth not my sayings: and the word which ye hear is not mine, but the Father's which sent me.

25 These things have I spoken unto you, being yet present with you.

26 But the Comforter, which is the Holy Ghost, whom the Father will send in my name, he shall teach you all things, and bring all things to your remembrance, whatsoever I have said unto you.

muhammad came in the name of his evil god, allah, NOT JESUS CHRIST! the Holy Spirit of GOD is given ONLY in the Name of Jesus Christ! (ACTS 2:38-39) (God, Jesus Christ, understands all languages, so whatever your language states for Him in Acts 2:38, as long as you are referring to Jesus Christ, who declares Himself in the Holy Bible, in your language; then God honors His Promise to Give His Holy Spirit to you to testify to the world about Him! Acts 1:8; 4:12)

37When the people heard this, they were cut to the heart and asked Peter and the other apostles, "Brothers, what shall we do?" 38 Peter replied, "Repent and be baptized, every one of you, in the name of Jesus Christ for the forgiveness of your sins, and you will receive the gift of the Holy Spirit. 39This promise belongs to you and your children and to all who are far off—to all whom the Lord our God will call to Himself."...
https://biblehub.com/acts/2-38.htm

God, Jesus Christ, gives us His Holy Spirit to COMFORT us in this wicked world! and He gives us His Holy Spirit of Truth to empower us to TESTIFY THAT JESUS CHRIST IS THE ONE TRUE GOD!

The Ascension
...7Jesus replied, "It is not for you to know times or seasons that the Father has fixed by His own authority. 8But you will receive power when the Holy Spirit comes upon you, and you will be My witnesses in Jerusalem, and in all Judea and Samaria, and to the ends of the earth."
https://biblehub.com/acts/1-8.htm

muhammad was WICKED; not HOLY!
https://www.thereligionofpeace.com/pages/articles/jesusmuhammad.aspx so wicked that muhammad was more like the devil, than he was like Jesus Christ, the One True God!

Jesus Christ is the TRUTH:

John 14:6-9

New King James Version

6 Jesus said to him, "I am the way, the truth, and the life. No one comes to the Father except through Me.

The Father Revealed

7 "If you had known Me, you would have known My Father also; and from now on you know Him and have seen Him."

8 Philip said to Him, "Lord, show us the Father, and it is sufficient for us."

9 Jesus said to him, "Have I been with you so long, and yet you have not known Me, Philip? He who has seen Me has seen the Father; so how can you say, 'Show us the Father'?

That's why His Spirit is called the Spirit of Truth! The Lord say He is the Truth and His Holy Spirit is the Spirit of Truth!

The Promise of the Holy Spirit

…12I still have much to tell you, but you cannot yet bear to hear it. 13However, when the Spirit of truth comes, He will guide you into all truth. For He will not speak on His own, but He will speak what He hears, and He will declare to you what is to come. 14He will glorify Me by taking from what is Mine and disclosing it to you.…
https://biblehub.com/john/16-13.htm

So only those testifying of Jesus Christ, the One True God, have His Holy Spirit of Truth!

The Ascension

…7Jesus replied, "It is not for you to know times or seasons that the Father has fixed by His own authority. 8But you will receive power when the Holy Spirit comes upon you, and you will be My witnesses in Jerusalem, and in

all Judea and Samaria, and to the ends of the earth."
https://biblehub.com/acts/1-8.htm

Living in the Spirit
8Those controlled by the flesh cannot please God. 9You, however, are controlled not by the flesh, but by the Spirit, if the Spirit of God lives in you. And if anyone does not have the Spirit of Christ, he does not belong to Christ. 10But if Christ is in you, your body is dead because of sin, yet your spirit is alive because of righteousness....
https://biblehub.com/romans/8-9.htm

muslims! stop believing and passing on lies! all liars end up in the lake of fire! Rev 21:8

https://www.facebook.com/photo/?fbid=6800758120003089&set=a.115635768515391 - Christians testify that Jesus Christ is the One True God, it's the reason they bear His Name and have His Holy Spirit of Truth. Christians isn't a name of insult like your cult teaches, it's a name of Glorious Praise to JESUS CHRIST! Those who bear His Name, should pray we live like He wants us to always. Amen.

The Ascension

...7Jesus replied, "It is not for you to know times or seasons that the Father has fixed by His own authority. 8But you will receive power when the Holy Spirit comes upon you, and you will be My witnesses in Jerusalem, and in all Judea and Samaria, and to the ends of the earth."
https://biblehub.com/acts/1-8.htm

So Christians in the region would say "Yeshua Christos Akbar!" not giving lipservice to the evil god, allah, of the muslims.

Living in the Spirit

8Those controlled by the flesh cannot please God. 9You, however, are controlled not by the flesh, but by the Spirit, if the Spirit of God lives in you. And if anyone does not have the Spirit of Christ, he does not belong to Christ. 10But if Christ is in you, your body is dead because of sin, yet your spirit is alive because of righteousness....
https://biblehub.com/romans/8-9.htm

IF ANYONE DOES NOT TESTIFY THAT JESUS CHRIST IS YHWH THE ONE TRUE GOD WHO CAME IN THE FLESH, THEY ARE NOT OF GOD! (not a Christian)

1 John 4:1-6

English Standard Version

Test the Spirits

4 Beloved, do not believe every spirit, but test the spirits to see whether they are from God, for many false prophets have gone out into the world. 2 By this you know the Spirit of God: every spirit that confesses that Jesus Christ has come in the flesh is from God, 3 and every spirit that does not confess Jesus is not from God. This is the spirit of the antichrist, which you heard was coming and now is in the world already. 4 Little children, you are from God and have overcome them, for he who is in you is greater than he who is in the world. 5 They are from the world; therefore they speak from the world, and the world listens to them. 6 We are from God. Whoever knows God listens to us; whoever is not from God does not listen to us. By this we know the Spirit of truth and the spirit of error.

So, no Christian gives the highest praise to anyone but Jesus Christ, the One True God! they certainly do not praise the name of any false gods, like the evil allah!

http://www.inthenameofallah.org

https://www.hope-of-israel.org/baaloftheOT.html

When muslims testify of allah and muhammad they bear false witness of a false prophet and his imaginary evil god, the contents of the quran and hadiths are just stories some of which were copied and others completely untrue and so the testimony of muslims is meaningless. muhammad and allah have nothing whatsoever in common with the Prophets in the Holy Bible and YHWH/JESUS CHRIST. If they did, there would be no muslims and certainly not the ones that have been attacking and murdering Holy Bible believers throughout history to this very day.

Jesus Christ is God who came in the flesh, just as the Holy Bible tells us. The fact all muslims deny the One True God, for their evil allah instead, shows us that islam comes from the devil, the spirit of err/antichrist and is why muslims deny Christ, and fight Christians to this very day.

https://www.thereligionofpeace.com/pages/articles/jesusmuhammad.aspx - muhammad was a lying false prophet, and allah is just another name for the devil.

This is why raping, robbing, slaving, murdering muslims attacked innocent people from the foundation of islam:
https://www.youtube.com/watch?v=I_To-cV94Bo

This is why there were centuries of brutal islamic slavery on earth:
https://www.google.com/search?client=opera&q=centuries+of+islamic+slave+trade&sourceid=opera&ie=UTF-8&oe=UTF-8

This is why muhammad was a racist who had slaves: https://www.youtube.com/watch?v=1HbOhLJHcFo

and it's why hundreds of millions of innocent people have been murdered by muslims: https://www.politicalislam.com/tears-of-jihad/

It's why muslims are still burning churches even to this very day: https://www.google.com/search?client=opera&q=muslims+burn+churches&sourceid=opera&ie=UTF-8&oe=UTF-8

and is why the evil quran advocates openly all these crimes: https://www.thereligionofpeace.com/pages/quran/index.aspx

And is why you muslims yourself offer lip service to the Prophets in the Holy Bible while openly calling them all liars, choosing to believe the lying quran over the Holy Bible.

It's why Jesus Christ the One True God, calls all muslims, antichrists, on their way to the lake of fire, because muslims are in fact, His enemies, and the enemies of His People who are in the Holy Bible and to this very day are His Disciples, known as Christians.

Beware of Antichrists

...21I have not written to you because you lack knowledge of the truth, but because you have it, and because no lie comes from the truth. 22Who is the liar, if it is not the one who denies that Jesus is the Christ? This is the antichrist, who denies the Father and the Son. 23Whoever denies the Son does not have the Father, but whoever confesses the Son has the Father as well.... https://biblehub.com/1_john/2-22.htm

ANYONE DENYING JESUS CHRIST IS THE ONE TRUE GOD, WHO CAME IN THE FLESH, IS AN ANTICHRIST! all such wicked persons will be cast into the lake of fire, if they refuse to repent and receive Jesus Christ as the Lord and Savior that He is.

1 John 4:1-6

Test the Spirits

4 Beloved, do not believe every spirit, but test the spirits to see whether they are from God, for many false prophets have gone out into the world. 2 By this you know the Spirit of God: every spirit that confesses that Jesus Christ has come in the flesh is from God, 3 and every spirit that does not confess Jesus is not from God. This is the spirit of the antichrist, which you heard was coming and now is in the world already. 4 Little children, you are from God and have overcome them, for he who is in you is greater than he who is in the world. 5 They are from the world; therefore they speak from the world, and the world listens to them. 6 We are from God. Whoever knows God listens to us; whoever is not from God does not listen to us. By this we know the Spirit of truth and the spirit of error.

A New Heaven and a New Earth

…7The one who overcomes will inherit all things, and I will be his God, and he will be My son. 8But to the cowardly and unbelieving and abominable and murderers and sexually immoral and sorcerers and idolaters and all liars, their place will be in the lake that burns with fire and sulfur. This is the second death." https://biblehub.com/revelation/21-8.htm

Peter and John Before the Council

…11This Jesus is 'the stone you builders rejected, which has become the cornerstone.' 12 Salvation exists in no one else, for there is no other name under heaven given to men by which we must be saved."
https://biblehub.com/acts/4-12.htm

Jesus Christ is the Truth; His Spirit is the Spirit of Truth. The scriptures make this redundantly clear and this quote from the Holy Bible is most definitely not about the criminal muhammad.

John 14:6-9

New King James Version

6 Jesus said to him, "I am the way, the truth, and the life. No one comes to the Father except through Me.

The Father Revealed

7 "If you had known Me, you would have known My Father also; and from now on you know Him and have seen Him."

8 Philip said to Him, "Lord, show us the Father, and it is sufficient for us."

9 Jesus said to him, "Have I been with you so long, and yet you have not known Me, Philip? He who has seen Me has seen the Father; so how can you say, 'Show us the Father'?

Jesus Promises the Holy Spirit

...16And I will ask the Father, and He will give you another Advocate to be with you forever— 17the Spirit of truth. The world cannot receive Him, because it neither sees Him nor knows Him. But you do know Him, for He abides with you and will be in you. 18I will not leave you as orphans; I will come to you.... https://biblehub.com/john/14-17.htm

muhammad was a criminal in the flesh, muhammad was a liar; not a comforter at all, has nothing whatsoever to do with Jesus Christ who is the Truth. Virtually, everything muslims are taught to reject Jesus Christ as GOD is due to muhammad's LIES.

https://www.thereligionofpeace.com/pages/articles/jesusmuhammad.aspx

In the context above, Jesus Christ PLAINLY tells us the SPIRIT OF TRUTH will be inside of us because HE IS SPIRIT and tells us that is Jesus Christ, when He concludes by saying "I WILL COME TO YOU." in other words Jesus Christ is the Truth and His Spirit is the Holy Spirit of Truth and that is how Jesus Christ lives inside of us. HIS HOLY SPIRIT IS WITH EVERYONE WHO IS A TRUE CHRISTIAN! Rom 8:8-10 That's why He said,"...in as much as you did it to the least of these, you did it unto ME!" and also why He said, to those who did not do unto the least of these, you did it NOT UNTO ME! God is with all who trust in Him, who have Repented of their Sins and gotten Baptized in His Name!

John 14:20-26
English Standard Version
20 In that day you will know that I am in my Father, and you in me, and I in you. 21 Whoever has my commandments and keeps them, he it is who loves me. And he who loves me will be loved by my Father, and I will love him and manifest myself to him." 22 Judas (not Iscariot) said to him, "Lord, how is it that you will manifest yourself to us, and not to the world?" 23 Jesus answered him, "If anyone loves me, he will keep my word, and my Father will love him, and we will come to him and make our home with him. 24 Whoever does not love me does not keep my words. And the word that you hear is not mine but the Father's who sent me.

25 "These things I have spoken to you while I am still with you. 26 But the Helper, the Holy Spirit, whom the Father will send in my name, he will teach you all things and bring to your remembrance all that I have said to you.

The scriptures are crystal clear that the Holy Spirit of Jesus Christ is given in HIS NAME! (not muhammad)

37When the people heard this, they were cut to the heart and asked Peter and the other apostles, "Brothers, what shall we do?" 38 Peter replied, "Repent and be baptized, every one of you, in the name of Jesus Christ for the forgiveness of your sins, and you will receive the gift of the Holy Spirit. 39This promise belongs to you and your children and to all who are far off—to all whom the Lord our God will call to Himself."...
https://biblehub.com/acts/2-38.htm

It is the very REAL PRESENCE of JESUS CHRIST in our lives by HIS HOLY SPIRIT OF TRUTH that makes us a true Christian, a Disciple of Jesus Christ, a follower of the One True God.

Living in the Spirit
8Those controlled by the flesh cannot please God. 9You, however, are controlled not by the flesh, but by the Spirit, if the Spirit of God lives in you. And if anyone does not have the Spirit of Christ, he does not belong to Christ. 10But if Christ is in you, your body is dead because of sin, yet your spirit is alive because of righteousness....
https://biblehub.com/romans/8-9.htm

So, the Holy Spirit of Truth is obviously the Spirit of Jesus Christ, the One True God, Himself.

Peter and John Before the Council
...11This Jesus is 'the stone you builders rejected, which has become the cornerstone.' 12 Salvation exists in no one else, for there is no other name under heaven given to men by which we must be saved." 13When they saw the boldness of Peter and John and realized that they were unschooled, ordinary men, they marveled and took note that these men had been with Jesus.... https://biblehub.com/acts/4-12.htm

another common lie muslims are taught is to claim muhammad was prophesied of in Deuteronomy 18 but no! absolutely not!

when muslims post the lies they believe, it only exposes them as liars. If you believe lies, you become a liar. You need to make sure that what you believe is absolutely true and the only way anyone can be certain of that is by knowing the One who tells us He is the Truth! Jn 14:6-9, Jn 8:32-36

muhammad was not from among the brothers of Moses. Beginning with Moses and his Brothers on down, were ALL Israelites. (not ishmaelites at all) so no, muhammad has nothing whatsoever to do with this prophecy.

Instead, the scriptures plainly tell us Jesus Christ is the Prophet that ALL MUST listen to.

https://www.oneforisrael.org/bible-based-teaching-from-israel/21-waysyeshua-is-a-prophet-like-moses/ - Jesus Christ

https://answersingenesis.org/jesus/who-is-prophet-like-moses/ - Jesus Christ clearly.

Virtually every day, I see muslims posting lies online. Like the common one where they falsely claim Jesus Christ isn't God because He didn't tell us the day and hour of His Return in the Holy Bible. So muslims COMPLETELY IGNORE THE ENTIRE CONTENTS OF THE HOLY BIBLE TO DENY THE ONE TRUE GOD, JESUS CHRIST, WHO TELLS US HE IS GOD HUNDREDS OF TIMES IN THOSE CONTENTS AND PROVED IT LIKE NO ONE ELSE IN THE ENTIRE HISTORY OF THE WORLD, just to rip His Words out of context to twist them, just like the devil did with Eve.

So when God came in the flesh as the Messiah, Jesus Christ, He tells us He emptied Himself (https://biblehub.com/philippians/2-7.htm) and that obviously included such Divine Knowledge as the day and hour of His Return. So no, it doesn't mean any nonsense muslims believe at all, such as denying the Divinity of Jesus Christ. Why? because Jesus Christ tells us He is God plainly MANY TIMES OVER IN THE HOLY BIBLE and Proved it beyond all reasonable doubt! He ever lives to answer any and all with enough sense to call upon Him.

In the Holy Bible, He tells us reasons why He doesn't tell us the hour of His Return:

1 Thessalonians 5

King James Version

5 But of the times and the seasons, brethren, ye have no need that I write unto you.

2 For yourselves know perfectly that the day of the Lord so cometh as a thief in the night.

3 For when they shall say, Peace and safety; then sudden destruction cometh upon them, as travail upon a woman with child; and they shall not escape.

4 But ye, brethren, are not in darkness, that that day should overtake you as a thief.

5 Ye are all the children of light, and the children of the day: we are not of the night, nor of darkness.

6 Therefore let us not sleep, as do others; but let us watch and be sober.

7 For they that sleep sleep in the night; and they that be drunken are drunken in the night.

8 But let us, who are of the day, be sober, putting on the breastplate of faith and love; and for an helmet, the hope of salvation.

9 For God hath not appointed us to wrath, but to obtain salvation by our Lord Jesus Christ,

2 Thessalonians 2

King James Version

2 Now we beseech you, brethren, by the coming of our Lord Jesus Christ, and by our gathering together unto him,

2		That ye be not soon shaken in mind, or be troubled, neither by spirit, nor by word, nor by letter as from us, as that the day of Christ is at hand.

3		Let no man deceive you by any means: for that day shall not come, except there come a falling away first, and that man of sin be revealed, the son of perdition;

4		Who opposeth and exalteth himself above all that is called God, or that is worshipped; so that he as God sitteth in the temple of God, shewing himself that he is God.

5		Remember ye not, that, when I was yet with you, I told you these things?

6		And now ye know what withholdeth that he might be revealed in his time.

7		For the mystery of iniquity doth already work: only he who now letteth will let, until he be taken out of the way.
8		And then shall that Wicked be revealed, whom the Lord shall consume with the spirit of his mouth, and shall destroy with the brightness of his coming:

9		Even him, whose coming is after the working of Satan with all power and signs and lying wonders,

10		And with all deceivableness of unrighteousness in them that perish; because they received not the love of the truth, that they might be saved.

11   And for this cause God shall send them strong delusion, that they should believe a lie:

12   That they all might be damned who believed not the truth, but had pleasure in unrighteousness.

So, God tells us the reason why He doesn't tell us the day or hour of His Return is that He is going to respond furiously with all those who refused His Commandment to Repent of their wicked ways, when He told them to do so, by the proclamation of His Gospel in the Holy Bible. So, His Day of Vengeance takes the wicked by surprise.

1As God's fellow workers, then, we urge you not to receive God's grace in vain. 2For He says: "In the time of favor I heard you, and in the day of salvation I helped you." Behold, now is the time of favor; now is the day of salvation! 3We put no obstacle in anyone's way, so that no one can discredit our ministry.... https://biblehub.com/2_corinthians/6-2.htm

In other words, anyone refusing to Repent of their wicked ways and obey our Living Lord Jesus Christ IMMEDIATELY, is rebelling against God and turning themselves into His enemies and so is risking His Wrath and the flames of damnation. REPENT NOW! is His Commandment, not tomorrow or the next day or the next or just before He Descends from Heaven Above, BUT NOW! RIGHT NOW! because no one knows if God is going to give them another breath, let alone another day.

muslims are online constantly posting the same false claims and lies islam has taught them all, so I am just compiling my responses so that people can just hand them the book that refutes their common false claims about the contents of the Holy Bible. Like these three locations they use to deny Jesus Christ is God, who said He is God and Proved He is God like no one else in the entire history of the world. So, one of them was citing these three passages claiming that it's reason not to worship Jesus Christ even though Jesus Christ is God who has always been worshiped. Jesus Christ ALWAYS receives worship, because He is God!

https://www.openbible.info/topics/worshipping_jesus so interpreting anything He said as recorded in the Holy Bible as somehow denial of that fact is MISINTERPRETATION!

Peter Speaks in Solomon's Colonnade

…12And when Peter saw this, he addressed the people: "Men of Israel, why are you surprised by this? Why do you stare at us as if by our own power or godliness we had made this man walk? 13The God of Abraham, Isaac, and Jacob, the God of our fathers, has glorified His servant Jesus. You handed Him over and rejected Him before Pilate, even though he had decided to release Him. 14You rejected the Holy and Righteous One and asked that a murderer be released to you.… https://biblehub.com/acts/3-13.htm

In your first citation you completely ignore the context that tells us that the Apostle healed someone by the Power of Jesus Christ and in His Name (a Divine Miracle is proof of Divinity) and furthermore refers to Jesus Christ as "the Holy and Righteous One" which is a reference directly to God. God serves Himself. Jesus Christ is the Servant of servants; it is not a reference in the scriptures to assuming Jesus Christ isn't God because the scriptures tell us all plainly, HE IS SUPREME IN EVERYTHING! Col 1:15-19 So that passage is teaching us that Jesus Christ is God who empowers even His Disciples to do Divine Miracles in His Name.

(God serves Himself.)

Luke 6:12-16

The Twelve Apostles

12 In these days he went out to the mountain to pray, and all night he continued in prayer to God. 13 And when day came, he called his disciples and chose from them twelve, whom he named apostles: 14 Simon, whom he named Peter, and Andrew his brother, and James and John, and Philip, and Bartholomew, 15 and Matthew, and Thomas, and James the son of

Alphaeus, and Simon who was called the Zealot, 16 and Judas the son of James, and Judas Iscariot, who became a traitor.

In the second citation God chooses His Twelve Apostles, those who testified to the whole world that Jesus Christ is God.

The humanity of Jesus Christ when He came in the flesh still prayed to His Divinity as His Way of leading us all by example. His Eternal Existence is invisible, pervasive and transcendent upon all creation - Eph 4:6. GOD EMPTIED HIMSELF to walk in the flesh as One of us, among us and so prays to His Eternal Existence as one of us, again never changing the fact that He is God. Phil 2:7 And so leads us not just by His Words, but by His EXAMPLE, His Deeds.

Jesus Appears to Thomas

…27Then Jesus said to Thomas, "Put your finger here and look at My hands. Reach out your hand and put it into My side. Stop doubting and believe." 28Thomas replied, "My Lord and my God!" 29Jesus said to him, "Because you have seen Me, you have believed; blessed are those who have not seen and yet have believed."… https://biblehub.com/john/20-28.htm

20And we know that the Son of God has come and has given us understanding, so that we may know Him who is true; and we are in Him who is true— in His Son Jesus Christ. He is the TRUE God and eternal life. 21Little children, keep yourselves from idols.…
https://biblehub.com/1_john/5-20.htm

Eyewitnesses of His Majesty

15And I will make every effort to ensure that after my departure, you will be able to recall these things at all times. 16For we did not follow cleverly devised fables when we made known to you the power and coming of our Lord Jesus Christ, but we were eyewitnesses of His majesty. 17For He received honor and glory from God the Father when the voice came to Him from the Majestic Glory, saying, "This is My beloved Son, in whom I am well pleased."... https://biblehub.com/2_peter/1-16.htm

God's Grace Brings Salvation

...12It instructs us to renounce ungodliness and worldly passions, and to live sensible, upright, and godly lives in the present age, 13as we await the blessed hope and glorious appearance of our great God and Savior Jesus Christ. 14He gave Himself for us to redeem us from all lawlessness and to purify for Himself a people for His own possession, zealous for good deeds.... https://biblehub.com/titus/2-13.htm

Peter and John Before the Council

...11This Jesus is 'the stone you builders rejected, which has become the cornerstone.' 12 Salvation exists in no one else, for there is no other name under heaven given to men by which we must be saved." 13When they saw the boldness of Peter and John and realized that they were unschooled, ordinary men, they marveled and took note that these men had been with Jesus.... https://biblehub.com/acts/4-12.htm

And your third citation:

Matthew 7:21-23

I Never Knew You

21 "Not everyone who says to me, 'Lord, Lord,' will enter the kingdom of heaven, but the one who does the will of my Father who is in heaven. 22

On that day many will say to me, 'Lord, Lord, did we not prophesy in your name, and cast out demons in your name, and do many mighty works in your name?' 23 And then will I declare to them, 'I never knew you; depart from me, you workers of lawlessness.'

Plainly states that not EVERYONE who calls Jesus Christ "LORD" is going to enter the Kingdom of Heaven, but only those who obey Him; only those who KNOW Him.

Jesus Christ DECLARES to us the WILL OF THE FATHER (Jn 14:6-9, Jn 12:49-50, Jn 8:28,29) and tells us HIS COMMANDMENTS. Jesus Christ GAVE US HIS COMMANDMENTS and so He is telling us it's not just enough to acknowledge He is Lord, BUT WE MUST OBEY HIM!

In other words, this is about the many religious people (like yourself) who offer lip service to Jesus Christ but don't even know Him, let alone obey Him. It's more specifically about false Christians who go to church and do the churchy things but have no personal relationship with Jesus Christ whatsoever.

In other words, true Christians, KNOW the Savior, and that HE ALONE HAS SAVED THEM! So, they don't attempt to justify themselves by any of their own things that they have done.

Ephesians 2:1-10 ESV

And you were dead in the trespasses and sins in which you once walked, following the course of this world, following the prince of the power of the air, the spirit that is now at work in the sons of disobedience— among whom we all once lived in the passions of our flesh, carrying out the desires of the body and the mind, and were by nature children of wrath, like the rest of mankind. But God, being rich in mercy, because of the great love with which he loved us, even when we were dead in our trespasses, made us alive together with Christ—by grace you have been saved— and raised us up with him and seated us with him in the heavenly places in Christ Jesus, so that in the coming ages he might show the immeasurable riches of his grace in kindness toward us in Christ Jesus. For by grace you have been saved through faith. And this is not your own doing; it is the gift of God, not a result of works, so that no one may boast. For we are his workmanship, created in Christ Jesus for good works, which God prepared beforehand, that we should walk in them.

https://biblehub.com/acts/4-12.htm

Next, another muslim was falsely claiming they respect Jesus Christ and was asking why Christians don't respect muhammad.

Denying Jesus Christ is the One True God that He showed Himself to be, is disrespecting Him and everyone who knows Him. When you call Jesus Christ, His Prophets and His Disciples in the Holy Bible ALL LIARS, in order to believe the lies of muhammad in the quran, you are disrespecting the One True God and all His Witnesses, and actually serving the devil instead. (the devil is the father of lies -
https://www.biblegateway.com/passage/?search=John%208%3A43-45&version=KJV)
https://www.thereligionofpeace.com/pages/articles/jesusmuhammad.aspx - muhammad is the liar that has deceived all muslims into denying the One True God, Jesus Christ. muhammad was a murderer, slaver, robber, pedophile and was a perverse criminal in all respects, not a prophet; he deserves NO RESPECT!

muslims are simply deluding themselves about their god, their so-called prophet and about the facts of history and reality. When you believe the lies of the devil, you are serving the devil.

Jesus Christ, the One True God is the only ONE who can set you free!

John 8:32-36
King James Version
32 And ye shall know the truth, and the truth shall make you free.

33 They answered him, We be Abraham's seed, and were never in bondage to any man: how sayest thou, Ye shall be made free?

34 Jesus answered them, Verily, verily, I say unto you, Whosoever committeth sin is the servant of sin.

35 And the servant abideth not in the house for ever: but the Son abideth ever.

36 If the Son therefore shall make you free, ye shall be free indeed.

The Lord's Approved Workman
…25He must gently reprove those who oppose him, in the hope that God may grant them repentance leading to a knowledge of the truth. 26Then they will come to their senses and escape the snare of the devil, who has taken them captive to his will. https://biblehub.com/2_timothy/2-26.htm

In other words, not one muslim hears, sees or knows God and that is because the lying muhammad taught them all to deny the One True God, Jesus Christ, who is the only One who can set them free from the lying devil!

…19We know that we are of God, and that the whole world is under the power of the evil one. 20And we know that the Son of God has come and has given us understanding, so that we may know Him who is true; and we are in Him who is true— in His Son Jesus Christ. He is the TRUE God and eternal life. 21Little children, keep yourselves from idols.…
https://biblehub.com/1_john/5-20.htm

Peter and John Before the Council
...11This Jesus is 'the stone you builders rejected, which has become the cornerstone.' 12 Salvation exists in no one else, for there is no other name under heaven given to men by which we must be saved."
https://biblehub.com/acts/4-12.htm

muslims are crying victims and complaining that the Israelites are occupying land that belongs to them, but this isn't true at all.

muslims came into this world centuries AFTER the Israelites, Jesus Christ, Jews and Christians, and they murdered - ATTACKED ANCIENT ISRAEL! muslims have NO RIGHT whatsoever to that land! they were just wicked criminals who murdered innocent people and drove them away! https://www.youtube.com/watch?v=I_To-cV94Bo - islam was founded by muhammad and his gang of rapists, robbers, slavers and murderers that raided the civilized world and murdered mass millions of innocent people. muslims have been attacking innocent people from the foundation of islam to this very day. muslims just don't know the facts of their entire history, they're all told muhammad was something wonderful, when he was detestable!

The ISRAELITES were given the LAND OF ISRAEL BY GOD HIMSELF! and were an ancient nation IN THAT LAND for many thousands of years before raping, robbing, murdering muslims attacked them.

https://www.google.com/search?client=opera&q=maps+of+ancient+Israel&sourceid=opera&ie=UTF-8&oe=UTF-8 - when criminal muslims attacked the Israelites, they showed themselves to be demonic, being ruled by the devil, by taking the name of the philistines and so called the land palestine, when in fact it's called Israel by God Himself who gave that land by covenant to Jacob/Israel and His Descendents.

The Renaming of Abraham

...7I will establish My covenant as an everlasting covenant between Me and you and your descendants after you, to be your God and the God of your descendants after you. 8And to you and your descendants I will give the land where you are residing— all the land of Canaan— as an eternal possession; and I will be their God." https://biblehub.com/genesis/17-8.htm

Genesis 15:18

On that day the LORD made a covenant with Abram, saying, "To your descendants I have given this land--from the river of Egypt to the great River Euphrates-- (note that muslims are occupying an enormous amount of land that the Israelites have a right to by Divine Covenant.)

and that land passed to Jacob/Israel -

The Command to Leave Horeb

...7Resume your journey and go to the hill country of the Amorites; go to all the neighboring peoples in the Arabah, in the hill country, in the foothills, in the Negev, and along the seacoast to the land of the Canaanites and to Lebanon, as far as the great River Euphrates. 8See, I have placed the land before you. Enter and possess the land that the LORD swore He would give to your fathers Abraham, Isaac, and Jacob, and to their descendants after them." https://biblehub.com/deuteronomy/1-8.htm

So that land belongs to Israel, by Divine Covenant, from the One True God, NOT ANY MUSLIMS! In fact, the true borders of Israel are much larger and if I were them, I would insist on those borders because those borders belong to the Israelites by Divine Agreement and Decree from the One

True God. Make certain NO MUSLIMS are allowed in your borders and tear down the abomination of desolation - the mosque to the demonic god of muslims in the temple mount! The holocaust survivors should tell their leaders and the rest of the world, that land belongs to the Israelites by Divine Covenant! muslims have many thousands of times the land mass of Israel to resettle in (the expenses of resettlements and organizing the proper borders of Israel, should be carried about by United Nations agreement), and so any muslims wanting to rebel against God by warring with Him and His People are risking not just their lives in the flesh but their everlasting souls (being cast away as the enemies of God and His People that they are showing themselves to be by warring against the Israelites.)

https://img.jagranjosh.com/images/2021/May/2052021/greaterisrael.jpg

Next a common objection from muslims is that Jesus Christ could not have suffered and died for us because no man can die for another, each must bear their own consequences for their own sins. So, this is what they ignore in the Holy Bible:

No sinner can die for another sinner because all such guilty persons are already under their own death sentence by God for sinning against Him, but Jesus Christ is GOD Himself who came in the flesh. Jesus Christ is HOLY, Sinless, Righteous, the ONLY ONE who could take upon Himself the penalty for the sins of mankind.

In His Law and Prophecies, He tells us all He is our Redeemer.

https://bible.knowing-jesus.com/topics/God,-As-Redeemer

According to His Law of Redemption, someone can indeed pay the price for another. Regarding the sins of mankind, ONLY GOD could pay that price in full and that is what He did. Everyone SHOULD BE GRATEFUL! but instead FAR TOO MANY wickedly deny His Forgiveness, Love, Mercy, Redemption and Salvation.

https://www.preceptaustin.org/tetelestai_paid_in_full

Peter and John Before the Council
...11This Jesus is 'the stone you builders rejected, which has become the cornerstone.' 12 Salvation exists in no one else, for there is no other name under heaven given to men by which we must be saved."
https://biblehub.com/acts/4-12.htm

Jesus Christ, the One True God, is the ONLY SAVIOR, because ONLY HE COULD FULFILL HIS LAW AND PROPHECIES, including His Law and Prophecies of being OUR REDEEMER!

https://www.accordingtothescriptures.org/prophecy/353prophecies.html
The Fulfillment of the Law
16In the same way, let your light shine before men, that they may see your good deeds and glorify your Father in heaven. 17Do not think that I have come to abolish the Law or the Prophets. I have not come to abolish them, but to fulfill them. 18For I tell you truly, until heaven and earth pass away, not a single jot, not a stroke of a pen, will disappear from the Law until everything is accomplished.... https://biblehub.com/matthew/5-17.htm

Jesus Opens the Scriptures
25Then Jesus said to them, "O foolish ones, how slow are your hearts to believe all that the prophets have spoken! 26 Was it not necessary for the Christ to suffer these things and then to enter His glory?" 27And beginning with Moses and all the Prophets, He explained to them what was written in all the Scriptures about Himself.... https://biblehub.com/luke/24-26.htm

Sadly, muslims are constantly posting lies because that's what they've all been taught. Like they make claims like they love and obey Jesus Christ, but not one muslim actually does or they wouldn't be muslims! instead, they would all be Christians!

The Great Commission

...15And He said to them, "Go into all the world and preach the gospel to every creature. 16Whoever believes and is baptized will be saved, but whoever does not believe will be condemned.
https://biblehub.com/mark/16-16.htm

"Brothers, what shall we do?" 38 Peter replied, "Repent and be baptized, every one of you, in the name of Jesus Christ for the forgiveness of your sins, and you will receive the gift of the Holy Spirit. 39This promise belongs to you and your children and to all who are far off—to all whom the Lord our God will call to Himself."... https://biblehub.com/acts/2-38.htm

Peter and John Before the Council

...11This Jesus is 'the stone you builders rejected, which has become the cornerstone.' 12 Salvation exists in no one else, for there is no other name under heaven given to men by which we must be saved."
https://biblehub.com/acts/4-12.htm

...the disciples were first called Christians at Antioch. Acts 11:26

So if any muslims actually obeyed Jesus Christ, they would be Christians.
No muslims, you do not love our Lord Jesus Christ, none of them do as He commands! Mt 28:18-20

muslims are constantly denying the historicity of the Holy Bible, especially regarding the life, death, crucifixion, resurrection and ascension of Jesus Christ.

islam is a world of lies. https://coldcasechristianity.com/writings/is-thereany-evidence-for-jesus-outside-the-bible/ - the life, death, crucifixion, resurrection and ascension of Jesus Christ are some of the strongest, most attested facts in all ancient history.
https://www.youtube.com/watch?v=ay_Db4RwZ_M

Anyone who denies those facts is not just showing themselves to be ignorant but are in open denial of well verified history. (are deceived and self-deluded)

https://youtu.be/LLnClp3OVmE?t=1884 - not just the most thoroughly studied and verified book in all the world (the Holy Bible) plainly tells us Jesus Christ was crucified, but His Burial Cloth is the most studied artifact in all the world and confirms it. (So muslims have their heads full of so many lies that they appear to be not just ignorant, but delusional.)

I respond to these common lies not to insult muslims, but with the hope they will all choose to stop believing the many lies islam has taught them, and learn to call upon Jesus Christ who is the Truth instead. (Holy Bible = True; quran = false)

Today a muslim was asking another common question, I've seen many times: why did Jesus pray in the Garden of Gethsemane? (it is their common way of asking why if Jesus is God who came in the flesh why did He pray?) and my common response is that God teaches not just by His Words, but by His Example/Deeds.

The scriptures teach us all that while we are in the flesh we have to keep our bodies in subjection to our spirits, especially the HOLY SPIRIT of GOD.

Living in the Spirit
8Those controlled by the flesh cannot please God. 9You, however, are controlled not by the flesh, but by the Spirit, if the Spirit of God lives in you. And if anyone does not have the Spirit of Christ, he does not belong to Christ. 10But if Christ is in you, your body is dead because of sin, yet your spirit is alive because of righteousness....
https://biblehub.com/romans/8-9.htm

So, when God came into this world as the Humble Servant Messiah, a Man, He tells us He emptied Himself.

The Attitude of Christ
...6Who, existing in the form of God, did not consider equality with God something to be grasped, 7but emptied Himself, taking the form of a servant, being made in human likeness. 8And being found in appearance as a man, He humbled Himself and became obedient to death—even death on a cross.... https://biblehub.com/philippians/2-7.htm

Jesus Christ KNEW He was going to be crucified; He told His Own Apostles that fact numerous times:

The Resurrection
...6He is not here; He has risen! Remember how He told you while He was still in Galilee: 7 'The Son of Man must be delivered into the hands of sinful men, and be crucified, and on the third day rise again.'" 8Then they remembered His words.... https://biblehub.com/luke/24-7.htm

Matthew 16:21

From that time on Jesus began to show His disciples that He must go to Jerusalem and suffer many things at the hands of the elders, chief priests, and scribes, and that He must be killed and on the third day be raised to life.

Luke 24:26
Was it not necessary for the Christ to suffer these things and then to enter His glory?"

Luke 24:46
And He told them, "This is what is written: The Christ will suffer and rise from the dead on the third day,

you (muslim) are not a prophet, but if you were, you would know EXACTLY what it FEELS like if you knew your own death before it even happened. So, in the moment when Christ KNEW HE MUST GO THROUGH WITH IT, He still battled His Own Flesh, BECAUSE HE KNEW EXACTLY what He was going to go through BEFORE it even happened! THAT'S LOVE! THAT'S COURAGE! So of course He prayed for Strength from His Spirit, to make His Body go through with what He KNEW HE MUST DO!

But I keep under my body, and bring it into subjection: lest that by any means, when I have preached to others, I myself should be a castaway. - https://biblehub.com/1_corinthians/9-27.htm

God came in the flesh and showed us how to go through things we could not go through without Him.
https://www.accordingtothescriptures.org/prophecy/353prophecies.html

https://tile.loc.gov/storageservices/public/gdcmassbookdig/foxesbookofmart00fo/foxesbookofmart00fo.pdf

it is improper of muslims to rip the Words of God out of context in order to go on denying Jesus Christ is God, when He tells us that fact throughout the entire Holy Bible.

Jesus Appears to Thomas
...27Then Jesus said to Thomas, "Put your finger here and look at My hands. Reach out your hand and put it into My side. Stop doubting and believe." 28Thomas replied, "My Lord and my God!" 29Jesus said to him, "Because you have seen Me, you have believed; blessed are those who have not seen and yet have believed."... https://biblehub.com/john/20-28.htm

John 5:39-40
39 You search the Scriptures because you think that in them you have eternal life; and it is they that bear witness about me, 40 yet you refuse to come to me that you may have life.

So God, Jesus Christ, fully understands the battle we all go through in the flesh.

Jesus the Great High Priest
14Therefore, since we have a great high priest who has passed through the heavens, Jesus the Son of God, let us hold firmly to what we profess. 15For we do not have a high priest who is unable to sympathize with our weaknesses, but we have one who was tempted in every way that we are, yet was without sin. 16Let us then approach the throne of grace with

confidence, so that we may receive mercy and find grace to help us in our time of need.... https://biblehub.com/hebrews/4-15.htm

Because muslims belong to an evil cult and criminal organization, they all the time look at the world through their own defiled minds and so look even at the Holy Bible wickedly. Constantly, they falsely accuse Jesus Christ of wrong doing, just like so many who don't know Him yet all over this world. One of the passages they cite is when Christ asked His Disciples to sell their clothes to buy a sword. So today another muslim was making that post and false accusation.

you read that two swords are enough and you compare that to outright bloodshed of islam?
https://www.thereligionofpeace.com/pages/quran/violence.aspx
Scriptures Must Be Fulfilled in Jesus

35 And he said to them, "When I sent you out with no moneybag or knapsack or sandals, did you lack anything?" They said, "Nothing." 36 He said to them, "But now let the one who has a moneybag take it, and likewise a knapsack. And let the one who has no sword sell his cloak and buy one. 37 For I tell you that this Scripture must be fulfilled in me: 'And he was numbered with the transgressors.' For what is written about me has its fulfillment." 38 And they said, "Look, Lord, here are two swords." And he said to them, "It is enough."
https://www.biblegateway.com/passage/?search=Luke%2022&version=ESV

In the days of Jesus Christ, there were armed rebels who were considered transgressors; so, Christ was asking if any of His Disciples had a sword so that the prophesy would be fulfilled "that he was numbered with the transgressors". That's why He said only two swords among them all was enough.

So, this passage is not advocating anything evil such as violently attacking innocent people and shedding innocent blood, like the quran does. It was simply enough to be numbered as among the transgressors in the prophecy above.
https://www.thereligionofpeace.com/pages/quran/index.aspx

Today, 11-09-23, a muslim was asking why Jesus Christ was likened to the serpent that Moses lifted up to save the Israelites in the wilderness.

Christ Redeemed Us
...12The law, however, is not based on faith; on the contrary, "The man who does these things will live by them." 13Christ redeemed us from the curse of the law by becoming a curse for us. For it is written: "Cursed is everyone who is hung on a tree." 14He redeemed us in order that the blessing promised to Abraham would come to the Gentiles in Christ Jesus, so that by faith we might receive the promise of the Spirit....
https://biblehub.com/galatians/3-13.htm

The War in Heaven
...9And the great dragon was hurled down—that ancient serpent called the devil and Satan, the deceiver of the whole world. He was hurled to the earth, and his angels with him. 10And I heard a loud voice in heaven saying: "Now have come the salvation and the power and the kingdom of our God, and the authority of His Christ. For the accuser of our brothers has been thrown down— he who accuses them day and night before our God. 11They have conquered him by the blood of the Lamb and by the word of their testimony. And they did not love their lives so as to shy away from death.... https://biblehub.com/revelation/12-10.htm

Alive in Christ
...13When you were dead in your trespasses and in the uncircumcision of your sinful nature, God made you alive with Christ. He forgave us all our trespasses, 14having canceled the debt ascribed to us in the decrees that

stood against us. He took it away, nailing it to the cross! 15And having disarmed the powers and authorities, He made a public spectacle of them, triumphing over them by the cross.... https://biblehub.com/colossians/2-14.htm

So, what we see in the Holy Bible is what we see in courts of law all over this world.

The criminals stand trial and is accused of breaking the law(s). There is a Judge, a Prosecutor/Accuser, and an Advocate for the accused.

The accuser tells of how the accused has broken the law and must be punished! While the Advocate pleads the defense of the accused. (there are false accusations from the devil but also true accusations by God through Moses)

Jesus Our Advocate
1My little children, I am writing these things to you so that you will not sin. But if anyone does sin, we have an advocate before the Father— Jesus Christ, the Righteous One. 2He Himself is the atoning sacrifice for our sins, and not only for ours but also for the sins of the whole world....
https://biblehub.com/1_john/2-1.htm

If anyone rejects Jesus Christ, they have no Advocate to defend them and stand convicted as lawbreakers and so are punished for dying in their sins.

Everyone MUST receive Jesus Christ as their Savior or they are condemned!

https://www.preceptaustin.org/tetelestai-paid_in_full

So, when Jesus Christ was crucified, He was nailing to the cross all our violations of His Law and thereby also defeating the false accuser, the devil. If you or anyone rejects Jesus Christ crucified, you have no Advocate, no hope and are condemned in your sins.

So, Christ Crucified in our behalf not only SAVES us but HEALS us and is why His Crucifixion is likened unto the serpent that Moses held up to heal and save the Israelites back when they had been bitten by snakes. (unclean spirits, sins, are like poison to us, death to our bodies) He takes the sin, the serpent's (devil's) accusations, and NAILS IT TO THE CROSS in our behalf, so all who look to Him there are SAVED and HEALED. That is why the cross (Christ Crucified) is THE POWER OF GOD to everyone who believes! 1 Corinthians 1:18-31

Christ Crucified Is God's Power and Wisdom

[18] For the message of the cross is foolishness to those who are perishing, but to us who are being saved it is the power of God. [19] For it is written:

"I will destroy the wisdom of the wise;
   the intelligence of the intelligent I will frustrate."[a]

[20] Where is the wise person? Where is the teacher of the law? Where is the philosopher of this age? Has not God made foolish the wisdom of the world? [21] For since in the wisdom of God the world through its wisdom did not know him, God was pleased through the foolishness of what was preached to save those who believe. [22] Jews demand signs and Greeks look for wisdom, [23] but we preach Christ crucified: a stumbling block to Jews and foolishness to Gentiles, [24] but to those whom God has called, both Jews and Greeks, Christ the power of God and the wisdom of God. [25] For the foolishness of God is wiser than human wisdom, and the weakness of God is stronger than human strength.

[26] Brothers and sisters, think of what you were when you were called. Not many of you were wise by human standards; not many were influential;

not many were of noble birth. ²⁷ But God chose the foolish things of the world to shame the wise; God chose the weak things of the world to shame the strong. ²⁸ God chose the lowly things of this world and the despised things—and the things that are not—to nullify the things that are, ²⁹ so that no one may boast before him. ³⁰ It is because of him that you are in Christ Jesus, who has become for us wisdom from God—that is, our righteousness, holiness and redemption. ³¹ Therefore, as it is written: "Let the one who boasts boast in the Lord."[b]

24That is why I told you that you would die in your sins. For unless you believe that I am He, you will die in your sins." 25"Who are You?" they asked. "Just what I have been telling you from the beginning," Jesus replied.... https://biblehub.com/john/8-24.htm

John 3:15-21
King James Version
15		That whosoever believeth in him should not perish, but have eternal life.

16		For God so loved the world, that he gave his only begotten Son, that whosoever believeth in him should not perish, but have everlasting life.

17		For God sent not his Son into the world to condemn the world; but that the world through him might be saved.

18		He that believeth on him is not condemned: but he that believeth not is condemned already, because he hath not believed in the name of the only begotten Son of God.

19		And this is the condemnation, that light is come into the world, and men loved darkness rather than light, because their deeds were evil.

20		For every one that doeth evil hateth the light, neither cometh to the light, lest his deeds should be reproved.

21   But he that doeth truth cometh to the light, that his deeds may be made manifest, that they are wrought in God.

And if you don't repent and accept Jesus Christ as your Lord and Savior before you die, you will perish in your sins and be cast into the lake of fire.

A New Heaven and a New Earth
...7The one who overcomes will inherit all things, and I will be his God, and he will be My son. 8But to the cowardly and unbelieving and abominable and murderers and sexually immoral and sorcerers and idolaters and all liars, their place will be in the lake that burns with fire and sulfur. This is the second death." https://biblehub.com/revelation/21-8.htm

...35The Father loves the Son and has placed all things in His hands. 36Whoever believes in the Son has eternal life. Whoever rejects the Son will not see life. Instead, the wrath of God remains on him."
https://biblehub.com/john/3-36.htm

12But to all who did receive Him, to those who believed in His name, He gave the right to become children of God— 13children born not of blood, nor of the desire or will of man, but born of God....
https://biblehub.com/john/1-12.htm

Every detail is important:

Numbers 21:4-9

Contemporary English Version

Moses Makes a Bronze Snake

4
   The Israelites had to go around the territory of Edom, so when they left Mount Hor, they headed south toward the Red Sea.[a] But along the way, the people became so impatient **5** that they complained against God and said to Moses, "Did you bring us out of Egypt, just to let us die in the desert? There's no water out here, and we can't stand this awful food!"
6
   Then the Lord sent poisonous snakes that bit and killed many of them.
7
   Some of the people went to Moses and admitted, "It was wrong of us to insult you and the Lord. Now please ask him to make these snakes go away."

Moses prayed, **8** and the Lord answered, "Make a snake out of bronze and place it on top of a pole. Anyone who gets bitten can look at the snake and be saved from death."
9
   Moses obeyed the Lord. And all of those who looked at the bronze snake lived, even though they had been bitten by the poisonous snakes.

So just speaking against God and His Words in the Holy Bible is sinful and brings consequences upon all doing so wickedly. Notice those who had sinned were bitten by poisonous snakes. Generally, people so bitten suffer and die, but death isn't immediate. Neither is death immediate for sinners although it comes soon enough. We have a short time to see Christ crucified in our behalf and be saved. Think about it! Why didn't God tell Moses to just kill one of the many vipers and put the dead carcass on a stick? No. instead He commands Moses to make one out of bronze, molten metal, purified by heat. Christ wasn't one of those poisonous serpents causing suffering and death to those who had sinned but instead was the Holy One, who resisted all the trials and temptations of the devil and was without sin, who alone was worthy to suffer and die for the sins of mankind.

And why the form of a serpent? Because Even though Christ was Perfect and Sinless, He was made to be cursed for us, and Himself bore the consequences of our sins on the cross. Bronze because He was tried and tested and found without sin, and yet in the form of a serpent because He was defeating the lying, false accusing devil and all sins on the cross, nailing the violations of His Law right there, such that all who recognize Jesus Christ as our Redeemer and Savior have their sins forever nailed there. We are Healed and Saved by understanding this Truth, Jesus Christ who knew no sin, bore our sins on the cross, and the Holy One Most Blessed, was cursed in our behalf on the cross. Bronze - tested and pure; form of a serpent - because all the accusations of the devil against us, everything that brings suffering and death was nailed to the cross.

If you receive that Truth, you are Healed/Saved/Redeemed and restored back alive with God; if you don't, you will bear your own sins, be condemned as a lawbreaker/sinner/criminal and be cast into the lake of fire accordingly.

a common lie from muslims is that Jesus Christ isn't God and isn't worshiped but the Holy Bible says He is quite clearly:

Jesus Christ not only is worshiped as God throughout the entire Holy Bible:

https://www.openbible.info/topics/worshipping_jesus

but openly complains when people should have done so and didn't:

The Ten Lepers

...16He fell facedown at Jesus' feet in thanksgiving to Him—and he was a Samaritan. 17"Were not all ten cleansed?" Jesus asked. "Where then are the other nine? 18Was no one found except this foreigner to return and give glory to God?"... https://biblehub.com/luke/17-17.htm

He even said the rocks would if people didn't:

The Triumphal Entry
35Then they led the colt to Jesus, threw their cloaks over it, and put Jesus on it. 36As He rode along, the people spread their cloaks on the road. 37And as He approached the descent from the Mount of Olives, the whole multitude of disciples began to praise God joyfully in a loud voice for all the miracles they had seen: 38"Blessed is the King who comes in the name of the Lord!" "Peace in heaven and glory in the highest!"39But some of the Pharisees in the crowd said to Him, "Teacher, rebuke Your disciples!" 40"I tell you," He answered, "if they remain silent, the very stones will cry out."
https://biblehub.com/luke/19-40.htm

John 5:39-40

39 You search the Scriptures because you think that in them you have eternal life; and it is they that bear witness about me, 40 yet you refuse to come to me that you may have life.

So, Jesus Christ tells us the entire Holy Bible is all about Him, the One who has Eternal Life (GOD!).

13You call Me Teacher and Lord, and rightly so, because I am.
https://biblehub.com/john/13-13.htm

8But Jesus answered, "It is written: 'Worship the Lord your God and serve Him only.'" https://biblehub.com/luke/4-8.htm

Jesus Appears to Thomas

...27Then Jesus said to Thomas, "Put your finger here and look at My hands. Reach out your hand and put it into My side. Stop doubting and believe." 28Thomas replied, "My Lord and my God!" 29Jesus said to him, "Because you have seen Me, you have believed; blessed are those who have not seen and yet have believed."... https://biblehub.com/john/20-28.htm

So clearly Jesus Christ stated He is Lord and God and that we should worship only Him.

So someone wrote today on facebook, "If I believe jesus was a special man sent from god,,,but not a god himself what religion am I really"

And so, I responded: one that isn't true.
https://www.facebook.com/photo.php?fbid=6800758120003089&set=pb.100002069048072.-2207520000&type=3

The way anyone can tell whether or not their current beliefs are true or not, is to ask themselves if they hear, see, know and are learning from the One who said He is the Truth.

John 14
6 Jesus said to him, "I am the way, and the truth, and the life. No one comes to the Father except through me. 7 If you had known me, you would have known my Father also.[d] From now on you do know him and have seen him."

8 Philip said to him, "Lord, show us the Father, and it is enough for us." 9 Jesus said to him, "Have I been with you so long, and you still do not know me, Philip? Whoever has seen me has seen the Father. How can you say, 'Show us the Father'? 10 Do you not believe that I am in the Father and the Father is in me? The words that I say to you I do not speak on my own

authority, but the Father who dwells in me does his works. 11 Believe me that I am in the Father and the Father is in me, or else believe on account of the works themselves.

12 "Truly, truly, I say to you, whoever believes in me will also do the works that I do; and greater works than these will he do, because I am going to the Father. 13 Whatever you ask in my name, this I will do, that the Father may be glorified in the Son. 14 If you ask me[e] anything in my name, I will do it.

Jesus Promises the Holy Spirit

15 "If you love me, you will keep my commandments. 16 And I will ask the Father, and he will give you another Helper,[f] to be with you forever, 17 even the Spirit of truth, whom the world cannot receive, because it neither sees him nor knows him. You know him, for he dwells with you and will be[g] in you.

18 "I will not leave you as orphans; I will come to you. 19 Yet a little while and the world will see me no more, but you will see me. Because I live, you also will live. 20 In that day you will know that I am in my Father, and you in me, and I in you. 21 Whoever has my commandments and keeps them, he it is who loves me. And he who loves me will be loved by my Father, and I will love him and manifest myself to him." 22 Judas (not Iscariot) said to him, "Lord, how is it that you will manifest yourself to us, and not to the world?" 23 Jesus answered him, "If anyone loves me, he will keep my word, and my Father will love him, and we will come to him and make our home with him. 24 Whoever does not love me does not keep my words. And the word that you hear is not mine but the Father's who sent me.

25 "These things I have spoken to you while I am still with you. 26 But the Helper, the Holy Spirit, whom the Father will send in my name, he will teach you all things and bring to your remembrance all that I have said to you.

John 8:32-36

32 And ye shall know the truth, and the truth shall make you free.

33 They answered him, We be Abraham's seed, and were never in bondage to any man: how sayest thou, Ye shall be made free?

34 Jesus answered them, Verily, verily, I say unto you, Whosoever committeth sin is the servant of sin.

35 And the servant abideth not in the house for ever: but the Son abideth ever.

36 If the Son therefore shall make you free, ye shall be free indeed.

So if your beliefs are true and correct, you KNOW they are because you learned those things from the One who is the Truth. And if your beliefs are not, then you do not know the One who is the Truth.

27And as for you, the anointing you received from Him remains in you, and you do not need anyone to teach you. But just as His TRUE and genuine anointing teaches you about all things, so remain in Him as you have been taught. https://biblehub.com/1_john/2-27.htm

I have often seen muslims accusing Christians of colonialism and slavery, when it is their own cult that openly practices such evil for centuries of history and to this very day.

https://www.google.com/search?client=opera&q=centuries+of+islamic+slave+trade&sourceid=opera&ie=UTF-8&oe=UTF-8 - islam actually teaches slavery and muhammad himself had black slaves.
https://www.youtube.com/watch?v=1HbOhLJHcFo

https://www.thereligionofpeace.com/pages/quran/slavery.aspx

It was very sad that some Europeans joined in the islamic slave trade; especially after muslims had murdered and enslaved even them:

https://www.youtube.com/watch?v=l_To-cV94Bo slavery still persists today but instead of calling it slavery, we say things like "human trafficking".

So evil cults are definitely a form of brutal slavery and colonialism on earth. But slavery and colonialism as such are DEFINITELY NOT THE TEACHINGS OF JESUS CHRIST, Christianity. And so, no one should be blaming either for them.

Luke 4:18-21 King James Version (KJV)
The Spirit of the Lord is upon me, Because he hath anointed me to preach the gospel to the poor; He hath sent me to heal the brokenhearted, to preach deliverance to the captives, And recovering of sight to the blind, To set at liberty them that are bruised, To preach the acceptable year of the Lord. And he closed the book, and he gave it again to the minister, and sat down. And the eyes of all them that were in the synagogue were fastened on him. And he began to say unto them, This day is this scripture fulfilled in your ears.

So, Jesus Christ came to end such things as slavery. And is why He isn't responsible for such evil, nor any of His Disciples. People take such things a servants obey your Masters, instead of just realizing employee and Employers are what those scriptures are talking about, or instead of just realizing that while God is ending this world as we know it with all the evil in it, there are still some people practicing the evil He preaches against. And as such Christians are to be obedient and shows no sign of disrespect to their employers, masters, or whomever they serve. They are to show in all ways righteous living. With the hopes their masters, employers will convert to Christianity and realize slavery or bad employer relationships of maltreating their servants (continuing to offer slave wages that are below the cost of living) are just wrong.

So, while islam spread through bloodshed and violence, slavery and colonialism, the teachings of Jesus Christ were spread by His Eyewitnesses who gave their lives to torture and death telling the world He is the One

True God. (muslims tend to think that people outside their nations are all Christians, when that isn't the case at all, and so nations had colonization just as a matter of that nation's government, irrespective of Christianity.)

Jesus Christ Founded Christianity
Jesus Christ clearly founded Christianity! so yes, Jesus Christ is Christian by definition.

The recorded and verified facts of history tell us in no uncertain terms Jesus Christ founded Christianity:

https://www.youtube.com/watch?v=ay_Db4RwZ_M - the New Testament was written by the Eyewitness Apostles and Disciples of Jesus Christ.

In addition, there are external sources; other historians that verify not only did Jesus Christ exist at the time indicated in the Holy Bible, but that there were indeed eyewitnesses, His Apostles and Disciples, that began Preaching the Gospel of Jesus Christ immediately following His Resurrection (Pentecost as noted in the Book of Acts):
https://coldcasechristianity.com/writings/is-there-any-evidence-for-jesusoutside-the-bible/ and
https://biblearchaeologyreport.com/2022/11/18/top-ten-historicalreferences-to-jesus-outside-of-the-bible/

so was not spread by violent conquest and slavery, but instead by God and His Eyewitness Apostles and Disciples. This world and everyone in it, belongs to Him and yet He gives us each the choice whether or not to Love or hate Him.
https://tile.loc.gov/storageservices/public/gdcmassbookdig/foxesbookofmart00fo/foxesbookofmart00fo.pdf

Those who love God, Jesus Christ, accept and obey His Commandments in the Holy Bible, whereas those who don't still are lost in a world of ignorance, wickedness, suffering and death.

John 14:6-9
New King James Version
6 Jesus said to him, "I am the way, the truth, and the life. No one comes to the Father except through Me.

The Father Revealed
7 "If you had known Me, you would have known My Father also; and from now on you know Him and have seen Him."

8 Philip said to Him, "Lord, show us the Father, and it is sufficient for us."

9 Jesus said to him, "Have I been with you so long, and yet you have not known Me, Philip? He who has seen Me has seen the Father; so how can you say, 'Show us the Father'?

The Great Commission
…15And He said to them, "Go into all the world and preach the gospel to every creature. 16Whoever believes and is baptized will be saved, but whoever does not believe will be condemned.

"Brothers, what shall we do?" 38 Peter replied, "Repent and be baptized, every one of you, in the name of Jesus Christ for the forgiveness of your sins, and you will receive the gift of the Holy Spirit. 39This promise belongs to you and your children and to all who are far off—to all whom the Lord our God will call to Himself."… https://biblehub.com/acts/2-38.htm

Peter and John Before the Council
…11This Jesus is 'the stone you builders rejected, which has become the cornerstone.' 12 Salvation exists in no one else, for there is no other name under heaven given to men by which we must be saved."
https://biblehub.com/acts/4-12.htm

Our Lord Jesus Christ clearly is against slavery and all forms of evil on earth:

15He taught in their synagogues and was glorified by everyone. **16**Then Jesus came to Nazareth, where He had been brought up. As was His custom, He entered the synagogue on the Sabbath. And when He stood up to read, **17**the scroll of the prophet Isaiah was handed to Him. Unrolling it, He found the place where it was written: **18**"The Spirit of the Lord is on Me, because He has anointed Me to preach good news to the poor. He has sent Me to proclaim liberty to the captives and recovery of sight to the blind, to release the oppressed, **19**to proclaim the year of the Lord's favor." **20**Then He rolled up the scroll, returned it to the attendant, and sat down. The eyes of everyone in the synagogue were fixed on Him, **21**and He began by saying,
"Today this Scripture is fulfilled in your hearing."...
https://biblehub.com/luke/4-18.htm

muslims constantly misinterpret the contents of the Holy Bible and one of the more common misinterpretations is their faulty understanding of Matthew 7:22,23. like today a muslim was trying to claim Jesus Christ is condemning Christians for worshipping Him as God, when that isn't the case at all. Jesus Christ is God and He has always been worshiped as such; so, I responded to his tirade and false accusation accordingly:

For example, you cite verses from the Holy Bible that don't mean anything at all like you imagine they mean. Jesus Christ ALWAYS receives worship as God, because He is God:

https://www.openbible.info/topics/worshipping_jesus

He even complains when people should have worshipped Him and didn't:

The Ten Lepers

...16He fell facedown at Jesus' feet in thanksgiving to Him—and he was a Samaritan. 17"Were not all ten cleansed?" Jesus asked. "Where then are the other nine? 18Was no one found except this foreigner to return and give glory to God?"... https://biblehub.com/luke/17-17.htm

muhammad worshiped the devil, which is why the quran and all muslims are still bowing to allah, instead of Jesus Christ, the One True God. (muhammad was an extremely wicked criminal, muslims are taught that they cannot criticize him on pain of death, so someone like myself has to tell you the truth) muhammad came along over 6 centuries after Jesus Christ and His Eyewitness Apostles and Disciples in the Holy Bible and yet muslims choose to believe muhammad and his lies in the quran over God, the Messiah, the Prophets and His Eyewitness Apostles and Disciples in the Holy Bible. The Prophets, Apostles and Disciples of Jesus Christ, the One True God, recorded in the Holy Bible, were not child molesters, rapists, robbers and murderers but muhammad was all those things and worse.

http://www.answeringmuslims.com/2014/03/muhammad-and-thighingof-aisha.html and

http://www.annaqed.com/en/muslims-under-the-microscope/muhammad-and-his-crimes-against-humanity and

https://www.youtube.com/watch?v=1HbOhLJHcFo

not one muslim, even yourself, hears, sees or knows God, because you are all believing lies and denying Him instead.

https://www.facebook.com/photo.php?fbid=6809546799124221&set=pb.100002069048072.-2207520000&type=3

and so the verses you cited:

Matthew 7:22 On that day many will say to me, 'Lord, Lord, did we not prophesy in your name, and cast out demons in your name, and do many mighty works in your name? ' 23 And then will I declare to them, 'I never knew you; depart from me, you workers of lawlessness.

Actually, shows you that you are one of those who will hear Him say to you to depart from Him, because you do not know Him and imagine that your own deeds somehow make you right with Him. (Unless you repent of your present state of ignorance and wickedness and learn to trust and obey our Lord and Savior Jesus Christ.)

In other words, you miss the real reason why Jesus Christ, the One True God, tells them to depart from Him (and casts them into the lake of fire Rev 21:8). Here these people were CLAIMING they had done all kinds of things in His Name but those who Know Jesus Christ, knows that He ALONE is our Savior, it is HIM and WHAT HE HAS DONE that Saves us; not anything we do.

Ephesians 2:1-10 ESV
And you were dead in the trespasses and sins in which you once walked, following the course of this world, following the prince of the power of the air, the spirit that is now at work in the sons of disobedience— among whom we all once lived in the passions of our flesh, carrying out the desires of the body and the mind, and were by nature children of wrath, like the rest of mankind. But God, being rich in mercy, because of the great love with which he loved us, even when we were dead in our trespasses, made us alive together with Christ—by grace you have been saved— and raised us up with him and seated us with him in the heavenly places in Christ Jesus, so that in the coming ages he might show the immeasurable riches of his grace in kindness toward us in Christ Jesus. For by grace you have been saved through faith. And this is not your own doing; it is the gift of God, not a result of works, so that no one may boast. For we are his workmanship, created in Christ Jesus for good works, which God prepared beforehand, that we should walk in them.

You don't KNOW the Savior, Jesus Christ, you have NOT received His Holy Spirit of Truth, you are NOT SAVED! Likewise, false christians, who imagine they are saved by their own works, are NOT SAVED! Christians don't do good works to EARN their Salvation; they do them as A RESULT THAT THE SAVIOR HAS SAVED THEM AND CALLS THEM TO A RIGHTEOUS LIFE! They do them because God has filled them with His Love.

"Brothers, what shall we do?" 38 Peter replied, "Repent and be baptized, every one of you, in the name of Jesus Christ for the forgiveness of your sins, and you will receive the gift of the Holy Spirit. 39This promise belongs to you and your children and to all who are far off—to all whom the Lord our God will call to Himself."... https://biblehub.com/acts/2-38.htm

ONLY THOSE WHO REPENT AND RECEIVE JESUS CHRIST, AS LORD AND SAVIOR THAT HE IS, ARE SAVED!

The Great Commission
...15And He said to them, "Go into all the world and preach the gospel to every creature. 16Whoever believes and is baptized will be saved, but whoever does not believe will be condemned.
https://biblehub.com/mark/16-16.htm

Peter and John Before the Council
...11This Jesus is 'the stone you builders rejected, which has become the cornerstone.' 12 Salvation exists in no one else, for there is no other name under heaven given to men by which we must be saved."
https://biblehub.com/acts/4-12.htm

12But to all who did receive Him, to those who believed in His name, He gave the right to become children of God— 13children born not of blood,

nor of the desire or will of man, but born of God....
https://biblehub.com/john/1-12.htm

muslims wrongly believe muhammad and the quran over God Almighty, the Messiah, His Prophets and Eyewitness Apostles and Disciples in the Holy Bible. According to what God plainly tells us in the Holy Bible, muhammad was an accursed antichrist and likewise all who believe his many lies and evil instructions in the quran and follow him instead of our Lord and Savior Jesus Christ and His Holy and Righteous Divine Commandments in the Holy Bible.

The Holy Bible is the tried and tested literary truth given mankind by the One True God; not the quran.

The recorded and verified facts of history tell us in no uncertain terms Jesus Christ founded Christianity:

https://www.youtube.com/watch?v=ay_Db4RwZ_M - the New Testament was written by the Eyewitness Apostles and Disciples of Jesus Christ.

In addition, there are external sources; other historians that verify not only did Jesus Christ exist at the time indicated in the Holy Bible, but that there were indeed eyewitnesses, His Apostles and Disciples, that began Preaching the Gospel of Jesus Christ immediately following His Resurrection (Pentecost as noted in the Book of Acts):
https://coldcasechristianity.com/writings/is-there-any-evidence-for-jesusoutside-the-bible/ and
https://biblearchaeologyreport.com/2022/11/18/top-ten-historicalreferences-to-jesus-outside-of-the-bible/

The quran was written by men that came along many centuries AFTER Jesus Christ and His Eyewitness Apostles and Disciples in the Holy Bible who plainly told us that if ANYONE even an angel contradicts what is given to us in the Holy Bible they are under a DIVINE CURSE and are antichrists!

Galatians 1:6-9

No Other Gospel

6 I am astonished that you are so quickly deserting him who called you in the grace of Christ and are turning to a different gospel— 7 not that there is another one, but there are some who trouble you and want to distort the gospel of Christ. 8 But even if we or an angel from heaven should preach to you a gospel contrary to the one we preached to you, let him be accursed. 9 As we have said before, so now I say again: If anyone is preaching to you a gospel contrary to the one you received, let him be accursed.

Beware of Antichrists

...21I have not written to you because you lack knowledge of the truth, but because you have it, and because no lie comes from the truth. 22Who is the liar, if it is not the one who denies that Jesus is the Christ? This is the antichrist, who denies the Father and the Son. 23Whoever denies the Son does not have the Father, but whoever confesses the Son has the Father as well.... https://biblehub.com/1_john/2-22.htm

1 John 4:1-6

Test the Spirits

4 Beloved, do not believe every spirit, but test the spirits to see whether they are from God, for many false prophets have gone out into the world. 2 By this you know the Spirit of God: every spirit that confesses that Jesus Christ has come in the flesh is from God, 3 and every spirit that does not confess Jesus is not from God. This is the spirit of the antichrist, which you heard was coming and now is in the world already. 4 Little children, you are from God and have overcome them, for he who is in you is greater than he who is in the world. 5 They are from the world; therefore they speak from the world, and the world listens to them. 6 We are from God.

Whoever knows God listens to us; whoever is not from God does not listen to us. By this we know the Spirit of truth and the spirit of error.

"Christ" is the Greek word for "Messiah" and Messiah means God in the flesh! - https://hebrew4christians.com/Names_of_Gd/Messiah/messiah.html

...25The woman said, "I know that Messiah" (called Christ) "is coming. When He comes, He will explain everything to us." 26 Jesus answered, "I who speak to you am He." https://biblehub.com/john/4-26.htm

So as long as anyone remains in the evil, lying cult of islam, they are accursed antichrists, on their way to the lake of fire. ALL MUSLIMS MUST REPENT AND BE BAPTIZED IN THE NAME OF JESUS CHRIST, THE ONE TRUE GOD, OUR LORD AND SAVIOR AND RECEIVE HIS HOLY SPIRIT OF TRUTH OR THEY WILL PERISH IN THEIR SINS AND BE CAST INTO THE LAKE OF FIRE!
...7The one who overcomes will inherit all things, and I will be his God, and he will be My son. 8But to the cowardly and unbelieving and abominable and murderers and sexually immoral and sorcerers and idolaters and all liars, their place will be in the lake that burns with fire and sulfur. This is the second death." https://biblehub.com/revelation/21-8.htm

Overcoming the World
...4because everyone born of God overcomes the world. And this is the victory that has overcome the world: our faith. 5Who then overcomes the world? Only he who believes that Jesus is the Son of God. 6This is the One who came by water and blood, Jesus Christ—not by water alone, but by water and blood. And it is the Spirit who testifies to this, because the Spirit is the truth.... https://biblehub.com/1_john/5-5.htm

12But to all who did receive Him, to those who believed in His name, He gave the right to become children of God— 13children born not of blood, nor of the desire or will of man, but born of God....
https://biblehub.com/john/1-12.htm

The Great Commission
...18Then Jesus came to them and said, "All authority in heaven and on earth has been given to Me. 19Therefore go and make disciples of all nations, baptizing them in the name of the Father, and of the Son, and of the Holy Spirit, 20and teaching them to obey all that I have commanded you. And surely I am with you always, even to the end of the age."...
https://biblehub.com/matthew/28-19.htm

"Brothers, what shall we do?" 38 Peter replied, "Repent and be baptized, every one of you, in the name of Jesus Christ for the forgiveness of your sins, and you will receive the gift of the Holy Spirit. 39This promise belongs to you and your children and to all who are far off—to all whom the Lord our God will call to Himself."... https://biblehub.com/acts/2-38.htm

Peter and John Before the Council
...11This Jesus is 'the stone you builders rejected, which has become the cornerstone.' 12 Salvation exists in no one else, for there is no other name under heaven given to men by which we must be saved."
https://biblehub.com/acts/4-12.htm

muslims are believing the lying criminal muhammad over the facts of history recorded in the Holy Bible and by external historians already mentioned, when they falsely claim that it only appeared that Jesus Christ was crucified and died on the cross. This is my reply to such incredible nonsense:

His own mother saw Jesus Christ crucified, and the eyewitnesses who saw Jesus Christ crucified and resurrected gave their lives over their testimonies in that regard. The historians in the region, that were not those who penned the Gospels, confirm those facts occurred; so muhammad, who was a criminal that came along centuries after those facts of history that he denied and instead claimed the entire world was deceived, including Mary, mother of Jesus Christ, Himself, is laughable, if it wasn't so sad that muslims actually believe God Almighty is a liar and deceiver by believing such incredible nonsense. If we can't trust God Almighty who tells us He NEVER lies, and His Words in the Holy Bible, we can't trust anyone or anything!

So, I told that to this particular muslim online and he was STILL claiming God Himself deceived the whole world! people that ignorant, blasphemous and wicked really bother me. He just doesn't understand that if God was a DECEIVER, then there is no Truth, there is NOTHING we can trust, SO GOD CANNOT BE A DECEIVER! And did not deceive the world EVER! The Holy Bible is telling us all the truth! I often wonder why God allows them to live and breathe. ALL muslims should thank Our Lord Jesus Christ for His Patience and Mercy! He was trying to claim that Jesus Christ couldn't have been crucified because people saw Him after His Crucifixion. He wasn't understanding that Jesus Christ had resurrected Himself just as He said He would; as proof He is God! (In other words, this person was deliberately trying to undermine the most important facts in the history of the world.)

so, I replied to this muslim, blaspheming God Almighty by claiming God had deceived the world (instead of the fact that the lies of muhammad had deceived him):

No, when the Apostles and Disciples saw Jesus Christ after His Crucifixion, DEATH and BURIAL, it is due to the FACT, HE ROSE FROM THE DEAD, JUST LIKE HE SAID HE WOULD, PROVING BEYOND ALL REASONABLE DOUBT that HE IS GOD! It's the reason, His Disciples SAY SO!

Jesus Appears to Thomas

...27Then Jesus said to Thomas, "Put your finger here and look at My hands. Reach out your hand and put it into My side. Stop doubting and believe." 28Thomas replied, "My Lord and my God!" 29Jesus said to him, "Because you have seen Me, you have believed; blessed are those who have not seen and yet have believed."... https://biblehub.com/john/20-28.htm

It's the reason they went preaching and telling the whole world that they had SEEN AND HEARD GOD FIRST HAND! It's the reason they accepted torture and death rather than recant of one word of their testimonies in the Holy Bible.

https://tile.loc.gov/storageservices/public/gdcmassbookdig/foxesbookofmart00fo/foxesbookofmart00fo/foxesbookofmart00fo.pdf

It's not just the most CERTAIN FACTS IN ALL ANCIENT HISTORY, but we have the most studied artifact on earth, the Burial Cloth of Jesus Christ, as external physical evidence He was CRUCIFIED, DEAD AND BURIED AND ROSE FROM THE DEAD JUST AS THE HOLY BIBLE SAYS!

https://youtu.be/LLnClp3OVmE?t=1884

So like I already said, muslims look like absolute evil fools, for claiming God Almighty deceived the world (muslims are calling GOD a liar, a deceiver! they are ALL evil blasphemers!), and choosing to believe a criminal like muhammad and the many evil lies in the quran over GOD HIMSELF, JESUS CHRIST and His Prophets and EYEWITNESSES in the Holy Bible, AND dismissing the EVIDENCE THAT IS THROUGHOUT HISTORY TO THIS DAY all confirming the historicity and veracity of the Holy Bible (like the Shroud of Turin, the most scientifically studied artifact in all the world for all time.)

JESUS CHRIST EVER LIVES TO CONFIRM HE IS THE ONE TRUE GOD TO ALL WHO SEEK TO KNOW HIM! I think it's a shame that anyone on earth would imagine God Almighty who gives them life and breath and every good thing, would deceive anyone. GOD ALWAYS TELLS THE TRUTH! We KNOW our Eternal Creator is Good and Righteous by examining His Words and Deeds throughout all history! For goodness to exist in this world God has to be Good! God is Omniscient and Omnibenevolent, not willing that any should perish, but if you turn yourself into an unrepentant rebellious, deluded wicked person who imagines they are serving the Creator by murdering other people who the Creator made, you are showing the world that you are DECEIVED by the evil devil! And it's a shame that the entire world doesn't tell you that fact! It's a shame that our once Christian nation has fallen so far from the truth, that they are welcoming people who hold to such awful and foolish notions as islam and the quran teaches. Our LAWS including the Bill of Rights are only for a lawful nation! You have the right to free speech, as long as your free speech does not include EXORTATION TO MURDER OTHER PEOPLE! You have the right to your religion just as long as your religion isn't worshipping any proposed god, goddess, or imaginary idol that demands that you worship that god BY MURDERING OTHER PEOPLE! MURDER IS INHERENTLY UNLAWFUL! Considering other people as less than yourselves, just to murder them, IS UNLAWFUL! DO NOT MURDER! If you disagree about important matters, speak and defend your reasons! BUT DO NOT MURDER! If you imagine muhammad and islam is a peaceful religion, then WHY DO MUSLIMS MURDER OTHER PEOPLE! (and why does their quran encourage muslims to murder other people?) why did the Saudis celebrate a mass murderer at their so-called holy site kaaba, mecca. Islam is a criminal organization plain and simple and it's a crying shame that the rest of the world doesn't pay attention enough to recognize that fact.
https://www.thereligionofpeace.com/pages/quran/index.aspx - tens of thousands of violent terrorist attacks by muslims since 911 and millions of them throughout history, islam has been at nonstop war with the rest of humanity since it's inception.

muhammad came along centuries after the facts recorded in the Holy Bible and so had no firsthand, personal knowledge of them whatsoever. On top of this he was a rapist, a robber, a child molester, slaver and mass murderer (liars and murderers are children of the devil! John 8:43-45). muslims look like absolute fools of the worst kind to believe muhammad over Jesus Christ, His Eyewitness Apostles and Disciples, and all His Prophets in the Holy Bible. ALL muslims need to repent and be baptized in the Name of our Lord and Savior, Jesus, the Christ and be filled with His Holy Spirit of Truth and frankly should burn all their vile, lying qurans! that evil book has led far too many souls away from the One True God, Jesus Christ; into the flames of damnation! every unrepentant muslim will be cast into the lake of fire for being so evil as to believe the lying criminal muhammad over the facts of history so clearly recorded in the Holy Bible. (if you believe lies, you pass them on and that makes you a LIAR! ALL LIARS WILL BE CAST INTO THE LAKE OF FIRE! Rev 21:8 JESUS CHRIST is TRUTH! NO ONE ESLE! (especially not wicked muhammad!)) I'm not saying all muslims are evil fools, I'm trying to say IF YOU BELIEVE your qurans OVER the HOLY BIBLE, God and all His Prophets, then you are one. You are not taking the proverb every tree that bears bad fruit IS BAD! Muhammad was a criminal! Don't believe a lying criminal like muhammad OVER JESUS CHRIST AND ALL HIS PROPHETS! Islam has generated the largest number of violent terrorists in the history of the world because islam is evil! Plain and simple truth!

Beware of Antichrists

...**21**I have not written to you because you lack knowledge of the truth, but because you have it, and because no lie comes from the truth. **22**Who is the liar, if it is not the one who denies that Jesus is the Christ? This is the antichrist, who denies the Father and the Son. **23**Whoever denies the Son does not have the Father, but whoever confesses the Son has the Father as well.... https://biblehub.com/1_john/2-22.htm

Another extremely common deceitful practice of muslims, is to rip words out of context from the Holy Bible to make false claims. Like one of the more common practices is for them to use the passage in Ezekiel that tells us everyone will be accountable for their own sins, a father cannot die for a son, and sons cannot die for a father but each must die for their own sins. They quote this passage to falsely claim Jesus Christ didn't die for us.

muslims seem to miss "...every man shall be put to death for his own sin." (Deut 24:16, Ezek 18:20, Jer 31:30) in other words, no GUILTY PERSON (sinner) can die for another BECAUSE THEY ARE ALREADY UNDER THEIR OWN DEATH SENTENCE.

But God, Jesus Christ, was Holy and Sinless and He tells us MANY TIMES He is our Redeemer: https://bible.knowing-jesus.com/topics/God,-As-Redeemer

So ONLY GOD could PAY THE PRICE in full for the sins of mankind, and that is what He did!

https://www.preceptaustin.org/tetelestai-paid_in_full - Jesus Paid it All!

ANYONE REJECTING JESUS CHRIST AND HIS REDEMPTION/SALVATION IS STILL UNDER THEIR OWN DEATH SENTENCE FOR THEIR OWN SINS AND WILL BE CAST INTO THE LAKE OF FIRE ACCORDINGLY IF THEY FAIL TO REPENT AND ACCEPT OUR LORD AND SAVIOR JESUS CHRIST!

24That is why I told you that you would die in your sins. For unless you believe that I am He, you will die in your sins." 25"Who are You?" they asked. "Just what I have been telling you from the beginning," Jesus replied.... https://biblehub.com/john/8-24.htm

...35The Father loves the Son and has placed all things in His hands. 36Whoever believes in the Son has eternal life. Whoever rejects the Son will not see life. Instead, the wrath of God remains on him."
https://biblehub.com/john/3-36.htm

A New Heaven and a New Earth
...7The one who overcomes will inherit all things, and I will be his God, and he will be My son. 8But to the cowardly and unbelieving and abominable and murderers and sexually immoral and sorcerers and idolaters and all liars, their place will be in the lake that burns with fire and sulfur. This is the second death." https://biblehub.com/revelation/21-8.htm

I wouldn't have believed it unless I personally encountered it, but a muslim was actually using the warnings of Jesus Christ about false christs to imagine He was warning us against Himself! UNBELIEVABLE that islam is so evil that ANYONE could be that deceived! But this muslim was insisting the reason he would never obey Jesus Christ and become a Christian was due to this passage:

The Abomination of Desolation
...**23**At that time, if anyone says to you, 'Look, here is the Christ!' or 'There He is!' do not believe it. **24**For false Christs and false prophets will appear and perform great signs and wonders that would deceive even the elect, if that were possible. **25**See, I have told you in advance....
https://biblehub.com/matthew/24-24.htm

So why is Jesus, THE CHRIST? and who are "false christs"? THE CHRIST comes from the Greek Christos which is the Greek for the Hebrew Messiah, the Anointed One, God, who came in the flesh.

https://biblescan.com/search.php?q=christ - Christ is English for the Greek Christos - https://biblehub.com/greek/5547.htm which is the equivalent of the Hebrew word Messiah.

Jesus and the Samaritan Woman

...**25**The woman said, "I know that Messiah" (called Christ) "is coming. When He comes, He will explain everything to us." **26** Jesus answered, "I who speak to you am He."
https://biblehub.com/john/4-26.htm

THE CHRIST speaks only the TRUE WORDS OF GOD.
Belief and Unbelief
...**47**As for anyone who hears My words and does not keep them, I do not judge him. For I have not come to judge the world, but to save the world. **48**There is a judge for the one who rejects Me and does not receive My words: The word that I have spoken will judge him on the last day. **49**I have not spoken on My own, but the Father who sent Me has commanded Me what to say and how to say it. **50**And I know that His command leads to eternal life. So I speak exactly what the Father has told Me to say."...
https://biblehub.com/john/12-49.htm

ONLY GOD ALWAYS SPEAKS HIS WORDS EXACTLY IN THE WAY HE WANTS THEM SPOKEN! Which is why THE CHRIST, THE MESSIAH, is GOD ALMIGHTY WHO CAME IN THE FLESH and is why the scriptures make it very clear that anyone denying that Jesus Christ, is God who came in the flesh, is an antichrist!

https://hebrew4christians.com/Names_of_G-d/Messiah/messiah.html - The Messiah, Jesus Christ, IS GOD WHO CAME IN THE FLESH! Declared Himself to mankind, showed Himself to mankind and proved Himself to mankind beyond any reasonable doubt! NO ONE ELSE IN THE ENTIRE HISTORY OF THE WORLD DID THE MANY MIRACLES JESUS CHRIST DID AS PROOF HE IS THE ONE TRUE GOD! NO ONE! unbelievers who heard Him speak personally, understood quite plainly that Jesus Christ claimed to be GOD!

The Unbelief of the Jews
*...**32**But Jesus responded, "I have shown you many good works from the Father. For which of these do you stone Me?" **33**" We are not stoning*

You for any good work," said the Jews, "but for blasphemy, because You, who are a man, declare Yourself to be God."...
...**37**If I am not doing the works of My Father, then do not believe Me. **38**But if I am doing them, even though you do not believe Me, believe the works themselves, so that you may know and understand that the Father is in Me, and I am in the Father."
https://biblehub.com/john/10-33.htm

And the response of Jesus Christ was to say LOOK AT THE MIRACLES! NO ONE ELSE HAS EVER CLAIMED TO BE GOD AND THEN PROVED IT JUST BY SPEAKING AND CHANGING REALITY INSTANTLY! HEALING ENTIRE CROWDS OF SICK PEOPLE! Even people born with birth defects! Raised the dead! Stopped storms! transformed water into wine! walked on stormy seas! And as His final proof He is the One who has Eternal Life, He publicly died, then raised His Body from the Grave, transfigured it, Made it Immortal and Glorious and Ascended into Heaven in front of eyewitnesses! Those eyewitnesses penned the New Testament and were so convinced they had heard and seen God Almighty first hand that they gave their lives to torturous demises rather than repent of one word of their testimonies, the contents of the Holy Bible!

30 Large crowds came to Him, bringing the lame, the blind, the crippled, the mute, and many others, and laid them at His feet, and He healed them. **31**The crowd was amazed when they saw the mute speaking, the crippled restored, the lame walking, and the blind seeing. And they glorified the God of Israel....

https://tile.loc.gov/storageservices/public/gdcmassbookdig/foxesbookofmart00fo/foxesbookofmart0 0fo.pdf - THEY SAW AND HEARD GOD IN THE FLESH! It's why the scriptures are crystal clear that ANYONE denying Jesus Christ is God who came in the flesh is a liar and an antichrist!

Beware of Antichrists

...**21**I have not written to you because you lack knowledge of the truth, but because you have it, and because no lie comes from the truth. **22**Who is the liar, if it is not the one
who denies that Jesus is the Christ? This is the antichrist, who denies the Father and the Son. **23**Whoever denies the Son does not have the Father, but whoever confesses the Son has the Father as well....
https://biblehub.com/1_john/2-22.htm

muslims have become liars and antichrists BECAUSE THEY ARE FOLLOWING A false teacher, false prophet, false christ! muhammad and his lies in the quran! CHRIST IS GOD IN THE FLESH, so anyone who claims to speak for God and tells lies is a FALSE teacher, FALSE prophet, FALSE christ! muslims are so deceived that they actually are doing exactly what JESUS CHRIST warned them NOT to do! following a lying antichrist!

https://www.thereligionofpeace.com/pages/articles/jesusmuhammad.aspx - who denies the Gospel of Jesus Christ in the Holy Bible and instead proclaimed that denial as the real one in the quran!

muhammad was a CRIMINAL who came along over six centuries AFTER the well-established FACTS in the Holy Bible! he had no personal knowledge of those facts whatsoever! but muslims are actually believing muhammad OVER THE EYEWITNESSES OF GOD! muslims are deceived and obviously so.

To twist the Words of God in the Holy Bible to the point where any of them could imagine He was warning against Himself and His Own Disciples, Christians, is truly so deceived they look like children of the devil to all who know the Living God and have already received His Holy Spirit of Truth. It will be no small miracle for any muslim, who is presently a lying antichrist, to actually repent, become a Disciple of Jesus Christ, the One True God, and escape the lake of fire. BUT PLEASE PRAY GOD WORKS SUCH MIRACLES and saves the ones that just don't realize they've been deceived by the evil cult of islam and the lies in the quran! if the zeal some muslims have for their false god and false prophet was placed where it belongs with the One True God, Jesus Christ, they would be great witnesses of the Truth, instead of lying antichrists.

Western civilization, Christian nations, NEED TO REALIZE, islam is SO EVIL that some islamic nations have banned the Holy Bible, the Words of God Almighty! muslims are enemies of God and all lawful citizens! They should not be loose in the world! islam is SO EVIL that their vile cult threatens to murder anyone who tries to leave it! (islamic apostasy laws)

https://www.google.com/search?client=opera&q=islamic+apostasy+death+penalty+nations&sourceid=opera&ie=UTF-8&oe=UTF-8 - so there is no freedom under the oppressive evil, criminal organization of islam. islam is that antithetical to our laws, culture and civilization! If I had my way, islam would be internationally banned as the criminal organization that it is and muslims would be forced to undergo deprogramming from their lying cult! any islamic terrorists so deceived, deranged and deluded that they imagine their evil god wants them to murder other people, would be properly imprisoned until and unless they realized God who creates life doesn't want anyone murdered. islamic terrorism would end globally.

islam is SO EVIL that it has founded the largest number of violent terrorist organizations in the history of the world! so many that the list is alphabetized!

https://www.google.com/search?client=opera&q=list+of+islamic+terrorist+groups&sourceid=opera&ie=UTF-8&oe=UTF-8

the quran openly advocates for ongoing crimes against humanity! - https://www.thereligionofpeace.com/pages/quran/index.aspx so the quran comes from the lying devil and obviously so!

In other words, anyone who practices the dogmas and doctrines of the quran becomes a violent criminal. islam is that evil. So, the majority of muslims would leave islam if the rest of humanity just understood these facts about that cult and properly recognized islam is a criminal organization in doctrine and practice and therefore not lawful and should not be allowed worldwide!

Today a muslim was telling me that he could show me the difference between words from satan and words from God; to which I responded:

I know God, and because I know Him, I know that no muslim in all the world knows Him or they wouldn't be a muslim, they'd be a Christian.

https://www.facebook.com/photo.php?fbid=6389305527815019&set=pb.100002069048072.-2207520000&type=3

muslims cannot tell the difference between truth and lies, God and the devil, or they wouldn't be a muslim. In other words, only by knowing Jesus Christ, who is the Truth (John 14:6-9, Acts 4:12, John 8:32-36) can anyone properly know Truth and be certain of Truth (1Jn 2:20-27). As such, those who do not know Jesus Christ are being deceived by the devil and so you sadly cannot tell me which words are from God and which are from the devil, because if you knew the difference, you wouldn't be a muslim, you'd be a Christian, filled with the Holy Spirit of Truth (Jesus Christ) and telling the entire world Jesus Christ is the One True God. (Acts 1:8; 4:12)

muslims are constantly online making ridiculous claims like "God has no Sons." I say if their god has no children, then it's obvious their god is not the One True Real God at all!

muslims need to discard the many lies of islam out of their heads. Understand God Created the Heavens and earth and all therein. He's the

One who THOUGHT of families, fathers, mothers, sons and daughters! HE CREATED AND MADE THEM and ALL CREATION BELONGS TO HIM! So yes, God LITERALLY has Sons and Daughters, HIS FAMILY! More than this He tells us His Sons and Daughters are those who know and love Him by the presence of His Spirit. So not just the whole world full of children belongs to God, but He specifically tells us those who know and love Him are His Sons and Daughters:

12But to all who did receive Him, to those who believed in His name, He gave the right to become children of God— 13children born not of blood, nor of the desire or will of man, but born of God....
https://biblehub.com/john/1-12.htm

People who have been born not just of flesh but of His Spirit, because they received the Holy Spirit of Truth (Jesus Christ) into their own existence.

John 3:1-21

English Standard Version

You Must Be Born Again

3 Now there was a man of the Pharisees named Nicodemus, a ruler of the Jews. 2 This man came to Jesus[a] by night and said to him, "Rabbi, we know that you are a teacher come from God, for no one can do these signs that you do unless God is with him." 3 Jesus answered him, "Truly, truly, I say to you, unless one is born again[b] he cannot see the kingdom of God." 4 Nicodemus said to him, "How can a man be born when he is old? Can he enter a second time into his mother's womb and be born?" 5 Jesus answered, "Truly, truly, I say to you, unless one is born of water and the Spirit, he cannot enter the kingdom of God. 6 That which is born of the flesh is flesh, and that which is born of the Spirit is spirit.[c] 7 Do not marvel that I said to you, 'You[d] must be born again.' 8 The wind[e] blows where it wishes, and you hear its sound, but you do not know where it comes from or where it goes. So it is with everyone who is born of the Spirit."

9 Nicodemus said to him, "How can these things be?" 10 Jesus answered him, "Are you the teacher of Israel and yet you do not understand these things? 11 Truly, truly, I say to you, we speak of what we know, and bear witness to what we have seen, but you[f] do not receive our testimony. 12 If I have told you earthly things and you do not believe, how can you believe if I tell you heavenly things? 13 No one has ascended into heaven except he who descended from heaven, the Son of Man.[g] 14 And as Moses lifted up the serpent in the wilderness, so must the Son of Man be lifted up, 15 that whoever believes in him may have eternal life.[h]

God is plainly telling us that in the same way He shows us that when a man and woman come together and give birth to children so also when Creator and His Creation come together, they give birth by His Spirit. That is more specifically, when the seed of a man enters the egg of a woman, a child is born of the flesh; likewise, when the SEED of GOD, Jesus Christ, enters our lives by His Holy Spirit of Truth, we are "born again" of His Holy Spirit and are true Sons and Daughters of God.

https://biblehub.com/interlinear/galatians/3-16.htm - notice the original language uses "spermati" for Seed of God, in other words, Jesus Christ is the genetic makeup, the exact representation of God (Hebrews 1:3) and as such those who receive His Holy Spirit of Truth are "born again" by the will of God and so Know God as their Heavenly Father. His Holy Spirit of Jesus Christ, the One True God, communicates with those who receive Him and tells them they are His Sons and Daughters:

Heirs with Christ

...15For you did not receive a spirit of slavery that returns you to fear, but you received the Spirit of sonship, by whom we cry, "Abba! Father!" 16The Spirit Himself testifies with our spirit that we are God's children. 17And if we are children, then we are heirs: heirs of God and co-heirs with Christ— if indeed we suffer with Him, so that we may also be glorified with Him....
https://biblehub.com/romans/8-16.htm

Which is why everyone rejecting Jesus Christ as the Lord and Savior that He is, does not see, hear or know God, because Jesus Christ and receiving Him into your life by His Holy Spirit is the ONLY Way to be "born of His Holy Spirit"; just like the only way to be a child of your father or mother is to actually be one by birth, or become one by adoption.

muslims are constantly falsely claiming the Holy Bible is confusing when it isn't. It is very clear and concise when you actually study the entire contents rather than ripping bits and pieces out of it to make false claims. For example, how muslims will take every title of God, Jesus Christ, that seems to make Him to be less than He is, (servant, messenger, man, prophet, and other such words completely out of context) while ignoring such plain statements as below:

The Eternal God, Jesus Christ, is Supreme in Everything and as such ALL Honorable Titles belong to Him, which is why the Holy Bible has many hundreds of those titles in its contents.

John 14:6-9
New King James Version
6 Jesus said to him, "I am the way, the truth, and the life. No one comes to the Father except through Me.

The Father Revealed
7 "If you had known Me, you would have known My Father also; and from now on you know Him and have seen Him."

8 Philip said to Him, "Lord, show us the Father, and it is sufficient for us."

9 Jesus said to him, "Have I been with you so long, and yet you have not known Me, Philip? He who has seen Me has seen the Father; so how can you say, 'Show us the Father'?

God is Eternal, "the Father" refers to His Invisible, Pervasive and Transcendent aspect of Him (Ephesians 4:6) and "the Son" refers to His Visible Image.

Colossians 1:15-19
The Supremacy of the Son of God
15 The Son is the image of the invisible God, the firstborn over all creation. 16 For in him all things were created: things in heaven and on earth, visible and invisible, whether thrones or powers or rulers or authorities; all things have been created through him and for him. 17 He is before all things, and in him all things hold together. 18 And he is the head of the body, the church; he is the beginning and the firstborn from among the dead, so that in everything he might have the supremacy. 19 For God was pleased to have all his fullness dwell in him,

So Jesus Christ is SUPREME in EVERYTHING, which means He is the: God of gods, Man of men, Angel of angels, Spirit of spirits, Father of fathers, Son of sons, Servant of servants, Messenger of messengers, Prophet of prophets, First and Last, Beginning and End, Star of stars, Sun of suns, Gate of gates, Door of doors, Heaven of heavens, Holy of holies, Prophet of prophets, King of kings, Lord of lords, etc. etc. etc. which is why all these titles and more are written plainly in the contents of the Holy Bible.

muslims like to IMAGINE that the many lies they are taught in islam are actually true and so they all IMAGINE they have something to teach the rest of the world other than that they are all deceived by the devil. So, a muslim was posting today how they actually imagine Jesus Christ is going to return and punish those who have been worshiping Him as the One True God that He is (muslims are overt enemies of Jesus Christ and Christians) and they indicate that fact not only by the evil history of islam but by such incredibly evil imaginations like this. God punishing His Own Loving Devoted Disciples! LUDICROUS! but muslims really are that obviously deceived by the devil.

https://www.openbible.info/topics/worshipping_jesus - Jesus Christ has always received worship as God, because that is who He is.

not one muslim sees, hears or knows God Almighty personally, so they have no idea that they are actually bowing down to the lying devil as long as they remain in islam. How can the world look at islam, FORCED To Bow, 5 times daily, in the direction of the kaaba, a black stone, COMMITTING OPEN IDOLATRY, in the site of the entire world! Following a rapist, robber, slaver, murderer and child molester, a perverse criminal, and his many evil lies in the quran; yet imagining that that muslims haven't been enslaved by the evil devil and his many lies! FACE REALITY PEOPLE, the Holy Bible is telling us all the absolute truth! 1Jn 5:19,20 If you know Jesus Christ because His Holy Spirit is inside of you; revealing Him and His Words of Truth to you, you are FREE, you are SAVED, you are FORGIVEN, but if you do not know Jesus Christ who is the Truth, you are being deceived by the deceiver, the devil. Jn 8:43-45, 1Jn 2:20-27, Acts 2:38-39, Jn 14:6-26, Acts 4:12, Acts 10:34-43, Jn 16:13, Jn 17:17

So, when our Lord and Savior, JESUS, the Christ, returns He will be putting an end to the devil and all his many lies in this world once and for all, judging all souls and casting the devil and all who followed him by believing his lies (like muslims) and so perished in their sins into the lake of fire. 2Th 1:8,9; Rev 21:8

Jesus Christ is God and He tells us He is the One who fulfills all His Law and Prophecies, which includes Judging all souls, and casting the devil and all believing and passing on his lies, making themselves to be liars also into the lake of fire:

2 Thessalonians 1:8-9

King James Version

8   In flaming fire taking vengeance on them that know not God, and that obey not the gospel of our Lord Jesus Christ:

9   Who shall be punished with everlasting destruction from the presence of the Lord, and from the glory of his power;

Notice it says that Jesus Christ will be taking vengeance ON ALL THOSE WHO DO NOT KNOW GOD! KNOW! not believe in, not have a good idea of, not have head knowledge about, BUT ON ALL THOSE WHO DO NOT KNOW HIM!

The only way to KNOW God, is to KNOW JESUS CHRIST PERSONALLY, BECAUSE THAT IS WHO HE IS!

THE ONLY WAY TO KNOW JESUS CHRIST PERSONALLY IS TO REPENT! turn from every evil thought, word, way and deed, WHICH INCLUDES DENYING THAT HE IS GOD! and be ready to love and obey Him now and forever! And then to get baptized in His Name so that He will give you His Own Holy Spirit of Truth whereby you will KNOW HIM PERSONALLY and GOD WILL BE TEACHING YOU PERSONALLY FROM THAT MOMENT FOREVER! Jn 14:20-26, Jn 16:13, Acts 2:38,39, Matt 28:18-20, Acts 4:12, 1Jn 2:27

The quran was written by men that came along many centuries AFTER Jesus Christ and His Eyewitness Apostles and Disciples in the Holy Bible who plainly told us that if ANYONE even an angel contradicts what is given to us in the Holy Bible they are under a DIVINE CURSE and are antichrists!

Galatians 1:6-9
No Other Gospel
6 I am astonished that you are so quickly deserting him who called you in the grace of Christ and are turning to a different gospel— 7 not that there is another one, but there are some who trouble you and want to distort the gospel of Christ. 8 But even if we or an angel from heaven should preach to you a gospel contrary to the one we preached to you, let him be accursed. 9 As we have said before, so now I say again: If anyone is

preaching to you a gospel contrary to the one you received, let him be accursed.

Beware of Antichrists
...21I have not written to you because you lack knowledge of the truth, but because you have it, and because no lie comes from the truth. 22Who is the liar, if it is not the one who denies that Jesus is the Christ? This is the antichrist, who denies the Father and the Son. 23Whoever denies the Son does not have the Father, but whoever confesses the Son has the Father as well.... https://biblehub.com/1_john/2-22.htm

1 John 4:1-6
Test the Spirits
4 Beloved, do not believe every spirit, but test the spirits to see whether they are from God, for many false prophets have gone out into the world. 2 By this you know the Spirit of God: every spirit that confesses that Jesus Christ has come in the flesh is from God, 3 and every spirit that does not confess Jesus is not from God. This is the spirit of the antichrist, which you heard was coming and now is in the world already. 4 Little children, you are from God and have overcome them, for he who is in you is greater than he who is in the world. 5 They are from the world; therefore they speak from the world, and the world listens to them. 6 We are from God. Whoever knows God listens to us; whoever is not from God does not listen to us. By this we know the Spirit of truth and the spirit of error.

"Christ" is the Greek word for "Messiah" and Messiah means God in the flesh! -
https://hebrew4christians.com/Names_of_Gd/Messiah/messiah.html

...25The woman said, "I know that Messiah" (called Christ) "is coming. When He comes, He will explain everything to us." 26 Jesus answered, "I who speak to you am He." https://biblehub.com/john/4-26.htm

So as long as anyone remains in the evil, lying cult of islam, they are accursed antichrists, on their way to the lake of fire. ALL MUSLIMS MUST REPENT AND BE BAPTIZED IN THE NAME OF JESUS CHRIST, THE ONE TRUE GOD, OUR LORD AND SAVIOR AND RECEIVE HIS HOLY SPIRIT OF TRUTH OR THEY WILL PERISH IN THEIR SINS AND BE CAST INTO THE LAKE OF FIRE!
...7The one who overcomes will inherit all things, and I will be his God, and he will be My son. 8But to the cowardly and unbelieving and abominable and murderers and sexually immoral and sorcerers and idolaters and all liars, their place will be in the lake that burns with fire and sulfur. This is the second death." https://biblehub.com/revelation/21-8.htm

Pretending that islam is an acceptable, lawful religion, is lying to muslims (and everyone else) all over the world and is actually hating them intensely, to let them believe that lying nonsense islam has taught them (brainwashed them with) to the point where they say untrue things even as their foundational statements about their imaginary god; to let them go on in their sins separated from our Eternal Creator. We have to tell people the TRUTH even if they hate us for it. Only then are we loving God and everyone else as He commanded us. Only the TRUTH sets us free and keeps us free from the lying devil! (evil thoughts and imaginations)

Overcoming the World
...4because everyone born of God overcomes the world. And this is the victory that has overcome the world: our faith. 5Who then overcomes the world? Only he who believes that Jesus is the Son of God. 6This is the One who came by water and blood, Jesus Christ—not by water alone, but by water and blood. And it is the Spirit who testifies to this, because the Spirit is the truth.... https://biblehub.com/1_john/5-5.htm

12But to all who did receive Him, to those who believed in His name, He gave the right to become children of God— 13children born not of blood, nor of the desire or will of man, but born of God....
https://biblehub.com/john/1-12.htm

The Great Commission

...18Then Jesus came to them and said, "All authority in heaven and on earth has been given to Me. 19Therefore go and make disciples of all nations, baptizing them in the name of the Father, and of the Son, and of the Holy Spirit, 20and teaching them to obey all that I have commanded you. And surely I am with you always, even to the end of the age."...
https://biblehub.com/matthew/28-19.htm

"Brothers, what shall we do?" 38 Peter replied, "Repent and be baptized, every one of you, in the name of Jesus Christ for the forgiveness of your sins, and you will receive the gift of the Holy Spirit. 39This promise belongs to you and your children and to all who are far off—to all whom the Lord our God will call to Himself."... https://biblehub.com/acts/2-38.htm

Peter and John Before the Council

...11This Jesus is 'the stone you builders rejected, which has become the cornerstone.' 12 Salvation exists in no one else, for there is no other name under heaven given to men by which we must be saved."
https://biblehub.com/acts/4-12.htm

https://www.biblegateway.com/passage/?search=John%2014%3A2026&version=ESV

John 14:20-26

English Standard Version

20
    In that day you will know that I am in my Father, and you in me, and I in you. 21 Whoever has my commandments and keeps them, he it is who loves me. And he who loves me will be loved by my Father, and I will love him and manifest myself to him." 22 Judas (not Iscariot) said to him, "Lord, how is it that you will manifest yourself to us, and not to the world?" 23 Jesus answered him, "If anyone loves me, he will keep my word, and my

Father will love him, and we will come to him and make our home with him. [24] Whoever does not love me does not keep my words. And the word that you hear is not mine but the Father's who sent me.

[25] "These things I have spoken to you while I am still with you. [26] But the Helper, the Holy Spirit, whom the Father will send in my name, he will teach you all things and bring to your remembrance all that I have said to you.

LOOK I'M TELLING YOU ALL ABOUT MUSLIMS NOT BECAUSE I WANT THE WORLD TO HATE THEM, BECAUSE MOST MUSLIMS JUST DON'T KNOW THE TRUTH ABOUT THEIR OWN CULT OR THEY WOULDN'T BE MUSLIMS! I'M TRYING TO TELL YOU ALL THAT NOT ALL RELIGIONS ARE THE SAME AND THAT ISLAM REALLY ISN'T LAWFUL TO PRACTICE AT ALL! so, I'm warning humanity about this lie because so many people just don't study history or the most important knowledge on earth, the contents of the Holy Bible! Any cult that celebrates the death of innocent men, women and children is obviously evil, of the devil. (a demonic cult) - https://www.thereligionofpeace.com/pages/articles/ahlam-tamimi-haj.aspx

I want the world to KNOW JESUS CHRIST the ONE TRUE GOD and to NOT BE DECEIVED! Learn to Live Righteously! Always speak truthfully with each other! If we cannot defend what we believe with facts, evidence, and right conduct, then what we believe isn't worth defending and we need to change our beliefs in that regard. If we know the Truth, that is we know our Eternal Creator, who came in the flesh, is the One known in the English Language as our Lord Jesus Christ who taught us all to Love Him and each other, THAT TRUTH is worth defending with our lives, to ensure our children grow up in a world where they know the Truth and can speak the Truth freely, instead of being raped by persons who call it child marriage; as in islamic nations. (bacha bazi, aisha, and
https://www.nairaland.com/1086492/ayatollah-khomeinis-book-sex-shias) growing up in a world as wicked as islam is why the One True God destroyed this world in the days of the flood!) Pretending that islam is a lawful religion, is dooming the entire world to becoming enslaved by the evil devil! Islam is EVIL, THOROUGHLY SO! Allowing muslims to go on

practicing their evil cult, is damning us all! We must SPEAK OUT against anything so overtly evil as islam! And frankly not do business with such persons until and unless they repent of such immoral wickedness! All while pretending to be holier than all the rest of mankind! Children need to be free to grow up and choose who they want to spend the rest of their lives with! Not be forced into marriage before they have even entered puberty! EVIL! And it's a crying shame any of us should have to say so! Child rape, and calling it marriage just because the pedophiles won't control their perverse, sexual urges. The dark ages, were called such because the darkness of islam had crept over the entire world making it dark! So much torture and death! So many plagues ravaged mankind in those dark days! Thankfully great men stood against such evil, and with the printing press, came along the Words of God, the Holy Bible, in common languages enlightening mankind! We have God and His Words in the Holy Bible to thank for everything commendable about western civilization! Presently this departure from God and His Words of Truth in the Holy Bible is bringing back darkness and evil things to our nation, suffering, plagues, diseases, destruction and death, including this modern influx of islamic immigration. CHRISTIANS SHOULD BE THE ONES MARCHING IN SOLIDARITY FOR OUR NATIONS AND THE LIVES OF INNOCENT PERSONS WORLDWIDE! Instead of the lgtbq movement with their defiant rainbow waving in front of God's Face, taunting our Eternal Creator, "you said you wouldn't destroy us again, by flood"; not realizing that God Almighty tells us all that if mankind becomes that wicked again, they will be destroyed by FIRE!

Far too many muslims just parrot the lies islam has taught them and when they do that, they show themselves to be unthinking individuals, believing lies and passing them on, makes muslims to be notorious liars. One of their common tactics is to rip a few Words of God out of the Holy Bible to make false claims about those words, for example they often insist that Jesus Christ was sent ONLY to the Israelites; acting like the rest of the entire Bible doesn't exist in the process.

muslims act like their reading comprehension and thinking skills are extremely challenged when they make such overtly false claims. When your Mommy and Daddy sent you off to grade school, did that mean you were ONLY sent to grade school for all eternity? of course not, so don't take one sentence said on one day at one point and time to mean that. Especially when God, JESUS CHRIST, is crystal clear He is LORD of ALL and His Gospel is for ALL.

The Great Commission
...18Then Jesus came to them and said, "All authority in heaven and on earth has been given to Me. 19Therefore go and make disciples of all nations, baptizing them in the name of the Father, and of the Son, and of the Holy Spirit, 20and teaching them to obey all that I have commanded you. And surely I am with you always, even to the end of the age."...
https://biblehub.com/matthew/28-19.htm

Acts 10:34-43
Gentiles Hear the Good News
34 So Peter opened his mouth and said: "Truly I understand that God shows no partiality, 35 but in every nation anyone who fears him and does what is right is acceptable to him. 36 As for the word that he sent to Israel, preaching good news of peace through Jesus Christ (he is Lord of all), 37 you yourselves know what happened throughout all Judea, beginning from Galilee after the baptism that John proclaimed: 38 how God anointed Jesus of Nazareth with the Holy Spirit and with power. He went about doing good and healing all who were oppressed by the devil, for God was with him. 39 And we are witnesses of all that he did both in the country of the Jews and in Jerusalem. They put him to death by hanging him on a tree, 40 but God raised him on the third day and made him to appear, 41 not to all the people but to us who had been chosen by God as witnesses, who ate and drank with him after he rose from the dead. 42 And he commanded us to preach to the people and to testify that he is the one appointed by God to be judge of the living and the dead. 43 To him all the prophets bear witness that everyone who believes in him receives forgiveness of sins through his name."

verse 36 Jesus Christ is LORD OF ALL and verse 43 ALL PROPHETS SAY SO! AND THAT FORGIVENESS OF SINS IS ONLY THROUGH HIM, BY NAME! Acts 4:12

Jesus is Coming

...**12**"Behold, I am coming soon, and My reward is with Me, to give to each one according to what he has done. **13**I am the Alpha and the Omega, the First and the Last, the Beginning and the End."

https://www.biblegateway.com/passage/?search=Matthew%2025%3A31-46&version=ESV - So the scriptures are crystal clear that Jesus Christ is Lord of All and He will Judge EVERYONE, ALL NATIONS! each person one by one! He Judges us by His Words! So, no one should be ignoring the Holy Bible! NO ONE! - Jn 12:48-50 unless they have a strangely stupid, self-destructive desire to experience the Wrath of God Almighty and end up in the lake of fire. John 3:36; 8:24-25; 2Th 1:8-9, Rev 21:8

Far too many today are committing blasphemy constantly these days by speaking wickedly against God, Jesus Christ, His Prophets and His Words in the Holy Bible. (they are fulfilling prophecies that portend to their own doom and destruction when they do so - https://www.biblegateway.com/passage/?search=2%20Timothy%203%3A1-5&version=AKJV)

Every time a muslim says God would never do this or that, like God would never be born, God would never eat, God would never sleep, God would never do anything we all do naturally, they don't seem to realize they are INSULTING HIM! HE CREATED AND MADE ALL THOSE THINGS! So when they speak bad about just the facts of nature, the facts of reality, they are blaspheming! And muslims do that constantly, in fact muslims do just about everything God tells us NOT to do in the Holy Bible. He says don't offer lip service, make repetitive prayers, practice vain religious traditions, instead of His Commandments. but muslims are all the time "PBUH" this and that, bowing by force multiple times daily, wearing robes to be seen of others, DOING EVERYTHING GOD DESPISES! Mt 6:7, 15:8 so as a standard of daily practice muslims are doing exactly what Jesus Christ said not to! It's why God calls muslims liars and antichrists, they offer lip service but do not obey Him; they do not have His Holy Spirit of Truth. 1Jn 2:20-27; 1Jn 4:1-6 Instead, muslims spend their time sneering down upon everyone else, especially Christians, and falsely accusing them. By so doing, they manifest they are children of the devil (unless they repent of their wicked ways and become Christians, Disciples of Jesus Christ, muslims will be cast into the lake of fire) - the false accuser of Christians is the devil, so when muslims spend all their time doing that, they are showing the devil is in their lives. Rev 12:10 Furthermore, islamic nations are so evil, some of them have banned the Holy Bible! (The Holy Bible contains the Words of our Good Lord Jesus Christ and provably so - read my book **_The Holy Bible is Provably and Verifiably Divinely Inspired_**.) People need to understand the facts of history. islam began by gangs of rapists, robbers, murderers, slavers and child molesters. The highest aspiration of the muslim is to end up in their depraved notion of paradise, where their evil god, allah, promises to give them endless erections to molest virgins with. virgins, in their culture, are little boys and girls, so islam is just a revival of ancient baalism, a perverse sex cult, the kind of evil that God drowned in the flood and incinerated in the past.

https://www.hope-of-israel.org/baaloftheOT.html it's why things like bachi bazi exist and https://www.nairaland.com/1086492/ayatollahkhomeinis-book-sex-shias fatwas of all manner of sexual immorality. islam in doctrine and practice doesn't just sow to the flesh in all manner of perversions, but is thoroughly evil and deceitful; otherwise known as demonic! Jn 8:43-45

https://www.youtube.com/watch?v=htshvId51UE and https://www.youtube.com/watch?v=pu_YlJdwpao - muslims are all the time in denial of the facts of history. their bloody cult has been violent from its inception to this day! www.youtube.com/watch?v=l_To-cV94Bo it began in violence and innocent bloodshed and spawned centuries of brutal slavery and oppression - https://www.google.com/search?client=opera&q=centuries+of+islamic+slave+trade&sourceid=opera&ie=UTF-8&oe=UTF-8 islam is so evil that people are not allowed to say so in islamic nations! NO FREE SPEECH THERE! Freedom only comes from Jesus Christ and His Words in the Holy Bible! John 8:32-36

When raping, robbing, enslaving, murdering muslims invaded Europe, brave Christian crusaders gave their lives to defending those nations or the world would have fallen into complete darkness under islam. (The USA would have never been founded if not for the Christian Crusaders!) To allow muslims into western Christian nations is a betrayal to those honorable souls who gave their lives in that battle. IT'S TREASON! Not one muslim or mosque belongs in Christian nations! islamic nations have banned the Holy Bible and burned churches! muslims have been violent enemies of all that is good from the very foundation of their demonic cult on earth! The entire world NEEDS TO RECOGNIZE THAT islam is a CRIMINAL ORGANIZATION in doctrine and practice!

https://www.thereligionofpeace.com/pages/quran/index.aspx - I'm not saying all muslims are violent, sexually perverse criminals, I'm saying that the cult of islam is so evil, it threatens the lives of anyone who tries to leave it! -
https://www.google.com/search?client=opera&q=islamic+apostasy+death+penalty+nations&sourceid=opera&ie=UTF-8&oe=UTF-8 - Since people living in islamic nations are not allowed to tell the truth about islam, THE REST OF THE ENTIRE WORLD NEEDS TO EDUCATE THEMSELVES AND SAY SO! No to islam! no muslims in our nations! no demonic mosques in the borders of any lawful country on earth! The only way a muslim should be allowed to immigrate is if they burn their quran, formerly renounce its evil dogmas, and vow before our Living Lord Jesus Christ to never practice the evil of islam ever again! I'm serious! Do you all want to see bloodshed, rubble and ruin, death and destruction?! then just keep letting the lying snake slither into your nations! SAY NO TO THE DEVIL! islam is evil and obviously so! -
https://www.youtube.com/results?search_query=islamic+rape+victims+speak+out

Some people make categorical errors, like saying some Christians, some Jews, some Atheists, some Hindus, some Buddhists etc also commit murder. The difference is those under the Righteous Law of God in Holy Bible can commit such crimes IN VIOLATION of God's Commandments, they know it's wrong! But in islam muslims are so brainwashed they commit murder in the name of their evil god! So islam as long as it exists will create violent murderers! It's why it's so dangerous! It's why it's founded the largest number of violent terrorist organizations in the history of the world!

islam was factually founded by rapists, child molesters, robbers, slavers and murderers and is why the quran openly advocates such crimes against humanity. muhammad used the name of a pagan idol, to deceive people and con other like-minded criminals into joining his gang. so islam is a sexually perverse cult that is mostly about gratifying the sexually perverse desires of wicked men like muhammad. women are just objects to be owned, used and abused in islam. But just in case any of them might learn to read, islam allows them to join the muslim males with their perpetual erections in their depraved notions of the afterlife... that is just as long as the women don't get in the way of the muslim men raping little boys and girls. yes! islam is that evil! the best idea they can come up with for their idea of heaven is perpetual boners to molest virgins with and yes! in islam virgins are little boys and girls! so islam is a damnable cult of child molesters, rapists, robbers and murderers those are the kind of criminals that founded it and those are the kinds of criminals that have perpetuated it throughout history to this day. islam is in NO WAY acceptable!

READ AND LEARN AND STOP REMAINING SO IGNORANT THAT YOU'RE RISKING YOUR LIVES AND THAT OF YOUR CHILDREN!
https://www.thereligionofpeace.com/pages/quran/index.aspx

People need to understand that the REAL GOD, JESUS CHRIST, FORBIDS every form of evil CLEARLY in the Holy Bible! that the imaginary evil allah encourages in the quran!

God tells us all plainly His Two Greatest Commandments are to Love Him and each other and that ALL His other Commandments are based on those two! So, anyone falsely accusing God of commanding any kind of unrighteous, evil act in the Holy Bible is WRONG!

Matthew 22:36-40

³⁶ "Teacher, which is the great commandment in the Law?" And he said to him, "You shall love the Lord your God with all your heart and with all your soul and with all your mind. ³⁸ This is the great and first commandment. ³⁹ And a second is like it: You shall love your neighbor as yourself. ⁴⁰ On these two commandments depend all the Law and the Prophets."

islam and the quran has generated the largest number of violent terrorist organizations in the history of the world! THOSE VIOLENT CRIMINALS ARE DOING WHAT THEIR evil allah TELLS THEM TO DO in the quran! Anyone committing such crimes in Christian nations IS BREAKING THE COMMANDMENTS OF JESUS CHRIST IN THE HOLY BIBLE! Which is why the Holy Bible, Jesus Christ and His Disciples, Christians, have founded and funded the largest number of humanitarian charities and organizations in the history of the world. IN SHORT, EVERYTHING THAT'S GOOD AND RIGHT ABOUT CIVILIZATION IS DUE TO GOD ALMIGHTY AND HIS COMMANDMENTS IN THE HOLY BIBLE! AND THE PEOPLE THAT KNOW, LOVE AND OBEY HIM! and everything that's evil and wrong in this world is due to how many souls are still ignoring His Divine Instructions given to mankind in the contents of the Holy Bible.

After the attacks on the towers, muslims were seen cheering with delight that thousands of innocent Americans had died. and what followed? an islamic president slithered into office, and allowed an islamic mosque to be built at ground zero, released islamic terrorists from Gitmo and flew in record numbers of muslims into our nation. Putting a mosque at ground zero is the ultimate insult to the innocent Americans who died there! It was an open sign of submission to the diabolical cult of islam! OUTRAGEOUS! Sure, muslims couldn't have done those attacks without traitors in our nation allowing it, but the fact that muslims cheered when it happened, SHOWS THEY ARE ENEMIES OF AMERICA! so, what obama did and what those in power allowed thereafter was at best betrayal of the innocent Americans who lost their lives in the tragedy of 911 and at worst committed acts of treason, while the rest of our nation watched. My

stomach turns every time I think about it. What western governments have done by allowing muslims to invade our nations when their cult is the antithesis of our laws, their dogmas and laws in islamic nations are defined as CRIMES by our laws! I'm wondering if the world is just so busy, so distracted that they just are oblivious to these facts? Clearly these recent actions of leaders governing Christian nations, shows either massive ignorance of islam and history to a dangerous degree or they were indeed bribed by oil rich islamic nations into committing treason. All manner of universities and companies have been accepting "donations" from islamic nations which precipitated a massive influx of muslims into western Christian nations. Christians worldwide should be arming themselves and writing letters to their authorities telling them in no uncertain terms that islam is not a lawful religion, it cannot be legally practiced under our laws. It is subversive to our laws, our freedoms and a danger to our civilization and lives. (muslims are criminals, the so-called "moderate" muslims that aren't directly engaging in violent acts of terrorism, also are not arresting the violent islamic terrorists themselves, they still identify themselves with their demonic cult and enabling/funding such violence in this world. If they are not practicing what islam teaches, or the doctrines of crimes in their qurans and as such are not muslims and should formerly leave that lying, wicked cult. Just associating with the cult as a muslim is enabling violent terrorism to continue worldwide). Brigette Gabriel warns the world that muslims only pretended to be friendly until they violently attacked and overturned Christian Lebanon into an islamic state.
https://www.google.com/search?client=opera&q=brigette+gabriel+leban on+islamic+betrayal&sourceid=opera&ie=UTF-8&oe=UTF-8

The world needs to take the evil of islam seriously, because sadly people just don't know enough to know better. The quran is essentially a manifesto of endless evil and crimes against humanity, that encourages muslims to never stop their quest for global domination by any means, including deceit and violence. If the nations of the world stopped buying petrol from islamic nations, muslims would starve to death! That's how obvious the One True God, is telling muslims that their cult is unacceptable! He doesn't provide food enough for them to even live without imports! So, letting that kind of evil into our Christian nations only brings suffering, destruction and death! PURE SELF-DESTRUCTIVE STUPIDITY! America was founded as a Christian nation! DEPARTING FROM THE ONE TRUE GOD, JESUS CHRIST, means DOOM! DEATH AND

DESTRUCTION! Deut 28. Cities lying in smoldering ashes, rubble and ruin! INSANITY!

I understand the vast majority of muslims are not deliberately evil people, but pretending the cult of islam is remotely acceptable or lawful only allows the deliberately evil "extremists" and "terrorists" criminals in it, to continue to get away with crimes against humanity and go on oppressing people in islamic nations! And allows ignorant people to call themselves a muslim without even understanding its doctrines, its history, or its criminal ways. The ones that do, "the extremists" wear the cloak of those ignorant muslims to continue to get away with their crimes. islam NEEDS TO BE RECOGNIZED AS THE CRIMINAL ORGANIZATION THAT IT IS! and banned worldwide!

https://www.google.com/search?client=opera&q=woman+beaten+to+death+for+not+wearing+hijab&sourceid=opera&ie=UTF-8&oe=UTF-8 - beating women for not wearing hot garb in the desert sun and whipping raped VICTIMS instead of punishing the rapists!
https://www.google.com/search?client=opera&q=woman+raped+given+200+lashes&sourceid=opera&ie=UTF-8&oe=UTF-8 islam is SO EVIL it punishes VICTIMS of violent crimes instead of the criminals!
https://www.google.com/search?client=opera&q=acid+faces+of+islam&sourceid=opera&ie=UTF-8&oe=UTF-8 - islam is SO EVIL it has UNIQUE evils to its cult! like acid throwing, scarring innocent women for life! so called "honor killings" where family members kill other family members unless they bow to the demonic cult of islam for life! LOOK! the quran OPENLY ENCOURAGES CRIMES AGAINST HUMANITY! - https://www.thereligionofpeace.com/pages/quran/index.aspx - torture, slavery, murder, suicide bombings etc. are all ENCOURAGED in islam! THOSE ARE CRIMES! SERIOUS CRIMES! so islam is NOT LEGAL TO PRACTICE IN ANY LAWFUL NATIONS (non-islamic). Which means there should be no mosques, no qurans and no muslims in America or Europe; no ifs, ands or buts! confine muslims to their criminal nations until islam hopefully passes away by educating/deprogramming them through broadcast media, satellites and the Internet. Otherwise, God Himself will incinerate islamic nations when He returns in Glory. 2Th 1:8-9

When muslims come into our nations and attempt to establish their own regions of control, so-called sharia law, they are showing us plainly that muslims are NOT integrating and obeying our laws! they have NO DESIRE to do so! THEY ARE SUBVERSIVE ENEMIES IN OUR MIDST!

To one who knows the facts about islam, its doctrines and history, it is such an obvious criminal organization that in my own thinking any and all muslims should be under arrest by the rest of humanity. The ones that have just been brainwashed with the many lies of islam need to be properly educated/deprogrammed from their criminal cult. islam is so overtly evil, that if I was in charge, islamic mosques would be razed to the ground worldwide. To me, anyone in western Christian nations that would dare join the demonic cult and criminal organization of islam is not just someone who is either lacking so much knowledge that they're a danger to themselves and others, but if they know how evil islam is and join it anyway, is someone that should be under immediate arrest. They look like the very worst kind of traitor to God and their countries. Realize the only reason we have freedom from the evil oppression of islam is that Christian patriots of western nations GAVE THEIR LIVES AND FOUGHT TO THE DEATH AGAINST lying, raping, robbing, child-molesting, enslaving, murdering muslims!

https://www.youtube.com/watch?v=l_To-cV94Bo

I don't hate muslims, I just think that the majority of them would leave islam instantly if they actually understood the true history of islam (over a thousand years of brutal slavery and oppression, and hundreds of millions of innocent people slain - https://www.politicalislam.com/tears-of-jihad/ and
http://materiaislamica.com/index.php/List_of_Wars_in_Pax_Islamic_History_(c._624—c._1999)), the teachings of the quran and hadiths, and heard from the rest of humanity THAT ISLAM IS EVIL! TOTALLY UNACCEPTABLE! because most of them have been brainwashed from birth to the point where many of them act like they can't tell fact from fiction, truth from lies, good from evil or God Almighty from the devil. (islam is so demonic that the devil turns the minds of muslims practically into unthinking

people who can only seem to parrot what was ingrained into them. - https://www.google.com/search?client=opera&q=child+abuse+in+islam+children+beaten+for+not+memorizing+the+quran&sourceid=opera&ie=UTF-8&oe=UTF-8) I'm not saying there are no intelligent muslims, I'm saying their cult is so perverse that inbreeding has caused birth defects, and lowered intelligence levels in huge numbers of them. Illiteracy is still widespread, or large percentages of muslims are barely literate among the islamic nations. In other words, islam continues to exist due to ignorance, a lack of correct information, and so much so, that when someone like myself cares enough to tell muslims the truth, they wrongly imagine I must be lying instead. The REAL GOD, JESUS CHRIST represents Himself as LOVE and TRUTH; only Virtuous and Good, so He Commands us to Love everyone enough to tell them the truth, we MUST tell muslims they are in a lying, evil cult and criminal organization! Love muslims enough to at least attempt to deprogram them from the vile antichristian, demonic cult of islam 1Jn 2:21-23; to save them from being cast into the lake of fire. Rev 21:8 Pretending islam is acceptable in any way is actually hating muslims.

Western Christian nations need to comprehend that islamic culture is so completely opposite to our own that they ban the Holy Bible! The Word of God in the Holy Bible is the foundation for our entire western Christian civilization! (YES! anyone saying otherwise is ignorant of the most important facts of history! I blame public education today for FAILING to teach the Words of God as COMMANDED by Him to all children! and how our own nations owe our freedoms and everything good about them to Him and His Words in the Holy Bible and the brave men and women that gave their lives in defense of our nations and God-given freedoms!) islam is TOTALLY INCOMPATIBLE with Christianity! (it's the reason muslims violently attacked us at the founding of their cult! it's also the reason they burn churches to this day in islamic nations! THEY ARE ENEMIES OF ALL LAWFUL CHRISTIAN NATIONS!) anyone allowing muslims to immigrate into our nations are DANGEROUSLY IGNORANT at best, and outright traitors at worst! Until islamic nations do away with "islamic apostasy laws" and "islamic blasphemy laws" and all their verses condoning violence toward others, murder, torture, decapitation, etc etc. and allow other religions to remain free without persecution, they are criminals and cannot be allowed to immigrate into our nations! (Essentially islamic nations have to STOP being islamic!)

muslims are taught to chant that their evil allah has no children and no partners. when they say that, I think to myself GREAT! then islam and muslims shouldn't exist! if their allah has no children, then muslims are openly acknowledging allah is not the REAL GOD. The REAL GOD Created and Made a world full of billions of children! ALL CREATION BELONGS TO THE REAL GOD! so the REAL GOD, JESUS CHRIST, has CHILDREN, HE PLAINLY SAID SO!

13Then the little children were brought to Jesus for Him to place His hands on them and pray for them. And the disciples rebuked those who brought them. **14**But **Jesus said, "Let the little children come to Me, and do not hinder them! For the kingdom of heaven belongs to such as these."**...
https://biblehub.com/matthew/19-13.htm

and when muslims say evil allah has no partners, I think that they should show that by NOT DOING ANYTHING allah asks them to! or you are a partner by definition! (In other words, islam is so evil, it brainwashes muslims into denying reality before their own eyes and into saying things repeatedly that are obviously not true.)

islam is just a revival of ancient perverse sex cults of the past (that the One True God flooded and incinerated), it's why child marriages/rape is common in islamic nations and polygamy. islam is so perverse sexually that their idea of "janna" is to have perpetual erections to molest virgins endlessly with. (When someone has the idea of raping innocent children, THOSE ARE CRIMES, crimes that One True God, tells us such persons:

Temptations and Trespasses
1Jesus said to His disciples, "It is inevitable that stumbling blocks will come, but woe to the one through whom they come! **2**It would be better for him to have a millstone hung around his neck and to be thrown into the sea than to cause one of these little ones to stumble. **3**Watch yourselves. If your brother sins, rebuke him; and if he repents, forgive him....

Oh and as a side note, women can join them in their perverse notion of paradise; just as long as they don't get in the way of raping innocent children. In other words, islam and the quran is about rapists, robbers, slavers and murderers gratifying their sexual perversities. (so NO! if you imagine that Heaven is to gratify your sexual immoralities (especially abusing innocent children), YOU ARE ON YOUR WAY TO THE FLAMES OF DAMNATION! Rev 21:8) none of this evil here on earth is welcome in Heaven. No one will be raped, abused, beaten, sexually molested, to satisfy your selfish, wicked ways.)

https://www.nairaland.com/1086492/ayatollah-khomeinis-book-sex-shias - fatwas in islam for zoophilia, necrophilia and worse - https://www.youtube.com/watch?v=2TkV5clbokQ

https://www.hope-of-israel.org/baaloftheOT.html

https://www.youtube.com/watch?v=pu_YlJdwpao - of course muslims will DENY the facts, but anyone can read the evil instructions in the quran for themselves. anyone denying that islam is a perverse sex cult is denying reality, the history and doctrines of islam.

https://www.thereligionofpeace.com/pages/quran/index.aspx - muslims actually think it's okay to rape children because their evil false prophet did -

http://www.answeringmuslims.com/2014/03/muhammad-and-thighing-of-aisha.html muhammad raped a little kid still playing with dolls. islam is that perverse, that wrong, that evil. muslims are taught to idolize and imitate muhammad who used the name of a pagan idol, as his means of controlling the weak-minded and other perverse criminals who joined his cult.

https://www.youtube.com/watch?v=dkCM5_qGEuo as far as I can tell youtube has employed subversives and traitors of America because they keep censoring people like David Wood for merely telling the truth about islam. I myself have been censored by them as well. Public forums on the Internet are the last bastion of free speech, and yet these companies make policies that violate the highest laws of our nation. No one telling truthful information should be censored. (even if other people falsely accuse them of what is modern day knows as "hate speech" – telling the truth is not hateful, it's loving people enough to tell them the facts!) American politicians, businesses, and universities have received donations/bribes from islamic nations, and is the reason for so much islamic immigration into our nations. So, our freedoms are ALREADY UNDER ATTACK! Companies and politicians making unlawful policies and decrees, are attempting to change this nation into one that is criminal. People accusing Christians of hate speech, should look at the entire world statistics, Christians have founded and funded the largest number of humanitarian charities in the history of the world, and yet Christians remain to be some of the most seriously persecuted people on earth! (Being murdered for loving people enough to tell them the Truth and being censored by other persons in our Christian nation! You're the ones who are guilty of hating not the Christians who are loving you all enough to tell you the Truth!) This corruption in America and Europe is nothing short of subversive and perhaps rises to acts of treason. His channel sadly has been removed from youtube, David was educating people who are dangerously ignorant about islam and in my opinion, was saving lives; so, it's a crying shame anyone would dare censor him. Americans accepting islamic money to subvert our laws and culture are factually traitors and if I was in power would be under arrest! Censoring Americans by companies on American soil should be resulting in arrests for attempting to subvert the highest laws of our nation. Bill of Rights Number One! censoring people for merely telling the truth, is an extremely evil thing to do, especially when they are seriously trying to save lives. So, companies in America employing muslims and taking money from islamic nations in order to subvert our laws especially our Constitution are in fact guilty of subversion and treason and those people responsible should be under arrest. muslims shouldn't be in our nation(s), but and if the people in the west are so foolish as to allow them to immigrate, they at least should be demanding that they leave their qurans, their damnable, demonic cult behind them PERMANENTLY and pledge allegiance to our laws; become law abiding loyal citizens! (muslims are subversive! they hold allegiance to their evil god allah, which is just another name of the lying devil!) under the One True GOD, Jesus Christ, who declares Himself to all mankind plainly in the contents of the Holy Bible! STOP BUYING OIL FROM ISLAMIC NATIONS, THEY'RE USING THAT

MONEY TO BRIBE CORRUPT PERSONS IN OUR NATIONS! And are already subverting our laws! THE BILL OF RIGHTS! And enacting unlawful laws, that cannot be justly upheld under the LAW OF GOD (The Holy Bible), that our nation was founded on! https://www.youtube.com/watch?v=fVgJFt5htBQ

Look! muhammad was like the devil in the flesh! the OPPOSITE of our LORD and SAVIOR, JESUS CHRIST! https://www.thereligionofpeace.com/pages/articles/jesusmuhammad.aspx so muslims aren't just incompatible, but so much so, that they are DIAMETRICALLY OPPOSED to everything about Christian culture! (or they wouldn't ban the Holy Bible and burn churches in islamic nations).

muslims are always asking why was it necessary for God to come in the flesh, show Himself, prove Himself and suffer and die for us on the cross? (If God hadn't done so, mankind wouldn't know who God is.)

Generally, God tells us that all of us put Him on the Cross by sinning, disobeying Him and so it was necessary for Him to Redeem and Save us according to His Own Law and Prophecies; specifically, it was a conspiracy between the unbelieving jews and the romans, but Jesus Christ ALLOWED it to happen to Prove He is God. (1Cor 2:7-9)

Jesus Comforts Martha and Mary

...24Martha replied, "I know that he will rise again in the resurrection at the last day." 25 Jesus said to her, "I am the resurrection and the life. Whoever believes in Me will live, even though he dies. 26And everyone who lives and believes in Me will never die. Do you believe this?"...
https://biblehub.com/john/11-25.htm

John 5:39-40

39 You search the Scriptures because you think that in them you have eternal life; and it is they that bear witness about me, 40 yet you refuse to come to me that you may have life.

John 14:4-9

4 And where I go you know, and the way you know."

5 Thomas said to Him, "Lord, we do not know where You are going, and how can we know the way?"

6 Jesus said to him, "I am the way, the truth, and the life. No one comes to the Father except through Me.

The Father Revealed

7 "If you had known Me, you would have known My Father also; and from now on you know Him and have seen Him."

8 Philip said to Him, "Lord, show us the Father, and it is sufficient for us."

9 Jesus said to him, "Have I been with you so long, and yet you have not known Me, Philip? He who has seen Me has seen the Father; so how can you say, 'Show us the Father'?

So, Jesus Christ had claimed to be God, the Way to Heaven, the One who has Eternal Life and the Power to Raise the dead back to life, and then He proved it by publicly dying, raising His Body from the Grave, transfiguring it, making it Immortal and Glorious and Ascending into Heaven in front of eyewitnesses. It's why the New Testament was written and Christianity began. Acts 1:7-11; Matthew 28:18-20; Acts 2:38-39; 4:12; 10:34-43

<u>Jesus Appears to Thomas</u>
...**27**Then Jesus said to Thomas, "Put your finger here and look at My hands. Reach out your hand and put it into My side. Stop doubting and believe." **28**<u>Thomas replied, "My Lord and my God!"</u> **29**Jesus said to him,

"Because you have seen Me, you have believed; blessed are those who have not seen and yet have believed."... https://biblehub.com/john/20-28.htm

God, Jesus Christ, fulfills His Law and Prophecies thereby Mt. 5:17-18; including His Law and Prophecies about Redemption and Salvation.

https://bible.knowing-jesus.com/topics/God,-As-Redeemer and https://www.preceptaustin.org/tetelestai-paid_in_full and https://www.accordingtothescriptures.org/prophecy/353prophecies.html

I once was asked about the "unforgiveable sin" and my personal perspective is that, as long as people are still breathing, God is allowing them the chance to truly repent and at least ask Him to forgive them of any and all sins. If you ignore God and His Commandments in the Holy Bible, you cannot be Saved. If you refuse to Repent of your sins: wicked and evil thoughts, words, ways and deeds, you cannot be Saved. If you deny Jesus Christ is the One True God, the Only Savior of mankind, you cannot be Saved. My point is that my opinion of the real unforgiveable "blasphemy against the Holy Ghost/Spirit" is to call God, Jesus Christ, His Words in the Holy Bible, a liar lifelong; unto your dying breath. (By ignoring, or deliberately disobeying, or denying Him and His Words therein.) NEVERTHELESS, I have heard or rather have seen some people saying/typing/writing such incredibly evil things, that I distance myself from them because God says He is going to pour out His Wrath upon such persons IN FLAMING FIRE. 2Th 1:8-9 If you have ever spoken badly about Jesus Christ and/or His Words and Commandments in the Holy Bible, you need to repent immediately. You are tempting the Wrath of the Living God by doing so wickedly. People die unexpectedly all over the world; don't be someone who perishes in your sins, when Jesus Christ is willing to forgive you; provided you repent and turn from your wicked ways and learn to love and obey Him and His Righteous Commandments given us all in the Holy Bible.

In other words, if someone who is presently ruled by the devil utters demonic blasphemies against God, Jesus Christ, His Words in the Holy Bible, then it might just be the devil speaking through them, rather than they themselves. So, if God is still giving breath to anyone on earth, I encourage them all to humbly ask God, Jesus Christ, to forgive them of any and all sins and to save their souls from the flames of damnation, where the lying devil and all wicked, unrepentant persons will be cast. Rev 20:10; 21:8

Everyone, Everywhere, should Pray fervently that God will change them by His Grace and Power to be Good, Holy, Inherently Righteous and Perfect as Himself. And that even now He would cleanse us all from all unrighteousness and ever abide with us by the Presence of His Holy Spirit of Truth in our lives.

I tend to think that if anyone, anywhere was truly guilty of "unforgiveable sin", they wouldn't be breathing any longer. By that I mean, if you spend your entire life disbelieving God, His Words in the Holy Bible, that exist because of His Holy Spirit who was upon men and women in the past, making them to be true Prophets, then you spent you entire lifetime calling God, Jesus Christ, His Prophets in the Holy Bible, all liars, and you committed the unforgiveable sin of calling His Holy Spirit a liar your entire life, which is why all such persons die in their sins and end up in the lake of fire.

24That is why I told you that you would die in your sins. For unless you believe that I am He, you will die in your sins." 25"Who are You?" they asked. "Just what I have been telling you from the beginning," Jesus replied.... https://biblehub.com/john/8-24.htm

So, no matter what anyone has done, if they have true sorrow before God for their sins, and truly wish to sin no more, are truly repentant and humble before Him, then I believe they can still be Saved and that is because if they couldn't be Saved, they would be dead already.

Hebrews 3:8-15

8 Harden not your hearts, as in the provocation, in the day of temptation in the wilderness:

9 When your fathers tempted me, proved me, and saw my works forty years.

10 Wherefore I was grieved with that generation, and said, They do alway err in their heart; and they have not known my ways.

11 So I sware in my wrath, They shall not enter into my rest.)

12 Take heed, brethren, lest there be in any of you an evil heart of unbelief, in departing from the living God.

13 But exhort one another daily, while it is called To day; lest any of you be hardened through the deceitfulness of sin.

14 For we are made partakers of Christ, if we hold the beginning of our confidence stedfast unto the end;

15 While it is said, To day if ye will hear his voice, harden not your hearts, as in the provocation.

In other words, EVERYONE SHOULD REPENT, while God still gives them breath and life to do so. EVERYONE EVERYWHERE should obey His Commandment to Repent and Be Baptized in His Name and be filled with His Holy Spirit, so God Himself will be working in their souls from that moment forward and empowering them to resist the devil and all evil sins and be leading them onward to Victory; to Heaven to be with Him forever! If you reject Jesus Christ your entire life and deny He is the One True God then you have called His Holy Spirit of Truth, a liar, your entire life, and so have blasphemed God, His Holy Spirit, who testifies that Jesus Christ is the One True God, in all the world. Doing that unto your dying breath is unforgiveable and will result in your damnation. Rev 21:8; Jn 3:36

...7The one who overcomes will inherit all things, and I will be his God, and he will be My son. 8But to the cowardly and unbelieving and abominable and murderers and sexually immoral and sorcerers and idolaters and all liars, their place will be in the lake that burns with fire and sulfur. This is the second death." https://biblehub.com/revelation/21-8.htm

Overcoming the World

...4because everyone born of God overcomes the world. And this is the victory that has overcome the world: our faith. 5Who then overcomes the world? Only he who believes that Jesus is the Son of God. 6This is the One who came by water and blood, Jesus Christ—not by water alone, but by water and blood. And it is the Spirit who testifies to this, because the Spirit is the truth.... https://biblehub.com/1_john/5-5.htm

12But to all who did receive Him, to those who believed in His name, He gave the right to become children of God— 13children born not of blood, nor of the desire or will of man, but born of God....
https://biblehub.com/john/1-12.htm

The Great Commission

...18Then Jesus came to them and said, "All authority in heaven and on earth has been given to Me. 19Therefore go and make disciples of all nations, baptizing them in the name of the Father, and of the Son, and of the Holy Spirit, 20and teaching them to obey all that I have commanded you. And surely I am with you always, even to the end of the age."...
https://biblehub.com/matthew/28-19.htm

"Brothers, what shall we do?" 38 Peter replied, "Repent and be baptized, every one of you, in the name of Jesus Christ for the forgiveness of your sins, and you will receive the gift of the Holy Spirit. 39This promise belongs to you and your children and to all who are far off—to all whom the Lord our God will call to Himself."... https://biblehub.com/acts/2-38.htm

Peter and John Before the Council

…11This Jesus is 'the stone you builders rejected, which has become the cornerstone.' 12 Salvation exists in no one else, for there is no other name under heaven given to men by which we must be saved."
https://biblehub.com/acts/4-12.htm

https://www.biblegateway.com/passage/?search=John%2014%3A2026&version=ESV

That said, people should be absolutely terrified of speaking against God and His Words in the Holy Bible, committing blasphemy, because no one knows if those will be the last words they will ever utter or express and hell is not a pleasant place for anyone to end up.

https://www.facebook.com/photo.php?fbid=6169704459775128&set=pb.100002069048072.-2207520000&type=3 and

https://www.facebook.com/photo.php?fbid=5496574817088099&set=pb.100002069048072.-2207520000&type=3

muslims are online constantly blaspheming and mocking the Living God, Jesus Christ, by false claiming He couldn't protect Himself, when He had no intention of doing so.

muslims are just plain wrong and in the most serious way (lake of fire, Wrath of God wrong.) Jesus Christ is God and proved it beyond all reasonable doubt.

The Betrayal of Jesus

...52 "Put your sword back in its place," Jesus said to him. "For all who draw the sword will die by the sword. 53 Are you not aware that I can call on My Father, and He will at once put at My disposal more than twelve legions of angels? 54 But how then would the Scriptures be fulfilled that say it must happen this way?"... https://biblehub.com/matthew/26-53.htm

He didn't intend on protecting Himself, He intended to publicly die and raise His Body from the Grave, transfigure it, make it Immortal and Ascend into Heaven as Proof He is God, which is exactly what He did.

Jesus the Good Shepherd

...17 The reason the Father loves Me is that I lay down My life in order to take it up again. 18 No one takes it from Me, but I lay it down of My own accord. I have authority to lay it down and authority to take it up again. This charge I have received from My Father."
https://biblehub.com/john/10-18.htm

Jesus Comforts Martha and Mary

...24 Martha replied, "I know that he will rise again in the resurrection at the last day." 25 Jesus said to her, "I am the resurrection and the life. Whoever believes in Me will live, even though he dies. 26 And everyone who lives and believes in Me will never die. Do you believe this?"...
https://biblehub.com/john/11-25.htm

John 5:39-40

39 You search the Scriptures because you think that in them you have eternal life; and it is they that bear witness about me, 40 yet you refuse to come to me that you may have life.

Jesus Christ plainly said the entire Holy Bible is about Him, the One who has Eternal Life and the One everyone MUST come to in order to have that Life. He said any and all who refuse to do so will die in their sins and be cast into the lake of fire.

John 8:24-25
24 I told you that you would die in your sins, for unless you believe that I am he you will die in your sins." 25 So they said to him, "Who are you?" Jesus said to them, "Just what I have been telling you from the beginning.

8But to the cowardly and unbelieving and abominable and murderers and sexually immoral and sorcerers and idolaters and all liars, their place will be in the lake that burns with fire and sulfur. This is the second death."
https://biblehub.com/revelation/21-8.htm

Unless muslims repent and stop denying the One True God, Jesus Christ, the ONLY One who can Save them, they will all end up in the lake of fire.

"Brothers, what shall we do?" 38 Peter replied, "Repent and be baptized, every one of you, in the name of Jesus Christ for the forgiveness of your sins, and you will receive the gift of the Holy Spirit. 39This promise belongs to you and your children and to all who are far off—to all whom the Lord our God will call to Himself."... https://biblehub.com/acts/2-38.htm

Peter and John Before the Council
...11This Jesus is 'the stone you builders rejected, which has become the cornerstone.' 12 Salvation exists in no one else, for there is no other name under heaven given to men by which we must be saved."
https://biblehub.com/acts/4-12.htm

The Great Commission
...15And He said to them, "Go into all the world and preach the gospel to every creature. 16Whoever believes and is baptized will be saved, but whoever does not believe will be condemned.

https://biblehub.com/mark/16-16.htm

...35The Father loves the Son and has placed all things in His hands. 36Whoever believes in the Son has eternal life. Whoever rejects the Son will not see life. Instead, the wrath of God remains on him."
https://biblehub.com/john/3-36.htm

2 Thessalonians 1:8-9

8   In flaming fire taking vengeance on them that know not God, and that obey not the gospel of our Lord Jesus Christ:

9   Who shall be punished with everlasting destruction from the presence of the Lord, and from the glory of his power;

Today as in many prior, another muslim was telling us their false interpretation of John 17:3; claiming that Jesus Christ was somehow denying all His many claims of being God throughout the entire Holy Bible.

When muslims deny that Jesus Christ tells us all He is God in the Holy Bible that somehow, they can rip His Words out of context in order to deny that fact, they are showing themselves to be lying antichrists.

John 5:39-40

39 You search the Scriptures because you think that in them you have eternal life; and it is they that bear witness about me, 40 yet you refuse to come to me that you may have life.

Jesus Christ plainly says the entire Holy Bible is all about Him, the One who has Eternal Life and the One to whom we all must go to likewise have it ourselves. So, John 17:3 isn't saying anything else but a repeat of this statement!

In other words, "ONLY TRUE GOD" are linked together with "JESUS CHRIST" by the word "kai", which means "AND, EVEN, ALSO, NAMELY" and in all four of those connotations Jesus Christ is saying He is the definition of Eternal Life and the ONLY TRUE GOD!

So muslims rip His Words out of context to lie to themselves and the entire world which makes them all LIARS and antichrists just as the scriptures plainly teach!

Beware of Antichrists

...21I have not written to you because you lack knowledge of the truth, but because you have it, and because no lie comes from the truth. 22Who is the liar, if it is not the one who denies that Jesus is the Christ? This is the antichrist, who denies the Father and the Son. 23Whoever denies the Son does not have the Father, but whoever confesses the Son has the Father as well.... https://biblehub.com/1_john/2-22.htm

Jesus Christ is the TRUTH; if you don't KNOW Him; it's due to the fact you are believing lies!

John 14:6-9
New King James Version
6 Jesus said to him, "I am the way, the truth, and the life. No one comes to the Father except through Me.

The Father Revealed

7 "If you had known Me, you would have known My Father also; and from now on you know Him and have seen Him."

8 Philip said to Him, "Lord, show us the Father, and it is sufficient for us."

9 Jesus said to him, "Have I been with you so long, and yet you have not known Me, Philip? He who has seen Me has seen the Father; so how can you say, 'Show us the Father'?

John 8:32-36
King James Version
32 And ye shall know the truth, and the truth shall make you free.

33 They answered him, We be Abraham's seed, and were never in bondage to any man: how sayest thou, Ye shall be made free?

34 Jesus answered them, Verily, verily, I say unto you, Whosoever committeth sin is the servant of sin.

35 And the servant abideth not in the house for ever: but the Son abideth ever.

36 If the Son therefore shall make you free, ye shall be free indeed.

muslims openly deny Jesus Christ is our Lord and Savior even though the Holy Bible makes that fact explicitly clear: https://bible.knowing-jesus.com/topics/God,-As-Redeemer - **God tells us He is our Redeemer/Savior not just in the New Testament but in the Old Testament also.**

A Redeemer is someone who pays what His Law requires in behalf of another. For example, if you owed money to someone under Old Testament Law someone else could pay off your debt for you.

No one but God Himself could pay off our debt of death for breaking His Law and so He came in the flesh as the Messiah and did so.

https://www.preceptaustin.org/tetelestai-paid_in_full

muslims like to quote Ezekiel and other locations in the Holy Bible that tell us no guilty person can die for another guilty person but each must die for their own sins as their reason for rejecting Jesus Christ as our Redeemer, but Jesus Christ was NOT a guilty sinner, He is the HOLY ONE, THE SINLESS ONE, who ALONE was WORTHY to suffer and die for the sins of mankind!

God is not a liar; so, when people sinned, they died (became separated from Him who is the Holy One, Truth, and Eternal Life). https://biblehub.com/isaiah/59-2.htm

The Only One who could therefore restore us to Himself is God. When He came in the flesh and publicly suffered and died for us, He was showing the inevitable results of sin (suffering and death) and how much He hates sin, but also how much He loves us!

So those rejecting Jesus Christ crucified are still in their sins and are still dead to Him:

24That is why I told you that you would die in your sins. For unless you believe that I am He, you will die in your sins." 25"Who are You?" they asked. "Just what I have been telling you from the beginning," Jesus replied.... https://biblehub.com/john/8-24.htm

Only those who accept Jesus Christ and His Redemption by suffering and dying for us on the Cross, are restored back to Him, forgiven and cleansed from their sins by Him. It's why the scriptures make it very clear that Redemption/Salvation is in no one else!

Ephesians 2:1-10 ESV
And you were dead in the trespasses and sins in which you once walked, following the course of this world, following the prince of the power of the air, the spirit that is now at work in the sons of disobedience— among whom we all once lived in the passions of our flesh, carrying out the desires of the body and the mind, and were by nature children of wrath, like the rest of mankind. But God, being rich in mercy, because of the great love with which he loved us, even when we were dead in our trespasses, made us alive together with Christ—by grace you have been saved— and raised us up with him and seated us with him in the heavenly places in Christ Jesus, so that in the coming ages he might show the immeasurable riches of his grace in kindness toward us in Christ Jesus. For by grace, you have been saved through faith. And this is not your own doing; it is the gift of God, not a result of works, so that no one may boast. For we are his workmanship, created in Christ Jesus for good works, which God prepared beforehand, that we should walk in them.

12But to all who did receive Him, to those who believed in His name, He gave the right to become children of God— 13children born not of blood, nor of the desire or will of man, but born of God....
https://biblehub.com/john/1-12.htm

The Great Commission
...15And He said to them, "Go into all the world and preach the gospel to every creature. 16Whoever believes and is baptized will be saved, but whoever does not believe will be condemned.
https://biblehub.com/mark/16-16.htm

"Brothers, what shall we do?" 38 Peter replied, "Repent and be baptized, every one of you, in the name of Jesus Christ for the forgiveness of your sins, and you will receive the gift of the Holy Spirit. 39This promise belongs to you and your children and to all who are far off—to all whom the Lord our God will call to Himself."... https://biblehub.com/acts/2-38.htm

Peter and John Before the Council
...11This Jesus is 'the stone you builders rejected, which has become the cornerstone.' 12 Salvation exists in no one else, for there is no other name under heaven given to men by which we must be saved."
https://biblehub.com/acts/4-12.htm

When I post facts of history about islam and the contents of their quran and hadiths, muslims tend to call them all lies instead and that is evidence of the severity of their brainwashing. muslims have been so thoroughly brainwashed/deceived that they are provably a danger to themselves and others. So, I responded to yet another muslim today denying their own hadiths from their own so called most trusted sources.

muslims like yourself are why the rest of humanity should arrest you all, if for nothing more than proper deprogramming from your cult. You are shown facts of history and imagine those facts are all lies; it's proof of mass brainwashing. The rest of mankind needs to arrest muslims to deliver you all from the evil cult of islam and give you all a proper education. islam and its many lies and evil instructions have caused too much harm to date, the worst of which is over a billion people who don't know God, don't see, hear or know Him at all; wrongly imagine that they aren't all headed to the lake of fire for denying Him as their evil cult has taught them all to do. (1Jn 2:22; Rev 21:7,8; 1Jn 5)

https://www.thereligionofpeace.com/pages/articles/jesusmuhammad.aspx - anyone following muhammad instead of Jesus Christ, the One True God, has been so thoroughly brainwashed they are acting like they can't tell truth from lies, facts from fiction, good from evil or God Almighty from the devil and as such are a danger to themselves and the rest of mankind and provably so.

https://www.google.com/search?client=opera&q=islamic+apostasy+death+penalty+nations&sourceid=opera&ie=UTF-8&oe=UTF-8   -   muslims threaten to murder other people who even try to leave their wicked cult, so islam is factually a criminal organization of murderers.

No, the Holy Bible doesn't have this. About 3500 years ago, God led the Israelites out of Egyptian Bondage by Miracles in the Exodus. He then, since the Israelites ALL KNEW HIM, commanded that if anyone should tell them to worship another god, they should not listen to them and stone them and not pity them. When Jesus Christ came, He was confronted with sins and instead of choosing to stone everyone He practiced forgiveness as the scriptures state MERCY TRIUMPHS OVER JUDGEMENT. So even that archaic law is not practiced BECAUSE no one alive today saw God first hand deliver them like those who He gave that law to and so no one is stoned to death. So, everything under the Law of God is tempered with MERCY AND FORGIVENESS. He only states capital offenses as His Way of telling us certain sins are more heinous than others and that if you don't avail yourself of HIS REDEMPTION AND SALVATION His Law still sentences you because you have not availed yourself of HIS MERCY AND FORGIVENESS. This is why EVERYONE is commanded to Repent and Believe on our Lord Jesus Christ! It's why SALVATION is ONLY IN HIM (Acts 4:12). All of HIS LAW is based on Loving Him and each other, so it does not condone evil in any way. So, you cannot compare this to muslims killing other muslims TODAY for islamic apostasy since their allah, no one has ever seen or heard! allah is just the name of pagan idol!
https://www.bible.ca/islam/islam-allahs-daughters.htm   it is just murder plain and simple! islamic apostasy death penalty and all their other violence are just CRIMES!

https://www.thereligionofpeace.com/pages/quran/index.aspx - the quran is full of instructions that are defined as crimes by the sane and educated part of humanity. So islam is a criminal organization historically and to this day and advocates crimes openly in doctrine and practice. It's a crying shame islam ever even came into existence.

muhammad was a criminal and obviously so:

http://www.answeringmuslims.com/2014/03/muhammad-and-thighingof-aisha.html - muslims venerate a child molester, totally unacceptable.

https://www.youtube.com/watch?v=1HbOhLJHcFo - most muslims are barely literate so when they finally learn to read and begin to educate themselves they come across the fact that muhammad was a slaver! their first reaction is to call such facts of history all lies, because they can't believe a billion people could be so thoroughly deceived as to speak well of muhammad. But this is why muslims need to be arrested worldwide (made to undergo deprogramming from their evil cult, and get a proper education from our Eternal Creator and those who KNOW Him. They need to understand that they need to toss away their lying qurans and instead study the Truthful Words of Almighty God in the Holy Bible; learn to Love our Eternal Creator and love each other as He Commands), they are indeed that ignorant, illiterate and are indeed lacking a proper education and dangerously so. http://www.annaqed.com/en/muslims-under-themicroscope/muhammad-and-his-crimes-against-humanity - muhammad and his gang of rapists, slavers, robbers, child molesters and murderers began islam through bloodshed of innocent people - https://www.politicalislam.com/tears-of-jihad/ - centuries of brutal slavery - https://www.google.com/search?client=opera&q=centuries+of+islamic+slave+trade&sourceid=opera&ie=UTF-8&oe=UTF-8 and is why the quran advocates such evil clearly in its vile contents:
https://www.youtube.com/watch?v=htshvId51UE

So islam is OBVIOUSLY and THOROUGHLY evil. About the only reasons it sadly still exists today is due to massive ignorance and wickedness among humanity.

muslims just don't seem to grasp that as long as they deny the One True God, there is no hope for them whatsoever:

The Supremacy of the Son
…7Now about the angels He says: "He makes His angels spirits, His servants flames of fire." 8But about the Son He says: "Your throne, O God, endures forever and ever, and justice is the scepter of Your kingdom. 9You have loved righteousness and hated wickedness; therefore God, Your God, has anointed You above Your companions with the oil of joy."…
https://biblehub.com/hebrews/1-8.htm

When the scriptures speak of "the Son of God" THE SON OF GOD, they are speaking about the Visible Image of God, still God/YHWH, but God/YHWH who came in the flesh!
https://www.biblegateway.com/passage/?search=Colossians%201%3A1519&version=NIV

So, the scriptures refer to "the Son" as the "ONE AND ONLY" or "ONLY BEGOTTEN" to indicate this uniqueness about Jesus Christ as GOD INCARNATE and in reference to His Visible Image.
https://biblehub.com/interlinear/john/3-16.htm

So YWHW/(English our LORD JESUS CHRIST) spoke to His Prophets telling them what He would say and do when He came in the flesh as the Messiah. He was speaking with His Prophets since He created Adam and Eve and is why He tells us:

John 5:39-40
39 You search the Scriptures because you think that in them you have eternal life; and it is they that bear witness about me, 40 yet you refuse to come to me that you may have life.

https://www.accordingtothescriptures.org/prophecy/353prophecies.html

In other words, God/YHWH told us all how to recognize Him when He came in the flesh for centuries in advance! and is why He said:

The Fulfillment of the Law
16In the same way, let your light shine before men, that they may see your good deeds and glorify your Father in heaven. 17Do not think that I have come to abolish the Law or the Prophets. I have not come to abolish them, but to fulfill them. 18For I tell you truly, until heaven and earth pass away, not a single jot, not a stroke of a pen, will disappear from the Law until everything is accomplished.... https://biblehub.com/matthew/5-17.htm

and

24That is why I told you that you would die in your sins. For unless you believe that I am He, you will die in your sins." 25"Who are You?" they asked. "Just what I have been telling you from the beginning," Jesus replied.... https://biblehub.com/john/8-24.htm

and

https://www.biblegateway.com/passage/?search=John%208%3A48-59&version=ESV

It's also why He calls anyone denying Jesus Christ is God who came in the flesh is an antichrist, an enemy, and if they refuse to repent will die in their sins and be cast into the lake of fire.

https://hebrew4christians.com/Names_of_G-d/Messiah/messiah.html

1 John 4:1-6
Test the Spirits
4 Beloved, do not believe every spirit, but test the spirits to see whether they are from God, for many false prophets have gone out into the world. 2 By this you know the Spirit of God: every spirit that confesses that Jesus Christ has come in the flesh is from God, 3 and every spirit that does not confess Jesus is not from God. This is the spirit of the antichrist, which you heard was coming and now is in the world already. 4 Little children, you are from God and have overcome them, for he who is in you is greater than he who is in the world. 5 They are from the world; therefore they speak from the world, and the world listens to them. 6 We are from God. Whoever knows God listens to us; whoever is not from God does not listen to us. By this we know the Spirit of truth and the spirit of error.

Beware of Antichrists
...21I have not written to you because you lack knowledge of the truth, but because you have it, and because no lie comes from the truth. 22Who is the liar, if it is not the one who denies that Jesus is the Christ? This is the antichrist, who denies the Father and the Son. 23Whoever denies the Son does not have the Father, but whoever confesses the Son has the Father as well.... https://biblehub.com/1_john/2-22.htm

Jesus and the Samaritan Woman

...25The woman said, "I know that Messiah" (called Christ) "is coming. When He comes, He will explain everything to us." 26 Jesus answered, "I who speak to you am He." https://biblehub.com/john/4-26.htm

Again, "Christ/Messiah" is YHWH/God who came in the flesh: https://hebrew4christians.com/Names_of_G-d/Messiah/messiah.html

Jesus Opens the Scriptures
...26Was it not necessary for the Christ to suffer these things and then to enter His glory?" 27And beginning with Moses and all the Prophets, He explained to them what was written in all the Scriptures about Himself. https://biblehub.com/luke/24-27.htm

and is why Salvation is in no one else.

Peter and John Before the Council
...11This Jesus is 'the stone you builders rejected, which has become the cornerstone.' 12 Salvation exists in no one else, for there is no other name under heaven given to men by which we must be saved."
https://biblehub.com/acts/4-12.htm

It's why His Apostles and Disciples who saw and heard Jesus Christ personally gave their lives telling everyone He is the One True God.

Jesus Appears to Thomas
...27Then Jesus said to Thomas, "Put your finger here and look at My hands. Reach out your hand and put it into My side. Stop doubting and believe." 28Thomas replied, "My Lord and my God!" 29Jesus said to him,

"Because you have seen Me, you have believed; blessed are those who have not seen and yet have believed."... https://biblehub.com/john/20-28.htm

https://tile.loc.gov/storageservices/public/gdcmassbookdig/foxesbookofmart00fo/foxesbookofmart0 0fo.pdf

The scriptures tell us we need to KNOW God our Savior, our Lord Jesus Christ; not just "believe in" Him.

2 Thessalonians 1:8-9
King James Version
8	In flaming fire taking vengeance on them that know not God, and that obey not the gospel of our Lord Jesus Christ:

9	Who shall be punished with everlasting destruction from the presence of the Lord, and from the glory of his power;

Mourning Turned to Joy
...33"But this is the covenant I will make with the house of Israel after those days, declares the LORD. I will put My law in their minds and inscribe it on their hearts. And I will be their God, and they will be My people. 34No longer will each man teach his neighbor or his brother, saying, 'Know the LORD,' because they will all know Me, from the least of them to the greatest, declares the LORD. For I will forgive their iniquities and will remember their sins no more." 35Thus says the LORD, who gives the sun for light by day, who sets in order the moon and stars for light by night, who stirs up the sea so that its waves roar—the LORD of Hosts is His name:... https://biblehub.com/jeremiah/31-34.htm

I for one am looking forward to seeing a global outpouring of His Holy

Spirit in such abundance that people are preaching everywhere, "KNOW THE LORD! KNOW THE LORD!"

https://www.biblegateway.com/passage/?search=John%2014%3A2026&version=ESV - we need to KNOW God, Jesus Christ, and be learning from Him by the presence of His Holy Spirit of Truth in our lives.

John 8:32-36
King James Version
32 And ye shall know the truth, and the truth shall make you free.

33 They answered him, We be Abraham's seed, and were never in bondage to any man: how sayest thou, Ye shall be made free?

34 Jesus answered them, Verily, verily, I say unto you, Whosoever committeth sin is the servant of sin.

35 And the servant abideth not in the house for ever: but the Son abideth ever.

36 If the Son therefore shall make you free, ye shall be free indeed.

Jesus Christ is the Truth we all must KNOW.

John 14:6-9
New King James Version
6 Jesus said to him, "I am the way, the truth, and the life. No one comes to the Father except through Me.

The Father Revealed
7 "If you had known Me, you would have known My Father also; and from now on you know Him and have seen Him."

8 Philip said to Him, "Lord, show us the Father, and it is sufficient for us."

9 Jesus said to him, "Have I been with you so long, and yet you have not known Me, Philip? He who has seen Me has seen the Father; so how can you say, 'Show us the Father'?

Today another muslim was imagining I only have "beliefs" instead of certain personal knowledge and experience with God.

https://www.accordingtothescriptures.org/prophecy/353prophecies.html for centuries God told His Prophets He would come in the flesh to Redeem/Save us: https://bible.knowing-jesus.com/topics/God,-AsRedeemer and so God showed Himself and Proved Himself to us quite clearly and even though He did so, you and mass billions still today have not obeyed Him and do not know Him.
https://www.preceptaustin.org/tetelestai-paid_in_full

John 5:39-40
39 You search the Scriptures because you think that in them you have eternal life; and it is they that bear witness about me, 40 yet you refuse to come to me that you may have life.

Which is why all of us who do know God personally are telling all you who don't that the reason you don't is that you are refusing to obey His very clear instructions in the Holy Bible on how to KNOW HIM PERSONALLY and BE LEARNING FROM HIM PERSONALLY! (So no, not one word in the Holy Bible is strange to me at all, instead I know every word in it comes from God and is absolutely true.)

In other words, you are known to us by your words and your deeds. When we look at your body we see a visible image of your invisible spirit; so, when God came in the flesh to show Himself to the world, it isn't anything that He hasn't caused all of us to do. (Nothing strange in the least.)

The Great Commission
...18Then Jesus came to them and said, "All authority in heaven and on earth has been given to Me. 19Therefore go and make disciples of all nations, baptizing them in the name of the Father, and of the Son, and of the Holy Spirit, 20and teaching them to obey all that I have commanded you. And surely I am with you always, even to the end of the age."...
https://biblehub.com/matthew/28-19.htm

I know God, Jesus Christ, personally beyond all doubt, so not you or the entire world can change that fact. (In other words, I write from absolute KNOWLEDGE, not personal "beliefs".) And it's because I obeyed Jesus Christ and repented of my sins and got baptized in His Name and He gave me His Holy Spirit of Truth, just as He promised!

37When the people heard this, they were cut to the heart and asked Peter and the other apostles, "Brothers, what shall we do?" 38 Peter replied, "Repent and be baptized, every one of you, in the name of Jesus Christ for the forgiveness of your sins, and you will receive the gift of the Holy Spirit. 39This promise belongs to you and your children and to all who are far off—to all whom the Lord our God will call to Himself."...
https://biblehub.com/acts/2-38.htm

Which is why I've been telling everyone I can ever since that they must do the same!

Peter and John Before the Council
...11This Jesus is 'the stone you builders rejected, which has become the cornerstone.' 12 Salvation exists in no one else, for there is no other name

under heaven given to men by which we must be saved."
https://biblehub.com/acts/4-12.htm

John 14:20-26
20 In that day you will know that I am in my Father, and you in me, and I in you. 21 Whoever has my commandments and keeps them, he it is who loves me. And he who loves me will be loved by my Father, and I will love him and manifest myself to him." 22 Judas (not Iscariot) said to him, "Lord, how is it that you will manifest yourself to us, and not to the world?" 23 Jesus answered him, "If anyone loves me, he will keep my word, and my Father will love him, and we will come to him and make our home with him. 24 Whoever does not love me does not keep my words. And the word that you hear is not mine but the Father's who sent me.

25 "These things I have spoken to you while I am still with you. 26 But the Helper, the Holy Spirit, whom the Father will send in my name, he will teach you all things and bring to your remembrance all that I have said to you.

Notice God tells us He will pour out His Wrath on everyone who does not KNOW Him!

2 Thessalonians 1:8-9
8   In flaming fire taking vengeance on them that know not God, and that obey not the gospel of our Lord Jesus Christ:

9   Who shall be punished with everlasting destruction from the presence of the Lord, and from the glory of his power;

And that's because He came in the flesh, told us He is God, proved He is God by publicly dying and raising His Own Body from the Grave, transfigured it gloriously and ascended into Heaven in front of eyewitnesses who then immediately began telling the whole world that they had seen and heard God firsthand! (It's how the Holy Bible came to be and how Christianity began.) The Apostles who saw and heard Jesus Christ firsthand testified to the world that He is GOD to the point where the people that had crucified Jesus Christ, threatened to murder them likewise and one by one, the Apostles gave their lives to torture and death rather than repent of one word of the Gospels!

https://tile.loc.gov/storageservices/public/gdcmassbookdig/foxesbookofmart00fo/foxesbookofmart0 0fo.pdf - so God came in the flesh, just like He said He would, and even though you don't know Him, you presume to argue with those who do. Not just you, but every single muslim worldwide needs to stop following the lies of muhammad and the quran and instead follow our Lord Jesus Christ, the Truth, and His Commandments in the Holy Bible.
https://www.thereligionofpeace.com/pages/articles/jesusmuhammad.aspx

Then a muslim was asking why Jesus Christ suffered and died in the worst way.

The Servant Exalted
13Behold, My Servant will prosper; He will be raised and lifted up and highly exalted. 14Just as many were appalled at Him— His appearance was disfigured beyond that of any man, and His form was marred beyond human likeness — 15so He will sprinkle many nations. Kings will shut their mouths because of Him. For they will see what they have not been told, and they will understand what they have not heard....
https://biblehub.com/isaiah/52-14.htm

It was just one of hundreds of prophecies God told us about Himself.
https://www.accordingtothescriptures.org/prophecy/353prophecies.html

John 5:39-40
39 You search the Scriptures because you think that in them you have eternal life; and it is they that bear witness about me, 40 yet you refuse to come to me that you may have life.

The scriptures tell us that God came down into this world He created and made and walked among us. That He faced the devil and all the evil in this world all by Himself and beat them all! The devils did the worst they could do to Him! And He just Rose from the Grave and shone like the sun!

VICTORY! over the devil! VICTORY! over all evil, even death! JESUS CHRIST SAID HE IS THE WAY, THE TRUTH AND THE LIFE, THE ONE WHO HAS AND GIVES ETERNAL LIFE AND THEN HE PROVED IT!

JESUS CHRIST IS LORD!!!!!!!! HALLELUYAH!!!!!!!!!!!!

https://www.youtube.com/watch?v=QDnzHfmUX0Q

Jesus Christ plainly states He is God from Genesis to Revelation.

John 5:39-40
39 You search the Scriptures because you think that in them you have eternal life; and it is they that bear witness about me, 40 yet you refuse to come to me that you may have life.

So, the entire Holy Bible tells us Jesus Christ is God quite plainly. Ripping any of His Words out of context to deny that fact only makes any and all doing so look either ignorant and deceived, or deliberate liars.

https://www.youtube.com/watch?v=0p2ZqRCipX4 - every location in the Holy Bible that says "YHWH"/"LORD" is a direct reference to Jesus Christ and is why He said:

The Fulfillment of the Law
16In the same way, let your light shine before men, that they may see your good deeds and glorify your Father in heaven. 17Do not think that I have come to abolish the Law or the Prophets. I have not come to abolish them, but to fulfill them. 18For I tell you truly, until heaven and earth pass away, not a single jot, not a stroke of a pen, will disappear from the Law until everything is accomplished.... https://biblehub.com/matthew/5-17.htm

(that He is the fulfillment of His Law and Prophecies)

Jesus is Coming
...12"Behold, I am coming soon, and My reward is with Me, to give to each one according to what he has done. 13I am the Alpha and the Omega, the First and the Last, the Beginning and the End."
https://biblehub.com/revelation/22-13.htm

So, from Genesis to Revelation Jesus Christ tells us many hundreds of times over that He is God.

Another passage muslims commonly abuse and misuse is Matthew 7:2123:

Matthew 7:21-23

English Standard Version

I Never Knew You

21
"Not everyone who says to me, 'Lord, Lord,' will enter the kingdom of heaven, but the one who does the will of my Father who is in heaven. 22 On that day many will say to me, 'Lord, Lord, did we
not prophesy in your name, and cast out demons in your name, and do many mighty works in your name?' 23 And then will I declare to them, 'I never knew you; depart from me, you workers of lawlessness.'

When God came in the flesh, He confronted the religious hypocrites who practice religion in vain, teaching doctrines of devils and men, rather than obeying God (like muslims).

So, when a deceived muslim reads such words, they imagine Jesus Christ was forbidding worshipping Him when that isn't the case at all. Jesus Christ is God and has always been worshipped. What He is condemning is people who offer Him lipservice but do not obey Him (like muslims). People who practice religion but don't even know Him. People who sin constantly because they don't know Him and do not have His Holy Spirit of Truth, but go to church and call themselves Christians. (they PRETEND to worship Him, by practicing such manmade religions as false, perverted versions of Christianity and islam and every other cult on earth where the people in those cults DO NOT KNOW JESUS CHRIST and ARE NOT OBEYING HIM, but practicing their religions **in vain** (SUCH FALSE PEOPLE WHO DO NOT KNOW GOD ARE NOT SAVED). We know they are not saved because they respond to the LORD who is JUDGING THEM by saying didn't I do this and didn't I do that? When everyone who is truly Saved by God, KNOWS THE LORD, because they obeyed His Commandment to Repent and Be Baptized in His Name; thereafter filled with His Own Holy Spirit of Truth; whereby all such persons KNOW GOD PERSONALLY! ALL TRULY SAVED

PEOPLE KNOW THEY ARE SAVED NOT BY ANYTHING THEY DO, BUT BECAUSE THE SAVIOR, JESUS CHRIST, SAVED THEM!

Ephesians 2:1-10 ESV
And you were dead in the trespasses and sins in which you once walked, following the course of this world, following the prince of the power of the air, the spirit that is now at work in the sons of disobedience— among whom we all once lived in the passions of our flesh, carrying out the desires of the body and the mind, and were by nature children of wrath, like the rest of mankind. But God, being rich in mercy, because of the great love with which he loved us, even when we were dead in our trespasses, made us alive together with Christ—by grace you have been saved— and raised us up with him and seated us with him in the heavenly places in Christ Jesus, so that in the coming ages he might show the immeasurable riches of his grace in kindness toward us in Christ Jesus. For by grace you have been saved through faith. And this is not your own doing; it is the gift of God, not a result of works, so that no one may boast. For we are his workmanship, created in Christ Jesus for good works, which God prepared beforehand, that we should walk in them.

The Great Commission
…15And He said to them, "Go into all the world and preach the gospel to every creature. 16Whoever believes and is baptized will be saved, but whoever does not believe will be condemned.
https://biblehub.com/mark/16-16.htm

37When the people heard this, they were cut to the heart and asked Peter and the other apostles, "Brothers, what shall we do?" 38 Peter replied, "Repent and be baptized, every one of you, in the name of Jesus Christ for the forgiveness of your sins, and you will receive the gift of the Holy Spirit. 39This promise belongs to you and your children and to all who are far off—to all whom the Lord our God will call to Himself."…
https://biblehub.com/acts/2-38.htm

Peter and John Before the Council
...11This Jesus is 'the stone you builders rejected, which has become the cornerstone.' 12 Salvation exists in no one else, for there is no other name under heaven given to men by which we must be saved."
https://biblehub.com/acts/4-12.htm
https://www.openbible.info/topics/worshipping_jesus - Jesus Christ is the One True God which is why He always receives worship as such.

So, He is condemning those who **"worship Him in vain";** in other words, they worship Him with their lips, sing His Praises, might say things like PBUH but none of those people worshiping Him IN VAIN even know Him.

GOD TELLS US WE MUST KNOW HIM IN ORDER TO TRULY WORSHIP HIM WITH OUR EXISTENCE "in Spirit and in Truth".

Jesus and the Samaritan Woman
...23But a time is coming and has now come when the true worshipers will worship the Father in spirit and in truth, for the Father is seeking such as these to worship Him. 24 God is Spirit, and His worshipers must worship Him in spirit and in truth." 25The woman said, "I know that Messiah" (called Christ) "is coming. When He comes, He will explain everything to us."26Jesus answered, "I who speak to you am He."...
https://biblehub.com/john/4-24.htm

So, when God says "in VAIN do they worship Me" He is talking about people who honor Him with their lips but their hearts and souls are far from Him "...depart from Me, you SINNERS! you LAWLESS ones! you wicked, unrepentant rebels! "

ONLY THOSE WHO KNOW THE SAVIOR WORSHIP HIM IN SPIRIT AND IN TRUTH (everyone else is only worshiping Him with their lips and some idol of their own imaginations because THEY DO NOT KNOW GOD!)

Tradition and Worship
...7You hypocrites! Isaiah prophesied correctly about you: 8'These people honor Me with their lips, but their hearts are far from Me. 9They worship Me in vain; they teach as doctrine the precepts of men.' "...
https://biblehub.com/matthew/15-8.htm

So, everyone worldwide that are in any form of religion that DO NOT KNOW GOD PERSONALLY cannot worship Him "in Spirit and in Truth" BECAUSE THEY DO NOT EVEN KNOW HIM! (so, they only are offering Him lipservice in vain, if at all.) TO BE SAVED YOU MUST KNOW THE SAVIOR!

This is why Jesus Christ plainly tells us all, His Wrath is upon ALL WHO DO NOT KNOW HIM!

2 Thessalonians 1:8-9
8   In flaming fire taking vengeance on them that know not God, and that obey not the gospel of our Lord Jesus Christ:

9   Who shall be punished with everlasting destruction from the presence of the Lord, and from the glory of his power;

So muslims wrongly think Jesus Christ is condemning His Own Disciples, True Christians, when instead He is condemning muslims, jews and all religious hypocrites, even false christians who do not know Him and yet are calling themselves by His Name, and instead are all following their own imaginations, traditions, false doctrines and beliefs.

EVERYONE MUST OBEY GOD AND REPENT AND BE BAPTIZED IN THE NAME OF OUR LORD AND SAVIOR, JESUS, THE CHRIST! EVERYONE! ONLY THEN WILL GOD BESTOW HIS OWN HOLY SPIRIT OF TRUTH UPON THEM AND ONLY THEN THEY WILL KNOW THEY ARE SAVED BY THE SAVIOR, THE ONE TRUE GOD, JESUS THE CHRIST!

A muslim was asking about why some Christians don't get circumcised.

63The Spirit gives life; the flesh profits nothing. The words I have spoken to you are spirit and they are life. https://biblehub.com/john/6-63.htm

When both the circumcised and uncircumcised die, their flesh returns to the dust of the earth, so this is why God tells us to have no confidence in our flesh.

7before the dust returns to the ground from which it came and the spirit returns to God who gave it. https://biblehub.com/ecclesiastes/12-7.htm

But rather let our confidence be in knowing Him and that our spirit has been made right with Him by His Grace and Power.

...23This is what the LORD says: "Let not the wise man boast in his wisdom, nor the strong man in his strength, nor the wealthy man in his riches. 24But let him who boasts boast in this, that he understands and knows Me, that I am the LORD, who exercises loving devotion, justice and righteousness on the earth— for I delight in these things," declares the LORD. 25"Behold, the days are coming," declares the LORD, "when I will punish all who are circumcised yet uncircumcised:... https://biblehub.com/jeremiah/9-24.htm

So here we read in the Prophets that God wants us all to KNOW HIM PERSONALLY! and that circumcision in our flesh is meaningless IF WE DO NOT KNOW HIM.

Which is why the Apostle further clarifies:

Freedom in Christ
...5But by faith we eagerly await through the Spirit the hope of righteousness. 6For in Christ Jesus neither circumcision nor uncircumcision has any value. All that matters is faith, expressed through love. 7You were running so well. Who has obstructed you from obeying the truth?...
https://biblehub.com/galatians/5-6.htm

Jeremiah 4:4
Circumcise yourselves to the LORD, and remove the foreskins of your hearts, O men of Judah and people of Jerusalem. Otherwise, My wrath will break out like fire and burn with no one to extinguish it, because of your evil deeds."

Romans 2:29
No, a man is a Jew because he is one inwardly, and circumcision is a matter of the heart, by the Spirit, not by the written code. Such a man's praise does not come from men, but from God.

Alive in Christ
...10And you have been made complete in Christ, who is the head over every ruler and authority. 11In Him you were also circumcised, in the putting off of your sinful nature, with the circumcision performed by Christ and not by human hands. 12And having been buried with Him in baptism,

you were raised with Him through your faith in the power of God, who raised Him from the dead.... https://biblehub.com/colossians/2-11.htm

So, ALL of God's Words are SPIRIT and to be understood by HIS SPIRIT in our lives and it is when we OBEY GOD and REPENT of every wicked, thought, word, way and deed and GET BAPTIZED in the Name of our LORD and SAVIOR, JESUS, the CHRIST, then GOD circumcises our wicked hearts and gives us clean and right hearts and minds instead. So, the Divine Instructions in the Old Testament Law and Prophets are explained by God when He came in the flesh as the Messiah, Jesus, the Christ and when He gave His Holy Spirit of Truth to His Apostles and Disciples in the New Testament. And when we read both, then we understand that those who are trying to understand His Words with their carnal minds are not understanding them correctly. It is only when we obey God and only when He gives us His Holy Spirit of Truth that we see His Instructions in the Old Testament are to be understood and kept SPIRITUALLY (because this flesh body is nothing but a body of sin and death and so flesh cannot please Him, it is only when we KNOW Him and Worship Him in Spirit and Truth that any of us please God.)

https://www.biblegateway.com/passage/?search=John%203%3A121&version=ESV - you MUST be born again of HIS HOLY SPIRIT!

12But to all who did receive Him, to those who believed in His name, He gave the right to become children of God— 13children born not of blood, nor of the desire or will of man, but born of God....
https://biblehub.com/john/1-12.htm

So, Everyone OBEY GOD and REPENT AND BE BAPTIZED IN THE NAME OF OUR LORD AND SAVIOR, JESUS THE CHRIST! (Matthew 28:18-20, Acts 2:38-39; 4:12)

Today a muslim was quoting from their quran that Christians cannot prove Jesus Christ is the only way to Heaven by quotes from the Holy Bible; so, I responded:

I Am the Good Shepherd
10 "Truly, truly, I say to you, he who does not enter the sheepfold by the door but climbs in by another way, that man is a thief and a robber. 2 But he who enters by the door is the shepherd of the sheep. 3 To him the gatekeeper opens. The sheep hear his voice, and he calls his own sheep by name and leads them out. 4 When he has brought out all his own, he goes before them, and the sheep follow him, for they know his voice. 5 A stranger they will not follow, but they will flee from him, for they do not know the voice of strangers." 6 This figure of speech Jesus used with them, but they did not understand what he was saying to them.

7 So Jesus again said to them, "Truly, truly, I say to you, I am the door of the sheep. 8 All who came before me are thieves and robbers, but the sheep did not listen to them. 9 I am the door. If anyone enters by me, he will be saved and will go in and out and find pasture. 10 The thief comes only to steal and kill and destroy. I came that they may have life and have it abundantly. 11 I am the good shepherd. The good shepherd lays down his life for the sheep. 12 He who is a hired hand and not a shepherd, who does not own the sheep, sees the wolf coming and leaves the sheep and flees, and the wolf snatches them and scatters them. 13 He flees because he is a hired hand and cares nothing for the sheep. 14 I am the good shepherd. I know my own and my own know me, 15 just as the Father knows me and I know the Father; and I lay down my life for the sheep. 16 And I have other sheep that are not of this fold. I must bring them also, and they will listen to my voice. So there will be one flock, one shepherd. 17 For this reason the Father loves me, because I lay down my life that I may take it up again. 18 No one takes it from me, but I lay it down of my own accord. I have authority to lay it down, and I have authority to take it up again. This charge I have received from my Father."

In My Father's House are Many Rooms

...2In My Father's house are many rooms. If it were not so, would I have told you that I am going there to prepare a place for you? 3And if I go and prepare a place for you, I will come back and welcome you into My presence, so that you also may be where I am. 4You know the way to the place where I am going."... https://biblehub.com/john/14-3.htm

John 14:6-9
New King James Version
6 Jesus said to him, "I am the way, the truth, and the life. No one comes to the Father except through Me.

The Father Revealed
7 "If you had known Me, you would have known My Father also; and from now on you know Him and have seen Him."

8 Philip said to Him, "Lord, show us the Father, and it is sufficient for us."

9 Jesus said to him, "Have I been with you so long, and yet you have not known Me, Philip? He who has seen Me has seen the Father; so how can you say, 'Show us the Father'?

In My Father's house are many mansions; if it were not so, I would have told you. I go to prepare a place for you. And if I go and prepare a place for you, I will come again and receive you to Myself; that where I am, there you may be also. And where I go you know, and the way you know." Thomas said to Him, "Lord, we do not know where You are going, and how can we know the way?" Jesus said to him, "I am the way, the truth, and the life. No one comes to the Father except through Me.

John 14:2-6 NKJV

Christ died and the Ascended into Heaven, showing He is the WAY THERE! And He told us He is preparing Heaven just for us!   Jn 14:1-**3**-9, Acts 1:7-11

The Ascension
...**7**Jesus replied, "It is not for you to know times or seasons that the Father has fixed by His own authority. **8**But you will receive power when the Holy Spirit comes upon you, and you will be My witnesses in Jerusalem, and in all Judea and Samaria, and to the ends of the earth." **9After He had said this, they watched as He was taken up, and a cloud hid Him from their sight. 10** They were looking intently into the sky as He was going, when suddenly two men dressed in white stood beside them. **11"Men of Galilee," they said, "why do you stand here looking into the sky? This same Jesus, who has been taken from you into heaven, will come back in the same way you have seen Him go into heaven."...**
https://biblehub.com/acts/1-8.htm

Peter and John Before the Council
...11This Jesus is 'the stone you builders rejected, which has become the cornerstone.' 12 Salvation exists in no one else, for there is no other name under heaven given to men by which we must be saved."
https://biblehub.com/acts/4-12.htm

So, Jesus Christ has made it very clear that He is the Only Way to Eternal Life in His Kingdom, Heaven.

John 5:39-40
39 You search the Scriptures because you think that in them you have eternal life; and it is they that bear witness about me, 40 yet you refuse to come to me that you may have life.

Paul Before the Areopagus
...23For as I walked around and examined your objects of worship, I even found an altar with this inscription: TO AN UNKNOWN GOD. Therefore what you worship as something unknown, I now proclaim to you. 24The God who made the world and everything in it is the Lord of heaven and earth and does not live in temples made by human hands. 25Nor is He

served by human hands, as if He needed anything, because He Himself gives everyone life and breath and everything else....
https://biblehub.com/acts/17-24.htm

Jesus is Coming
...12"Behold, I am coming soon, and My reward is with Me, to give to each one according to what he has done. 13I am the Alpha and the Omega, the First and the Last, the Beginning and the End." 14Blessed are those who wash their robes, so that they may have the right to the tree of life and may enter the city by its gates.... https://biblehub.com/revelation/22-13.htm

He plainly states that anyone who tries to get in any other way is a thief and robber. Such criminals will be cast into the lake of fire:

A New Heaven and a New Earth
...7The one who overcomes will inherit all things, and I will be his God, and he will be My son. 8But to the cowardly and unbelieving and abominable and murderers and sexually immoral and sorcerers and idolaters and all liars, their place will be in the lake that burns with fire and sulfur. This is the second death." https://biblehub.com/revelation/21-8.htm

Jesus Christ and Jesus Christ alone is THE WAY, THE TRUTH and THE LIFE! Everyone must KNOW Him! Obey His Commandments! REPENT AND BE BAPTIZED IN HIS NAME! PRAY TO RECEIVE HIS HOLY SPIRIT OF TRUTH!

The Great Commission
...15And He said to them, "Go into all the world and preach the gospel to every creature. 16Whoever believes and is baptized will be saved, but whoever does not believe will be condemned.
https://biblehub.com/mark/16-16.htm

"Brothers, what shall we do?" 38 Peter replied, "Repent and be baptized, every one of you, in the name of Jesus Christ for the forgiveness of your sins, and you will receive the gift of the Holy Spirit. 39This promise belongs to you and your children and to all who are far off—to all whom the Lord our God will call to Himself."... https://biblehub.com/acts/2-38.htm

Ask, Seek, Knock
...12Or if he asks for an egg, will give him a scorpion? 13So if you who are evil know how to give good gifts to your children, how much more will your Father in heaven give the Holy Spirit to those who ask Him!" https://biblehub.com/luke/11-13.htm

Yet another muslim was online today falsely accusing me of not understanding the Holy Bible. So, I responded to his quotes (all completely out of context):

You are repeating the same verses and not understanding them so I will go over them one by one because your reading comprehension is lacking.

Galatians 1:8 is the reason ALL MUSLIMS ARE CURSED! you are preaching a different Gospel! you are believing a different Gospel than the Holy Bible!

Galatians 1:6-9
No Other Gospel
6 I am astonished that you are so quickly deserting him who called you in the grace of Christ and are turning to a different gospel— 7 not that there is another one, but there are some who trouble you and want to distort the gospel of Christ. 8 But even if we or an angel from heaven should preach to you a gospel contrary to the one we preached to you, let him be

accursed. 9 As we have said before, so now I say again: If anyone is preaching to you a gospel contrary to the one you received, let him be accursed.

Here is the Gospel of Jesus Christ (Summarized):

1 Corinthians 15
The Gospel of Jesus Christ
15 Now I would remind you, brothers, of the gospel I preached to you, which you received, in which you stand, 2 and by which you are being saved, if you hold fast to the word I preached to you—unless you believed in vain.

3 For I delivered to you as of first importance what I also received: that Christ died for our sins in accordance with the Scriptures, 4 that he was buried, that he was raised on the third day in accordance with the Scriptures, 5 and that he appeared to Cephas, then to the twelve. 6 Then he appeared to more than five hundred brothers at one time, most of whom are still alive, though some have fallen asleep. 7 Then he appeared to James, then to all the apostles. 8 Last of all, as to one untimely born, he appeared also to me. 9 For I am the least of the apostles, unworthy to be called an apostle, because I persecuted the church of God. 10 But by the grace of God I am what I am, and his grace toward me was not in vain. On the contrary, I worked harder than any of them, though it was not I, but the grace of God that is with me. 11 Whether then it was I or they, so we preach and so you believed.

muslims DENY the Gospel of Jesus Christ, they DENY He is God, they DENY the Father and the Son, they are all accursed antichrists! (including YOU!)

Beware of Antichrists
...21I have not written to you because you lack knowledge of the truth, but because you have it, and because no lie comes from the truth. 22Who is the liar, if it is not the one who denies that Jesus is the Christ? This is the antichrist, who denies the Father and the Son. 23Whoever denies the Son

does not have the Father, but whoever confesses the Son has the Father as well.... https://biblehub.com/1_john/2-22.htm

I have been telling you the truth! you are believing lies! which makes you a liar! and not just any liar but an accursed antichrist BECAUSE YOU ARE LYING ABOUT GOD AND HIS WORDS IN THE HOLY BIBLE! and as such are on your way to the flames of damnation!

A New Heaven and a New Earth
...7The one who overcomes will inherit all things, and I will be his God, and he will be My son. 8But to the cowardly and unbelieving and abominable and murderers and sexually immoral and sorcerers and idolaters and all liars, their place will be in the lake that burns with fire and sulfur. This is the second death." https://biblehub.com/revelation/21-8.htm

So, what you are quoting from the Holy Bible doesn't mean anything you wrongly imagine! You are quoting things that CONDEMN YOU AS A LIAR AND AN ANTICHRIST! (for lying about GOD And His Gospel in the Holy Bible!)

muhammad was a lying criminal ONLY FOOLS would follow him! https://www.thereligionofpeace.com/pages/articles/jesusmuhammad.aspx when I say FOOL, I mean it! only a fool would believe a lying criminal who came along over six centuries after Jesus Christ and His Eyewitness Apostles in the Holy Bible! (obviously muhammad had NO PERSONAL KNOWLEDGE whatsoever of the FACTS recorded in the Holy Bible!) so muslims are all FOOLS! extreme FOOLS! for believing muhammad over GOD ALMIGHTY AND HIS HAND-PICKED WITNESSES IN THE HOLY BIBLE! I am using this expression not to insult anyone, but to cause everyone to STOP BEING SO FOOLISH!

Understand I'm not calling muslims all fools to insult them; I'm telling you the truth, BECAUSE SOMEONE NEEDS TO! If you all don't come to your senses and Repent and Be Baptized in the Name of our Lord and Savior, Jesus, the Christ, you will all end up in the lake of fire! DON'T BE A FOOL! (Note: a fool is NOT my brother! only when someone stops acting the fool will they be my brother. Only when someone repents and serves the Lord Jesus Christ will they no longer be a fool on their way to the flames of damnation!)

Your next quote taken out of context:

John 14:6-9
6 Jesus said to him, "I am the way, the truth, and the life. No one comes to the Father except through Me.

The Father Revealed
7 "If you had known Me, you would have known My Father also; and from now on you know Him and have seen Him."

8 Philip said to Him, "Lord, show us the Father, and it is sufficient for us."

9 Jesus said to him, "Have I been with you so long, and yet you have not known Me, Philip? He who has seen Me has seen the Father; so how can you say, 'Show us the Father'?

let it penetrate your deceived mind! Jesus Christ is TRUTH! Jesus Christ is THE WAY! Jesus Christ is LIFE! to SEE JESUS CHRIST IS TO SEE GOD! (John chapter 14 verses 6-9; abbreviated - Jn 14:6-9)

So, NOTHING you quote from the Holy Bible means what you imply it means or imagine it means INSTEAD YOU ARE QUOTING PROOFS THAT JESUS CHRIST IS GOD!

The phrases "Son of Man" and "Son of God" (capitalized) are all references to GOD as the Messiah (God in the flesh) they are direct titles and quotes Jesus Christ told the prophets about Himself before He came in the flesh.

https://www.gotquestions.org/One-like-a-Son-of-Man.html - the phrase "Son of Man" refers to the fact God came in the flesh as a MAN, the Messiah, the phrase "Son of God" refers to His Divinity that He is in fact the One True God, incarnated and walked among us humbly as a man. ("SON OF GOD" specifically refers to the VISIBLE IMAGE OF GOD)

John 14:6-9
New King James Version
6 Jesus said to him, "I am the way, the truth, and the life. No one comes to the Father except through Me.

The Father Revealed
7 "If you had known Me, you would have known My Father also; and from now on you know Him and have seen Him."

8 Philip said to Him, "Lord, show us the Father, and it is sufficient for us."

9 Jesus said to him, "Have I been with you so long, and yet you have not known Me, Philip? He who has seen Me has seen the Father; so how can you say, 'Show us the Father'?

Colossians 1:15-19
The Supremacy of the Son of God
15 The Son is the image of the invisible God, the firstborn over all creation. 16 For in him all things were created: things in heaven and on earth, visible and invisible, whether thrones or powers or rulers or authorities; all things have been created through him and for him. 17 He is before all things, and in him all things hold together. 18 And he is the head of the body, the church; he is the beginning and the firstborn from among the

dead, so that in everything he might have the supremacy. 19 For God was pleased to have all his fullness dwell in him,

So let it penetrate your deceived mind! JESUS CHRIST IS GOD WHO CREATED THE HEAVENS AND EARTH, TOLD THE PROPHETS HE WOULD COME IN THE FLESH AS THE MESSIAH AND DID SO!

Jesus Appears to Thomas
...27Then Jesus said to Thomas, "Put your finger here and look at My hands. Reach out your hand and put it into My side. Stop doubting and believe." 28Thomas replied, "My Lord and my God!" 29Jesus said to him, "Because you have seen Me, you have believed; blessed are those who have not seen and yet have believed."... https://biblehub.com/john/20-28.htm

It's why Jesus Christ never once refused worship as GOD!

https://www.openbible.info/topics/worshipping_jesus

He even expressed dissatisfaction when people that should have worshipped Him didn't!

The Ten Lepers
...16He fell facedown at Jesus' feet in thanksgiving to Him—and he was a Samaritan. 17"Were not all ten cleansed?" Jesus asked. "Where then are the other nine? 18Was no one found except this foreigner to return and give glory to God?"... https://biblehub.com/luke/17-17.htm

The Holy Bible plainly tells us all Jesus Christ is God from Genesis to Revelation! So, NOTHING He says is a denial of that fact!

Jesus is Coming
...12"Behold, I am coming soon, and My reward is with Me, to give to each one according to what he has done. 13I am the Alpha and the Omega, the First and the Last, the Beginning and the End."
https://biblehub.com/revelation/22-13.htm

1 John 5:20
20 And we know that the Son of God has come and has given us understanding, so that we may know shim who is true; and we are in him who is true, in his Son Jesus Christ. He is the true God and eternal life.

You are ripping the Words of God out of context to LIE about God! that is EVIL!

next you quote:

The Faith of the Canaanite Woman
...23But Jesus did not answer a word. So His disciples came and urged Him, "Send her away, for she keeps crying out after us." 24 He answered, " I was sent only to the lost sheep of the house of Israel." 25The woman came and knelt before Him. "Lord, help me!" she said.26But Jesus replied, "It is not right to take the children's bread and toss it to the dogs." 27"Yes, Lord," she said, " even the dogs eat the crumbs that fall from their master's table." 28"O woman," Jesus answered, "your faith is great! Let it be done for you as you desire." And her daughter was healed from that very hour....
https://biblehub.com/matthew/15-24.htm

This is a passage you and every muslim should treasure because Jesus Christ is saying He will save even muslims who have been wickedly denying Him if they will but humble themselves before Him and approach Him in FAITH!

the Canaanites are ancient enemies of the Israelites and the descendants of the Canaanites (like the Philistines who became known as Palestinians) trace their physical ancestry back to these ancient enemies of God (many muslims are descended from those bloodlines) it's why they attacked Israel, Jews and Christians and are still arguing with us to this very day!

https://www.youtube.com/watch?v=I_To-cV94Bo

In short, virtually NONE of the many lies the quran has taught muslims is true. The lies are hidden in abundance amidst things that were copied from the Holy Bible to make those lies seem plausible but the gist of it is that it's all a bunch of lies and lies of the worst kind, LIES ABOUT GOD!

It's why God calls muslims liars and antichrists in the Holy Bible, because that is what they are! When you believe the lies of the devil, lies from anyone like muhammad (who led a gang of rapists, robbers, slavers, child molesters and murderers) you are turning yourself into an enemy of God an enemy of Truth! (your head is full of lies from the devil) it's the reason Jesus Christ says we ALL need to know HIM because HE IS THE TRUTH that sets us FREE FROM THE LIES OF THE DEVIL!

John 8:32-36
32 And ye shall know the truth, and the truth shall make you free.

33 They answered him, We be Abraham's seed, and were never in bondage to any man: how sayest thou, Ye shall be made free?

34 Jesus answered them, Verily, verily, I say unto you, Whosoever committeth sin is the servant of sin.

35 And the servant abideth not in the house for ever: but the Son abideth ever.

36 If the Son therefore shall make you free, ye shall be free indeed.

this is what should be done with all lying qurans worldwide:
https://www.youtube.com/watch?v=htshvId51UE

muslims like to act like they are stupid when it comes to reading the Holy Bible or assume the rest of us are by telling us that finding a place where Jesus makes a comment on one specific day and time that somehow means for all eternity that must be the case. When I say "stupid" I am referring to the fact we all know that if our mothers or fathers sent us to grade school as a child, it doesn't mean we are to ONLY GO TO GRADE SCHOOL FOREVER, or if we send ourselves to get groceries at the market that we intend to ONLY GO TO THE MARKET FOREVER. But that is what muslims want us to believe about this passage where Jesus Christ tells the Canaanite woman He was sent to the Children of Israel. When we can all read passages that tell us plainly Jesus Christ is LORD of ALL and His Commandments are for ALL NATIONS; EVERYONE WORLDWIDE!

The Great Commission
...18Then Jesus came to them and said, "All authority in heaven and on earth has been given to Me. 19Therefore go and make disciples of all nations, baptizing them in the name of the Father, and of the Son, and of the Holy Spirit, 20and teaching them to obey all that I have commanded you. And surely I am with you always, even to the end of the age."...
https://biblehub.com/matthew/28-19.htm

The Lamb is Worthy
...8When He had taken the scroll, the four living creatures and the twenty-four elders fell down before the Lamb. Each one had a harp, and they were holding golden bowls full of incense, which are the prayers of the saints.

9And they sang a new song: "Worthy are You to take the scroll and open its seals, because You were slain, and by Your blood You purchased for God those from every tribe and tongue and people and nation. 10You have made them to be a kingdom and priests to serve our God, and they will reign upon the earth."... https://biblehub.com/revelation/5-9.htm

9After this I looked and saw a multitude too large to count, from every nation and tribe and people and tongue, standing before the throne and before the Lamb. They were wearing white robes and holding palm branches in their hands. 10And they cried out in a loud voice: "Salvation to our God, who sits on the throne, and to the Lamb!"... https://biblehub.com/revelation/7-9.htm

So muslims stop lying to yourselves and the world by ripping the Words of God out of context to make false claims. It only makes you all look either stupid on purpose or evil, wicked liars!

Then you quote Jesus Christ sending the devil away, which is another proof He is God!

HE is the ONE who is worshiped; not satan!
https://www.openbible.info/topics/worshipping_jesus

And then you quote Jesus Christ giving us His Two Greatest Commandments to Love Him and each other. (for some reason you imagine Jesus Christ issuing Divine Commandments and quoting Himself from the Old Testament isn't proof He is God!)

Then you quote that He told us plainly that He was giving Himself as a ransom to Save many (that means Jesus Christ is our Redeemer and Savior!)

https://bible.knowing-jesus.com/topics/God,-As-Redeemer - in fulfillment of His Law and Prophecies!

https://www.preceptaustin.org/tetelestai-paid_in_full - the reason you don't here, see, or know God, is due to the fact you haven't obeyed Him and instead are denying Him! Jesus Christ, the One True God, PAID THE PRICE IN FULL for your sins and the sins of each of us, BUT IF YOU REFUSE TO BE GRATEFUL TO HIM AND INSTEAD DENY HIM, you must die for your own sins (dead to God and is why you don't know Him, you are still lost in your sins)

Jesus Christ, the One True God, is our Redeemer and Savior; NO ONE ELSE! you either Obey His Commandment to Repent and Be Baptized in His Name or you are a disobedient enemy, a lying antichrist! one who will end up in the lake of fire!

So, you have not understood correctly anything in the Holy Bible you have quoted and that is due to the fact the spirit of err is deceiving you. CALL ON JESUS CHRIST, He is the ONLY ONE who can kick the devil out of your life! (He sent the devil away in the passage you quoted and yet you still didn't realize that's because He's GOD! no mere mortal can send the devil away or you wouldn't be lost in his lies!)

Then you quote a passage where He said:

Tradition and Worship
...8'These people honor Me with their lips, but their hearts are far from Me. 9 They worship Me in vain; they teach as doctrine the precepts of men.'" 10Jesus called the crowd to Him and said, "Listen and understand.11A man is not defiled by what enters his mouth, but by what comes out of it." 12Then the disciples came to Him and said, "Are You aware that the Pharisees were offended when they heard this?" 13But Jesus replied, "Every plant that My heavenly Father has not planted will be pulled up by its roots.... https://biblehub.com/matthew/15-9.htm

Mark 7:14-23
What Defiles a Person
14 And he called the people to him again and said to them, "Hear me, all of you, and understand: 15 There is nothing outside a person that by going into him can defile him, but the things that come out of a person are what defile him."[a] 17 And when he had entered the house and left the people, his disciples asked him about the parable. 18 And he said to them, "Then are you also without understanding? Do you not see that whatever goes into a person from outside cannot defile him, 19 since it enters not his heart but his stomach, and is expelled?"[b] (Thus he declared all foods clean.) 20 And he said, "What comes out of a person is what defiles him. 21 For from within, out of the heart of man, come evil thoughts, sexual immorality, theft, murder, adultery, 22 coveting, wickedness, deceit, sensuality, envy, slander, pride, foolishness. 23 All these evil things come from within, and they defile a person."

You're quoting a passage that's a double whammy against the cult of islam! muslims are all the time saying "PBUH" offering lipservice to God, to Jesus Christ, while they don't know Him, don't obey Him and obviously have not one clue what His Words in the Holy Bible mean. Because in this context Jesus Christ is condemning people who worship Him in VAIN (not condemning those who worship Him in Spirit and Truth, who KNOW Him and as such are worshipping Him TRUTHFULLLY. As opposed to those who offer Him lipservice (like muslims) who do NOT know Him! and do NOT obey Him) muslims are all the time DOING THE VERY THING CHRIST SAID NOT TO DO! Taking pride in their flesh! are you circumcised? going around making pretentious accolade by reiteration to their imaginary god? pray 5 times and make it known? you are all the time doing what God says NOT to do!

The second whammy is that God, Jesus Christ, plainly tells us nothing we eat defiles us, but muslims are more concerned about eating a sausage and pepperoni pizza then they are about following a rapist, child molester, robber, murderer, lying cult leader who had slaves!

muslims are the very religious hypocrites JESUS CHRIST CONDEMNS! teaching lying doctrines of muhammad instead of obeying HIM!

http://www.annaqed.com/en/muslims-under-themicroscope/muhammad-and-his-crimes-against-humanity - muhammad was a criminal of the worst kind, not anyone to venerate or imitate.

http://www.answeringmuslims.com/2014/03/muhammad-and-thighingof-aisha.html - even hardened criminals consider child molesters the lowest of the low! muhammad was wicked!
https://www.youtube.com/watch?v=1HbOhLJHcFo - according to islam's most reliable sources muhammad was a racist slaver and began the diabolical cult of islam in which followed many centuries of brutal slavery - https://www.google.com/search?client=opera&q=centuries+of+islamic+slave+trade&sourceid=opera&ie=UTF-8&oe=UTF-8

so muhammad and his gang of criminals began islam and is why islam is criminal in doctrine and practice to this very day.

https://www.thereligionofpeace.com/pages/quran/index.aspx - the quran contains hundreds of verses that openly advocate crimes against humanity. If the rest of humanity understood islam, it's history, it's doctrines and practices, it would be declared a criminal organization and unlawful to practice anywhere on earth! it's that evil! - https://www.politicalislam.com/tears-of-jihad/

It's warped your thinking to the point where you read passages out of the Holy Bible that are refuting your beliefs and you don't even realize it!

Then you quote Jesus Christ uttering the Words He told us He would utter by the Prophets on the Cross:

"My God, my God, why have you forsaken me?" - https://www.biblegateway.com/passage/?search=Psalm%2022&version=ESV

Just one of hundreds of Prophecies fulfilled by Jesus Christ, God in the flesh, as the Messiah:
https://www.accordingtothescriptures.org/prophecy/353prophecies.html
But muslims like yourself IGNORE ALL of them, to go on DENYING Him instead.

The Fulfillment of the Law and Prophets
17Do not think that I have come to abolish the Law or the Prophets. I have not come to abolish them, but to fulfill them. 18For I tell you truly, until heaven and earth pass away, not a single jot, not a stroke of a pen, will disappear from the Law until everything is accomplished....
https://biblehub.com/matthew/5-17.htm

ONLY GOD CAN FULFILL ALL HIS LAW AND PROPHECIES! NO ONE ELSE!

Then you quote the struggle of Christ to go through with being Scourged and Crucified, even as He had told the Prophets and even as He had told the Apostles numerous times. NO ONE would want to be scourged and crucified, it's one of the very worst methods of death the devil and evil people ever concocted! So, God prayed, yes, God, the Son, prayed! He tells us EVERY WORD HE SPOKE WAS GOD SPEAKING so here God showed us when we face trials and tribulations, we must pray to Him for Strength! The humanity (his then mortal body of flesh) of the Messiah was seeking strength from His Holy Spirit, to go forward with the scourging and crucifixion, which He knew He must do or He would have broken His Own Law and Prophecies! SO YES, JESUS CHRIST WAS SCOURGED AND CRUCIFIED! He subsequently RAISED HIS OWN BODY FROM THE GRAVE AND TRANSFIGURED IT INTO AN IMMORTAL, GLORIOUS ONE! It's the reason His Apostles and Disciples immediately began telling the world that they had seen and heard God Almighty, the Messiah firsthand as living eyewitnesses! Those who penned the contents of the Holy Bible GAVE THEIR LIVES TELLING THE WORLD THAT THEY HAD SEEN AND HEARD GOD IN THE FLESH AND WATCHED HIM PUBLICLY DIE AND THEN RAISE HIS BODY FROM THE GRAVE JUST AS HE PROPHESIED AND THEN WATCHED HIM ASCEND BODILY INTO HEAVEN! THEY GAVE THEIR LIVES TO TORTUROUS DEMISES RATHER THAN RECANT OF ONE WORD!

https://tile.loc.gov/storageservices/public/gdcmassbookdig/foxesbookofmart00fo/foxesbookofmart0 0fo.pdf - so Jesus Christ and His Eyewitness Apostles in the Holy Bible are telling us all the TRUTH; not wicked, lying muhammad and the quran!

Let this sink in! The Holy Bible contains the most important facts in all history; it has been THOROUGHLY STUDIED like no other book in all the world! The contents of the Holy Bible inspired the invention of the printing press; so, the Holy Bible is the reason other books even exist! The Gospel of Jesus Christ in the Holy Bible is the most strongly attested fact in the history of the world! Those contents are backed by God Almighty Himself! And His Chosen Eyewitnesses GAVE THEIR LIVES to pass that TRUTH onto us! Not only does the most studied book on earth tell us plainly that Jesus Christ, is the One True God, and that He suffered and died to Redeem and Save us, that He Rose from the dead and Transfigured

His Own Body (made it immortal and glorious AGAIN PROVING HE IS GOD!) but ascended into Heaven and then poured out His Own Holy Spirit upon His Apostles to Empower them to be His Witnesses! The Holy Bible PLAINLY TELLS US ALL THESE FACTS, and it is the MOST STUDIED BOOK IN THE ENTIRE WORLD! So, the most studied book on earth tells us Jesus Christ is God and that He really was scourged, crucified, dead and buried and that He really rose from the dead proving He is the One who has Eternal Life and is the Way to Eternal Life. He really ascended straight into Heaven in front of eyewitnesses, proving He is the Way to Heaven! So not just the most studied book in all the world plainly tells us all these things but the most studied artifact, His Burial Cloth, confirms it! SO, ANYONE DENYING JESUS CHRIST CRUCIFIED AND RESURRECTED IS LYING TO THEMSELVES AND THE WORLD!!!!!!!!

https://youtu.be/LLnClp3OVmE?t=1884

GET IT STRAIGHT muslims! JESUS CHRIST IS GOD AND OBVIOUSLY SO! HE EVER LIVES TO ANSWER ANY AND ALL WITH ENOUGH SENSE TO CALL UPON HIM!

Then you quote the Son saying He does nothing without the Father. How can Jesus Christ say to see Him is to see the Father (John 14:9) and that He and the Father are ONE (John 10:30) if the Father and Son are TWO separate Persons instead?

So, when the Son says He does nothing without the Father that is similar to the fact that your own body does nothing without your spirit. We cannot see your spirit (unless God enables us to) but we can see your body. This is why the scriptures plainly say Jesus Christ is the Image of the Invisible God!

Colossians 1:15-19

The Supremacy of the Son of God
15 The Son is the image of the invisible God, the firstborn over all creation. 16 For in him all things were created: things in heaven and on earth, visible and invisible, whether thrones or powers or rulers or authorities; all things have been created through him and for him. 17 He is before all things, and in him all things hold together. 18 And he is the head of the body, the church; he is the beginning and the firstborn from among the dead, so that in everything he might have the supremacy. 19 For God was pleased to have all his fullness dwell in him,

TO SEE JESUS CHRIST IS TO SEE GOD!

John 14:6-9
6 Jesus said to him, "I am the way, the truth, and the life. No one comes to the Father except through Me.

The Father Revealed
7 "If you had known Me, you would have known My Father also; and from now on you know Him and have seen Him."

8 Philip said to Him, "Lord, show us the Father, and it is sufficient for us."

9 Jesus said to him, "Have I been with you so long, and yet you have not known Me, Philip? He who has seen Me has seen the Father; so how can you say, 'Show us the Father'?

READ VERSE 9 AS MANY TIMES AS IT TAKES!

So, when you then quote John 17:3 (again out of context)

https://biblehub.com/interlinear/john/17-3.htm - you act like you're making some kind of point other than that you are lying to yourself and the world in denying Jesus Christ is God.

LOOK!

John 5:39-40
39 You search the Scriptures because you think that in them you have eternal life; and it is they that bear witness about me, 40 yet you refuse to come to me that you may have life.

28I give them eternal life, and they will never perish. No one can snatch them out of My hand. 29My Father who has given them to Me is greater than all. No one can snatch them out of My Father's hand....
https://biblehub.com/john/10-28.htm

Again, IN CONTEXT "the Father" refers to the Eternal, Pervasive and Transcendent Existence of God (His Invisible Eternal Aspect of Himself - Ephesians 4:6) and "the Son" refers to His Visible Image! you cannot separate "the Father" and "the Son"; they are ONE! similar to how your own invisible spirit is one with your visible body!

Since the body does not speak, or do anything without the spirit, the spirit is greater than the body!

That said, DO NOT THINK FOR A SECOND THAT JESUS CHRIST ISN'T GOD! In the above passages He plainly tells us HE IS THE ONE THAT THE ENTIRE HOLY BIBLE IS ALL ABOUT! HE IS THE ONE WHO HAS AND GIVES ETERNAL LIFE! So, He doesn't suddenly say otherwise in John 17:3!

In that verse the words "...only true God..." and "...Jesus Christ..." are connected by the word "kai" (Greek) that word "kai" means "AND, EVEN, ALSO, NAMELY" so that verse tells us that ONLY TRUE GOD AND JESUS CHRIST are ONE AND ONLY TRUE GOD NAMELY JESUS CHRIST is how we have Eternal Life.

That's why the scriptures CONFIRM IT PLAINLY! JESUS CHRIST IS THE ONE TRUE GOD! THE ONE WHO HAS, GIVES AND IS ETERNAL LIFE!

20And we know that the Son of God has come and has given us understanding, so that we may know Him who is true; and we are in Him who is true— in His Son Jesus Christ. He is the TRUE God and eternal life. https://biblehub.com/1_john/5-20.htm

Jesus Christ REVEALS HIMSELF to those who LOVE and OBEY HIM! (John 14:20-26) the reason not one muslims sees, hears or knows God, Jesus Christ, is due to the fact they are all denying Him and bowing down to their imaginary "allah" instead. allah is the name of a pagan idol as a fact of history so all muslims are guilty of idolatry.

https://www.bible.ca/islam/islam-allahs-daughters.htm

At least you are consistent in your LYING and MISREPRESENTING the contents of the Holy Bible:

The Crucifixion

...29And those who passed by heaped abuse on Him, shaking their heads and saying, "Aha! You who are going to destroy the temple and rebuild it in three days, 30come down from the cross and save Yourself!" 31In the same way, the chief priests and scribes mocked Him among themselves, saying, "He saved others, but He cannot save Himself!...
https://biblehub.com/mark/15-30.htm

So, you quoted wicked people mocking the Lord of Creation as He hung on the Cross. (above)

and then quoted:

The Apostles Before the Council
...29But Peter and the other apostles replied, "We must obey God rather than men. 30The God of our fathers raised up Jesus, whom you had killed by hanging Him on a tree. 31God exalted Him to His right hand as Prince and Savior, in order to grant repentance and forgiveness of sins to Israel....
https://biblehub.com/acts/5-30.htm

And falsely claimed a contradiction when there is none.

You appear to be either totally deceived to the point where you don't understand anything you read in the Holy Bible or are so ruled by the wicked devil that you imagine you can deceive those of us who know better with your many lies. Either way you need to repent and call upon the Living Lord Jesus Christ. You and all muslims need to obey His Commandment to Repent and Be Baptized in the Name of our Lord and Savior, JESUS, the Christ and pray to receive His Holy Spirit of Truth, because right now you all demonstrate quite clearly that you are all deceived by the spirit of err (the lying devil).

Your quotes of the lying quran are useless. Everyone who knows Jesus Christ the Truth, immediately can tell the quran is good for nothing but as fuel for a fire: https://www.youtube.com/watch?v=htshvld51UE - Ann properly quotes the reasons she's disgusted by it and I agree with her in full. The quran is a wicked book full of lies and evil instructions from the lying devil, it's a crying shame that muslims act like they can't tell fact from fiction, truth from lies, good from evil, or God Almighty, Jesus Christ, from the damned devil (one of the devil's many lying names is obviously allah, and one of his many false prophets is obviously muhammad)!

I tell you this plainly ONE MORE TIME, you MUST obey GOD, JESUS CHRIST or you will perish in your sins!

The Great Commission
...15And He said to them, "Go into all the world and preach the gospel to every creature. 16Whoever believes and is baptized will be saved, but whoever does not believe will be condemned.
https://biblehub.com/mark/16-16.htm

The Great Commission
...18Then Jesus came to them and said, "All authority in heaven and on earth has been given to Me. 19Therefore go and make disciples of all nations, baptizing them in the name of the Father, and of the Son, and of the Holy Spirit, 20and teaching them to obey all that I have commanded you. And surely I am with you always, even to the end of the age."...
https://biblehub.com/matthew/28-19.htm

"Brothers, what shall we do?" 38 Peter replied, "Repent and be baptized, every one of you, in the name of Jesus Christ for the forgiveness of your sins, and you will receive the gift of the Holy Spirit. 39This promise belongs to you and your children and to all who are far off—to all whom the Lord our God will call to Himself."... https://biblehub.com/acts/2-38.htm

Peter and John Before the Council
...11This Jesus is 'the stone you builders rejected, which has become the cornerstone.' 12 Salvation exists in no one else, for there is no other name under heaven given to men by which we must be saved." 13When they saw the boldness of Peter and John and realized that they were unschooled, ordinary men, they marveled and took note that these men had been with Jesus.... https://biblehub.com/acts/4-12.htm

24That is why I told you that you would die in your sins. For unless you believe that I am He, you will die in your sins." 25"Who are You?" they asked. "Just what I have been telling you from the beginning," Jesus replied.... https://biblehub.com/john/8-24.htm

SO, IF YOU DON'T WANT TO END UP IN THE LAKE OF FIRE OBEY GOD! REPENT AND BE BAPTIZED IN THE NAME OF OUR LORD JESUS CHRIST! PRAY TO RECEIVE HIS HOLY SPIRIT OF TRUTH! DO IT NOW!

A New Heaven and a New Earth
...7The one who overcomes will inherit all things, and I will be his God, and he will be My son. 8But to the cowardly and unbelieving and abominable and murderers and sexually immoral and sorcerers and idolaters and all liars, their place will be in the lake that burns with fire and sulfur. This is the second death." https://biblehub.com/revelation/21-8.htm

Another common lie among muslims is that they wrongly assert that Jesus Christ never said to worship Him, when He absolutely does Command us to do so in the Holy Bible and expressly forbids worshipping anyone or anything else.

Exodus 20:1-17

English Standard Version

The Ten Commandments

20 And God spoke all these words, saying,

2 "I am the Lord your God, who brought you out of the land of Egypt, out of the house of slavery.

3 "You shall have no other gods before [a] me.

4 "You shall not make for yourself a carved image, or any likeness of anything that is in heaven above, or that is in the earth beneath, or that is in the water under the earth. **5** You shall not bow down to them or serve them, for I the Lord your God am a jealous God, visiting the iniquity of the fathers on the children to the third and the fourth generation of those who hate me, **6** but showing steadfast love to thousands[b] of those who love me and keep my commandments.

The Greatest Commandment
...**12** be careful not to forget the LORD who brought you out of the land of Egypt, out of the house of slavery. **13** Fear the LORD your God, serve Him only, and take your oaths in His name. **14** Do not follow other gods, the gods of the peoples around you.... https://biblehub.com/deuteronomy/6-13.htm

Every Location of LORD in all capitals in the Holy Bible is a reference to YHWH and YHWH is a reference to the English version of His Name, JESUS CHRIST.
https://www.youtube.com/results?search_query=behold+the+nail+behold+the+hand

Isaiah 43:11 no Savior but YHWH and Acts 4:12 Salvation ONLY IN JESUS CHRIST which means YHWH is JESUS CHRIST and JESUS CHRIST is YHWH!

The One True God (just different languages spoken at different times by different people on earth. JESUS CHRIST IS GOD. HE IS THE GOD WHO DECLARES HIMSELF IN BOTH OLD AND NEW TESTAMENTS.

Yes, Jesus Christ is the SAME GOD speaking in the Old Testament!

25"Who are You?" they asked. "Just what I have been telling you from the beginning," Jesus replied. https://biblehub.com/john/8-25.htm

John 5:39-40
39
   You search the Scriptures because you think that in them you have eternal life; and it is they that bear witness about me, **40** yet you refuse to come to me that you may have life.

8But Jesus answered, "It is written: 'Worship the Lord your God and serve Him only.'" https://biblehub.com/luke/4-8.htm

Jesus Appears to Thomas
...27Then Jesus said to Thomas, "Put your finger here and look at My hands. Reach out your hand and put it into My side. Stop doubting and believe." 28Thomas replied, "My Lord and my God!" 29Jesus said to him, "Because you have seen Me, you have believed; blessed are those who have not seen and yet have believed."... https://biblehub.com/john/20-28.htm

It's the reason Jesus Christ always accepts worship:
https://www.openbible.info/topics/worshipping_jesus

and even expressed dissatisfaction when people should have but didn't:

The Ten Lepers
...16He fell facedown at Jesus' feet in thanksgiving to Him—and he was a Samaritan. 17"Were not all ten cleansed?" Jesus asked. "Where then are the other nine? 18Was no one found except this foreigner to return and give glory to God?"... https://biblehub.com/luke/17-17.htm

Another typical rhetorical question from muslims is how can the Creator be killed by His Creation? (As one of their many ways and attempts at denying the Divinity of our Lord Jesus Christ.)

muslims often ask this question as if they don't realize that God created death and that Jesus Christ plainly said:

Jesus the Good Shepherd
...17The reason the Father loves Me is that I lay down My life in order to take it up again. 18No one takes it from Me, but I lay it down of My own accord. I have authority to lay it down and authority to take it up again. This charge I have received from My Father."
https://biblehub.com/john/10-18.htm

So not only did Jesus Christ, the One True God, fulfill His Own Law and Prophecies but He proved we can trust Him beyond death, by publicly dying and raising His Own Body from the Grave, transfiguring it, making it Immortal and rising into Heaven in front of eyewitnesses showing He is the Way to Heaven just as He claimed and also proving He is the One who has Eternal Life, just as He said.

https://www.accordingtothescriptures.org/prophecy/353prophecies.html

John 5:39-40
39 You search the Scriptures because you think that in them you have eternal life; and it is they that bear witness about me, 40 yet you refuse to come to me that you may have life.

Jesus Comforts Martha and Mary
...24Martha replied, "I know that he will rise again in the resurrection at the last day." 25 Jesus said to her, "I am the resurrection and the life. Whoever believes in Me will live, even though he dies. 26And everyone who lives and believes in Me will never die. Do you believe this?"...
https://biblehub.com/john/11-25.htm

No one else in all history both claimed to be God and Proved it like Jesus Christ.

Jesus Appears to Thomas
...27Then Jesus said to Thomas, "Put your finger here and look at My hands. Reach out your hand and put it into My side. Stop doubting and believe." 28Thomas replied, "My Lord and my God!" 29Jesus said to him, "Because you have seen Me, you have believed; blessed are those who have not seen and yet have believed."... https://biblehub.com/john/20-28.htm

Yet another muslim was falsely accusing the Apostle Paul (because God through Paul exposes islam as an accursed cult of antichrists)

Saul was a religious person hating on our Lord Jesus Christ and His Disciples, Christians. (much like religious muslims today) and Jesus Christ confronted Saul for doing that (Acts 8-9) Saul was converted by being blinded then healed by Jesus Christ and afterward spent time learning the Truth from God, Jesus Christ, personally. (Galatians 1:11-17)

Saul became the Apostle Paul. God wrought special miracles through the Apostle Paul, confirming His Conversion to Christianity: (that the Lord Jesus Christ had given the Apostle His Holy Spirit of Truth and was with Paul)

Paul Ministers in Ephesus
…10This continued for two years, so that everyone who lived in the province of Asia, Jews and Greeks alike, heard the word of the Lord. 11 God did extraordinary miracles through the hands of Paul, 12so that even handkerchiefs and aprons that had touched him were taken to the sick, and the diseases and evil spirits left them.... https://biblehub.com/acts/19-11.htm

God Taught and Commanded the Apostle Paul to Preach His Gospel to the world and Paul obeyed Him. As a result, the Words of God proclaimed by the Apostle Paul make up a significant portion of the New Testament.

So obviously the Apostle Paul is someone who has produced much good fruit to the Glory of God.

Stop Criticizing the Apostle Paul

muslims are in the very bad habit of falsely accusing the Apostle Paul. It makes them all look very evil when they do.

Paul was confronted by Jesus Christ and taught by His Holy Spirit and then afterward confirmed by the other Apostles; so, when muslims criticize the Apostle Paul, they are criticizing God and the entire Holy Bible.

https://www.biblegateway.com/passage/?search=Acts%209&version=KJV - Saul, who was persecuting Christians, was confronted for doing so by the Lord Jesus Christ Himself! (and subsequently became the Apostle Paul) Get it through your thick, brainwashed and deceived skulls muslims! Saul was persecuting Christians! meaning Christianity existed BEFORE He became the Apostle Paul! So, our Lord Jesus Christ clearly founded Christianity and even defended His Disciples by directly confronting the zealot Saul who was persecuting them!

Peter's Confession of Christ
...**17**Jesus replied, "Blessed are you, Simon son of Jonah! For this was not revealed to you by flesh and blood, but by My Father in heaven. **18**And I tell you that you are Peter, and on this rock I will build My church, and the gates of Hades will not prevail against it. **19**I will give you the keys of the kingdom of heaven. Whatever you bind on earth will be bound in heaven, and whatever you loose on earth will be loosed in heaven."...
https://biblehub.com/matthew/16-18.htm

After Saul was blinded by our Lord Jesus Christ and then healed by His Power, he was taught by His Holy Spirit the Gospel of Jesus Christ and became the Apostle Paul.

10   For do I now persuade men, or God? or do I seek to please men? for if I yet pleased men, I should not be the servant of Christ.

11   But I certify you, brethren, that the gospel which was preached of me is not after man.

12   For I neither received it of man, neither was I taught it, but by the revelation of Jesus Christ.

13   For ye have heard of my conversation in time past in the Jews' religion, how that beyond measure I persecuted the church of God, and wasted it:

14   And profited in the Jews' religion above many my equals in mine own nation, being more exceedingly zealous of the traditions of my fathers.

15   But when it pleased God, who separated me from my mother's womb, and called me by his grace,

16   To reveal his Son in me, that I might preach him among the heathen; immediately I conferred not with flesh and blood:

17   Neither went I up to Jerusalem to them which were apostles before me; but I went into Arabia, and returned again unto Damascus.

18   Then after three years I went up to Jerusalem to see Peter, and abode with him fifteen days.

https://www.biblegateway.com/passage/?search=Galatians%201&version=KJV - the Apostle Paul was taught the Gospel of Jesus Christ from Jesus Christ!

https://www.biblegateway.com/passage/?search=Galatians%202&version=KJV - After the Apostle Paul had matured in the Faith, he met with the other Apostles and even confronted them on certain issues!

…15Consider also that our Lord's patience brings salvation, just as our beloved brother Paul also wrote you with the wisdom God gave him. 16He writes this way in all his letters, speaking in them about such matters. Some parts of his letters are hard to understand, which ignorant and unstable people distort, as they do the rest of the Scriptures, to their own destruction. 17Therefore, beloved, since you already know these things, be on your guard so that you will not be carried away by the error of the lawless and fall from your secure standing.
https://biblehub.com/2_peter/3-16.htm

Personally, when people belonging to a cult as obviously evil as islam choose to consider the Apostle Paul as their nemesis, it only makes me esteem Paul even more than I already did. The Apostle Paul is a prime example of the Grace and Power of God, to transform even a deadly enemy into a very great ally and friend. So, the one muslims consider to be their nemesis, is probably the one (next to God Almighty) that they really need to take the most seriously. After all, Paul is an example to them that the One True God, Jesus Christ, will save even them if they will but repent and recognize the Lord Jesus Christ as the One True God that He is. (Instead of continuing to be idolaters by bowing down to the kaaba stone; to the evil false god, allah, and his false prophet, muhammad.)

So, the Lord Jesus Christ and the other Apostles knew the Apostle Paul AND CONFIRMED HIM AND HIS LETTERS! Get it straight muslims, to criticize the Apostle Paul is to criticize them all!

I Am the True Vine
John 15 "I am the true vine, and my Father is the vinedresser. 2 Every branch in me that does not bear fruit he takes away, and every branch that does bear fruit he prunes, that it may bear more fruit. 3 Already you are clean because of the word that I have spoken to you. 4 Abide in me, and I in you. As the branch cannot bear fruit by itself, unless it abides in the vine, neither can you, unless you abide in me. 5 I am the vine; you are the branches. Whoever abides in me and I in him, he it is that bears much fruit, for apart from me you can do nothing. 6 If anyone does not abide in me he is thrown away like a branch and withers; and the branches are gathered, thrown into the fire, and burned. 7 If you abide in me, and my words abide in you, ask whatever you wish, and it will be done for you. 8 By this my Father is glorified, that you bear much fruit and so prove to be my disciples.

So, another desperate muslim was trying to deny the Divinity of Jesus Christ by quoting part of 1 Cor 15 (ignoring the rest of the Holy Bible and the context as usual in order to do so)

As usual, you muslims fail to understand what you are reading in the Holy Bible.

LET THIS SINK IN UNTIL YOU UNDERSTAND IT!

John 5:39-40
39 You search the Scriptures because you think that in them you have eternal life; and it is they that bear witness about me, 40 yet you refuse to come to me that you may have life.

THE ENTIRE HOLY BIBLE IS ALL ABOUT JESUS CHRIST, THE ONE TRUE GOD, THE ONE WHO HAS ETERNAL LIFE AND THE ONE WE ALL MUST COME TO IN ORDER TO GET THAT LIFE!

Unto Us a Child is Born
…5For every trampling boot of battle and every garment rolled in blood will be burned as fuel for the fire. 6For unto us a child is born, unto us a son is given, and the government will be upon His shoulders. And He will be called Wonderful Counselor, Mighty God, Everlasting Father, Prince of Peace. 7Of the increase of His government and peace there will be no end. He will reign on the throne of David and over his kingdom, to establish and sustain it with justice and righteousness from that time and forevermore. The zeal of the LORD of Hosts will accomplish this.…
https://biblehub.com/isaiah/9-6.htm

John 14:6-9

New King James Version
6 Jesus said to him, "I am the way, the truth, and the life. No one comes to the Father except through Me.

The Father Revealed
7 "If you had known Me, you would have known My Father also; and from now on you know Him and have seen Him."

8 Philip said to Him, "Lord, show us the Father, and it is sufficient for us."

9 Jesus said to him, "Have I been with you so long, and yet you have not known Me, Philip? He who has seen Me has seen the Father; so how can you say, 'Show us the Father'?

Jesus Christ is GOD "the Father" who came in the flesh... of His Kingdom there is "no End".

When GOD, the Father, walked this earth IN THE FLESH, that VISIBLE IMAGE OF GOD, is called "the Son". The Son has ALL POWER AND AUTHORITY -

The Great Commission
...17When they saw Him, they worshiped Him, but some doubted. 18Then Jesus came to them and said, "All authority in heaven and on earth has been given to Me. 19Therefore go and make disciples of all nations, baptizing them in the name of the Father, and of the Son, and of the Holy Spirit,... https://biblehub.com/matthew/28-18.htm

(notice Jesus Christ NEVER ONCE forbids anyone from worshipping Him!) instead HE ACKNOWLEDGES HE IS LORD AND GOD!

Jesus Appears to Thomas
...27Then Jesus said to Thomas, "Put your finger here and look at My hands. Reach out your hand and put it into My side. Stop doubting and believe." 28Thomas replied, "My Lord and my God!" 29Jesus said to him, "Because you have seen Me, you have believed; blessed are those who have not seen and yet have believed."... https://biblehub.com/john/20-28.htm

So, GOD, "the Father", came into this world He created and made and walked among us humbly as the Messiah, "the Son", and when He finished His Act of Redemption and Salvation on the Cross, He transfigured His Own Mortal Body and Made it Immortal and Glorious and then Returned to Heaven where He is Reigning over all His Creation as GOD. GOD IS ALWAYS GOD, HE DOESN'T EVER CEASE BEING GOD!

So, God the Father indwells the Son and as such the Son is the Visible Image of God the Father as the scriptures plainly teach. So, all this passage is saying is that once God, Jesus Christ, finishes Judging all souls, and once He perfects us and makes us all immortal and glorious like Himself, destroying death, then will we all Know God the Father fully and completely and actually be ONE with God in us all, around us all and through us all. (All Creation will be the Perfect Expression of our Eternal Creator.) As such, we will ALL be the Image of the Invisible, Eternal Creator and He will be our Father Forever. (It is STILL Jesus Christ! only instead of "the Son" (unique visible image of God, the First and the Last) having dominion exclusively over us all, It is His Pleasure to Give Us His Kingdom such that we ALL (all who love and obey Him and are not among those who are cast into the lake of fire) are ONE with Him.)

Do Not Worry
...31But seek His kingdom, and these things will be added unto you. 32Do not be afraid, little flock, for your Father is pleased to give you the kingdom. https://biblehub.com/luke/12-32.htm

A New Heaven and a New Earth

...7The one who overcomes will inherit all things, and I will be his God, and he will be My son. 8But to the cowardly and unbelieving and abominable and murderers and sexually immoral and sorcerers and idolaters and all liars, their place will be in the lake that burns with fire and sulfur. This is the second death." https://biblehub.com/revelation/21-8.htm

So read the entire CONTEXT of 1Cor 15 and you will see it begins with telling us all the Gospel of Jesus Christ summarized, but then talks about the End of this Present Age after the Resurrection. When He does that, gives us immortal, incorruptible bodies like His Own, He is conferring upon us His Power and Glory, we are UNITING WITH GOD as ONE.

John 17:21-23

21   That they all may be one; as thou, Father, art in me, and I in thee, that they also may be one in us: that the world may believe that thou hast sent me.

22   And the glory which thou gavest me I have given them; that they may be one, even as we are one:

23   I in them, and thou in me, that they may be made perfect in one; and that the world may know that thou hast sent me, and hast loved them, as thou hast loved me.

ONLY AFTER JESUS CHRIST, the ONE TRUE GOD, PERFECTS US, GLORIFIES US, AND MAKES US TO BE INCORRUPTIBLE AND IMMORTAL LIKE HIMSELF DO WE ALL SHARE HIS KINGDOM (CREATION PERFECTED) AND HAVE EVERY GOOD THING JUST AS GOD DOES. AND SO ONLY THEN DOES THE ONE WHO CREATED AND MADE US TELL US THAT THE FATHER (HIS INVISIBLE, ETERNAL, PERVASIVE AND TRANSCENDENT EXISTENCE) WILL BE OUR FATHER, OUR GOD; ALL IN ALL.

When the Son (God in the flesh) tells us that He didn't know the hour of His Return, it was His Way of not telling us for similar reasons parents often don't answer everything their children ask them! Like when a child asks questions about matters that are beyond their age or when a parent tells them that if they are very good, they will get a big surprise and the child wants to know when.

In other words, God knows many of us are procrastinators, so doesn't tell us when He is coming back because His Message is for all of us to REPENT NOW! IMMEDIATELY and live righteously all our lives as if He could return at any moment! So, nothing you have quoted in any way is reason to deny the facts:

1) Jesus Christ is God who came in the flesh (the scriptures are redundantly clear on this. (1Tim 3:16, https://www.accordingtothescriptures.org/prophecy/353prophecies.html)

2) Jesus Christ is the One who will Judge your soul and determine whether or not you have eternal life with Him or will be cast into the lake of fire. (Jn 5:22)

3) Everyone needs to obey the Commandments of Jesus Christ in the Holy Bible and stop trying to think they worship God by ignoring and denying Him. (muslims, like yourself). (Mt 28:18-20)

UNTIL HE PERFECTS US AND DESTROYS DEATH THE LAST ENEMY, JESUS CHRIST IS THE ONE WE ALL BOW TO AS THE LIVING GOD OVER HIS CREATION. When we unite with Him AFTER He Perfects us, THEN and not until THEN will we be ONE WITH GOD IN ALL HIS POWER AND GLORY.

I want to be crystal clear about what God, Jesus Christ (English), tells us about Himself and His Creation in the contents of the Holy Bible. From Genesis to Revelation God is telling us the END from the BEGINNING. And when we read those contents, we realize that the aspect of God He refers to as "the Father" is ETERNAL, INVISIBLE, PERVASIVE and TRANSCENDENT above ALL HIS CREATION. (God, the Father, is Greater than ALL His Creation- Ephesians 4:6) THAT SAME ETERNAL, INVISIBLE, PERVASIVE and TRANSCENDENT GOD, ALSO HAS A VISIBLE IMAGE, called "the Son". THE FATHER INDWELLS THE SON, so the Father and the Son are ONE, similar to how our own invisible spirit is one with our visible body! ONE GOD, NOT TWO! He is just letting us know that He is much more than just that Visible Image, but is ETERNAL and EVERYWHERE (so it's IMPOSSIBLE to SEE that aspect of God!, but He declares Himself to us VISIBLY in JESUS, the Christ!) In other words, "the Son" is the Visible Image of "the Father" similar to how your own body is the visible image of your invisible spirit.

When we OBEY GOD, JESUS CHRIST, and REPENT and are BAPTIZED in His Name, He imparts to us His Holy Spirit of Truth, the Holy Spirit of God, of Jesus Christ, enters us and we SPIRITUALLY UNITE with Him, He begins REVEALING HIMSELF to us (Matthew 28:18-20, Mark 16:15-16; Acts 2:38,39, John 14:20-26)! That Divine Revelation gives us a proper understanding of Him and His Words in the Holy Bible such that we understand what He is telling us about Himself and what He is Doing in Creating, Making and Perfecting His Creation. So, we become ONE WITH GOD, JESUS CHRIST, when we RECEIVE HIM, BY HIS HOLY SPIRIT OF TRUTH, SPIRITUALLY! BUT WE ARE NOT YET PERFECTED BY HIM, SO WE ARE NOT YET ONE WITH HIM IN POWER AND GLORY, (in Essence)! That happens AFTER He Resurrects us AT THE END OF THIS AGE!

WHEN His Creation (His Bride) is PERFECTED, HOLY and GLORIOUS, like our Eternal Creator, JESUS (English for Yahoshuah/Yeshua/YHWH in the Hebrew), "the Father", will be all in all; STILL JESUS, but His Visible Image "the Son" will have given us all things (Himself) and we will ALL be ONE in not just Spirit, but in Power and Glory (Elohim). (Creation ONE with our Eternal Creator) So God is telling us He intends to Perfect us to the state where we are ONE with Him in not just our thoughts, not just our spirits, but in Power and Glory, like unto Himself. When that Happens, we will know God, the Father, as our own, we will understand He is IN ALL, THROUGH ALL, ABOVE ALL and we belong to Him, perfectly united as ONE with our Eternal Creator.

I have been in Heaven and I have seen Jesus Christ face to face and when I was there His INVISIBLE, ETERNAL SELF was permeating EVERYTHING so tangibly I could feel His Love EVERYWHERE, IMMERSED IN GOD! I could feel Him and His Virtues Permeating EVERYONE and EVERYTHING, even myself! And YET, there was no mistaking that ALL of that Power and Glory was coming from and radiating from JESUS CHRIST! So, when the scriptures tell us God is giving us every Good thing, HIMSELF and ALL HIS CREATION, it is not saying that JESUS CHRIST isn't GOD! It's merely telling us that we are not to think that His VISIBLE IMAGE, the SON, is ALL THAT HE IS! (yes, and no) yes, in that the scriptures tell us the FULLNESS OF GOD indwells the Son, but no, in that God is ETERNAL, INVISIBLE, PERVASIVE and TRANSCENDENT (can't SEE that aspect of Him). So the Father indwells the Son and that is why the scriptures refer to Him as the Visible Image of God, the UNIQUE ONE AND ONLY Visible Image of God, similar to how each of our own bodies are unique to our own invisible spirits. So, this is why JESUS CHRIST is the ONE NAME of the ONE GOD who describes Himself as "the Father", "the Son" and "the Holy Spirit".

We exist in His INVISIBLE, ETERNAL, PERVASIVE AND TRANSCENDENT self: God, the Father, (STILL JESUS) is all around us! But we do not see God until we look at "the Son", the Image of God. This is why the SON is the ONLY WAY to the FATHER, because the Father and the Son are ONE, just like the only way to know your invisible spirit is by interacting with your visible body, listening to what you have to say, watching what you do. WE KNOW GOD, ONLY BY THE FACT HE DECLARES HIMSELF TO US PLAINLY THROUGH JESUS CHRIST! (In other words, how would you feel if everyone imagined you were someone or something else other than who you declare yourself to be?) But that is what everyone who is rejecting Jesus Christ as the One True God is doing, they are idolizing their own imaginations of their imaginary god(s) in their heads, and are rejecting the REAL ONE!

So God, JESUS CHRIST who is "the Father", "the Son" and "the Holy Spirit" is STILL WORKING, STILL CREATING, MAKING and TRANSFORMING/PERFECTING His Creation! As long as His Creation is still in process, HE IS REIGNING EVEN NOW OVER IT ALL! King of kings and Lord of lords! BUT WHEN He RESURRECTS US, when The Final Judgment of Souls is over, when He transfigures the bodies of the Saved and gives us immortal and incorruptible ones like His Own, THEN His Kingdom, His Creation, will be PERFECTED and ONE with His Eternal, Invisible, Pervasive and Transcendent Self (called the Father - STILL JESUS!). And as such the Son will no longer be the ONE and ONLY (emphasis on ONLY) UNIQUE VISIBLE IMAGE of GOD, but God, the FATHER (STILL JESUS!) will be all in all, and all His Creation a Visible Expression of Him in Power and Glory. (this is what the passage in 1Cor 15:20-28 is telling us about the Son delivering His Kingdom to God, the Father, (STILL JESUS; again, "the Father" refers to His Eternal, Invisible, Pervasive and Transcendent Existence - Ephesians 4:6. so never imagine that "the Father" and "the Son" are two different Persons/Gods/Beings; no more than your own body and spirit are two different persons!) that the Father is all in all.)

In other words, NOTHING in the Holy Bible ever teaches us that Jesus Christ isn't the ONE TRUE GOD (the ENTIRE Holy Bible is all about Him! - Jn 5:39-40), anyone interpreting His Words to imagine God is someone other than Jesus Christ, is MISINTERPRETING THEM. JESUS CHRIST IS GOD! JESUS IS THE FATHER, THE SON and THE HOLY SPIRIT! that's why there is only ONE NAME for "the Father", "the Son", and "the Holy Spirit" those are all titles and aspects of the ONE GOD, JESUS CHRIST! (Matthew 28:1820, Acts 2:38; 4:12 and Isaiah 43:11 ONE GOD, ONE SAVIOR, JESUS CHRIST. (JESUS the CHRIST is English for YHWH in ancient Hebrew))

GOD, Jesus Christ, describes Himself as our Redeemer, our Savior, our Shepherd, our Teacher, our Provider, our Healer, our Creator, our Maker, our King, our Lord, etc. in the contents of the Holy Bible BECAUSE HE IS! THAT'S the TRUTH! He also says He is our Heavenly Father, our Friend, our Brother, our Servant, our Ambassador, our Advocate, our Comforter, etc. etc. BECAUSE HE IS! GOD IS OUR EVERYTHING! Without Jesus Christ there is no Creation! without our Eternal Creator, Lord and Savior, there would be NOTHING!

So people who rip His Words out of context not realizing God, Jesus Christ, is telling us He is ALL things to us, Life itself, Truth itself, the ONLY WAY TO KNOW HIM (John 14-17; Col 1:14-19); to instead focus on those aspects that they imagine are somehow less than God, like HOW LOVING AND HUMBLE HE IS to walk among us as one of us, SERVING OUR WANTS AND NEEDS (John 13:12-14)! THAT'S INCREDIBLE! GOD! WHO HAS ALL POWER AND ALL AUTHORITY! LOVING AND CARING ABOUT US! COMING TO PERSONALLY WALK WITH US! SHOW HIMSELF TO US! TEACH US BY HIS WORDS AND DEEDS! GOD IS SO GOOD that many people just can't grasp HOW GOOD because they are not obeying Jesus Christ, so that they can KNOW HIM AS HE IS!

So, some might ask if God, Jesus Christ, is in all, through all and above all, why do so many still don't know Him? And that is due to the fact God gives us His Holy Spirit of Truth WHEN WE OBEY HIS COMMANDMENT TO TURN FROM OUR SINS, OUR WICKED THOUGHTS, WORDS, WAYS, AND DEEDS! WHEN WE OBEY HIM AND REPENT OF THINKING WE KNOW BETTER THAN HIM AND ARE READY TO LISTEN TO AND OBEY HIM AND HIS COMMANDMENTS IN THE HOLY BIBLE! WHEN WE ACTUALLY GO AND GET BAPTIZED IN HIS NAME, SHOWING HIM AND THE WORLD THAT WE ARE FINALLY OBEYING HIM! THEN HE KICKS THE DEVIL, THE DECEIVER, OUT OF OUR LIVES along with all the many lies we've been believing instead of JESUS CHRIST, the ONE TRUE GOD, and His Words in the Holy Bible! Until then God tells us He is HOLY and that our many sins SEPARATE US FROM HIM (Isaiah 59) and we are dead to God, Jesus Christ; lost in our sins, until we Repent and Receive Him (Ephesians 2:1-10). He doesn't come into our lives by His Holy Spirit UNTIL WE REPENT AND ARE BAPTIZED IN HIS NAME, UNTIL WE NO LONGER WANT TO SIN ANY MORE AND INSTEAD WANT TO LIVE RIGHTEOUSLY BY HIS GRACE AND POWER! THEN and ONLY THEN does our Lord Jesus Christ come into our lives by the Presence of His Holy Spirit of Truth! Then we begin to Hear Him Speaking to us, like He Spoke with all His Prophets Since the Beginning! Then and only then does He begin teaching us in dreams and visions, Divine Revelations, just like the ones we read about in the Holy Bible! SO, IF ANYONE REALLY WANTS TO KNOW GOD ALMIGHTY PERSONALLY, THEY MUST OBEY OUR LIVING LORD JESUS CHRSIT AND HIS COMMANDMENTS IN THE HOLY BIBLE! MUST! THERE IS NO OTHER WAY, BECAUSE JESUS CHRIST IS THE ONE TRUE REAL GOD! (no one else! Acts 4:12, 1Jn 5:20, Rev 22:12-14)

Jesus is Coming Rev 22-

...**12**"Behold, I am coming soon, and My reward is with Me, to give to each one according to what he has done. **13**I am the Alpha and the Omega, the First and the Last, the Beginning and the End."

SO, REMEMBER JESUS CHRIST IS THE ONE WHO WILL JUDGE US ALL AND DETERMINE WHETHER OR NOT WE SPEND ETERNITY IN PARADISE WITH HIM OR ARE CAST INTO THE LAKE OF FIRE FOR REFUSING TO REPENT OF OUR WICKED WAYS! (Jn 5:22; Rev 21:8) JESUS CHRIST IS THE TRUTH! if you don't know Him, it's because you are believing lies! (John 14:6-9; 8:32-36; 1Jn 2:20-27; 5:19-21)

John 10:30 I and the Father are ONE. (so, stop trying to separate God from God)

Col 1:14-19 the Son is the Image of the Invisible God (so to look at Jesus Christ is to see God)

Heb 1:3 the Son is the EXACT REPRESENTATION OF GOD (again, stop trying to deny Him)

You WILL BOW BEFORE HIM, you can either do it now to your everlasting Joy or you can do it when He judges your wicked soul to your everlasting shame, but you and all souls will bow before Jesus Christ and confess with your mouths that JESUS CHRIST IS LORD! (LORD in the Holy Bible refers to YHWH/GOD)

The Attitude of Christ

...9Therefore God exalted Him to the highest place and gave Him the name above all names, 10that at the name of Jesus every knee should bow, in heaven and on earth and under the earth, 11and every tongue confess that Jesus Christ is Lord, to the glory of God the Father....
https://biblehub.com/philippians/2-10.htm

Yet another muslim was slamming the Holy Bible and singing their praises about their vile quran; so, I responded:

It takes a muslim to believe the criminal muhammad who came along over 6 centuries AFTER the FACTS published in the Holy Bible (and so had NO PERSONAL KNOWLEDGE OF THOSE FACTS WHATSOEVER) and his many lies in the quran over God Almighty, Jesus Christ, His Prophets and His Chosen Eyewitness Apostles in the Holy Bible.

https://www.thereligionofpeace.com/pages/articles/jesusmuhammad.aspx

So, another day passes and another muslim was posting yet more islamic lies; claiming the Holy Bible was manmade doctrines and ripping a verse out of scripture where Christ was condemning those who worship Him IN VAIN (muslims imagine He is forbidding worship because they completely ignore the context of His Words):

LET THIS SINK IN UNTIL YOU UNDERSTAND IT!

John 5:39-40

39 You search the Scriptures because you think that in them you have eternal life; and it is they that bear witness about me, 40 yet you refuse to come to me that you may have life.

THE ENTIRE HOLY BIBLE IS ALL ABOUT JESUS CHRIST, THE ONE TRUE GOD, THE ONE WHO HAS ETERNAL LIFE AND THE ONE WE ALL MUST COME TO IN ORDER TO GET THAT LIFE!

The Holy Bible is not "manmade" doctrines! your quran is! (Only muslims believe a lying criminal and his many lies in the quran over God Almighty, Jesus Christ, His Prophets and His Chosen Eyewitness Apostles in the Holy Bible! muslims are OBVIOUSLY believing lies and by believing lies and passing them on are all LIARS! https://www.thereligionofpeace.com/pages/articles/jesusmuhammad.aspx)

Matthew 15:1-20

Traditions and Commandments

15 Then Pharisees and scribes came to Jesus from Jerusalem and said, 2 "Why do your disciples break the tradition of the elders? For they do not wash their hands when they eat." 3 He answered them, "And why do you break the commandment of God for the sake of your tradition? 4 For God commanded, 'Honor your father and your mother,' and, 'Whoever reviles father or mother must surely die.' 5 But you say, 'If anyone tells his father or his mother, "What you would have gained from me is given to God,"[a] 6 he need not honor his father.' So for the sake of your tradition you have made void the word[b] of God. 7 You hypocrites! Well did Isaiah prophesy of you, when he said:

8 "'This people honors me with their lips,

but their heart is far from me; 9 in vain

do they worship me,

teaching as doctrines the commandments of men.'"

What Defiles a Person

10 And he called the people to him and said to them, "Hear and understand: 11 it is not what goes into the mouth that defiles a person, but what comes out of the mouth; this defiles a person." 12 Then the disciples came and said to him, "Do you know that the Pharisees were offended when they heard this saying?" 13 He answered, "Every plant that my heavenly Father has not planted will be rooted up. 14 Let them alone; they are blind guides.[c] And if the blind lead the blind, both will fall into a pit." 15 But Peter said to him, "Explain the parable to us." 16 And he said, "Are you also still without understanding? 17 Do you not see that whatever goes into the mouth passes into the stomach and is expelled?[d] 18 But what comes out of the mouth proceeds from the heart, and this defiles a person. 19 For out of the heart come evil thoughts, murder, adultery, sexual immorality, theft, false witness, slander. 20 These are what defile a person. But to eat with unwashed hands does not defile anyone."

Mark 7:14-23

What Defiles a Person

14 And he called the people to him again and said to them, "Hear me, all of you, and understand: 15 There is nothing outside a person that by going into him can defile him, but the things that come out of a person are what defile him."[a] 17 And when he had entered the house and left the people, his disciples asked him about the parable. 18 And he said to them, "Then are you also without understanding? Do you not see that whatever goes into a person from outside cannot defile him, 19 since it enters not his heart but his stomach, and is expelled?"[b] (Thus he declared all foods clean.) 20 And he said, "What comes out of a person is what defiles him. 21 For from within, out of the heart of man, come evil thoughts, sexual immorality, theft, murder, adultery, 22 coveting, wickedness, deceit, sensuality, envy, slander, pride, foolishness. 23 All these evil things come from within, and they defile a person."

Jesus Christ is God and He ALWAYS has been worshiped!

https://www.openbible.info/topics/worshipping_jesus - not only did God, Jesus Christ, receive worship even when He walked among us in the flesh but He was displeased when people should have done so and didn't:

The Ten Lepers

...16He fell facedown at Jesus' feet in thanksgiving to Him—and he was a Samaritan. 17"Were not all ten cleansed?" Jesus asked. "Where then are the other nine? 18Was no one found except this foreigner to return and give glory to God?"... https://biblehub.com/luke/17-17.htm

So, the passage is about religious hypocrites (like muslims) who go around saying things like PBUH ritually without even KNOWING Him and set aside His Commandments in the Holy Bible for your manmade lying doctrines in the quran! (yes, I know I am redundant in this book, but muslims are in need of DEPROGRAMMING from the lies of their cult! redundancy is in my opinion necessary!) STUDY THE TRUTH, THE WORDS OF GOD, IN THE HOLY BIBLE LIFELONG!

You quote a passage that condemns you as the very religious hypocrite He was speaking against (people who honor Him with their lips but don't even KNOW Him or OBEY Him!)

Notice He doesn't condemn anyone for worshiping Him, He is condemning those who worship Him **in VAIN** (with mere words, rather than knowing, loving and obeying Him "in Spirit and in Truth".)

He is pointing out how wrong it is to be going around condemning people for what they feed their flesh bodies (like muslims sneering at those who eat a sausage and pepperoni pizza) while they are SETTING ASIDE HIS

COMMANDMENTS for their own rituals, traditions and doctrines, AND LYING ABOUT HIM AND HIS COMMANDMENTS in the Holy Bible (like you just did).

muslims must repent and be baptized in the Name of our Lord and Savior, JESUS, the Christ or they will be cast into the lake of fire for lying about Him and His Words in the Holy Bible and all their other sins.

The Great Commission

...15And He said to them, "Go into all the world and preach the gospel to every creature. 16Whoever believes and is baptized will be saved, but whoever does not believe will be condemned.
https://biblehub.com/mark/16-16.htm

"Brothers, what shall we do?" 38 Peter replied, "Repent and be baptized, every one of you, in the name of Jesus Christ for the forgiveness of your sins, and you will receive the gift of the Holy Spirit. 39This promise belongs to you and your children and to all who are far off—to all whom the Lord our God will call to Himself."... https://biblehub.com/acts/2-38.htm

Beware of Antichrists

...21I have not written to you because you lack knowledge of the truth, but because you have it, and because no lie comes from the truth. 22Who is the liar, if it is not the one who denies that Jesus is the Christ? This is the antichrist, who denies the Father and the Son. 23Whoever denies the Son does not have the Father, but whoever confesses the Son has the Father as well.... https://biblehub.com/1_john/2-22.htm

A New Heaven and a New Earth

...7The one who overcomes will inherit all things, and I will be his God, and he will be My son. 8But to the cowardly and unbelieving and abominable and murderers and sexually immoral and sorcerers and idolaters and all liars, their place will be in the lake that burns with fire and sulfur. This is the second death." https://biblehub.com/revelation/21-8.htm

So, if muslims don't want to end up in the lake of fire they all need to Repent and Be Baptized in the Name of our Lord and Savior Jesus Christ, they all need to receive Him into their lives by His Holy Spirit of Truth! Only when a muslim becomes a Disciple of Jesus Christ (a true Christian), who KNOWS, LOVES and OBEYS Him, will they be Saved! (Acts 2:38,39; 4:12, Jn 14:20-26) until then they are all acting like lying children of the lying devil (John 8:43-45).

Yet another muslim was today online telling Christians to repent and be saved by islam; so, I responded:

islam isn't salvation, it's damnation.

God, Jesus Christ, is the ONLY SAVIOR! Is 43:11; Acts 4:12 (not islam, not your imaginary evil allah of the quran (just another name for the devil), or the lying criminal muhammad!)

Peter and John Before the Council
...11This Jesus is 'the stone you builders rejected, which has become the cornerstone.' 12 Salvation exists in no one else, for there is no other name under heaven given to men by which we must be saved."
https://biblehub.com/acts/4-12.htm

https://www.thereligionofpeace.com/pages/articles/jesusmuhammad.aspx

Jesus Christ tells us all muslims are lying antichrists on their way to the lake of fire:

Beware of Antichrists
...21I have not written to you because you lack knowledge of the truth, but because you have it, and because no lie comes from the truth. 22Who is the liar, if it is not the one who denies that Jesus is the Christ? This is the antichrist, who denies the Father and the Son. 23Whoever denies the Son does not have the Father, but whoever confesses the Son has the Father as well.... https://biblehub.com/1_john/2-22.htm

A New Heaven and a New Earth
...7The one who overcomes will inherit all things, and I will be his God, and he will be My son. 8But to the cowardly and unbelieving and abominable and murderers and sexually immoral and sorcerers and idolaters and all liars, their place will be in the lake that burns with fire and sulfur. This is the second death." https://biblehub.com/revelation/21-8.htm

So, unless muslims repent and obey Jesus Christ, they will all end up in the flames of damnation.

The Great Commission
...18Then Jesus came to them and said, "All authority in heaven and on earth has been given to Me. 19Therefore go and make disciples of all nations, baptizing them in the name of the Father, and of the Son, and of the Holy Spirit, 20and teaching them to obey all that I have commanded you. And surely I am with you always, even to the end of the age."...
https://biblehub.com/matthew/28-19.htm

"Brothers, what shall we do?" 38 Peter replied, "Repent and be baptized, every one of you, in the name of Jesus Christ for the forgiveness of your sins, and you will receive the gift of the Holy Spirit. 39This promise belongs to you and your children and to all who are far off—to all whom the Lord our God will call to Himself."... https://biblehub.com/acts/2-38.htm

So only when a muslim repents and receives our Lord and Savior, Jesus, the Christ (becoming a Christian) are they Saved. Otherwise, they are all under His Wrath for denying Him and refusing to Obey His Commandments in the Holy Bible.

2 Thessalonians 1:8-9
8   In flaming fire taking vengeance on them that know not God, and that obey not the gospel of our Lord Jesus Christ:

9   Who shall be punished with everlasting destruction from the presence of the Lord, and from the glory of his power;

24That is why I told you that you would die in your sins. For unless you believe that I am He, you will die in your sins." 25"Who are You?" they asked. "Just what I have been telling you from the beginning," Jesus replied.... https://biblehub.com/john/8-24.htm

...35The Father loves the Son and has placed all things in His hands. 36Whoever believes in the Son has eternal life. Whoever rejects the Son will not see life. Instead, the wrath of God remains on him." https://biblehub.com/john/3-36.htm

Another question muslims often ask is why the Son said He does nothing without the Father if Jesus Christ is God who came in the flesh?

muslims have a hard time perceiving the LOVE of God for us, because the cult of islam is devoid of it.

It was the LOVE of God that compelled Him to come into this world He Created and Made to suffer and die for us. It was His Love and Virtues that put Him on the Cross where He showed us all how much He hates sin, but still loves us sinners.

Christ's Sacrifice for the Ungodly
...7Very rarely will anyone die for a righteous man, though for a good man someone might possibly dare to die. 8But God proves His love for us in this: While we were still sinners, Christ died for us. 9Therefore, since we have now been justified by His blood, how much more shall we be saved from wrath through Him!... https://biblehub.com/romans/5-8.htm

Once someone realizes that God knew He would need to come in the flesh to Redeem us to Save us, then they can see what Christ Crucified for them and us all really means - it means God hates sin that much, but also that He loves us that much!

When God came in the flesh as the Messiah, exactly like He told His Prophets he would do:

https://www.accordingtothescriptures.org/prophecy/353prophecies.html
in order to Redeem/Save us:

https://bible.knowing-jesus.com/topics/God,-As-Redeemer and
https://www.preceptaustin.org/tetelestai-paid_in_full

He condemned sin the flesh (no one can falsely accuse God of giving us impossible commandments, because He proved they can indeed be kept in the flesh, as a Man.)

Living in the Spirit
…2For in Christ Jesus the law of the Spirit of life set you free from the law of sin and death. 3For what the law was powerless to do in that it was weakened by the flesh, God did by sending His own Son in the likeness of sinful man, as an offering for sin. He thus condemned sin in the flesh, https://biblehub.com/romans/8-3.htm

When the Son says He does nothing, says nothing, without the Father, that's similar to the fact that our own body does nothing without our spirit.

26 As the body without the spirit is dead, so faith without deeds is dead. https://biblehub.com/james/2-26.htm

The Son is the Visible Image of the Father, similar to how our own body is the visible image of our invisible spirit:

John 14:6-9
6 Jesus said to him, "I am the way, the truth, and the life. No one comes to the Father except through Me.

The Father Revealed

7 "If you had known Me, you would have known My Father also; and from now on you know Him and have seen Him."

8 Philip said to Him, "Lord, show us the Father, and it is sufficient for us."

9 Jesus said to him, "Have I been with you so long, and yet you have not known Me, Philip? He who has seen Me has seen the Father; so how can you say, 'Show us the Father'?

Colossians 1:15-19
The Supremacy of the Son of God
15 The Son is the image of the invisible God, the firstborn over all creation. 16 For in him all things were created: things in heaven and on earth, visible and invisible, whether thrones or powers or rulers or authorities; all things have been created through him and for him. 17 He is before all things, and in him all things hold together. 18 And he is the head of the body, the church; he is the beginning and the firstborn from among the dead, so that in everything he might have the supremacy. 19 For God was pleased to have all his fullness dwell in him,

So even though His Body, the Son, didn't want to suffer and die, feel that tremendous evil, the sins of the world, He knew that He needed to and so He went through it just like He had said He would:

https://www.gotquestions.org/Jesus-predict-His-death.html

Jesus Christ claimed to be God who has Eternal Life and is the fulfillment of His Law and Prophecies:

John 5:39-40
39 You search the Scriptures because you think that in them you have eternal life; and it is they that bear witness about me, 40 yet you refuse to come to me that you may have life.

The Fulfillment of the Law
16In the same way, let your light shine before men, that they may see your good deeds and glorify your Father in heaven. 17Do not think that I have come to abolish the Law or the Prophets. I have not come to abolish them, but to fulfill them. 18For I tell you truly, until heaven and earth pass away, not a single jot, not a stroke of a pen, will disappear from the Law until everything is accomplished.... https://biblehub.com/matthew/5-17.htm

Jesus Christ openly claimed to have the Power of Resurrection and LIFE:

Jesus Comforts Martha and Mary
...24Martha replied, "I know that he will rise again in the resurrection at the last day." 25 Jesus said to her, "I am the resurrection and the life. Whoever believes in Me will live, even though he dies. 26And everyone who lives and believes in Me will never die. Do you believe this?"... https://biblehub.com/john/11-25.htm

He then publicly died and raised His Own Body from the Grave, transfigured it, making it Immortal and Glorious and then Ascended in front of eyewitnesses. Those Eyewitnesses were so convinced that Jesus Christ is the One True God that they gave their lives testifying of Him to everyone, everywhere, even those that had just crucified Him. That's how Christianity began and the Risen Lord Jesus Christ still gives His Holy Spirit of Truth to all who love and obey Him.

The Great Commission
...15And He said to them, "Go into all the world and preach the gospel to every creature. 16Whoever believes and is baptized will be saved, but whoever does not believe will be condemned.

https://biblehub.com/mark/16-16.htm

Three Thousand Believe

37When the people heard this, they were cut to the heart and asked Peter and the other apostles, "Brothers, what shall we do?" 38 Peter replied, "Repent and be baptized, every one of you, in the name of Jesus Christ for the forgiveness of your sins, and you will receive the gift of the Holy Spirit. 39This promise belongs to you and your children and to all who are far off—to all whom the Lord our God will call to Himself."…
https://biblehub.com/acts/2-38.htm

Peter and John Before the Council

…11This Jesus is 'the stone you builders rejected, which has become the cornerstone.' 12 Salvation exists in no one else, for there is no other name under heaven given to men by which we must be saved." 13When they saw the boldness of Peter and John and realized that they were unschooled, ordinary men, they marveled and took note that these men had been with Jesus.… https://biblehub.com/acts/4-12.htm

No one else in the entire history of the world both claimed and proved they are the One True God, like Jesus Christ. Everyone, everywhere needs to obey Him. EVERYONE! Repent and Be Baptized in the Name of Jesus Christ today and pray to receive His Holy Spirit of Truth until you KNOW HIM! (John 14:20-26, Luke 11:13)

I have yet to see any muslims post or comment anything true about God, the Holy Bible, or Jesus Christ and I have been reading their lies many years. Today one was saying because Jesus Christ said, "All Power in Heaven and earth is given unto me..." that means He isn't God. And also lying saying that Jesus Christ never claimed to be God in the Holy Bible.

Well does God call muslims liars and antichrists.

Beware of Antichrists

...21I have not written to you because you lack knowledge of the truth, but because you have it, and because no lie comes from the truth. 22Who is the liar, if it is not the one who denies that Jesus is the Christ? This is the antichrist, who denies the Father and the Son. 23Whoever denies the Son does not have the Father, but whoever confesses the Son has the Father as well.... https://biblehub.com/1_john/2-22.htm

Jesus Christ publicly stated:

John 5:39-40
39 You search the Scriptures because you think that in them you have eternal life; and it is they that bear witness about me, 40 yet you refuse to come to me that you may have life.
that the entire Holy Bible is about Him, the One who has Eternal Life and the One everyone must come to in order to have that Life.

John 8:48-59

Before Abraham Was, I Am
48 The Jews answered him, "Are we not right in saying that you are a Samaritan and have a demon?" 49 Jesus answered, "I do not have a demon, but I honor my Father, and you dishonor me. 50 Yet I do not seek my own glory; there is One who seeks it, and he is the judge. 51 Truly, truly, I say to you, if anyone keeps my word, he will never see death." 52 The Jews said to him, "Now we know that you have a demon! Abraham died, as did the prophets, yet you say, 'If anyone keeps my word, he will never taste death.' 53 Are you greater than our father Abraham, who died? And the prophets died! Who do you make yourself out to be?" 54 Jesus answered, "If I glorify myself, my glory is nothing. It is my Father who glorifies me, of whom you say, 'He is our God.'[a] 55 But you have not known him. I know him. If I were to say that I do not know him, I would be

a liar like you, but I do know him and I keep his word. 56 Your father Abraham rejoiced that he would see my day. He saw it and was glad." 57 So the Jews said to him, "You are not yet fifty years old, and have you seen Abraham?"[b] 58 Jesus said to them, "Truly, truly, I say to you, before Abraham was, I am." 59 So they picked up stones to throw at him, but Jesus hid himself and went out of the temple.

He used the Name of God referring to Himself!

Moses at the Burning Bush

…13Then Moses asked God, "Suppose I go to the Israelites and say to them, 'The God of your fathers has sent me to you,' and they ask me, 'What is His name?' What should I tell them?" 14God said to Moses, "I AM WHO I AM. This is what you are to say to the Israelites: 'I AM has sent me to you.'" 15God also told Moses, "Say to the Israelites, 'The LORD, the God of your fathers—the God of Abraham, the God of Isaac, and the God of Jacob—has sent me to you.' This is My name forever, and this is how I am to be remembered in every generation…. https://biblehub.com/exodus/3-14.htm

Those who didn't believe Him and who heard Him instantly understood He was claiming to be God, THEY SAID SO!

The Unbelief of the Jews
…32But Jesus responded, "I have shown you many good works from the Father. For which of these do you stone Me?" 33" We are not stoning You for any good work," said the Jews, "but for blasphemy, because You, who are a man, declare Yourself to be God." https://biblehub.com/john/10-33.htm

So, Jesus Christ said that every mention of God in the Holy Bible is referring to Him and He plainly acknowledged He is God -

Jesus Appears to Thomas

…27Then Jesus said to Thomas, "Put your finger here and look at My hands. Reach out your hand and put it into My side. Stop doubting and believe." 28Thomas replied, "My Lord and my God!" 29Jesus said to him, "Because you have seen Me, you have believed; blessed are those who have not seen and yet have believed."… https://biblehub.com/john/20-28.htm

The scriptures tell us when God came in the flesh He did so humbly as a Man (emptied Himself) in order to "condemn sin in the flesh" and to "fulfill the Law and Prophets".

In other words, no one can say to God that He gave us impossible commandments. He proved they can be kept as a Man.

The Attitude of Christ
…6Who, existing in the form of God, did not consider equality with God something to be grasped, 7but emptied Himself, taking the form of a servant, being made in human likeness. 8And being found in appearance as a man, He humbled Himself and became obedient to death—even death on a cross.… https://biblehub.com/philippians/2-7.htm

So, God left Heaven Above (John 1:1-14) to walk among us humbly as a Man, the Messiah, and then when He Returned to Heaven, He again was telling us plainly He is no longer just a humble Man like one of us, but is returning as the Omnipotent God that He is. Jesus Christ is the One who will Judge your soul, if you deny Him, you will be going to the lake of fire - Jn 8:24,25; Jn 3:36; 2Th 1:8-9; Rev 21:8; 22:13

Another common question muslims ask is why God came into this world to suffer and die?

The One True God, Jesus Christ, told His Prophets He would come into this world He created and made as the Messiah, centuries before He actually did so:

https://www.accordingtothescriptures.org/prophecy/353prophecies.html

The One True God, Jesus Christ, told us that He is the One who those scriptures, the Law and Prophecies are all about:

John 5:39-40
39 You search the Scriptures because you think that in them you have eternal life; and it is they that bear witness about me, 40 yet you refuse to come to me that you may have life.

That He is the Fulfillment of His Law and Prophecies:

The Fulfillment of the Law
16In the same way, let your light shine before men, that they may see your good deeds and glorify your Father in heaven. 17Do not think that I have come to abolish the Law or the Prophets. I have not come to abolish them, but to fulfill them. 18For I tell you truly, until heaven and earth pass away, not a single jot, not a stroke of a pen, will disappear from the Law until everything is accomplished.... https://biblehub.com/matthew/5-17.htm

which includes His Law of Redemption and His Prophecies of Salvation:

https://bible.knowing-jesus.com/topics/God,-As-Redeemer and https://www.preceptaustin.org/tetelestai-paid_in_full

God, Jesus Christ, stated plainly, He is the One who has and gives Eternal Life and that He is the Resurrection and the Life and then proved it by publicly dying and raising His Body from the Grave, transfiguring it; making it immortal and glorious and ascended into back into Heaven in front of eyewitnesses. No one else in the entire history of the world both claimed and proved they are God like Jesus Christ. If God had not done what He did, then the wild imaginations of mankind would be endlessly creating false gods and foolish notions. Instead, God showed Himself, proved Himself and told us all how to know Him beyond all doubt, so no one has any excuse.

The Hatred of the World
…23Whoever hates Me hates My Father as well. 24If I had not done among them the works that no one else did, they would not be guilty of sin; but now they have seen and hated both Me and My Father. 25But this is to fulfill what is written in their Law: 'They hated Me without reason.'… https://biblehub.com/john/15-24.htm

24That is why I told you that you would die in your sins. For unless you believe that I am He, you will die in your sins." 25"Who are You?" they asked. "Just what I have been telling you from the beginning," Jesus replied.… https://biblehub.com/john/8-24.htm

…24Martha replied, "I know that he will rise again in the resurrection at the last day." 25 Jesus said to her, "I am the resurrection and the life. Whoever believes in Me will live, even though he dies. 26And everyone who lives and believes in Me will never die. Do you believe this?"… https://biblehub.com/john/11-25.htm

https://www.facebook.com/photo.php?fbid=6609426679136235&set=pb.100002069048072.-2207520000&type=3

a muslim was asking why Christians don't repent? and I responded by saying that is a false accusation because anyone who hasn't repented isn't a Christian.

Every Good thing comes from God, Jesus Christ, even repentance.

Good and Perfect Gifts
…16Do not be deceived, my beloved brothers. 17Every good and perfect gift is from above, coming down from the Father of the heavenly lights, with whom there is no change or shifting shadow. 18He chose to give us birth through the word of truth, that we would be a kind of firstfruits of His creation.… https://biblehub.com/james/1-17.htm

John the Baptist preached Repentance:

Matthew 3
John the Baptist Prepares the Way
3   In those days John the Baptist came, preaching in the wilderness of Judea 2 and saying, "Repent, for the kingdom of heaven has come near." 3 This is he who was spoken of through the prophet Isaiah:

"A voice of one calling in the wilderness,
'Prepare the way for the Lord, make
straight paths for him.'"

4   John's clothes were made of camel's hair, and he had a leather belt around his waist. His food was locusts and wild honey. 5 People went out to him from Jerusalem and all Judea and the whole region of the Jordan. 6 Confessing their sins, they were baptized by him in the Jordan River.

7 But when he saw many of the Pharisees and Sadducees coming to where he was baptizing, he said to them: "You brood of vipers! Who warned you to flee from the coming wrath? 8 Produce fruit in keeping with repentance. 9 And do not think you can say to yourselves, 'We have Abraham as our father.' I tell you that out of these stones God can raise up children for Abraham. 10 The ax is already at the root of the trees, and every tree that does not produce good fruit will be cut down and thrown into the fire.

11 "I baptize you with water for repentance. But after me comes one who is more powerful than I, whose sandals I am not worthy to carry. He will baptize you with[c] the Holy Spirit and fire. 12 His winnowing fork is in his hand, and he will clear his threshing floor, gathering his wheat into the barn and burning up the chaff with unquenchable fire."

So, Repentance Prepares the Way for the Savior. WITHOUT REPENTANCE THERE IS NO SALVATION.

It's why the Divine Commandment is for everyone to REPENT (turn from our wicked thoughts, words, ways and deeds) back to God and His Good and Righteous, Holy Commandments.

Jesus Begins His Ministry
...16the people living in darkness have seen a great light; on those living in the land of the shadow of death, a light has dawned." 17From that time on Jesus began to preach, "Repent, for the kingdom of heaven is near."
https://biblehub.com/matthew/4-17.htm

It's why when Jesus Christ gave His Holy Spirit of Truth to His Apostles on Pentecost, He Commanded through them to EVERYONE:

"Brothers, what shall we do?" 38 Peter replied, "Repent and be baptized, every one of you, in the name of Jesus Christ for the forgiveness of your sins, and you will receive the gift of the Holy Spirit. 39This promise belongs to you and your children and to all who are far off—to all whom the Lord our God will call to Himself."... https://biblehub.com/acts/2-38.htm

So, unless a person REPENTS, the SAVIOR, JESUS CHRIST, will not come into their life by His Holy Spirit of Truth. A person MUST REPENT (be willing to stop sinning and to love and obey God, Jesus Christ, forever) in order to be given the Holy Spirit of Truth, of God, of Jesus Christ. Only when someone has received His Holy Spirit and KNOWS God, KNOWS Jesus Christ, and is learning from Him are they a Christian, and are Saved by the Savior. (John 14:6-26; 8:32-36)

Peter and John Before the Council
...11This Jesus is 'the stone you builders rejected, which has become the cornerstone.' 12 Salvation exists in no one else, for there is no other name under heaven given to men by which we must be saved."
https://biblehub.com/acts/4-12.htm

Romans 8:9-11
9 You, however, are not in the flesh but in the Spirit, if in fact the Spirit of God dwells in you. Anyone who does not have the Spirit of Christ does not belong to him. 10 But if Christ is in you, although the body is dead because of sin, the Spirit is life because of righteousness. 11 If the Spirit of him who raised Jesus from the dead dwells in you, he who raised Christ Jesus[a] from the dead will also give life to your mortal bodies through his Spirit who dwells in you.

So, the scriptures make it very clear that without Repentance there is no Salvation, and without the Savior, Jesus Christ, living in a person by His Holy Spirit of Truth, they are not a Christian. Which is why I stated that anyone who has not repented is not a Christian.

a muslim was falsely accusing Christians again today; this time it was about "original sin".

https://www.biblegateway.com/passage/?search=Romans%205&version=ESV
Everyone, even babes in the flesh can die, so you're not comprehending what the scriptures in the Holy Bible are telling us. (In other words, you're not understanding that reality itself shows us we are all born into bodies of death, what is attributed to the original sin of Adam and Eve.) Don't confuse the fact that all of us are born into bodies of death due to original sin, into thinking that babes and little children are not held innocent spiritually by God.

1) Adam and Eve were with God in the Garden of Eden (no death) 2) they sinned and fell (their very nature changed into a body of death, a body that dies) 3) so all those born through Adam and Eve are also automatically born into bodies of death (even babes and little children die)

The Incarnation of the Messiah was not in or through sin but was an Immaculate Conception, in which God chose to Incarnate through the virgin Mary. (different from all other births in all history, a sinless birth) So only Jesus Christ was conceived sinlessly.

The Sign of Immanuel
...13Then Isaiah said, "Hear now, O house of David! Is it not enough to try the patience of men? Will you try the patience of my God as well? 14Therefore the Lord Himself will give you a sign: Behold, the virgin will be with child and will give birth to a son, and will call Him Immanuel.
https://biblehub.com/isaiah/7-14.htm

Gabriel Foretells Jesus' Birth
...34"How can this be," Mary asked the angel, "since I am a virgin?" 35The angel replied, "The Holy Spirit will come upon you, and the power of the Most High will overshadow you. So the Holy One to be born will be called the Son of God. https://biblehub.com/luke/1-35.htm

So, the birth of Jesus Christ was sinless, unlike all the rest of us.

https://biblehub.com/interlinear/psalms/51-5.htm - ever since Adam and Eve, children are born into bodies of death, (these bodies of flesh all suffer and die, they are all temporal)

Nevertheless, even though our PHYSICAL bodies are sinful bodies of death (https://biblehub.com/romans/7-24.htm) the spirits of children are indeed innocent (until a person comes of age and knows the difference between good and evil, right and wrong, they are innocent.) We know that children are deemed innocent by God by such passages as:

Jesus Blesses the Children
13Then the little children were brought to Jesus for Him to place His hands on them and pray for them. And the disciples rebuked those who brought them. 14But Jesus said, "Let the little children come to Me, and do not hinder them! For the kingdom of heaven belongs to such as these." 15And after He had placed His hands on them, He went on from there....
https://biblehub.com/matthew/19-14.htm

and

David's Loss and Repentance
...22David answered, "While the child was alive, I fasted and wept, for I said, 'Who knows? The LORD may be gracious to me and let him live.' 23But now that he is dead, why should I fast? Can I bring him back again? I will go to him, but he will not return to me."
https://biblehub.com/2_samuel/12-23.htm

So, babes and little children are innocent and belong to God (go to Heaven). Sin is only imputed when people are old enough to understand they have indeed disobeyed God and broken His Commandments in thoughts, words and deeds. (Sin is not just violating all the DO NOTS but neglecting all the DOS. In other words, sins are by commission of crimes and the omission of righteous acts. Whether by deliberate intent or by apathy and neglect, God tells us all have sinned - Romans 3:23)

Abraham Receives the Promise
...14For if those who live by the law are heirs, faith is useless and the promise is worthless, 15because the law brings wrath. And where there is no law, there is no transgression. 16Therefore, the promise comes by faith, so that it may rest on grace and may be guaranteed to all Abraham's offspring—not only to those who are of the law, but also to those who are of the faith of Abraham. He is the father of us all....
https://biblehub.com/romans/4-15.htm

Romans 3:20
Therefore no one will be justified in His sight by works of the law. For the law merely brings awareness of sin.

Romans 5:13
For sin was in the world before the law was given; but sin is not taken into account when there is no law.

Romans 7:7
What then shall we say? Is the law sin? Certainly not! Indeed, I would not have been mindful of sin if not for the law. For I would not have been aware of coveting if the law had not said, "Do not covet."

Romans 7:10
So, I discovered that the very commandment that was meant to bring life actually brought death.

1 Corinthians 15:56
The sting of death is sin, and the power of sin is the law.

So, until a child is mature enough to understand the Law of God, and comprehend they have broken His Law/Commandments and thereby sinned, they are innocent.

(Babes and innocent little children who die go to Heaven to be with God, He doesn't punish little ones who haven't even matured enough to understand His Commandments, His Law and the Consequences for breaking it.)

Romans 2:12-16
God's Judgment and the Law
12 For all who have sinned without the law will also perish without the law, and all who have sinned under the law will be judged by the law. 13 For it is not the hearers of the law who are righteous before God, but the doers of the law who will be justified. 14 For when Gentiles, who do not have the law, by nature do what the law requires, they are a law to themselves, even though they do not have the law. 15 They show that the work of the law is written on their hearts, while their conscience also bears witness, and their conflicting thoughts accuse or even excuse them 16 on that day when, according to my gospel, God judges the secrets of men by Christ Jesus.

So, God tells us that even those who have never read His Words in the Holy Bible, have been given a conscience by Him (His law written on their hearts) and that when a person is old and mature enough, that conscience tells them whether or not they have violated His Commandments. In other words, no one has any excuse once they are convicted by their own conscience of having done something they know is wrong. ALL are commanded therefore to REPENT but only AFTER they receive the Knowledge of Truth, only AFTER they are mature enough to understand right and wrong and the need to REPENT of all wrongdoing. (This is why Christ wasn't baptized with the Baptism of Repentance until He was mature; as our example, even though He had nothing to repent of.)

So, we have all inherited a sinful nature (these temporal bodies of flesh, sin, lusts and death) BUT little children are still held as innocent in their spirits (Heaven Bound) until they reach a mature enough age to comprehend God, His Commandments and the Need to REPENT of any and all wrongdoing.

The Great Commission
...15And He said to them, "Go into all the world and preach the gospel to every creature. 16Whoever believes and is baptized will be saved, but whoever does not believe will be condemned.
https://biblehub.com/mark/16-16.htm

"Brothers, what shall we do?" 38 Peter replied, "Repent and be baptized, every one of you, in the name of Jesus Christ for the forgiveness of your sins, and you will receive the gift of the Holy Spirit. 39This promise belongs to you and your children and to all who are far off—to all whom the Lord our God will call to Himself."... https://biblehub.com/acts/2-38.htm

Yet another muslim was repeating their lying brainwashing today and claiming wrongly that Numbers 23:19 tells us God is not a Man. (PERIOD) which is not a correct rendering of that verse at all.

God tells us to study His Words:

The Lord's Approved Workman

14Remind the believers of these things, charging them before God to avoid quarreling over words, which succeeds only in leading the listeners to ruin. 15Make every effort to present yourself approved to God, an unashamed workman who accurately handles the word of truth. 16But avoid irreverent, empty chatter, which will only lead to more ungodliness,... https://biblehub.com/2_timothy/2-15.htm

And when you do, you read in the very first chapter:

26Then God said, "Let Us make man in Our image, after Our likeness, to rule over the fish of the sea and the birds of the air, over the livestock, and over all the earth itself and every creature that crawls upon it." 27So God created man in His own image; in the image of God He created him; male and female He created them.... https://biblehub.com/genesis/1-26.htm

https://biblehub.com/hebrew/1823.htm - image/likeness so even in the very first chapter of the Holy Bible God plainly tells us He is a Man and that men are gods. He confirms this elsewhere:

The Unbelief of the Jews

…33"We are not stoning You for any good work," said the Jews, "but for blasphemy, because You, who are a man, declare Yourself to be God." 34 Jesus replied, "Is it not written in your Law: 'I have said you are gods'? 35If he called them gods to whom the word of God came—and the Scripture cannot be broken— 36then what about the One whom the Father sanctified and sent into the world? How then can you accuse Me of blasphemy for stating that I am the Son of God? 37If I am not doing the works of My Father, then do not believe Me.…
https://biblehub.com/john/10-34.htm

God plainly told His Prophets hundreds of times He would come in the flesh as the Messiah, a Man:

https://www.accordingtothescriptures.org/prophecy/353prophecies.html

And when He did so, He said He is the God who spoke to His Prophets and whom all the Prophets testify of:

John 5:39-40

39 You search the Scriptures because you think that in them you have eternal life; and it is they that bear witness about me, 40 yet you refuse to come to me that you may have life.

Jesus Opens the Scriptures

...26Was it not necessary for the Christ to suffer these things and then to enter His glory?" 27And beginning with Moses and all the Prophets, He explained to them what was written in all the Scriptures about Himself.
https://biblehub.com/luke/24-27.htm

John 8:48-59

Before Abraham Was, I Am

48 The Jews answered him, "Are we not right in saying that you are a Samaritan and have a demon?" 49 Jesus answered, "I do not have a demon, but I honor my Father, and you dishonor me. 50 Yet I do not seek my own glory; there is One who seeks it, and he is the judge. 51 Truly, truly, I say to you, if anyone keeps my word, he will never see death." 52 The Jews said to him, "Now we know that you have a demon! Abraham died, as did the prophets, yet you say, 'If anyone keeps my word, he will never taste death.' 53 Are you greater than our father Abraham, who died? And the prophets died! Who do you make yourself out to be?" 54 Jesus answered, "If I glorify myself, my glory is nothing. It is my Father who glorifies me, of whom you say, 'He is our God.'[a] 55 But you have not known him. I know him. If I were to say that I do not know him, I would be a liar like you, but I do know him and I keep his word. 56 Your father Abraham rejoiced that he would see my day. He saw it and was glad." 57 So the Jews said to him, "You are not yet fifty years old, and have you seen Abraham?"[b] 58 Jesus said to them, "Truly, truly, I say to you, before Abraham was, I am." 59 So they picked up stones to throw at him, but Jesus hid himself and went out of the temple.

Acts 10:34-43

34 So Peter opened his mouth and said: "Truly I understand that God shows no partiality, 35 but in every nation anyone who fears him and does what is right is acceptable to him. 36 As for the word that he sent to Israel, preaching good news of peace through Jesus Christ (he is Lord of all), 37 you yourselves know what happened throughout all Judea, beginning from Galilee after the baptism that John proclaimed: 38 how God anointed Jesus of Nazareth with the Holy Spirit and with power. He went about doing good and healing all who were oppressed by the devil, for God was

with him. 39 And we are witnesses of all that he did both in the country of the Jews and in Jerusalem. They put him to death by hanging him on a tree, 40 but God raised him on the third day and made him to appear, 41 not to all the people but to us who had been chosen by God as witnesses, who ate and drank with him after he rose from the dead. 42 And he commanded us to preach to the people and to testify that he is the one appointed by God to be judge of the living and the dead. 43 To him all the prophets bear witness that everyone who believes in him receives forgiveness of sins through his name."

(Verse 36 Jesus Christ is LORD of ALL and verse 43 ALL PROPHETS BEAR WITNESS OF JESUS CHRIST, LORD OF ALL, and that FORGIVENESS OF SINS IS ONLY THROUGH HIM, BY NAME)

So Jesus Christ is God who came in the flesh as a Man and walked among us, showing us He is God, Proving He is God and telling us all how to know and learn from Him personally now and forever.

https://www.facebook.com/photo.php?fbid=6471680786244159&set=pb.100002069048072.-2207520000&type=3

So then when you actually do study the verses you cited:

https://biblehub.com/interlinear/numbers/23-19.htm - you see that the original language has no punctuation marks and that the first part of the verse refers to "ish" LIARS. So in modern English that reads God doesn't tell lies like sinful men do, and then the second part refers to a son of "Adam" so in the original language the verse says: God doesn't tell lies like sinful men do, and He doesn't need to repent even like the sons of Adam. (God is telling us He isn't a wicked liar, and also contrasting that He doesn't even make mistakes like the righteous sons of Adam do; in other words, God is Perfect, tells no lies, and makes no mistakes/sins like all the rest of us.) But what the verse doesn't say is "God is not a man." PERIOD. You have to STUDY! because sadly, too many make such a false claim as "God is not a man." PERIOD! which would require tossing out the entire Holy Bible.

God is a Man and men are gods, He says so quite plainly in the very first chapter and throughout the entire Holy Bible.

To clarify further:

Colossians 1:15-19

The Supremacy of the Son of God

15 The Son is the image of the invisible God, the firstborn over all creation. 16 For in him all things were created: things in heaven and on earth, visible and invisible, whether thrones or powers or rulers or authorities; all things have been created through him and for him. 17 He is before all things, and in him all things hold together. 18 And he is the head of the body, the church; he is the beginning and the firstborn from among the dead, so that in everything he might have the supremacy. 19 For God was pleased to have all his fullness dwell in him,

Jesus Christ is SUPREME in EVERYTHING which means He is the: God of gods, Man of men, Angel of angels, Spirit of spirits, King of kings, Lord of Lords, Father of fathers, Son of sons, Star of stars, Gate of gates, Door of doors, Teacher of teachers, Servant of servants, Prophet of prophets, First and Last, etc. etc. etc. which is why the scriptures refer to Him in all these ways and more.

Then another muslim was asking what makes someone a Prophet?

Prophets all have the Holy Spirit of Jesus Christ, the One True God, and testify of Him accordingly.

Eyewitnesses of His Majesty
…20Above all, you must understand that no prophecy of Scripture comes from one's own interpretation. 21For no such prophecy was ever brought forth by the will of man, but men spoke from God as they were carried along by the Holy Spirit. https://biblehub.com/2_peter/1-21.htm

2 Samuel 23:2
The Spirit of the LORD spoke through me; His word was on my tongue.

The Ascension
…7Jesus replied, "It is not for you to know times or seasons that the Father has fixed by His own authority. 8But you will receive power when the Holy Spirit comes upon you, and you will be My witnesses in Jerusalem, and in all Judea and Samaria, and to the ends of the earth."
https://biblehub.com/acts/1-8.htm

Acts 10:34-43
34 So Peter opened his mouth and said: "Truly I understand that God shows no partiality, 35 but in every nation anyone who fears him and does what is right is acceptable to him. 36 As for the word that he sent to Israel, preaching good news of peace through Jesus Christ (he is Lord of all), 37 you yourselves know what happened throughout all Judea, beginning from Galilee after the baptism that John proclaimed: 38 how God anointed Jesus of Nazareth with the Holy Spirit and with power. He went about doing good and healing all who were oppressed by the devil, for God was with him. 39 And we are witnesses of all that he did both in the country of the Jews and in Jerusalem. They put him to death by hanging him on a tree, 40 but God raised him on the third day and made him to appear, 41 not to all the people but to us who had been chosen by God as witnesses, who ate and drank with him after he rose from the dead. 42 And he commanded us to preach to the people and to testify that he is the one appointed by God to be judge of the living and the dead. 43 To him all the prophets bear witness that everyone who believes in him receives forgiveness of sins through his name."

(Verse 36 - Jesus Christ is LORD of ALL and verse 43 - ALL Prophets bear witness of Jesus Christ, Lord of All, and that forgiveness of sins is only through Him, by Name.)

The Marriage of the Lamb
...9Then the angel told me to write, "Blessed are those who are invited to the marriage supper of the Lamb." And he said to me, "These are the true words of God." 10So I fell at his feet to worship him. But he told me, "Do not do that! I am a fellow servant with you and your brothers who rely on the testimony of Jesus. Worship God! For the testimony of Jesus is the spirit of prophecy." https://biblehub.com/revelation/19-10.htm

THE TESTIMONY OF JESUS CHRIST IS THE SPIRIT OF PROPHECY!

https://biblehub.com/joel/2-28.htm - GOD, JESUS CHRIST, POURS OUT HIS HOLY SPIRIT UPON HIS PROPHETS TO EMPOWER THEM TO SPEAK HIS WORDS, TO TESTIFY THAT HE IS GOD!

Acts 2:17
In the last days, God says, I will pour out My Spirit on all people. Your sons and daughters will prophesy, your young men will see visions, your old men will dream dreams.

GOD, JESUS CHRIST, HAS PROMISED TO GIVE HIS HOLY SPIRIT OF TRUTH TO ALL WHO REPENT AND ARE BAPTIZED IN HIS NAME, SO THAT ALL CAN KNOW HIM, JUST LIKE THE PROPHETS!

37When the people heard this, they were cut to the heart and asked Peter and the other apostles, "Brothers, what shall we do?" 38 Peter replied,

"Repent and be baptized, every one of you, in the name of Jesus Christ for the forgiveness of your sins, and you will receive the gift of the Holy Spirit. 39This promise belongs to you and your children and to all who are far off—to all whom the Lord our God will call to Himself."…
https://biblehub.com/acts/2-38.htm

I REPEAT! YOU CAN BE A PROPHET OF GOD! YOU CAN KNOW GOD! OBEY HIM AND REPENT AND BE BAPTIZED IN THE NAME OF OUR LORD AND SAVIOR, JESUS, THE CHRIST!

John 14:20-26
20 In that day you will know that I am in my Father, and you in me, and I in you. 21 Whoever has my commandments and keeps them, he it is who loves me. And he who loves me will be loved by my Father, and I will love him and manifest myself to him." 22 Judas (not Iscariot) said to him, "Lord, how is it that you will manifest yourself to us, and not to the world?" 23 Jesus answered him, "If anyone loves me, he will keep my word, and my Father will love him, and we will come to him and make our home with him. 24 Whoever does not love me does not keep my words. And the word that you hear is not mine but the Father's who sent me.

25 "These things I have spoken to you while I am still with you. 26 But the Helper, the Holy Spirit, whom the Father will send in my name, he will teach you all things and bring to your remembrance all that I have said to you.

muslims aren't the only ones trying to interpret the Holy Bible with their carnal minds and connotations, but they are the ones most notoriously doing so. Today one of them was trying to justify polygamy with the Prophecy about the Messiah in Isaiah Ch. 4

It takes a muslim who is in a perverse sex cult, to imagine that the Holy Bible justifies their perversions, when it doesn't. (in other words, muslims are all about gratifying their lusts, their selfish desires of their carnal flesh, as evidenced that they are so perverse they imagine their depraved notion of paradise is all about constant erections to molest virgins endlessly) muslims are demonstrating depravity at completely unacceptable levels and is why they cannot understand the Words of God in the Holy Bible unless they all repent of such overt wickedness.

To be sure, ANYONE who interprets PROPHECIES through the eyes of the flesh (as if that prophecy is speaking about gratifying their fleshly lusts and depravity) is MISINTERPRETING Holy Writ!

Romans 8:7-9 NKJV
Because the carnal mind is enmity against God; for it is not subject to the law of God, nor indeed can be. So then, those who are in the flesh cannot please God. But you are not in the flesh but in the Spirit, if indeed the Spirit of God dwells in you. Now if anyone does not have the Spirit of Christ, he is not His.

(If you are thinking about gratifying your flesh, your sinful lusts and desires, you are still in your sins and are an enemy of God.)

If you, as a carnally minded person, still sinning in your thoughts, words and deeds, try and interpret Prophecies in the Holy Bible, which are given by the Holy Spirit of God, and must be understood by His Spirit (SPIRITUALLY) not carnally, then you are MISINTERPRETING His Words (lying about God and His Words given us).

Spiritual Wisdom
...13And this is what we speak, not in words taught us by human wisdom, but in words taught by the Spirit, expressing spiritual truths in spiritual words. 14 The natural man does not accept the things that come from the Spirit of God. For they are foolishness to him, and he cannot understand them, because they are spiritually discerned. 15The spiritual man judges

all things, but he himself is not subject to anyone's judgment....
https://biblehub.com/1_corinthians/2-14.htm
Only when someone REPENTS and is Baptized in the Name of our Lord and Savior, JESUS, the Christ, do they receive His HOLY SPIRIT of TRUTH! (Mark 16:15-16, Matthew 28:18-20; Acts 2:38-39; 4:12; Jn 14:20-26; 1Jn 2:20-27; Romans 8:8-10) and only then do they begin to understand His Words in the Holy Bible correctly!

John 14:17
the Spirit of truth. The world cannot receive Him, because it neither sees Him nor knows Him. But you do know Him, for He abides with you and will be in you.

1 Corinthians 1:18
For the message of the cross is foolishness to those who are perishing, but to us who are being saved it is the power of God.

1 Corinthians 1:21
For since in the wisdom of God the world through its wisdom did not know Him, God was pleased through the foolishness of what was preached to save those who believe.

1 Corinthians 1:23 but we preach Christ crucified, a stumbling block to Jews and foolishness to Gentiles,

1 Corinthians 1:25
For the foolishness of God is wiser than man's wisdom, and the weakness of God is stronger than man's strength.

1 Corinthians 3:1
Brothers, I could not address you as spiritual, but as worldly--as infants in Christ.

https://www.biblegateway.com/passage/?search=Isaiah%203&version=ESV - so when we read His Words, we understand God is talking about the sins of people leading them into serious Divine Consequences. (oppression, destruction, war and death)

and that afterward
https://www.biblegateway.com/passage/?search=Isaiah%204&version=ESV

https://www.icr.org/article/18767 - the Messiah, the Branch would come and be Glorified

https://juchre.org/isaiah53/branch.htm - the Branch (capitals in the Old Testament are references to God, the Messiah. (God IS the Messiah, the Savior of mankind; His Name in English, is Jesus the Christ.)

So, when judgment, oppression, death and destruction precedes the Prophecy of His Coming as the Messiah and is linked by the verse that talks of 7 women holding One Man, saying take away our reproach. That is a Prophecy of the Messiah and the 7 churches (written about in Revelation) who are all Redeemed and cleansed by God, the Messiah, the Branch - Jesus Christ. (has nothing whatsoever to do with carnal polygamy).
The Church is called the Bride of Christ -
https://www.biblegateway.com/passage/?search=Ephesians%205%3A22-33&version=ESV and
https://www.biblegateway.com/passage/?search=Revelation%2021&version=KJV (Rev 21:2)

And so, the seven churches in the Book of Rev Ch. 1-3 are the seven women taking hold of the Messiah, the Branch, saying take away our reproach. They come humbly, realizing how they have sinned before Him, saying, let us be called by your Name (Jesus Christ - Christians).

Again, no prophecy in the Holy Bible is about gratifying fleshly, carnal lusts and is all to be spiritually understood.

https://biblehub.com/john/6-63.htm

muslims are constantly denigrating the One True God, Jesus Christ, by wrongly imagining He was just another man like them. So they say things like how can he die for us? How can a man die for another man? So they falsely accuse the Holy Bible of making a contradiction when there is none.

No contradiction: if you owe 1000, and you cannot pay your own debt, then you can't pay the debt of someone else either. Likewise, if you are under your own death sentence, you cannot die for anyone else, because you must pay your own sentence.

So only God, who is Eternal and truly INNOCENT, could pay the debt for the sins of all mankind.

https://bible.knowing-jesus.com/topics/God,-As-Redeemer and that's what He did - https://www.preceptaustin.org/tetelestai-paid_in_full

If you choose to deny that He did so, you are welcome to die in your sins and end up in the lake of fire for your own sins.

24That is why I told you that you would die in your sins. For unless you believe that I am He, you will die in your sins." 25"Who are You?" they asked. "Just what I have been telling you from the beginning," Jesus replied.... https://biblehub.com/john/8-24.htm

If you choose to be a wicked ingrate for what God did to Save you, you are welcome to His Wrath:

2 Thessalonians 1:8-9

8	In flaming fire taking vengeance on them that know not God, and that obey not the gospel of our Lord Jesus Christ:

9	Who shall be punished with everlasting destruction from the presence of the Lord, and from the glory of his power;

A New Heaven and a New Earth
...7The one who overcomes will inherit all things, and I will be his God, and he will be My son. 8But to the cowardly and unbelieving and abominable and murderers and sexually immoral and sorcerers and idolaters and all liars, their place will be in the lake that burns with fire and sulfur. This is the second death." https://biblehub.com/revelation/21-8.htm

The wise choose to Obey Him instead:

The Great Commission
...15And He said to them, "Go into all the world and preach the gospel to every creature. 16Whoever believes and is baptized will be saved, but whoever does not believe will be condemned.
https://biblehub.com/mark/16-16.htm

37When the people heard this, they were cut to the heart and asked Peter and the other apostles, "Brothers, what shall we do?" 38 Peter replied, "Repent and be baptized, every one of you, in the name of Jesus Christ for the forgiveness of your sins, and you will receive the gift of the Holy Spirit. 39This promise belongs to you and your children and to all who are far off—to all whom the Lord our God will call to Himself."...
https://biblehub.com/acts/2-38.htm

Peter and John Before the Council
...11This Jesus is 'the stone you builders rejected, which has become the cornerstone.' 12 Salvation exists in no one else, for there is no other name under heaven given to men by which we must be saved."
https://biblehub.com/acts/4-12.htm

Another extremely evil thing that muslims do rather constantly is to falsely claim that we cannot trust the contents of the Holy Bible because mankind has somehow corrupted it.

https://carm.org/about-the-bible/manuscript-evidence-for-superior-newtestament-reliability/

Whenever muslims falsely allege the Holy Bible has been changed so that it's not true to the original, it makes them look ignorant and deceptive.

The Holy Bible has tens of thousands of ancient manuscripts to compare any and all versions to.

https://carm.org/about-the-bible/manuscript-evidence-for-superior-newtestament-reliability/

https://hc.edu/museums/dunham-bible-museum/tour-of-themuseum/past-exhibits/biblical-manuscripts/

So, the Holy Bible has remained true throughout the generations of mankind and provably so.

Likewise, in all translations the Holy Bible tells everyone how to know the One True God and learn from Him personally. So, the Holy Bible is not just historically true, but verifiably comes from God because it leads us all to KNOWING HIM AND LEARNING FROM HIM PERSONALLY! (is verifiably Divinely Inspired and True.)

https://www.facebook.com/photo/?fbid=1408899032522385&set=a.115635768515391

So, anyone claiming mere mortals changed His Words in the Holy Bible, He has caused to be written, published and translated worldwide, is saying God is impotent against mere mortals to preserve His Own Words. (blasphemy)

https://www.facebook.com/photo.php?fbid=4890242114388042&set=pb.100002069048072.-2207520000&type=3

So, anyone denigrating the contents of the Holy Bible in any way is lying to themselves and the world and is committing blasphemy against the One True God.

33 Heaven and earth will pass away, but My words will never pass away.
https://biblehub.com/luke/21-33.htm

Today another muslim was denying Jesus Christ is God, even though the entire Holy Bible says so quite plainly. His excuse was that Jesus didn't tell us the day and hour of His Return. I told him that the reason God didn't tell us the day and hour of His Return was that He Commands us all to REPENT NOW IMMEDIATELY and not to put it off, and he sneeringly responded that I must not state my opinion, but only scriptures. So here it is muslims:

"Brothers, what shall we do?" 38 Peter replied, "Repent and be baptized, every one of you, in the name of Jesus Christ for the forgiveness of your sins, and you will receive the gift of the Holy Spirit. 39This promise belongs to you and your children and to all who are far off—to all whom the Lord our God will call to Himself."... https://biblehub.com/acts/2-38.htm

Jesus Begins His Ministry
...16the people living in darkness have seen a great light; on those living in the land of the shadow of death, a light has dawned." 17From that time on Jesus began to preach, "Repent, for the kingdom of heaven is near."
https://biblehub.com/matthew/4-17.htm

2For He says: "In the time of favor I heard you, and in the day of salvation I helped you." Behold, now is the time of favor; now is the day of salvation!
https://biblehub.com/2_corinthians/6-2.htm

16Then Jesus came to Nazareth, where He had been brought up. As was His custom, He entered the synagogue on the Sabbath. And when He stood up to read, 17the scroll of the prophet Isaiah was handed to Him. Unrolling it, He found the place where it was written: 18"The Spirit of the Lord is on

Me, because He has anointed Me to preach good news to the poor. He has sent Me to proclaim liberty to the captives and recovery of sight to the blind, to release the oppressed, 19to proclaim the year of the Lord's favor."20Then He rolled up the scroll, returned it to the attendant, and sat down. The eyes of everyone in the synagogue were fixed on Him, 21and He began by saying, "Today this Scripture is fulfilled in your hearing."...
https://biblehub.com/luke/4-20.htm

The Parable of the Barren Fig Tree

[6] And he told this parable: "A man had a fig tree planted in his vineyard, and he came seeking fruit on it and found none. [7] And he said to the vinedresser, 'Look, for three years now I have come seeking fruit on this fig tree, and I find none. Cut it down. Why should it use up the ground?' [8] And he answered him, 'Sir, let it alone this year also, until I dig around it and put on manure. [9] Then if it should bear fruit next year, well and good; but if not, you can cut it down.'"

Everyone who doesn't obey God, Jesus Christ, and Repent of every evil thought, word, way and deed; every wicked way, and learn to live righteously by His Grace and Power is risking being cutoff and cast into the lake of fire. https://www.bible.com/bible/8/JHN.15.2-6.AMPC and https://www.biblegateway.com/passage/?search=Matthew+7%3A1520&version=ESV (muhammad was a criminal so muslims are following a false prophet (tree with bad fruit) that God warned us all about - https://www.thereligionofpeace.com/pages/articles/jesusmuhammad.aspx)

John 15:2-6 AMPC

Any branch in Me that does not bear fruit [that stops bearing] He cuts away (trims off, takes away); and He cleanses and repeatedly prunes every branch that continues to bear fruit, to make it bear more and richer and more excellent fruit. You are cleansed and pruned already, because of the word which I have given you [the teachings I have discussed with you].

Dwell in Me, and I will dwell in you. [Live in Me, and I will live in you.] Just as no branch can bear fruit of itself without abiding in (being vitally united to) the vine, neither can you bear fruit unless you abide in Me. I am the Vine; you are the branches. Whoever lives in Me and I in him bears much (abundant) fruit. However, apart from Me [cut off from vital union with Me] you can do nothing. If a person does not dwell in Me, he is thrown out like a [broken-off] branch, and withers; such branches are gathered up and thrown into the fire, and they are burned.

Matthew 7:15-20

A Tree and Its Fruit

15 "Beware of false prophets, who come to you in sheep's clothing but inwardly are ravenous wolves. **16** You will recognize them by their fruits. Are grapes gathered from thorn bushes, or figs from thistles? **17** So, every healthy tree bears good fruit, but the diseased tree bears bad fruit. **18** A healthy tree cannot bear bad fruit, nor can a diseased tree bear good fruit. **19** Every tree that does not bear good fruit is cut down and thrown into the fire. **20** Thus you will recognize them by their fruits.

The Great Commission
…15And He said to them, "Go into all the world and preach the gospel to every creature. 16Whoever believes and is baptized will be saved, but whoever does not believe will be condemned.
https://biblehub.com/mark/16-16.htm

So, the Commandment of God is for everyone to REPENT NOW! and Be Baptized in the Name of our Lord Jesus Christ IMMEDIATELY, otherwise you could perish in your sins and face His Wrath!

24That is why I told you that you would die in your sins. For unless you believe that I am He, you will die in your sins." **25**"Who are You?" they asked. "Just what I have been telling you from the beginning," Jesus replied.... https://biblehub.com/john/8-24.htm

The Great Commission
...18Then Jesus came to them and said, "All authority in heaven and on earth has been given to Me. 19Therefore go and make disciples of all nations, baptizing them in the name of the Father, and of the Son, and of the Holy Spirit, 20and teaching them to obey all that I have commanded you. And surely I am with you always, even to the end of the age."...
https://biblehub.com/matthew/28-19.htm

37When the people heard this, they were cut to the heart and asked Peter and the other apostles, "Brothers, what shall we do?" 38 Peter replied, "Repent and be baptized, every one of you, in the name of Jesus Christ for the forgiveness of your sins, and you will receive the gift of the Holy Spirit. 39This promise belongs to you and your children and to all who are far off—to all whom the Lord our God will call to Himself."...
https://biblehub.com/acts/2-38.htm

Peter and John Before the Council
...11This Jesus is 'the stone you builders rejected, which has become the cornerstone.' 12 Salvation exists in no one else, for there is no other name under heaven given to men by which we must be saved." 13When they saw the boldness of Peter and John and realized that they were unschooled, ordinary men, they marveled and took note that these men had been with Jesus.... https://biblehub.com/acts/4-12.htm

(not my opinion, GOD's COMMANDMENT!)

Philip and the Ethiopian

...35Then Philip began with this very Scripture and told him the good news about Jesus. 36 As they traveled along the road and came to some water, the eunuch said, "Look, here is water! What is there to prevent me from being baptized?" ... https://biblehub.com/acts/8-36.htm

Matthew 3:6
Confessing their sins, they were baptized by him in the Jordan River.

Matthew 3:11
I baptize you with water for repentance, but after me will come One more powerful than I, whose sandals I am not worthy to carry. He will baptize you with the Holy Spirit and with fire.

Acts 8:37
And Philip said, If thou believest with all thine heart, thou mayest. And he answered and said, I believe that Jesus Christ is the Son of God.

Acts 10:47
"Can anyone withhold the water to baptize these people? They have received the Holy Spirit just as we have!"

Anyone putting off obeying God's Commandment to REPENT NOW! TODAY! is risking His Wrath and the flames of damnation! Especially any so foolish as to wait for His Return. (so that's why He doesn't tell us the day or hour)

Be Watchful for the Day
34But watch yourselves, or your hearts will be weighed down by dissipation, drunkenness, and the worries of life—and that day will spring upon you suddenly like a snare. 35For it will come upon all who dwell on the face of all the earth. 36So keep watch at all times, and pray that you

may have the strength to escape all that is about to happen and to stand before the Son of Man."... https://biblehub.com/luke/21-35.htm

Psalm 11:6
Upon the wicked he shall rain snares, fire and brimstone, and an horrible tempest: this shall be the portion of their cup.

1 Thessalonians 5:1-6
The Day of the Lord
5 Now concerning the times and the seasons, brothers,[a] you have no need to have anything written to you. 2 For you yourselves are fully aware that the day of the Lord will come like a thief in the night. 3 While people are saying, "There is peace and security," then sudden destruction will come upon them as labor pains come upon a pregnant woman, and they will not escape. 4 But you are not in darkness, brothers, for that day to surprise you like a thief. 5 For you are all children[b] of light, children of the day. We are not of the night or of the darkness. 6 So then let us not sleep, as others do, but let us keep awake and be sober.

2 Thessalonians 1:8-9
8   In flaming fire taking vengeance on them that know not God, and that obey not the gospel of our Lord Jesus Christ:

9   Who shall be punished with everlasting destruction from the presence of the Lord, and from the glory of his power;

A New Heaven and a New Earth
...7The one who overcomes will inherit all things, and I will be his God, and he will be My son. 8But to the cowardly and unbelieving and abominable and murderers and sexually immoral and sorcerers and idolaters and all liars, their place will be in the lake that burns with fire and sulfur. This is the second death." https://biblehub.com/revelation/21-8.htm

Not one muslim sees, hears or knows God, and that's because they are all denying Him and disobeying Him instead. OBEY THE LIVING GOD muslims! REPENT AND GET BAPTIZED IN THE NAME OF OUR LORD JESUS CHRIST RIGHT NOW! for why will you perish in your sins?

muslims constantly misrepresent the contents of the Holy Bible, due to their islamic brainwashing. NOTHING in the Holy Bible justifies the lies of islam, such as how they imagine Matthew 7:21-23 is condemning anyone for worshipping Jesus Christ when that is not what He said at all.

Notice how lying muslims always change what is actually written in the Holy Bible to make false claims.

Matthew 7
Judging Others
7 "Judge not, that you be not judged. 2 For with the judgment you pronounce you will be judged, and with the measure you use it will be measured to you. 3 Why do you see the speck that is in your brother's eye, but do not notice the log that is in your own eye? 4 Or how can you say to your brother, 'Let me take the speck out of your eye,' when there is the log in your own eye? 5 You hypocrite, first take the log out of your own eye, and then you will see clearly to take the speck out of your brother's eye.

6   "Do not give dogs what is holy, and do not throw your pearls before pigs, lest they trample them underfoot and turn to attack you.

Ask, and It Will Be Given
7   "Ask, and it will be given to you; seek, and you will find; knock, and it will be opened to you. 8 For everyone who asks receives, and the one who seeks finds, and to the one who knocks it will be opened. 9 Or which one of you, if his son asks him for bread, will give him a stone? 10 Or if he asks for a fish, will give him a serpent? 11 If you then, who are evil, know how to give good gifts to your children, how much more will your Father who is in heaven give good things to those who ask him!

The Golden Rule

12 "So whatever you wish that others would do to you, do also to them, for this is the Law and the Prophets.

13 "Enter by the narrow gate. For the gate is wide and the way is easy[a] that leads to destruction, and those who enter by it are many. 14 For the gate is narrow and the way is hard that leads to life, and those who find it are few.

A Tree and Its Fruit

15 "Beware of false prophets, who come to you in sheep's clothing but inwardly are ravenous wolves. 16 You will recognize them by their fruits. Are grapes gathered from thornbushes, or figs from thistles? 17 So, every healthy tree bears good fruit, but the diseased tree bears bad fruit. 18 A healthy tree cannot bear bad fruit, nor can a diseased tree bear good fruit. 19 Every tree that does not bear good fruit is cut down and thrown into the fire. 20 Thus you will recognize them by their fruits.

I Never Knew You

21 "Not everyone who says to me, 'Lord, Lord,' will enter the kingdom of heaven, but the one who does the will of my Father who is in heaven. 22 On that day many will say to me, 'Lord, Lord, did we not prophesy in your name, and cast out demons in your name, and do many mighty works in your name?' 23 And then will I declare to them, 'I never knew you; depart from me, you workers of lawlessness.'

So, in context, our Lord Jesus Christ is talking about how to tell the difference between true and false people. (How to tell the difference especially between religious people who CLAIM to love Him from those who actually do.)

He starts off by telling us all not to act like we are God Himself in condemning others (especially falsely accusing like you have just done.)

Then He warns us of FALSE prophets (people who claim they love Him and speak for Him - people like muslims!) religious hypocrites who honor Him with their lips but do not OBEY Him. (instead, are without Him and His Commandments/Law and following the lies of wicked muhammad all while saying "PBUH" habitually.)

so muslims are the ones who honor/worship Him IN VAIN because THEY DO NOT DO AS HE COMMANDS!

Likewise, there are people who call themselves Christians, sing songs to Him but DO NOT DO AS HE COMMANDS!

Tradition and Worship
…7You hypocrites! Isaiah prophesied correctly about you: 8'These people honor Me with their lips, but their hearts are far from Me. 9They worship Me in vain; they teach as doctrine the precepts of men.' "…
https://biblehub.com/matthew/15-8.htm

So, ALL religious people pretending to worship God, but NOT DOING WHAT HE COMMANDS is who He is condemning.

IN VAIN do they honor/worship me, all while teaching commandments of men (muhammad) instead of obeying GOD, Jesus Christ!

IN VAIN do muslims say "PBUH" but do not do what He, Jesus Christ, the One True God, commands.

Likewise FALSE Christians, who sing His Praises but ignore His Commandments are who He is talking about.

We know He is talking about FALSE Christians because HE JUST WARNED US ALL HOW TO TELL THE DIFFERENCE BETWEEN TRUE AND FALSE! in the preceding verses.

So, Jesus Christ is NOT condemning those who love, worship and obey Him, He is condemning those who only honor/worship Him with their lips, instead of their lives.

To be sure Jesus Christ is not just condemning lip-service muslims, who say "PBUH" and falsely claim to love Him but do not know, love and obey Him in Spirit and Truth as He commands, but God is condemning all who practice their manmade religions in vain in this passage, religious hypocrites who have never truly repented, never stopped sinning and instead, imagine their claimed good deeds will somehow justify themselves before Him.

God knows everyone and everything; so, this means that He was addressing those who are false, religious people practicing their manmade religions, maybe even calling themselves Christians, but do not KNOW Him. Are not DOING what GOD Commands, and instead practicing their religion in vain. God often addressed the religious hypocrites that He said were like whitewashed tombs, all concerned about their outward appearances but were dead to Him inside; still lost in their sins.

Listen to what He tells us about how those people tried to justify themselves... Didn't I do this? and Didn't I do that?

When the scriptures make it crystal clear that we are Saved by what He did! His Grace! His Power! His Blood! not any of our deeds, done as religious dogmas or not. If we LOVE Him, we OBEY Him, not in any way to justify ourselves before Him, but strictly because He Loved us first and

Gave Himself to Save us, and so the very least we can do to thank Him, is humbly obey Him, seeking to Please Him out of the Love He gives us to Love Him and others in return. (Ephesians 2:1-10) if we don't Know Him, we are still dead to Him, still lost in our sins; still devoid of His Holy Spirit of Truth in our lives. (Rom 8:4-10, Acts 2:38-39; John 14:20-26; 1Jn 2:20-27, Acts 1:8)

What everyone who reads that passage, needs to ask themselves is, "Do you KNOW Him? Do you LOVE Him? Are you obeying Him?" or are you practicing religion in vain?

We can tell they do not KNOW Him because they try to justify themselves by claims of what they have done, rather than bowing before God, saying YOU ALONE are our LORD and SAVIOR, Saved by GRACE, not by our own efforts and works.

Ephesians 2:1-10 ESV
And you were dead in the trespasses and sins in which you once walked, following the course of this world, following the prince of the power of the air, the spirit that is now at work in the sons of disobedience— among whom we all once lived in the passions of our flesh, carrying out the desires of the body and the mind, and were by nature children of wrath, like the rest of mankind. But God, being rich in mercy, because of the great love with which he loved us, even when we were dead in our trespasses, made us alive together with Christ—by grace you have been saved— and raised us up with him and seated us with him in the heavenly places in Christ Jesus, so that in the coming ages he might show the immeasurable riches of his grace in kindness toward us in Christ Jesus. For by grace you have been saved through faith. And this is not your own doing; it is the gift of God, not a result of works, so that no one may boast. For we are his workmanship, created in Christ Jesus for good works, which God prepared beforehand, that we should walk in them.

So, when muslims cite this passage, they wrongly imagine Jesus Christ is telling people not to worship Him when that isn't what He is saying at all.

https://www.openbible.info/topics/worshipping_jesus - Jesus Christ never told anyone not to worship Him

Instead, He is condemning those who worship Him **IN VAIN** (honoring Him with only their lips, instead of their lives) living wickedly, teaching doctrines of men (like muslims) all while ignoring His Commandments and the fact that not one of them knows Him.

So, if you don't want to be someone God tells to depart from Him, you need to OBEY Him!

https://www.facebook.com/photo.php?fbid=6609426679136235&set=pb.100002069048072.-2207520000&type=3

Because everyone who doesn't know Him is still dead to God; still lost in their sins.

https://www.facebook.com/photo.php?fbid=6169704459775128&set=pb.100002069048072.-2207520000&type=3

And all who do not KNOW God, will incur His Wrath.

2 Thessalonians 1:8-9
8   In flaming fire taking vengeance on them that know not God, and that obey not the gospel of our Lord Jesus Christ:

9   Who shall be punished with everlasting destruction from the presence of the Lord, and from the glory of his power;

A New Heaven and a New Earth
...7The one who overcomes will inherit all things, and I will be his God, and he will be My son. 8But to the cowardly and unbelieving and abominable and murderers and sexually immoral and sorcerers and idolaters and all liars, their place will be in the lake that burns with fire and sulfur. This is the second death." https://biblehub.com/revelation/21-8.htm

So, if you don't want to be one of those people He tells to depart from Him into the flames of damnation, then OBEY HIM! (Learn to Love God and each other as He commands us all to do.)

The Great Commission
...15And He said to them, "Go into all the world and preach the gospel to every creature. 16Whoever believes and is baptized will be saved, but whoever does not believe will be condemned.
https://biblehub.com/mark/16-16.htm

The Great Commission
...18Then Jesus came to them and said, "All authority in heaven and on earth has been given to Me. 19Therefore go and make disciples of all nations, baptizing them in the name of the Father, and of the Son, and of the Holy Spirit, 20and teaching them to obey all that I have commanded you. And surely I am with you always, even to the end of the age."...
https://biblehub.com/matthew/28-19.htm

37When the people heard this, they were cut to the heart and asked Peter and the other apostles, "Brothers, what shall we do?" 38 Peter replied,

"Repent and be baptized, every one of you, in the name of Jesus Christ for the forgiveness of your sins, and you will receive the gift of the Holy Spirit. 39This promise belongs to you and your children and to all who are far off—to all whom the Lord our God will call to Himself."...
https://biblehub.com/acts/2-38.htm

Peter and John Before the Council
...11This Jesus is 'the stone you builders rejected, which has become the cornerstone.' 12 Salvation exists in no one else, for there is no other name under heaven given to men by which we must be saved."
https://biblehub.com/acts/4-12.htm

Another common lie muslims tell themselves and the world is that the Holy Bible has been corrupted and so they only pick bits and pieces of it and ignore whatever they feel like. Anything they disagree with or don't like they just ignore and call a lie.

There is no falsehood in the Holy Bible.

17Sanctify them by the truth; Your word is truth.
https://biblehub.com/john/17-17.htm

33 Heaven and earth will pass away, but My words will never pass away.
https://biblehub.com/luke/21-33.htm

The Fulfillment of the Law
17Do not think that I have come to abolish the Law or the Prophets. I have not come to abolish them, but to fulfill them. 18For I tell you truly, until heaven and earth pass away, not a single jot, not a stroke of a pen, will

disappear from the Law until everything is accomplished. 19So then, whoever breaks one of the least of these commandments and teaches others to do likewise will be called least in the kingdom of heaven; but whoever practices and teaches them will be called great in the kingdom of heaven.... https://biblehub.com/matthew/5-18.htm

So, God tells us that it's easier for the heavens and earth to vanish than His Words and also goes so far to say that it's easier for the heavens and earth to pass away than even for a tiny mark in His Words!

Anyone claiming the Holy Bible is not telling the Truth is calling God, Jesus Christ, a liar, and is saying He was impotent to preserve His Words as He plainly states.

https://www.facebook.com/photo.php?fbid=4890242114388042&set=pb.100002069048072.-2207520000&type=3 AND

https://www.facebook.com/photo/?fbid=1408899032522385&set=a.115635768515391 - the Holy Bible is PROVABLY and VERIFIABLY DIVINELY INSPIRED.

The Holy Bible calls muslims accursed, lying, antichrists (https://biblehub.com/1_john/2-22.htm and https://www.biblegateway.com/passage/?search=Galatians%201%3A6-9&version=ESV and https://www.biblegateway.com/passage/?search=1%20John%204%3A1-6&version=ESV) If you believe the lies of a criminal antichrist like muhammad, you become one. So muslims are constantly falsely claiming that the contents of the Holy Bible have been corrupted or otherwise trying to doubt any part of it that exposes the fact that islam and their quran is evil and full of lies. So, between the two books which is reliable?

The quran most definitely isn't, it has no original manuscripts, late copies that all disagree, and comes from criminals who deny the facts of history in the Holy Bible (the most certain and strongly attested facts of history in all the world).

https://youtu.be/abDnusXXoes?t=3728 - contrary to what muslims are brainwashed to believe, their quran has no original manuscripts and only a few copies that came long after muhammad and his gang of criminals who began islam. All of those copies and versions have significant differences.

The people who wrote the Holy Bible were put to torturous demises that they accepted rather than recant of even one word!
https://tile.loc.gov/storageservices/public/gdcmassbookdig/foxesbookofmart00fo/foxesbookofmart0 0fo.pdf

So, between lying muhammad and his criminals and the Eyewitnesses of God in the Holy Bible, the Holy Bible is by FAR more trustworthy, BY FAR!
https://www.thereligionofpeace.com/pages/articles/jesusmuhammad.aspx

The entire Old Testament was compiled at least a couple centuries prior to the advent of Jesus Christ, God coming in the flesh as the Messiah.

https://biblearchaeology.org/research/new-testament-era/4022-a-briefhistory-of-the-septuagint - the old testament Law and Prophets existed before Jesus Christ came in the flesh.

https://www.accordingtothescriptures.org/prophecy/353prophecies.html - so the hundreds of prophecies about Him are absolute proof of His Divinity.

https://www.icsv.at/one-chance-in-a-trillion-trillion-trillion-trillion-trilliontrillion-trillion-trillion-trillion-trillion-trillion-trillion-trillion - God told us centuries in advance what He would say and do when He came in the flesh as the Messiah. So, Jesus Christ is absolutely the God who spoke with His Prophets.

John 5:39-40
39 You search the Scriptures because you think that in them you have eternal life; and it is they that bear witness about me, 40 yet you refuse to come to me that you may have life.

Jesus Opens the Scriptures
...26Was it not necessary for the Christ to suffer these things and then to enter His glory?" 27And beginning with Moses and all the Prophets, He explained to them what was written in all the Scriptures about Himself. https://biblehub.com/luke/24-27.htm

Only God can fulfill all His Law and Prophecies:

The Fulfillment of the Law
16In the same way, let your light shine before men, that they may see your good deeds and glorify your Father in heaven. 17Do not think that I have come to abolish the Law or the Prophets. I have not come to abolish them, but to fulfill them. 18For I tell you truly, until heaven and earth pass away, not a single jot, not a stroke of a pen, will disappear from the Law until everything is accomplished.... https://biblehub.com/matthew/5-17.htm

And when He came, He handpicked Eyewitnesses who immediately began proclaiming the Gospel as He Commanded, despite persecution.

https://www.youtube.com/watch?v=ay_Db4RwZ_M - you have to LISTEN to the expert historians to understand how we know the Gospel was proclaimed immediately following the Resurrection and Ascension of Jesus Christ.

https://carm.org/about-the-bible/manuscript-evidence-for-superior-newtestament-reliability/ - there are tens of thousands of ancient manuscripts that are linked to real events and people throughout history proving that the contents of the Holy Bible are as true today as they were thousands of years ago.

https://manuscripts.csntm.org - just because someone uses radiometric dating, doesn't necessarily mean those dates are all accurate, but even so there are plenty of early fragments for Jesus Christ and His Words In the Holy Bible (far more than all other ancient literature in the entire world COMBINED!) so anyone questioning the Holy Bible may as well toss out all ancient history.

https://coldcasechristianity.com/writings/is-there-any-evidence-for-jesusoutside-the-bible/ - Jesus Christ is cited by numerous historians of that time and as such is a very real Person who factually existed in ancient history in the flesh on earth. (Some people today are lacking so much knowledge they try to falsely claim God never came in the flesh when He most certainly did.)

https://coldcasechristianity.com/videos/the-apostle-johns-chain-ofcustody-video/ - among the historic records there is a chain of custody throughout history such that real people knew the Eyewitness Apostles who wrote the contents of the Holy Bible.

Understand the ancient world didn't have computers, typewriters etc. and had to handwrite on papyrus or other materials every word! So even today it can take an author decades to write a book even with all the modern tools! So, the fact that there are tens of thousands of ancient manuscripts so early and close to the historic events in the Holy Bible makes those contents absolutely reliable and trustworthy.

On top of the historic facts that the words in the Holy Bible were proclaimed concurrently with those facts and thereafter throughout the generations to this day, God Himself told us He watches over His Words and that it's easier for the heavens and earth to vanish away than His Words (Luke 21:33). So, the Holy Bible is the most trustworthy reference book in all the world.

On top of the facts it contains, God tells us all how to know and learn from Him personally, so anyone can verify the words of God in the Holy Bible with Him personally! (Matthew 28:18-20; Mark 16:15,16; Acts 2:38-39; 4:12; John 14:20-26; Luke 11:13)

The contents of the Holy Bible therefore are intellectually reasonable, historically accurate and trustworthy (having been more thoroughly studied and verified than any other book in all the world BY FAR), and provably and verifiably Divinely Inspired. Anyone claiming it is unreliable, a work of fiction, inaccurate, or attempting to denigrate the Holy Bible in any way is at best, lacking correct information, and at worst, lying to themselves and the world.

https://www.facebook.com/photo/?fbid=4890242114388042&set=a.115635768515391 - never trust any spoken or written opinion from anyone over the contents of the Holy Bible.

https://www.facebook.com/photo/?fbid=1408899032522385&set=a.115635768515391 - the Holy Bible comes from the One True God and tells us all how to know Him personally; so no one has any excuse.
https://www.amazon.com/Bible-Provably-Verifiably-Divinely-Inspired/dp/1965173004/ref=tmm_pap_swatch_0?_encoding=UTF8&qid=&sr= - The Holy Bible is Provably and Verifiably Divinely Inspired!

Every day some muslim is making comments that show they are all deceived. Like today one was saying Christians lack guidance. All muslims need to understand the following:

Sorry, you are following a rapist, robber, slaver, child molester and murderer to the flames of damnation and Christians are following our Lord and Savior Jesus Christ into Heaven, yet you think they are the ones lacking guidance. You and all muslims are acting like incredible fools.

https://www.thereligionofpeace.com/pages/articles/jesusmuhammad.aspx

Jesus Christ is the ONLY ONE in ALL HISTORY who claimed to have Eternal Life and then proved it by publicly dying, raising His Body from the Grave and ascending into Heaven in front of eyewitnesses!

John 5:39-40
39 You search the Scriptures because you think that in them you have eternal life; and it is they that bear witness about me, 40 yet you refuse to come to me that you may have life.

The Ascension

...7Jesus replied, "It is not for you to know times or seasons that the Father has fixed by His own authority. 8But you will receive power when the Holy Spirit comes upon you, and you will be My witnesses in Jerusalem, and in all Judea and Samaria, and to the ends of the earth." 9After He had said this, they watched as He was taken up, and a cloud hid Him from their sight.10They were looking intently into the sky as He was going, when suddenly two men dressed in white stood beside them. 11"Men of Galilee," they said, "why do you stand here looking into the sky? This same Jesus, who has been taken from you into heaven, will come back in the same way you have seen Him go into heaven." https://biblehub.com/acts/1-8.htm

So, you and all muslims can ignorantly or deliberately follow the lying criminal muhammad into the flames of damnation if you want, but don't ever imagine Christians are lacking guidance for following Jesus Christ into Eternal Life and Heaven.

...35The Father loves the Son and has placed all things in His hands. 36Whoever believes in the Son has eternal life. Whoever rejects the Son will not see life. Instead, the wrath of God remains on him."
https://biblehub.com/john/3-36.htm

A New Heaven and a New Earth
...7The one who overcomes will inherit all things, and I will be his God, and he will be My son. 8But to the cowardly and unbelieving and abominable and murderers and sexually immoral and sorcerers and idolaters and all liars, their place will be in the lake that burns with fire and sulfur. This is the second death." https://biblehub.com/revelation/21-8.htm

Overcoming the World
...4because everyone born of God overcomes the world. And this is the victory that has overcome the world: our faith. 5Who then overcomes the world? Only he who believes that Jesus is the Son of God. 6This is the One who came by water and blood, Jesus Christ—not by water alone, but by

water and blood. And it is the Spirit who testifies to this, because the Spirit is the truth.... https://biblehub.com/1_john/5-5.htm

12But to all who did receive Him, to those who believed in His name, He gave the right to become children of God— 13children born not of blood, nor of the desire or will of man, but born of God....
https://biblehub.com/john/1-12.htm

The Great Commission
...15And He said to them, "Go into all the world and preach the gospel to every creature. 16Whoever believes and is baptized will be saved, but whoever does not believe will be condemned.
https://biblehub.com/mark/16-16.htm

37When the people heard this, they were cut to the heart and asked Peter and the other apostles, "Brothers, what shall we do?" 38 Peter replied, "Repent and be baptized, every one of you, in the name of Jesus Christ for the forgiveness of your sins, and you will receive the gift of the Holy Spirit. 39This promise belongs to you and your children and to all who are far off—to all whom the Lord our God will call to Himself."...
https://biblehub.com/acts/2-38.htm

Peter and John Before the Council
...11This Jesus is 'the stone you builders rejected, which has become the cornerstone.' 12 Salvation exists in no one else, for there is no other name under heaven given to men by which we must be saved."
https://biblehub.com/acts/4-12.htm

20And we know that the Son of God has come and has given us understanding, so that we may know Him who is true; and we are in Him who is true— in His Son Jesus Christ. He is the TRUE God and eternal life.

https://biblehub.com/1_john/5-20.htm

The reason not one muslim sees, hears or knows the Living God, is that none of you are obeying Him. (you are following the lying criminal muhammad instead.)

https://www.facebook.com/photo.php?fbid=6606552169423686&set=pb.100002069048072.-2207520000&type=3

Then some muslim was trying to say that John 10:30 only meant that Jesus Christ was one "in purpose" not one in essence as God Himself.

Belief and Unbelief

...48There is a judge for the one who rejects Me and does not receive My words: The word that I have spoken will judge him on the last day. 49 I have not spoken on My own, but the Father who sent Me has commanded Me what to say and how to say it. 50And I know that His command leads to eternal life. So I speak exactly what the Father has told Me to say."...
https://biblehub.com/john/12-49.htm

...28So Jesus said, "When you have lifted up the Son of Man, then you will know that I am He, and that I do nothing on My own, but speak exactly what the Father has taught Me. 29 He who sent Me is with Me. He has not left Me alone, because I always do what pleases Him." 30As Jesus spoke these things, many believed in Him.... https://biblehub.com/john/8-29.htm

So, Jesus Christ said HE ALWAYS SPEAKS THE WORDS OF GOD EXACTLY IN THE WAY GOD WANTS THEM SPOKEN AND ALWAYS DOES THE WILL OF GOD EXACTLY!

John 14:6-9

6 Jesus said to him, "I am the way, the truth, and the life. No one comes to the Father except through Me.

The Father Revealed

7 "If you had known Me, you would have known My Father also; and from now on you know Him and have seen Him."

8 Philip said to Him, "Lord, show us the Father, and it is sufficient for us."

9 Jesus said to him, "Have I been with you so long, and yet you have not known Me, Philip? He who has seen Me has seen the Father; so how can you say, 'Show us the Father'?

THEN HE SAID TO LOOK AT HIM IS TO SEE GOD!

The Hatred of the World

...22If I had not come and spoken to them, they would not be guilty of sin. Now, however, they have no excuse for their sin. 23Whoever hates Me hates My Father as well. 24If I had not done among them the works that no one else did, they would not be guilty of sin; but now they have seen and hated both Me and My Father.25But this is to fulfill what is written in their Law: 'They hated Me without reason.'...
https://biblehub.com/john/15-24.htm

THEN HE SAID TO HATE HIM IS TO HATE GOD! Notice how "the Son" is talking about Himself and "the Father" in verse 24 but then says that "the Father" and "the Son" are just "Me" in verse 25

How can the Father and Son be One? and yet the Son say the Father is Greater? answer: the same way your own visible body is one with your invisible spirit! your body does NOTHING without your spirit!

26 As the body without the spirit is dead, so faith without deeds is dead. https://biblehub.com/james/2-26.htm

So, the scriptures are crystal clear that when Jesus Christ said "the Father" and "the Son" are ONE, that's exactly what He meant.

ONLY GOD ALWAYS SPEAKS HIS WORDS EXACTLY HOW HE WANTS THEM SPOKEN AND ONLY GOD ALWAYS DOES HIS WILL, HIS GOOD PLEASURE AND ONLY GOD SAYS AND DOES THE THINGS JESUS CHRIST SAYS AND DOES!

Jesus Appears to Thomas

…27Then Jesus said to Thomas, "Put your finger here and look at My hands. Reach out your hand and put it into My side. Stop doubting and believe." 28Thomas replied, "My Lord and my God!" 29Jesus said to him, "Because you have seen Me, you have believed; blessed are those who have not seen and yet have believed."… https://biblehub.com/john/20-28.htm

John 5:39-40
39 You search the Scriptures because you think that in them you have eternal life; and it is they that bear witness about me, 40 yet you refuse to come to me that you may have life.

The entire Holy Bible plainly tells us many hundreds of times over that Jesus Christ is the One True God.

He told His Prophets He would come in the flesh and that is exactly what He did:

https://www.accordingtothescriptures.org/prophecy/353prophecies.html

The Fulfillment of the Law

16In the same way, let your light shine before men, that they may see your good deeds and glorify your Father in heaven. 17Do not think that I have come to abolish the Law or the Prophets. I have not come to abolish them, but to fulfill them. 18For I tell you truly, until heaven and earth pass away, not a single jot, not a stroke of a pen, will disappear from the Law until everything is accomplished.... https://biblehub.com/matthew/5-17.htm

ONLY GOD CAN FULFILL ALL HIS LAW AND PROPHECIES! Including His Law and Prophecies of Redemption/Salvation.

https://bible.knowing-jesus.com/topics/God,-As-Redeemer and https://www.preceptaustin.org/tetelestai-paid_in_full

So yes, Jesus Christ is the One True God, just as the scriptures plainly state. (1John 5:20)

Another very common lie that muslims claim is that they pray like Jesus Christ and that they love Jesus Christ and some actually falsely boast more than Christians. None of those claims have any merit whatsoever. Anyone who truly loves Jesus Christ is a Christian, who Honors God by NAME. JESUS CHRIST IS LORD! Acts 1:8; 2:38,39; 4:12 CHRISTIAN! Acts 11:26 CHRISTIAN - Disciples of JESUS CHRIST! (muslims- followers of wicked, lying muhammad) so no, muslims do not Love Jesus Christ because not one of them follows Him or obeys Him. (John 14:6-15-26; and not one of them knows Him - 1Jn 2:20-27; 4:1-6) the scriptures instead call muslims liars and antichrists, accursed from God for believing a very different message/gospel. (Gal 1:6-9, Jn 3:36; 1Jn 2:22, Mt 28:18-20; 1Jn 4:1-6 and all such liars and antichrists will be cast into the lake of fire unless they repent and become Disciples of Jesus Christ/Christians - Rev 21:8)

Jesus Christ did nothing that muslims do with respect to the doctrines, beliefs and practices of islam and the quran.

https://www.thereligionofpeace.com/pages/articles/jesusmuhammad.aspx

Jesus Christ is God, when He prayed it was for our example and benefit and He told us how to pray; it's nothing at all like muslims:

(yes, Jesus Christ is God and obviously so: https://www.facebook.com/photo.php?fbid=6809546799124221&set=pb.100002069048072.-2207520000&type=3 and https://www.facebook.com/photo.php?fbid=6800758120003089&set=pb.100002069048072.-2207520000&type=3 and https://www.facebook.com/photo.php?fbid=6471680786244159&set=pb.100002069048072.-2207520000&type=3) the only reason the whole world doesn't already know Jesus Christ is the One True God, is that the devil is still filling people's heads with lies. But anyone who obeys Jesus Christ, can see, hear, know and learn from Him, personally!

https://www.facebook.com/photo.php?fbid=6609426679136235&set=pb.100002069048072.-2207520000&type=3 - everyone should pray God gives them true Repentance, because true Repentance from all evil prepares the Way for His Holy Spirit of Truth.

Jesus Christ taught us to pray in this manner and it has absolutely nothing to do with islam and the way muslims pray and bow down at the kaaba stone, or to their imaginary allah; nothing whatsoever.

Matthew 6:9-13
9   In this manner, therefore, pray:

Our Father in heaven,
Hallowed be Your name.
10 Your kingdom come.
Your will be done
On earth as it is in heaven.
11 Give us this day our daily bread. 12 And forgive us our debts, As we
    forgive our debtors.
13 And do not lead us into temptation, But
deliver us from the evil one.
[a]For Yours is the kingdom and the power and the glory forever. Amen.

So no, islam has nothing whatsoever to do with Jesus Christ because it comes from the lying criminal muhammad instead.

(that's NOT an insult; it's the truth! you muslims just don't understand you've all been deceived.)

muhammad was nothing good, he was not a prophet, he was a lying criminal who created a cult following to gratify his own evil desires.

https://www.youtube.com/watch?v=076LtW_ZSnw

Which is why the quran is full of evil instructions and lies:

https://www.thereligionofpeace.com/pages/quran/index.aspx

Another common question muslims ask, is why did Jesus Christ cry out on the cross, "My God! My God! Why have You forsaken Me?" if He is God?

God, Jesus Christ, told the Prophets what He would say and do when He came in the flesh:

https://www.accordingtothescriptures.org/prophecy/353prophecies.html
and one of those things was crying out, "My God! My God! why have You forsaken Me?"

Psalm 22
22 My God, my God, why hast thou forsaken me? ...

Only God fulfills ALL His Law and Prophecies:

John 5:39-40
39 You search the Scriptures because you think that in them you have eternal life; and it is they that bear witness about me, 40 yet you refuse to come to me that you may have life.

The Fulfillment of the Law
16In the same way, let your light shine before men, that they may see your good deeds and glorify your Father in heaven. 17Do not think that I have come to abolish the Law or the Prophets. I have not come to abolish them, but to fulfill them. 18For I tell you truly, until heaven and earth pass away, not a single jot, not a stroke of a pen, will disappear from the Law until everything is accomplished.... https://biblehub.com/matthew/5-17.htm

So, God, Jesus Christ, told His Prophets centuries in advance He would come into this world He created and made, humbly, as a Man, the Messiah, God in the flesh. and that when He did so, it would be for the purpose of fulfilling His Law and Prophecies; including His Law and Prophecies of Redemption and Salvation. Which is why He went to the Cross to suffer and die for the sins of mankind, to Redeem and Save all who are Grateful to Him, all who Love Him for doing so.

https://bible.knowing-jesus.com/topics/God,-As-Redeemer and https://www.preceptaustin.org/tetelestai-paid_in_full

So, God, Jesus Christ came humbly the first time as a Man, the Messiah:

The Attitude of Christ
...6Who, existing in the form of God, did not consider equality with God something to be grasped, 7but emptied Himself, taking the form of a servant, being made in human likeness. 8And being found in appearance as a man, He humbled Himself and became obedient to death—even death on a cross.... https://biblehub.com/philippians/2-7.htm

The scriptures tell us that the sins of the world were laid upon Christ in His dying moments on the cross and that is when He cried out: My God! My God! Why have You forsaken Me? in fulfillment of His Prophecies.

Jesus Our Advocate

1My little children, I am writing these things to you so that you will not sin. But if anyone does sin, we have an advocate before the Father—Jesus Christ, the Righteous One. **2** He Himself is the atoning sacrifice for our sins, and not only for ours but also for the sins of the whole world. **3**By this we can be sure that we have come to know Him: if we keep His commandments.... https://biblehub.com/1_john/2-2.htm

God tells us that not only did He come Humbly as a Man, the Messiah, in order to show Himself to us, fulfill His Law and Prophecies and Call us all back to Him, to Redeem and Save our souls, but also so that no one could falsely accuse Him of giving us impossible commandments; to "condemn sin in the flesh".

Living in the Spirit

...**2**For in Christ Jesus the law of the Spirit of life set you free from the law of sin and death. **3**For what the law was powerless to do in that it was weakened by the flesh, God did by sending His own Son in the likeness of sinful man, as an offering for sin. He thus condemned sin in the flesh, **4**so that the righteous standard of the law might be fulfilled in us, who do not walk according to the flesh but according to the Spirit....
https://biblehub.com/romans/8-3.htm

(muslims should really study the book of Romans because they are in a cult that sows to the flesh, instead of our spirits, and as such are on a path of suffering, death and destruction, and will end up in the lake of fire unless they all repent of following wicked muhammad (lies of the quran) and learn to follow our Lord and Savior, JESUS, the Christ instead (Words of God, Truth, in the Holy Bible).
https://www.thereligionofpeace.com/pages/articles/jesusmuhammad.aspx

But when He Returns, it will be in Glory and Power as the One True God! taking vengeance upon all His enemies, all who refused to obey Him and His Commandment to REPENT of every evil thought, word, way and deed and Get Baptized in His Name; filled with His Holy Spirit of Truth, so that they would KNOW Him and learn from Him thereafter.

2 Thessalonians 1:8-9
8	In flaming fire taking vengeance on them that know not God, and that obey not the gospel of our Lord Jesus Christ:

9	Who shall be punished with everlasting destruction from the presence of the Lord, and from the glory of his power;

The Great Commission
…15And He said to them, "Go into all the world and preach the gospel to every creature. 16Whoever believes and is baptized will be saved, but whoever does not believe will be condemned.
https://biblehub.com/mark/16-16.htm

"Brothers, what shall we do?" 38 Peter replied, "Repent and be baptized, every one of you, in the name of Jesus Christ for the forgiveness of your sins, and you will receive the gift of the Holy Spirit. 39This promise belongs to you and your children and to all who are far off—to all whom the Lord our God will call to Himself."… https://biblehub.com/acts/2-38.htm

John 14:20-26
20 In that day you will know that I am in my Father, and you in me, and I in you. 21 Whoever has my commandments and keeps them, he it is who loves me. And he who loves me will be loved by my Father, and I will love him and manifest myself to him." 22 Judas (not Iscariot) said to him, "Lord, how is it that you will manifest yourself to us, and not to the world?" 23 Jesus answered him, "If anyone loves me, he will keep my word, and my Father will love him, and we will come to him and make our home with

him. 24 Whoever does not love me does not keep my words. And the word that you hear is not mine but the Father's who sent me.

25 "These things I have spoken to you while I am still with you. 26 But the Helper, the Holy Spirit, whom the Father will send in my name, he will teach you all things and bring to your remembrance all that I have said to you.

…35The Father loves the Son and has placed all things in His hands. 36Whoever believes in the Son has eternal life. Whoever rejects the Son will not see life. Instead, the wrath of God remains on him."
https://biblehub.com/john/3-36.htm

(all muslims are taught by the lying devil and his evil criminal, muhammad, to DENY the Son and as such are ALL lying antichrists! unless muslims repent, they will all be cast into the lake of fire and feel the Wrath of the One True God!)

Beware of Antichrists
…21I have not written to you because you lack knowledge of the truth, but because you have it, and because no lie comes from the truth. 22Who is the liar, if it is not the one who denies that Jesus is the Christ? This is the antichrist, who denies the Father and the Son. 23Whoever denies the Son does not have the Father, but whoever confesses the Son has the Father as well.… https://biblehub.com/1_john/2-22.htm

A New Heaven and a New Earth
…7The one who overcomes will inherit all things, and I will be his God, and he will be My son. 8But to the cowardly and unbelieving and abominable and murderers and sexually immoral and sorcerers and idolaters and all

liars, their place will be in the lake that burns with fire and sulfur. This is the second death." https://biblehub.com/revelation/21-8.htm

Another lie muslims are taught in islam is that Jesus Christ wasn't really crucified, but that someone else was crucified in His place. (Even though we are told in the Holy Bible that His own mother, Mary, saw Him nailed to the cross. - John 19:25-27 and His Burial Cloth proves the Holy Bible is telling us all the truth; not the lying quran - https://youtu.be/LLnClp3OVmE?t=1884) So today a muslim was asking why His Disciples didn't prevent His Crucifixion or fight back; again, ignoring that Peter tried to - John 18:3–11; Matthew 26:47–56; Mark 14:43–50; Luke 22:47–53)

muslims just don't understand that the public scourging and crucifixion of Jesus Christ was His Purpose and Mission and that He had told His Prophets and His Disciples that's exactly what He would do as our Redeemer, Savior and Messiah.
https://www.accordingtothescriptures.org/prophecy/353prophecies.html - hundreds of prophecies about God coming in the flesh as the Messiah to Redeem/Save us.

https://bible.knowing-jesus.com/topics/God,-As-Redeemer - only the One True God could Redeem/Save us - https://www.preceptaustin.org/tetelestai-paid_in_full

https://www.gotquestions.org/Jesus-predict-His-death.html Jesus Christ told His Chosen Eyewitnesses, His Apostles and Disciples numerous times in advance how He would suffer and die.

He had said He was the One who had Eternal Life:

John 5:39-40
39 You search the Scriptures because you think that in them you have eternal life; and it is they that bear witness about me, 40 yet you refuse to come to me that you may have life.

and the One who had Power to Raise the dead back to Life:

Jesus Comforts Martha and Mary
…24Martha replied, "I know that he will rise again in the resurrection at the last day." 25 Jesus said to her, "I am the resurrection and the life. Whoever believes in Me will live, even though he dies. 26And everyone who lives and believes in Me will never die. Do you believe this?"… https://biblehub.com/john/11-25.htm

and then proved it by publicly dying and raising His Body from the Grave, transfiguring it, making it Immortal and Glorious and Ascending back into Heaven in front of eyewitnesses. PROVING HE IS THE ONE TRUE GOD!

Jesus Appears to Thomas
…27Then Jesus said to Thomas, "Put your finger here and look at My hands. Reach out your hand and put it into My side. Stop doubting and believe." 28Thomas replied, "My Lord and my God!" 29Jesus said to him, "Because you have seen Me, you have believed; blessed are those who have not seen and yet have believed."… https://biblehub.com/john/20-28.htm

Jesus Christ ever lives to answer any and all who have the good sense to obey His Commandment to Repent of their wicked ways and Call Upon Him to Save their souls!

Luke 13:1-9
Repent or Perish
13 There were present at that season some who told Him about the Galileans whose blood Pilate had mingled with their sacrifices. 2 And Jesus answered and said to them, "Do you suppose that these Galileans were worse sinners than all other Galileans, because they suffered such things? 3 I tell you, no; but unless you repent you will all likewise perish. 4 Or those eighteen on whom the tower in Siloam fell and killed them, do you think that they were worse sinners than all other men who dwelt in Jerusalem? 5 I tell you, no; but unless you repent you will all likewise perish."

The Parable of the Barren Fig Tree
6 He also spoke this parable: "A certain man had a fig tree planted in his vineyard, and he came seeking fruit on it and found none. 7 Then he said to the keeper of his vineyard, 'Look, for three years I have come seeking fruit on this fig tree and find none. Cut it down; why does it use up the ground?' 8 But he answered and said to him, 'Sir, let it alone this year also, until I dig around it and fertilize it. 9 And if it bears fruit, well. But if not, after that you can cut it down.' "

The Great Commission
...15And He said to them, "Go into all the world and preach the gospel to every creature. 16Whoever believes and is baptized will be saved, but whoever does not believe will be condemned.
https://biblehub.com/mark/16-16.htm

"Brothers, what shall we do?" 38 Peter replied, "Repent and be baptized, every one of you, in the name of Jesus Christ for the forgiveness of your sins, and you will receive the gift of the Holy Spirit. 39This promise belongs to you and your children and to all who are far off—to all whom the Lord our God will call to Himself."... https://biblehub.com/acts/2-38.htm

Peter and John Before the Council
…11This Jesus is 'the stone you builders rejected, which has become the cornerstone.' 12 Salvation exists in no one else, for there is no other name under heaven given to men by which we must be saved."
https://biblehub.com/acts/4-12.htm

Another muslim asked how can Jesus Christ be both Father and Son and how can the Creator be killed by His Creation?

1) God, Jesus Christ, is Supreme in EVERYTHING:

Colossians 1:15-19
The Supremacy of the Son of God
15 The Son is the image of the invisible God, the firstborn over all creation. 16 For in him all things were created: things in heaven and on earth, visible and invisible, whether thrones or powers or rulers or authorities; all things have been created through him and for him. 17 He is before all things, and in him all things hold together. 18

And he is the head of the body, the church; he is the beginning and the firstborn from among the dead, so that in everything he might have the supremacy. 19 For God was pleased to have all his fullness dwell in him,

this passage means Jesus Christ is the: God of gods, Man of men, Angel of angels, Spirit of spirits, Prophet of prophets, Father of fathers, Son of sons, Servant of servants, Teacher of teachers, King of kings, Lord of lords, First and Last, Beginning and End, etc. etc. which is why the Holy Bible refers to Him in all these ways and more.

2) Jesus the Good Shepherd

...17The reason the Father loves Me is that I lay down My life in order to take it up again. 18No one takes it from Me, but I lay it down of My own accord. I have authority to lay it down and authority to take it up again. This charge I have received from My Father."

Jesus Christ claimed to be God who came in the flesh in fulfillment of what He had told His Prophets:

John 5:39-40
39 You search the Scriptures because you think that in them you have eternal life; and it is they that bear witness about me, 40 yet you refuse to come to me that you may have life.
https://www.accordingtothescriptures.org/prophecy/353prophecies.html

Jesus Opens the Scriptures
...26Was it not necessary for the Christ to suffer these things and then to enter His glory?" 27And beginning with Moses and all the Prophets, He explained to them what was written in all the Scriptures about Himself.
https://biblehub.com/luke/24-27.htm

He had openly claimed to have Eternal Life and openly claimed to have the Power to raise the dead back to life and then proved it by publicly dying, raising His Body from the grave, transfigured it, making it Immortal and Glorious and then ascended back into Heaven in front of eyewitnesses; thereby proving He is the One True God He had said. (all 4 Gospels and Acts 1:1-11, 1 Cor 15)

Jesus Comforts Martha and Mary
...24Martha replied, "I know that he will rise again in the resurrection at the last day." 25 Jesus said to her, "I am the resurrection and the life. Whoever believes in Me will live, even though he dies. 26And everyone

who lives and believes in Me will never die. Do you believe this?"...
https://biblehub.com/john/11-25.htm

Jesus Appears to Thomas
...27Then Jesus said to Thomas, "Put your finger here and look at My hands. Reach out your hand and put it into My side. Stop doubting and believe." 28Thomas replied, "My Lord and my God!" 29Jesus said to him, "Because you have seen Me, you have believed; blessed are those who have not seen and yet have believed."... https://biblehub.com/john/20-28.htm

Some muslim was again today trying to tell us how wonderful their evil cult is. muslims need to comprehend that islam never saved anyone; only the One True God, Jesus Christ, can save your soul.

Peter and John Before the Council
...11This Jesus is 'the stone you builders rejected, which has become the cornerstone.' 12 Salvation exists in no one else, for there is no other name under heaven given to men by which we must be saved."
https://biblehub.com/acts/4-12.htm

muslims are all acting severely brainwashed and deceived; to the point of appearing to be mentally impaired. muhammad was a criminal who is dead and buried, he was no prophet but a con artist, that got together with a bunch of bandits and began the cult of islam. They raided small caravans, then their numbers grew, until they raided homesteads, outlying villages until their numbers were sufficient to raid and subjugate whole nations to islam. muhammad and his gang, raided, raped, murdered, took slaves, or otherwise made people pay them to stay alive (armed robbery in the form of "jizya tax"), islam is the largest gang of criminals in the history of the world. One thing is certain, as long as you remain a muslim, you are destined for the lake of fire. (Rev. 21:8) It has always been a criminal organization and will always be such. https://youtu.be/I_TocV94Bo islam is far from "wonderful".

Jesus Christ is Lord who stated He is the Way to Eternal Life and Heaven and then rose into Heaven Bodily in front of eyewitnesses after publicly dying and being buried in a grave as PROOF!

John 5:39-40
39 You search the Scriptures because you think that in them you have eternal life; and it is they that bear witness about me, 40 yet you refuse to come to me that you may have life.

Acts 1:8-11
8	But ye shall receive power, after that the Holy Ghost is come upon you: and ye shall be witnesses unto me both in Jerusalem, and in all Judaea, and in Samaria, and unto the uttermost part of the earth.

9	And when he had spoken these things, while they beheld, he was taken up; and a cloud received him out of their sight.

10	And while they looked stedfastly toward heaven as he went up, behold, two men stood by them in white apparel;

11	Which also said, Ye men of Galilee, why stand ye gazing up into heaven? this same Jesus, which is taken up from you into heaven, shall so come in like manner as ye have seen him go into heaven.

So, no one should be following muhammad into the flames of damnation; everyone should be following our Lord and Savior, Jesus Christ, into Eternal Life and Heaven!

https://www.thereligionofpeace.com/pages/articles/jesusmuhammad.aspx

Yet another muslim was lying to himself and the world today by falsely claiming the hundreds of verses in the quran and hadiths advocating violent crimes against humanity are all about self-defense and was mocking God for telling us to love even our enemies, in the Holy Bible. He did this in response to my citation of the fact that the quran openly advocates crimes against humanity, rape, slavery, robbery, wife and child abuse, torture, murder; virtually all manner of evil openly. So, he deflected away from facing those facts by attempting to lie about them all, and also to change the focus to the Holy Bible in which he was implying that God erred in some way by telling us to love our enemies. So, I responded:

You, like many who disobey God, choose to skip around the fact that you're doing that by changing the subject.

https://www.facebook.com/photo.php?fbid=7161653763913521&set=pb.100002069048072.-2207520000&type=3 - the Holy Bible encourages no crimes, no evil in any way. God tells us the various contexts He meant about "love your enemies" and it has nothing to do with loving the devil, or not to defend self and loved ones against people violently attacking them such as acts of war or terrorism, or otherwise failing to arrest criminals and everything to do with loving God and all persons still in the flesh enough to forgive them, pray for them, and tell them all to repent of every wicked, thought, word, way and deed while God still gives them breath to do so. If someone refuses to repent as God commands and shows themselves to be an antichrist, persons like Hitler committing genocides against innocent people, then the rest of mankind is under a Divine duty to oppose such wicked beings, by word and deed, forcefully. So, there are devils/antichrists in the flesh and no, we are not commanded by God to love devils/antichrists. (rather to hate all evil, all devils) - and as long as muslims refuse to obey God and repent and be baptized in the Name of our Lord Jesus Christ, they are showing themselves to be such antichrists, children of the devil, disobedient and rebellious against the One True God and His Commandments in the Holy Bible.

Beware of Antichrists
...21I have not written to you because you lack knowledge of the truth, but because you have it, and because no lie comes from the truth. 22Who is the liar, if it is not the one who denies that Jesus is the Christ? This is the antichrist, who denies the Father and the Son. 23Whoever denies the Son does not have the Father, but whoever confesses the Son has the Father as well.... https://biblehub.com/1_john/2-22.htm

The quran advocates crimes and sins - https://www.thereligionofpeace.com/pages/quran/index.aspx - since the quran openly advocates what is evil and wrong, it is not from God who is Good, but from the devil.

The reason why God, Jesus Christ, Commandment is to love even our enemies even our enemies is He is speaking from an Eternal Perspective. That there is no way for us all to exist harmoniously with Him forever UNLESS WE LEARN TO LOVE! hatred would have us all just killing each other until no one was left! It was His Love that He died for us while we were still estranged from God lost in our sins, so He shows us the way to conquer all evil is by LOVE! It's the reason FOR ALL HIS COMMANDMENTS, we have to stop being wicked and evil, thinking only of ourselves, and learn to love and care about others. When we commit sexual immorality, we are thinking about our personal gratification; regardless of others. When we are covetous, greedy, we again are thinking of ourselves selfishly, so God COMMANDS us to LEARN TO LOVE, because that is the only way for us all to exist harmoniously with Him and each other in ETERNITY. The martyr's prayed as Jesus did, Father forgive them for they... don't realize by killing those of us who love them, all that's left in the world is hatred and murderers like themselves! It means they are acting in a way to ensure their own demise. So, the martyr's prayed for those murdering them that they would LEARN TO LOVE! that God would forgive those doing so and reach them with His Love!

God tells us we have our lifetimes to learn this Truth and if we don't LEARN TO LOVE each other, if we REFUSE to do so, then we won't be able to spend eternity with Him and all who chose to LOVE, instead all such wicked, hateful people will be confined in the lake of fire.

islam is historically and fundamentally a criminal organization in doctrine and practice; so if I was in power, islam would be properly identified as such, mosques razed to the ground, and all violent islamic terrorists who have committed murder either given a sentence until and unless they repented or executed for their crimes against humanity. All other muslims would receive a proper education so as to deprogram them all from their evil cult.

islam has generated more violent terrorist organizations than any other worldview in the entire history of the world; proving it comes from the devil and is a criminal organization in essence. - https://www.google.com/search?client=opera&q=list+of+islamic+terrorist+groups&sourceid=opera&ie=UTF-8&oe=UTF-8 - the lists provided are not complete as islam forms more of them regularly all over the world.

whereas Bible Believers, those who acknowledge Jesus Christ is the One True God, have founded, funded and operate the largest number of humanitarian charities and organizations in the history of the world, proving Christianity comes from our Good Lord Jesus Christ. - https://www.google.com/search?client=opera&q=list+of+Christian+Humanitarian+Organizations&sourceid=opera&ie=UTF-8&oe=UTF-8

So, the Holy Bible and Christianity is plainly from God, Jesus Christ, and islam and the quran is plainly from the devil.

Today a muslim was asking, why should muslims accept Jesus Christ as God who came in the flesh, the Messiah, when the Jews didn't?

Yes, they did. Christianity began at Jerusalem among all the twelve tribes of Israel (the Jews); just read the Book of Acts that plainly tells us thousands from all the twelve tribes of Israel were added daily to the Disciples of Jesus Christ, Christians. https://jewsforjesus.org/our-stories - many from the twelve tribes of Israel are still testifying today.
https://www.facebook.com/photo.php?fbid=7161653763913521&set=pb.100002069048072.-2207520000&type=3

Those from among the Jews that didn't believe Jesus Christ is God who came in the flesh, the Messiah, He called children of the devil.

John 8:43-45
43 Why do you not understand what I say? It is because you cannot bear to hear my word. 44 You are of your father the devil, and your will is to do your father's desires. He was a murderer from the beginning, and does not stand in the truth, because there is no truth in him. When he lies, he speaks out of his own character, for he is a liar and the father of lies. 45 But because I tell the truth, you do not believe me.

Essentially God came in the flesh and told them they didn't understand His Words that He had already given them and were instead perverting them, living wickedly, by creating their own manmade rituals and doctrines instead of obeying Him and the true intent of His Words that He had given them in His Law and Prophecies.

John 5:39-40
39 You search the Scriptures because you think that in them you have eternal life; and it is they that bear witness about me, 40 yet you refuse to come to me that you may have life.

Those STILL rejecting Jesus Christ as the One True God, and STILL ignoring His Commandments in the Holy Bible, and instead creating their own religions (like islam and muslims), made by men and not Him, Jesus Christ, the One True God, are still acting just like the children of the devil, He exposed to their faces when He came in the flesh.

When the Jews, Israel, finally come to their senses and openly acknowledges Yeshua Ha Mashiach as their Messiah, then will come the anger of the devils on earth against them, and as the scriptures record, the nations will gather against them and God, Yeshua (Jesus Christ) will return in Glory to vanquish any and all that would dare attack His People, Israel.

https://www.biblegateway.com/passage/?search=Zechariah%2014&version=KJV - all those who fight against Israel will be destroyed.

Today, people wrongly think that those practicing Judaism are Jews, when that just isn't the case at least not in every connotation of the word. The scriptures tell us of twelve tribes, one of which was from Judah. So, there are those who are physically descended from Judah and the other patriarchs, sons of Israel. The scriptures go on to tell us that Christianity, not Judaism is the religion of the patriarchs, because all the Prophets knew and testified that Jesus Christ, Yeshua Ha Mashiach, is the One True God. (Acts 10:34-43 and https://www.accordingtothescriptures.org/prophecy/353prophecies.html)

I explain this truth further by His Grace given me in these citations: https://www.facebook.com/photo.php?fbid=6433644810047757&set=pb.100002069048072.-2207520000&type=3 - the people of God, the Prophets who knew Him, always testified of Yeshua, our Redeemer, who would come in the flesh and Save us.
https://www.facebook.com/photo.php?fbid=6800758120003089&set=pb.

100002069048072.-2207520000&type=3 and
https://www.facebook.com/photo.php?fbid=6471680786244159&set=pb.100002069048072.-2207520000&type=3

Another common lie muslims believe is that the Holy Bible has been corrupted (and in their thinking so much so that they believe the opposite of what it plainly states in all versions about many things).

If you believe and follow lying boneheads, you become like them.

God Himself said:

33 Heaven and earth will pass away, but My words will never pass away. https://biblehub.com/luke/21-33.htm

and

The Fulfillment of the Law

16In the same way, let your light shine before men, that they may see your good deeds and glorify your Father in heaven. 17Do not think that I have come to abolish the Law or the Prophets. I have not come to abolish them, but to fulfill them. 18For I tell you truly, until heaven and earth pass away, not a single jot, not a stroke of a pen, will disappear from the Law until everything is accomplished.... https://biblehub.com/matthew/5-17.htm

So no, the Holy Bible has not been "corrupted". In fact, any effort to prove otherwise, would mean there is an uncorrupted version still today. (it's an obviously false claim). In other words, versions and translations of the Holy Bible exist because languages change over time, even words in the same language change meaning over time. So just because the Holy Bible has been translated into many languages and versions, doesn't mean it isn't or wasn't true for that time and language. In all versions of the Holy Bible, we still have tens of thousands of ancient manuscripts to compare them with for veracity AND God Himself ever lives to answer any questions anyone might have about the contents in any language or version. So, His Words remain, because God, Jesus Christ, Himself is Eternal.

John 5:39-40

[39] You search the Scriptures because you think that in them you have eternal life; and it is they that bear witness about me, [40] yet you refuse to come to me that you may have life.

https://www.facebook.com/photo.php?fbid=4890242114388042&set=pb.100002069048072.-2207520000&type=3

Some muslims wrongly think that if Jesus Christ died for our sins, then everyone goes to Heaven or that you can go on sinning and no matter what you will go to Heaven, but that isn't what Jesus Christ tells us in the Holy Bible at all.

Everyone who rejects Jesus Christ and His Salvation is under His Wrath. Everyone who refuses to repent of their sins and wicked ways and to obey Him, will die in their sins and face serious Divine Consequences.

...35The Father loves the Son and has placed all things in His hands. 36Whoever believes in the Son has eternal life. Whoever rejects the Son will not see life. Instead, the wrath of God remains on him."
https://biblehub.com/john/3-36.htm

2 Thessalonians 1:8-9

8   In flaming fire taking vengeance on them that know not God, and that obey not the gospel of our Lord Jesus Christ:

9   Who shall be punished with everlasting destruction from the presence of the Lord, and from the glory of his power;

Everyone is commanded by God to repent and be baptized in His Name.

The Great Commission
...18Then Jesus came to them and said, "All authority in heaven and on earth has been given to Me. 19Therefore go and make disciples of all nations, baptizing them in the name of the Father, and of the Son, and of the Holy Spirit, 20and teaching them to obey all that I have commanded you. And surely I am with you always, even to the end of the age."...
https://biblehub.com/matthew/28-19.htm

37When the people heard this, they were cut to the heart and asked Peter and the other apostles, "Brothers, what shall we do?" 38 Peter replied, "Repent and be baptized, every one of you, in the name of Jesus Christ for the forgiveness of your sins, and you will receive the gift of the Holy Spirit. 39This promise belongs to you and your children and to all who are far off—to all whom the Lord our God will call to Himself."...
https://biblehub.com/acts/2-38.htm

Peter and John Before the Council
...11This Jesus is 'the stone you builders rejected, which has become the cornerstone.' 12 Salvation exists in no one else, for there is no other name under heaven given to men by which we must be saved."
https://biblehub.com/acts/4-12.htm

So, people either believe Him and obey Him or they perish in their sins.

24That is why I told you that you would die in your sins. For unless you believe that I am He, you will die in your sins." 25"Who are You?" they asked. "Just what I have been telling you from the beginning," Jesus replied.... https://biblehub.com/john/8-24.htm

And are cast into the lake of fire for refusing to repent and turn from their wicked ways and for refusing to obey the One True God.

Now Christians are commanded to live righteously by His Grace, we are not to go on sinning, no one who loves Him desires to sin, we are aware that when we sin, it is contrary to OUR SPIRITS MADE RIGHT BY HIM (the "new creation" spoke of in 2Cor 5:17), and so we then pray to Him, to forgive us and ask Him to strengthen us so that we do not sin again. (1Jn 1:7-9) Nevertheless, because none of us are perfect, we sin if not by acts of commission, by acts of omission. (Heb 4:14-16) God ever lives to forgive us once are under the Grace of our Lord Jesus Christ. It is certain, that no one who is a Christian, just thinks God will forgive me and commits something like muslims imply a murder, or something akin to what they do. Instead, sin is a battle for the Christian that we are destined to conquer in Christ! (Rom 7:23-25) It is that while we struggle against sin, we sometimes fall, something not so serious as the grievous kinds of sins like murder, but it can be serious GOD still tells us He forgives the truly repentant. But even seeming little sins like not doing something He wanted you to do, give to a charity or something, and you just didn't (Acts 5:3,4) can be serious with God and so we live with reverence trying our hardest not to sin because sin has consequences not just for us but others. We still pray for something that still convicts us that we have sinned against His Holy Spirit and so we pray each day to be more and more like God wants us to be, - HOLY, PURE, SINLESS, and SPOTLESS like Himself. The key word is REPENT! repent from all your sinful ways and TURN TO

GOD, OUR LORD JESUS CHRIST, and He will empower you to do what is Good and RIGHT in His Sight!

Those who have truly repented are manifest in that they no longer desire to sin but to live RIGHTEOUSLY BY THE GRACE OF GOD, so Christians are different from this sinful world changed by God's grace.

...**8**The one who practices sin is of the devil, because the devil has been sinning from the very start. This is why the Son of God was revealed, to destroy the works of the devil. **9**Anyone born of God refuses to practice sin, because God's seed abides in him; he cannot go on sinning, because he has been born of God. **10**By this the children of God are distinguished from the children of the devil: Anyone who does not practice righteousness is not of God, nor is anyone who does not love his brother.... https://biblehub.com/1_john/3-9.htm

So muslims are still so wicked that they imagine the Christian can do whatever they want and all is forgiven, when the truth is Christians filled with the Holy Spirit of God, are nothing like their cult of murderers, rapists, child molesters, wife beaters, acid-throwing, hijab misogynists, honor killings, suicide bombers and otherwise atrocities of hating others. Christians are righteous! They're the ones feeding orphans, and widows, the hungry, preaching Salvation even to prisoners, and championing all manner of civil rights issues in this world.

A New Heaven and a New Earth
...**7**The one who overcomes will inherit all things, and I will be his God, and he will be My son. **8**But to the cowardly and unbelieving and abominable and murderers and sexually immoral and sorcerers and idolaters and all liars, their place will be in the lake that burns with fire and sulfur. This is the second death." https://biblehub.com/revelation/21-8.htm

muslims are online constantly asking us where Jesus Christ tells us He is God in the Holy Bible. (Obviously they haven't read it, or if they have, haven't understood it.)

Anyone saying that the Holy Bible doesn't tell us plainly that Jesus Christ is God, hasn't read it or if they have, most definitely lacks proper reading comprehension.

https://www.facebook.com/photo/?fbid=6809546799124221&set=a.115635768515391 - muslims are taught obvious lies in islam, like this worst one, denying Jesus Christ is God.

muslims Ask, Where Does Jesus Christ Tell Us He is God and to Worship Him?

And those who know and testify of the fact that Jesus Christ is God because He has given us His Holy Spirit of Truth, respond that He tells us that in the entire contents of the Holy Bible from Genesis through Revelation.

NO ONE IS A PROPHET WITHOUT THE HOLY SPIRIT OF THE ONE TRUE GOD, JESUS CHRIST, WHICH IS WHY ALL PROPHETS TESTIFY OF JESUS CHRIST THE ONE TRUE GOD, WHO HAS BEEN SPEAKING WITH MANKIND FROM THE BEGINNING!

https://biblehub.com/revelation/19-10.htm - …9Then the angel told me to write, "Blessed are those who are invited to the marriage supper of the Lamb." And he said to me, "These are the true words of God." 10So I fell at his feet to worship him. But he told me, "Do not do that! I am a fellow servant with you and your brothers who rely on the testimony of Jesus. Worship God! For the testimony of Jesus is the spirit of prophecy."

1) JESUS CHRIST SPOKE TO ALL PROPHETS AND IS WHY ALL PROPHETS TESTIFY OF JESUS CHRIST, THE ONE TRUE GOD!

Jesus Promises the Holy Spirit
...19In a little while the world will see Me no more, but you will see Me. Because I live, you also will live. 20On that day you will know that I am in My Father, and you are in Me, and I am in you. 21Whoever has My commandments and keeps them is the one who loves Me. The one who loves Me will be loved by My Father, and I will love him and reveal Myself to him."... https://biblehub.com/john/14-20.htm

Jesus Christ plainly told His Disciples He would be living inside of them. He told us the way He lives inside of us is by giving us His Own Holy Spirit of Truth.

8But you will receive power when the Holy Spirit comes upon you, and you will be My witnesses in Jerusalem, and in all Judea and Samaria, and to the ends of the earth." https://biblehub.com/acts/1-8.htm

It's by the Holy Spirit of God, Jesus Christ, that we are one with Him and how we hear the Voice of His Spirit telling us what to say and what to write. (How and Why the Holy Bible exists.)

Eyewitnesses of His Majesty
...20Above all, you must understand that no prophecy of Scripture comes from one's own interpretation. 21For no such prophecy was ever brought forth by the will of man, but men spoke from God as they were carried along by the Holy Spirit. https://biblehub.com/2_peter/1-21.htm

2 Samuel 23:2
The Spirit of the LORD spoke through me; His word was on my tongue.

Luke 1:70 as He spoke through His holy prophets, those of ages past,

David knew Jesus Christ, the One True God, by the presence of His Holy Spirit upon and within him and is why He asked God, Jesus Christ, not to take His Holy Spirit from him!

Acts 1:16
"Brothers, the Scripture had to be fulfilled which the Holy Spirit foretold through the mouth of David concerning Judas, who became a guide for those who arrested Jesus.

Acts 3:18
But in this way God has fulfilled what He foretold through all the prophets, saying that His Christ would suffer.

Jesus Opens the Scriptures
...26Was it not necessary for the Christ to suffer these things and then to enter His glory?" 27And beginning with Moses and all the Prophets, He explained to them what was written in all the Scriptures about Himself. https://biblehub.com/luke/24-27.htm

Create in Me a Clean Heart, O God
...10Create in me a clean heart, O God, and renew a right spirit within me. 11Cast me not away from Your presence; take not Your Holy Spirit from me. 12Restore to me the joy of Your salvation, and sustain me with a willing spirit.... https://biblehub.com/psalms/51-11.htm

This is why ALL Prophets tell us Jesus Christ is LORD and SAVIOR (just as David did in the above citation):

https://www.accordingtothescriptures.org/.../353prophecie... - the Holy Spirit of Jesus Christ, the One True God, told the Prophets what to say about Him, even when He told them He would come in the flesh as the Messiah, centuries before He did so! THE MESSIAH, known in the English language as Jesus Christ, is YHWH who came in the flesh!

Acts 10:34-43
34 So Peter opened his mouth and said: "Truly I understand that God shows no partiality, 35 but in every nation anyone who fears him and does what is right is acceptable to him. 36 As for the word that he sent to Israel, preaching good news of peace through Jesus Christ (he is Lord of all), 37 you yourselves know what happened throughout all Judea, beginning from Galilee after the baptism that John proclaimed: 38 how God anointed Jesus of Nazareth with the Holy Spirit and with power. He went about doing good and healing all who were oppressed by the devil, for God was with him. 39 And we are witnesses of all that he did both in the country of the Jews and in Jerusalem. They put him to death by hanging him on a tree, 40 but God raised him on the third day and made him to appear, 41 not to all the people but to us who had been chosen by God as witnesses, who ate and drank with him after he rose from the dead. 42 And he commanded us to preach to the people and to testify that he is the one appointed by God to be judge of the living and the dead. 43 To him all the prophets bear witness that everyone who believes in him receives forgiveness of sins through his name."

verse 36 - Jesus Christ is LORD OF ALL verse 43 ALL PROPHETS TESTIFY THAT JESUS CHRIST IS LORD OF ALL AND THAT FORGIVENESS OF SINS IS ONLY THROUGH HIM, BY NAME!

SALVATION IS IN NO ONE AND NOTHING ELSE BUT JESUS CHRIST!

...11This Jesus is 'the stone you builders rejected, which has become the cornerstone.' 12 Salvation exists in no one else, for there is no other name under heaven given to men by which we must be saved."
https://biblehub.com/acts/4-12.htm

Anyone who knows God, Jesus Christ, because He has given them His Holy Spirit of Truth, speaks and writes His Words to others, not just in the past throughout history, but to this very day. True Christians are TESTIFYING ABOUT JESUS CHRIST, THE ONE TRUE GOD, to the entire world!

16Whoever listens to you listens to Me; whoever rejects you rejects Me; and whoever rejects Me rejects the One who sent Me." https://biblehub.com/luke/10-16.htm

IT'S DUE TO THE FACT GOD, JESUS CHRIST, IS REALLY WITH HIS DISCIPLES, TRUE CHRISTIANS, BECAUSE HE HAS GIVEN US HIS OWN HOLY SPIRIT OF TRUTH AND IS TELLING US WHAT TO SAY AND WRITE DOWN!

My Heart is Stirred by a Noble Theme
1For the choirmaster. To the tune of "The Lilies." A Maskil of the sons of Korah. A love song. My heart is stirred by a noble theme as I recite my verses to the king; my tongue is the pen of a skillful writer.
https://biblehub.com/psalms/45-1.htm

So that's why the ENTIRE contents of the Holy Bible come from Jesus Christ and are fulfilled by Jesus Christ, the One True God!

All Scripture is God-Breathed
...15From infancy you have known the Holy Scriptures, which are able to make you wise for salvation through faith in Christ Jesus. 16All Scripture is God-breathed and is useful for instruction, for conviction, for correction, and for training in righteousness, 17so that the man of God may be complete, fully equipped for every good work....
https://biblehub.com/2_timothy/3-16.htm

The Fulfillment of the Law
16In the same way, let your light shine before men, that they may see your good deeds and glorify your Father in heaven. 17Do not think that I have come to abolish the Law or the Prophets. I have not come to abolish them, but to fulfill them. 18For I tell you truly, until heaven and earth pass away, not a single jot, not a stroke of a pen, will disappear from the Law until everything is accomplished.... https://biblehub.com/matthew/5-17.htm

John 5:39-40
English Standard Version
39 You search the Scriptures because you think that in them you have eternal life; and it is they that bear witness about me, 40 yet you refuse to come to me that you may have life.

God, Jesus Christ, PLAINLY SAYS, the entire contents of the Holy Bible are all about Him, the One True God, who keeps His Own Law and Prophecies. NO ONE ELSE CAN, BECAUSE THEY ARE NOT THE ONE TRUE GOD! (It's why the very first verse tells us Jesus Christ, the Beginning and End(ALEPH-TAV in the first verse of the Holy Bible is the One who created the Heavens and Earth and in John 1:1-14 that ALEPH-TAV, One True God, who speaks and it is, came in the flesh!), is STILL the One True God and is why the very last verses in the Holy Bible, is STILL the SAME GOD, JESUS CHRIST, telling us all HE IS THE ALPHA-OMEGA (Greek for the Hebrew ALEPH-TAV in the first verse of the Holy Bible and throughout) who is coming back to Judge mankind, one by one!

So don't follow the damned fools who are running into the flames of damnation! Make sure you are RIGHT WITH GOD, by OBEYING THE COMMANDMENTS OF OUR LORD AND SAVIOR JESUS CHRIST, THE ONE TRUE GOD, WHO TELLS US HOW TO KNOW AND LEARN FROM HIM PERSONALLY IN THE CONTENTS OF THE HOLY BIBLE!

2) ANY AND ALL LOCATIONS THAT MENTION LORD, GOD, YHWH, JESUS CHRIST, SPIRIT OF GOD, SPIRIT OF TRUTH, HOLY SPIRIT, SPIRIT OF CHRIST, OR ANY AND ALL SUPREME TITLES LIKE: THE BEGINNING AND THE END, THE FIRST AND THE LAST, THE FIRSTBORN, THE ONE TRUE GOD, KING OF KINGS, LORD OF LORDS, THE FATHER, THE SON, THE PROPHET, THE HOLY GHOST, THE GOOD SHEPHERD, THE ETERNAL ONE, I AM THAT I AM, THE ANGEL OF THE LORD, THE SUN OF RIGHTEOUSNESS, any and ALL SUPREME TITLES are REFERRING TO GOD, WHO IS THE ONE CALLED (IN ENGLISH LANGUAGE) JESUS, THE CHRIST. JESUS CHRIST IS YHWH, THE ONE TRUE GOD, WHO CAME IN THE FLESH AS THE MESSIAH; JUST AS HE TOLD THE PROPHETS.
https://www.facebook.com/photo.php?fbid=6800758120003089&set=pb.100002069048072.-2207520000&type=3 - JESUS CHRIST IS THE SAME GOD WHO CREATED AND MADE THE HEAVENS AND EARTH AND HAS BEEN SPEAKING WITH MANKIND FROM THE BEGINNING.

24That is why I told you that you would die in your sins. For unless you believe that I am He, you will die in your sins." 25"Who are You?" they asked. "Just what I have been telling you from the beginning," Jesus replied.... https://biblehub.com/john/8-24.htm

Exodus 3:14
God said to Moses, "I AM WHO I AM. This is what you are to say to the Israelites: 'I AM has sent me to you.'"

John 8:48-59
English Standard Version
Before Abraham Was, I Am

48 The Jews answered him, "Are we not right in saying that you are a Samaritan and have a demon?" 49 Jesus answered, "I do not have a demon, but I honor my Father, and you dishonor me. 50 Yet I do not seek my own glory; there is One who seeks it, and he is the judge. 51 Truly, truly, I say to you, if anyone keeps my word, he will never see death." 52 The Jews said to him, "Now we know that you have a demon! Abraham died, as did the prophets, yet you say, 'If anyone keeps my word, he will never taste death.' 53 Are you greater than our father Abraham, who died? And the prophets died! Who do you make yourself out to be?" 54 Jesus answered, "If I glorify myself, my glory is nothing. It is my Father who glorifies me, of whom you say, 'He is our God.'[a] 55 But you have not known him. I know him. If I were to say that I do not know him, I would be a liar like you, but I do know him and I keep his word. 56 Your father Abraham rejoiced that he would see my day. He saw it and was glad." 57 So the Jews said to him, "You are not yet fifty years old, and have you seen Abraham?"[b] 58 Jesus said to them, "Truly, truly, I say to you, before Abraham was, I am." 59 So they picked up stones to throw at him, but Jesus hid himself and went out of the temple.

THERE IS NO DOUBT WHATSOEVER THAT JESUS CHRIST CLAIMED TO BE THE VERY SAME GOD WHO GAVE HIS LAW TO MOSES AND SPOKE WITH ALL THE PROPHETS FROM THE BEGINNING! THOSE WHO HEARD HIM SPEAKING THEIR OWN LANGUAGE QUOTING FROM THE WORDS HE HAD GIVEN THEM IN THEIR OWN SCROLLS, IMMEDIATELY UNDERSTOOD JESUS CHRIST WAS CLAIMING TO BE YHWH! IT'S WHY THOSE WHO DIDN'T BELIEVE HIM, IMMEDIATELY BENT DOWN TO PICK UP STONES AND STONE HIM!

So muslims, you can't say you believe in Jesus Christ, if you are denying He claimed to be GOD! you can't call Jesus Christ a Prophet and a liar! liars are NOT prophets! Bottom line, the Holy Bible, Christianity, is telling us all the Truth; not the quran and islam! In other words, not one muslim hears, sees or knows God and that is because they are believing lies and denying the One True God, our GOOD LORD Jesus Christ, and are following the lying muhammad and his false imaginary evil god, allah, instead! ALL true Prophets and ALL true Christians KNOW GOD PERSONALLY! Because they ALL have His SAME HOLY SPIRIT OF TRUTH! If anyone DOES NOT HAVE THE HOLY SPIRIT OF THE ONE TRUE GOD, JESUS CHRIST, THEY ARE NOT A CHRISTIAN! NOT A PROPHET! and instead are STILL in their sins, STILL being deceived by the spirit of err, the devil!

Living in the Spirit
8Those controlled by the flesh cannot please God. 9You, however, are controlled not by the flesh, but by the Spirit, if the Spirit of God lives in you. And if anyone does not have the Spirit of Christ, he does not belong to Christ. 10But if Christ is in you, your body is dead because of sin, yet your spirit is alive because of righteousness....
https://biblehub.com/romans/8-9.htm

If you do not have His Holy Spirit of Truth, you do not understand His Words correctly in the Holy Bible! You must listen to those who at least CLAIM they KNOW GOD and have His Holy Spirit of Truth! otherwise, you are being deceived by the spirit of err, to the point where you don't interpret what you read in the Holy Bible, correctly!

Testing the Spirits
...5They are of the world. That is why they speak from the world's perspective, and the world listens to them. 6We are from God. Whoever knows God listens to us; whoever is not from God does not listen to us. That is how we know the Spirit of truth and the spirit of deception.
https://biblehub.com/1_john/4-6.htm

Spiritual Wisdom
...13And this is what we speak, not in words taught us by human wisdom, but in words taught by the Spirit, expressing spiritual truths in spiritual words. 14 The natural man does not accept the things that come from the Spirit of God. For they are foolishness to him, and he cannot understand

them, because they are spiritually discerned. 15The spiritual man judges all things, but he himself is not subject to anyone's judgment....
https://biblehub.com/1_corinthians/2-14.htm

Romans 8:5-10

King James Version

5 For they that are after the flesh do mind the things of the flesh; but they that are after the Spirit the things of the Spirit.
6 For to be carnally minded is death; but to be spiritually minded is life and peace.
7 Because the carnal mind is enmity against God: for it is not subject to the law of God, neither indeed can be.
8 So then they that are in the flesh cannot please God.
9 But ye are not in the flesh, but in the Spirit, if so be that the Spirit of God dwell in you. Now if any man have not the Spirit of Christ, he is none of his.
10 And if Christ be in you, the body is dead because of sin; but the Spirit is life because of righteousness.

Heirs with Christ

...15For you did not receive a spirit of slavery that returns you to fear, but you received the Spirit of sonship, by whom we cry, "Abba! Father!" 16The Spirit Himself testifies with our spirit that we are God's children. 17And if we are children, then we are heirs: heirs of God and co-heirs with Christ— if indeed we suffer with Him, so that we may also be glorified with Him.... https://biblehub.com/romans/8-16.htm

If you do not KNOW GOD, Jesus Christ, PERSONALLY as your Heavenly Father, it is because you are believing lies and have not obeyed His Commandment to Repent and Be Baptized in His Name so that you could receive Him by His Own Holy Spirit of TRUTH! JESUS CHRIST IS THE TRUTH! HIS SPIRIT IS THE HOLY SPIRIT OF TRUTH!

John 14:6-9

New King James Version

6   Jesus said to him, "I am the way, the truth, and the life. No one comes to the Father except through Me.

The Father Revealed

7   "If you had known Me, you would have known My Father also; and from now on you know Him and have seen Him."

8   Philip said to Him, "Lord, show us the Father, and it is sufficient for us." 9 Jesus said to him, "Have I been with you so long, and yet you have not known Me, Philip? He who has seen Me has seen the Father; so how can you say, 'Show us the Father'?

JESUS CHRIST IS THE REVELATION OF THE FATHER GOD IN THE FLESH! IN OTHER WORDS "THE SON" IS THE VISIBLE IMAGE OF "THE FATHER" SIMILAR TO HOW YOUR OWN BODY IS THE VISIBLE IMAGE OF YOUR OWN INVISIBLE SPIRIT!

Colossians 1:15-19

The Supremacy of the Son of God

15 The Son is the image of the invisible God, the firstborn over all creation. 16 For in him all things were created: things in heaven and on earth, visible and invisible, whether thrones or powers or rulers or authorities; all things have been created through him and for him. 17 He is before all things, and in him all things hold together. 18 And he is the head of the body, the church; he is the beginning and the firstborn from among the dead, so that in everything he might have the supremacy. 19 For God was pleased to have all his fullness dwell in him,

Which is why the scriptures plainly say that those who receive Jesus Christ, who have His Holy Spirit of Truth, are the Children of God! God is with them by His Holy Spirit calling each of them His own Son or His own Daughter! (Romans 8:16)

...11He came to His own, and His own did not receive Him. 12But to all who did receive Him, to those who believed in His name, He gave the right to become children of God— 13children born not of blood, nor of the desire or will of man, but born of God.... https://biblehub.com/john/1-12.htm

Continue in Him
...26I have written these things to you about those who are trying to deceive you. 27And as for you, the anointing you received from Him remains in you, and you do not need anyone to teach you. But just as His TRUE and genuine anointing teaches you about all things, so remain in Him as you have been taught. 28And now, little children, remain in Christ, so that when He appears, we may be confident and unashamed before Him at His coming.... https://biblehub.com/1_john/2-27.htm

So when a Son or Daughter of God is praying to "Our Father, who is in Heaven..." we are praying to our Lord and Savior, Jesus Christ, the One True God! It's why He tells us every knee will bow before Him and acknowledge that fact! JESUS CHRIST, NAME ABOVE ALL NAMES!

...9Therefore God exalted Him to the highest place and gave Him the name above all names, 10that at the name of Jesus every knee should bow, in heaven and on earth and under the earth, 11and every tongue confess that Jesus Christ is Lord, to the glory of God the Father.... https://biblehub.com/philippians/2-10.htm

Psalm 95:6
O come, let us worship and bow down; let us kneel before the LORD our Maker.

Isaiah 45:23
By Myself I have sworn; truth has gone out from My mouth, a word that will not be revoked: Every knee will bow before Me, every tongue will swear allegiance.

Romans 14:11
It is written: "As surely as I live, says the Lord, every knee will bow before Me; every tongue will confess to God."

People actually ask me why I cite the contents of the Holy Bible and I'm astonished when they do, because there is no one in all creation to cite as a Greater Authority than God Almighty and His Words given us all in the contents of the Holy Bible! GOD ALMIGHTY, JESUS CHRIST, IS THE TRUTH AND HE DOESN'T LIE! everyone else He created and made not only has lied, but they are believing and passing on lies, if they don't know Him! EVERYONE on earth is lying to themselves and others, if they don't know GOD ALMIGHTY, JESUS CHRIST, WHO IS THE TRUTH AND NEVER LIES!

God's Unchangeable Promise
...17So when God wanted to make the unchanging nature of His purpose very clear to the heirs of the promise, He guaranteed it with an oath. 18Thus by two unchangeable things in which it is impossible for God to lie, we who have fled to take hold of the hope set before us may be strongly encouraged. 19We have this hope as an anchor for the soul, firm and secure. It enters the inner sanctuary behind the curtain,...
https://biblehub.com/hebrews/6-18.htm

Numbers https://biblehub.com/interlinear/numbers/23-19.htm - 23:19 SAYS IN THE ORIGINAL LANGUAGE that God doesn't tell lies like sinful men AND He doesn't even need to repent like the sons of Adam! God is telling us those who intentionally tell lies, especially about Him and His Words in the Holy Bible, are wicked! sinful! "ish"! wicked, sinful men are liars! BUT EVEN the righteous sons of Adam, still make mistakes and so still need to repent, BUT NOT GOD! NOT JESUS CHRIST! HE IS HOLY AND PERFECT! God tells us hundreds of times He would come as the Messiah, a Man, in the flesh!
https://www.accordingtothescriptures.org/prophecy/353prophecies.html
AND He tells us in the very first chapter of the Holy Bible that He created mankind in His Image and Likeness! So, God NEVER denies He is a Man in

essence! He is only telling us He doesn't tell lies, like wicked, sinners do and He has no need to repent, because He is Good and Perfect!

The Sixth Day
...26Then God said, "Let Us make man in Our image, after Our likeness, to rule over the fish of the sea and the birds of the air, over the livestock, and over all the earth itself and every creature that crawls upon it." 27So God created man in His own image; in the image of God He created him; male and female He created them. 28God blessed them and said to them, "Be fruitful and multiply, and fill the earth and subdue it; rule over the fish of the sea and the birds of the air and every creature that crawls upon the earth."... https://biblehub.com/genesis/1-27.htm

So when muslims deny Jesus Christ is the One True God, who came in the flesh, they are calling God, Jesus Christ, a liar, they are calling all His Prophets in the Holy Bible liars, they are calling His Eyewitness Apostles and Disciples (Christians) in the Holy Bible all liars and they are calling the billions of us who are plainly telling them all that Jesus Christ is the One True God because He has given us His Holy Spirit of Truth to empower us to testify about Him to everyone, everywhere (Acts 1:8) that He is the One True God, all liars. So muslims act like when they deny Jesus Christ as the One True God that He is, that they are not insulting Him or us, even though they are! We are telling muslims that they are lying to themselves and the whole world, not because we are insulting them, but because it's just plain true! muslims are believing lies about God and passing those lies on, which makes them all liars and antichrists.

Beware of Antichrists
...21I have not written to you because you lack knowledge of the truth, but because you have it, and because no lie comes from the truth. 22Who is the liar, if it is not the one who denies that Jesus is the Christ? This is the antichrist, who denies the Father and the Son. 23Whoever denies the Son does not have the Father, but whoever confesses the Son has the Father as well.... https://biblehub.com/1_john/2-22.htm

1 John 4:1-6
English Standard Version
Test the Spirits
4 Beloved, do not believe every spirit, but test the spirits to see whether they are from God, for many false prophets have gone out into the world. 2 By this you know the Spirit of God: every spirit that confesses that Jesus Christ has come in the flesh is from God, 3 and every spirit that does not confess Jesus is not from God. This is the spirit of the antichrist, which you heard was coming and now is in the world already. 4 Little children, you are from God and have overcome them, for he who is in you is greater than he who is in the world. 5 They are from the world; therefore they speak from the world, and the world listens to them. 6 We are from God. Whoever knows God listens to us; whoever is not from God does not listen to us. By this we know the Spirit of truth and the spirit of error.

So anyone who denies that Jesus Christ is YHWH who came in the flesh is a liar and an antichrist! Christ is the Greek for Messiah! Messiah is YHWH in the flesh!

Jesus and the Samaritan Woman
...24God is Spirit, and His worshipers must worship Him in spirit and in truth." 25The woman said, "I know that Messiah" (called Christ) "is coming. When He comes, He will explain everything to us." 26Jesus answered, "I who speak to you am He."... https://biblehub.com/john/4-25.htm

https://hebrew4christians.com/Names_of_G-d/Messiah/messiah.html - Messiah is YHWH (JESUS CHRIST) who came in the flesh!

...10"You are My witnesses," declares the LORD, "and My servant whom I have chosen, so that you may consider and believe Me and understand that I am He. Before Me no god was formed, and after Me none will come.

11I, yes I, am the LORD, and there is no Savior but Me. 12I alone decreed and saved and proclaimed—I, and not some foreign god among you. So you are My witnesses," declares the LORD, "that I am God....
https://biblehub.com/isaiah/43-11.htm

Peter and John Before the Council
...11This Jesus is 'the stone you builders rejected, which has become the cornerstone.' 12 Salvation exists in no one else, for there is no other name under heaven given to men by which we must be saved."
https://biblehub.com/acts/4-12.htm

3)So, ANY LOCATION IN THE HOLY BIBLE TELLING US "THUS SAYS THE LORD" IS JESUS CHRIST SPEAKING! FURTHERMORE, WHATEVER HIS APOSTLES SAID OR WROTE IN HIS NAME, UNDER INSPIRATION OF HIS HOLY SPIRIT OF TRUTH, IS STILL JESUS CHRIST SPEAKING! EVERYTHING THE HOLY SPIRIT OF GOD, JESUS CHRIST, TOLD HIS PROPHETS TO SAY AND WRITE DOWN IS STILL THE WORDS OF JESUS CHRIST! IN OTHER WORDS, THE ENTIRE CONTENTS OF THE HOLY BIBLE ARE THE WORDS OF JESUS CHRIST, THE ONE TRUE GOD! SO, THE HOLY BIBLE IS TELLING US THE TRUTH, BECAUSE IT COMES FROM THE ONE WHO IS TRUTH, JESUS CHRIST!

And in His Words, He tells us many HUNDREDS of times that He is the One True God, His very Name tells us He is the One True God, ALL His Prophets and Disciples tell us He is the One True God, and Jesus Christ ever lives to confirm He is the One True God, to any and all who have enough sense to call upon Him!

The Greatest Commandment
...3Hear, O Israel, and be careful to observe them, so that you may prosper and multiply greatly in a land flowing with milk and honey, just as the LORD, the God of your fathers, has promised you. 4Hear, O Israel: The LORD our God, the LORD is One. 5And you shall love the LORD your God

with all your heart and with all your soul and with all your strength....
https://biblehub.com/deuteronomy/6-4.htm

Matthew 22:37
Jesus declared, "'Love the Lord your God with all your heart and with all your soul and with all your mind.'

Mark 12:29
Jesus replied, "This is the most important: 'Hear O Israel, the Lord our God, the Lord is One.
Mark 12:30
Love the Lord your God with all your heart and with all your soul and with all your mind and with all your strength.'

Luke 10:27
He answered, "'Love the Lord your God with all your heart and with all your soul and with all your strength and with all your mind' and 'Love your neighbor as yourself.'"

John 10:30
I and the Father are one."

So, in EVERY LOCATION in the Holy Bible where God says He is GOD and to worship, love, serve and obey, only Him: THAT IS JESUS CHRIST! It's why He says to hate Him is to hate God! to hate "the Son" is to hate "the Father"! HE IS THE VISIBLE IMAGE OF GOD, THE EXACT REPRESENTATION OF GOD! YOU CANNOT SEPARATE HIS VISIBLE REPRESENTATION FROM HIS ETERNAL INVISIBLE EXISTENCE! When we bow before God, we will be bowing before JESUS CHRIST! This is why HE ALWAYS RECEIVES WORSHIP AS GOD!

The Greatest Commandment
...12be careful not to forget the LORD who brought you out of the land of Egypt, out of the house of slavery. 13 Fear the LORD your God, serve Him only, and take your oaths in His name. 14Do not follow other gods, the gods of the peoples around you.... https://biblehub.com/deuteronomy/6-

13.htm

Matthew 4:10
"Away from Me, Satan!" Jesus declared. "For it is written: 'Worship the Lord your God and serve Him only.'"

Luke 4:8
But Jesus answered, "It is written: 'Worship the Lord your God and serve Him only.'"

muslims like to imagine Jesus Christ wasn't quoting Himself when He makes these statements but He was! It's WHY HE ALWAYS RECEIVES WORSHIP AS GOD!

https://www.openbible.info/topics/worshipping_jesus - NEVER ONCE DOES JESUS CHRIST TELL ANYONE WORSHIPPING HIM TO STOP DOING SO! INSTEAD, HE COMPLAINS WHEN PEOPLE SHOULD HAVE AND DIDN'T!

The Ten Lepers
...16He fell facedown at Jesus' feet in thanksgiving to Him—and he was a Samaritan. 17"Were not all ten cleansed?" Jesus asked. "Where then are the other nine? 18Was no one found except this foreigner to return and give glory to God?"... https://biblehub.com/luke/17-17.htm

When Jesus Christ says things like "the Father is Greater" and "I speak the Words of the Father exactly in the Way the Father wants them to be spoken." and "I always do the will of the Father" and yet also says to look at Him is to see the Father and that He and the Father are One. THOSE ARE ALL JUST TRUTH! It is God saying do NOT think that this visible body of flesh and bones is all that I am! Instead, He is telling us that His Body, His Visible Image, the Messiah, is actually GOD in the flesh! And that His

Eternal, Pervasive, Transcendent Existence is what is causing His Flesh and Bone Body to SPEAK HIS WORDS EXACTLY ALWAYS! AND TO DO HIS MIRACLES! etc. etc.! It DOES NOT MEAN THAT JESUS CHRIST ISN'T GOD! IT JUST MEANS GOD IS TEACHING US NOT TO IMAGINE THAT HIS FLESH AND BONE VISIBLE BODY IS ALL THAT HE IS! GOD IS MUCH, MUCH MORE THAN WHAT HE APPEARS TO BE WHEN HE CAME HUMBLY AS A MAN, THE MESSIAH!

This is why He says things like hating Him is hating God.

The Hatred of the World
...22If I had not come and spoken to them, they would not be guilty of sin. Now, however, they have no excuse for their sin. 23Whoever hates Me hates My Father as well. 24If I had not done among them the works that no one else did, they would not be guilty of sin; but now they have seen and hated both Me and My Father. 25But this is to fulfill what is written in their Law: 'They hated Me without reason.'...
https://biblehub.com/john/15-24.htm

Notice Jesus Christ is speaking about Himself and His Father as if His Father could be someone other than Himself but then notice in verse 25 He refers to "Me and My Father" as just "Me". This is because His Visible Body is ONE with His Invisible Spirit, similar to how your own body is one with your own invisible spirit, and just as your body, doesn't live, breathe, speak or do anything without your spirit, so the Son (Visible Image of God) does nothing without the Father (Eternal, Invisible, Pervasive and Transcendent Existence of God - Ephesians 4:6)!

26 As the body without the spirit is dead, so faith without deeds is dead.
https://biblehub.com/james/2-26.htm

Since the body does NOTHING without the spirit, the spirit is GREATER than the body, even though spirit and body are one!

So, stop trying to make Jesus Christ to be someone other than the One True God that He is! it would be as ridiculous as you trying to claim your own body, your words and your deeds, don't represent yourself to the rest of the world!

Colossians 1:15-19
The Supremacy of the Son of God
15 The Son is the image of the invisible God, the firstborn over all creation. 16 For in him all things were created: things in heaven and on earth, visible and invisible, whether thrones or powers or rulers or authorities; all things have been created through him and for him. 17 He is before all things, and in him all things hold together. 18 And he is the head of the body, the church; he is the beginning and the firstborn from among the dead, so that in everything he might have the supremacy. 19 For God was pleased to have all his fullness dwell in him,

When the Scriptures PLAINLY STATE that Jesus Christ, is the Image of the Invisible God and is SUPREME in EVERYTHING then it follows that Jesus Christ is the: God of gods, Man of men, Spirit of spirits, Angel of angels, Father of fathers, Son of sons, Servant of servants, Prophet of prophets, First and Last, Beginning and End, King of kings, Lord of lords, Apostle of apostles, Disciple of disciples, Word of words, Shepherd of shepherds, Star of stars, Holy of holies, Heaven of heavens, Star of stars, Cup of cups, Thunder of thunders, Scroll of scrolls, Book of books, Gate of gates, etc. etc. etc. which is WHY the scriptures refer to Him in ALL these ways and MORE! HE HAS THE PREEMINENCE, IS SUPREME IN EVERYTHING!

So, stop ripping His Words out of context to make false claims about Him, because that is what the devil did and is still doing to this day. If you don't want to be known as a child of the devil, an antichrist, STOP LYING ABOUT GOD AND HIS WORDS IN THE HOLY BIBLE! (muslims! because muslims are the worst violators in this regard on earth today!)

JESUS CHRIST IS THE EXACT REPRESENTATION OF GOD, similar to how your own visible body represents you!

The Supremacy of the Son
...2But in these last days He has spoken to us by His Son, whom He appointed heir of all things, and through whom He made the universe. 3The Son is the radiance of God's glory and the exact representation of His nature, upholding all things by His powerful word. After He had provided purification for sins, He sat down at the right hand of the Majesty on high. 4So He became as far superior to the angels as the name He has inherited is excellent beyond theirs.... https://biblehub.com/hebrews/1-3.htm

Jesus Christ tells us that God is Spirit, that His Words are Spirit, and so it is IMPOSSIBLE for Jesus Christ to LITERALLY sit "at the right hand of God". It is an idiom that is still in use to this day as "right hand man" to mean one who is entrusted with power and authority. JUST LIKE HE TELLS US!

...62Then what will happen if you see the Son of Man ascend to where He was before? 63The Spirit gives life; the flesh profits nothing. The words I have spoken to you are spirit and they are life.
https://biblehub.com/john/6-63.htm

The Great Commission
...17When they saw Him, they worshiped Him, but some doubted. 18Then Jesus came to them and said, "All authority in heaven and on earth has been given to Me. 19Therefore go and make disciples of all nations, baptizing them in the name of the Father, and of the Son, and of the Holy Spirit,20and teaching them to obey all that I have commanded you. And surely I am with you always, even to the end of the age."...
https://biblehub.com/matthew/28-18.htm

So "the Son" does nothing without "the Father" similar to how our own bodies do nothing without our spirits. When we die, our flesh returns to the dust, while our spirit must give account to Jesus Christ, the One True God.

7before the dust returns to the ground from which it came and the spirit returns to God who gave it. https://biblehub.com/ecclesiastes/12-7.htm

The Father and the Son
...21For just as the Father raises the dead and gives them life, so also the Son gives life to whom He wishes. 22Furthermore, the Father judges no one, but has assigned all judgment to the Son, 23so that all may honor the Son just as they honor the Father. Whoever does not honor the Son does not honor the Father who sent Him.... https://biblehub.com/john/5-22.htm

Do you understand yet? WHEN GOD JUDGES YOUR SOUL, YOU WILL BE BOWING BEFORE JESUS CHRIST! not some imaginary, invisible, false god! BUT THE ONE TRUE GOD WHO CREATED AND MADE THE HEAVENS AND EARTH AND CAME IN THE FLESH AND SHOWED US ALL WHO HE IS!

Matthew 25:31-46
The Final Judgment
31 "When the Son of Man comes in his glory, and all the angels with him, he will sit on his glorious throne. 32 All the nations will be gathered before him, and he will separate the people one from another as a shepherd separates the sheep from the goats. 33 He will put the sheep on his right and the goats on his left.
34 "Then the King will say to those on his right, 'Come, you who are blessed by my Father; take your inheritance, the kingdom prepared for you since the creation of the world. 35 For I was hungry and you gave me something to eat, I was thirsty and you gave me something to drink, I was a stranger and you invited me in, 36 I needed clothes and you clothed me,

I was sick and you looked after me, I was in prison and you came to visit me.'

37 "Then the righteous will answer him, 'Lord, when did we see you hungry and feed you, or thirsty and give you something to drink? 38 When did we see you a stranger and invite you in, or needing clothes and clothe you? 39 When did we see you sick or in prison and go to visit you?' 40 "The King will reply, 'Truly I tell you, whatever you did for one of the least of these brothers and sisters of mine, you did for me.'

41 "Then he will say to those on his left, 'Depart from me, you who are cursed, into the eternal fire prepared for the devil and his angels. 42 For I was hungry and you gave me nothing to eat, I was thirsty and you gave me nothing to drink, 43 I was a stranger and you did not invite me in, I needed clothes and you did not clothe me, I was sick and in prison and you did not look after me.'

44 "They also will answer, 'Lord, when did we see you hungry or thirsty or a stranger or needing clothes or sick or in prison, and did not help you?' 45 "He will reply, 'Truly I tell you, whatever you did not do for one of the least of these, you did not do for me.'

46 "Then they will go away to eternal punishment, but the righteous to eternal life."

so muslims! stop ripping His Words out of context to try and deny that Jesus Christ claimed and proved He is GOD! He most definitely said so and did! Again, ALL the PROPHETS SAY SO! ALL HIS DISCIPLES SAY SO! HE SAYS SO!

Woes to Scribes and Pharisees
...7the greetings in the marketplaces, and the title of 'Rabbi' by which they are addressed. 8But you are not to be called 'Rabbi,' for you have one Teacher, and you are all brothers. 9And do not call anyone on earth your father, for you have one Father, who is in heaven....
https://biblehub.com/matthew/23-8.htm

So here God tells them to stop referring to each other by Titles that belong to Him! HE SAYS CALL NO ONE TEACHER/RABBI because only GOD is our

TRUE TEACHER/RABBI and call no one FATHER because ONLY GOD IS OUR TRUE FATHER! (Spiritually speaking, in other words we have earthly fathers and earthly teachers but you are to refer to no religious person by these words because only God, SPIRITUALLY SPEAKING, bears these most honorable titles! Col 1:15-19) So when Jesus Christ then says:

13You call Me Teacher and Lord, and rightly so, because I am.
https://biblehub.com/john/13-13.htm

He is ABSOLUTELY STATING HE IS GOD!

Jesus Appears to Thomas
…27Then Jesus said to Thomas, "Put your finger here and look at My hands. Reach out your hand and put it into My side. Stop doubting and believe." 28Thomas replied, "My Lord and my God!" 29Jesus said to him, "Because you have seen Me, you have believed; blessed are those who have not seen and yet have believed."… https://biblehub.com/john/20-28.htm

Just like when He says no one is Good but God and then preaches openly that He is the Good Shepherd!

The Rich Young Man
17As Jesus started on His way, a man ran up and knelt before Him. "Good Teacher," he asked, "what must I do to inherit eternal life?" 18"Why do you call Me good?" Jesus replied. "No one is good except God alone. 19You know the commandments: 'Do not murder, do not commit adultery, do not steal, do not bear false witness, do not cheat others, honor your father and mother.' "… https://biblehub.com/mark/10-18.htm John 10 English Standard Version
I Am the Good Shepherd

10 "Truly, truly, I say to you, he who does not enter the sheepfold by the door but climbs in by another way, that man is a thief and a robber. 2 But he who enters by the door is the shepherd of the sheep. 3 To him the gatekeeper opens. The sheep hear his voice, and he calls his own sheep by name and leads them out. 4 When he has brought out all his own, he goes before them, and the sheep follow him, for they know his voice. 5 A stranger they will not follow, but they will flee from him, for they do not know the voice of strangers." 6 This figure of speech Jesus used with them, but they did not understand what he was saying to them. 7 So Jesus again said to them, "Truly, truly, I say to you, I am the door of the sheep. 8 All who came before me are thieves and robbers, but the sheep did not listen to them. 9 I am the door. If anyone enters by me, he will be saved and will go in and out and find pasture. 10 The thief comes only to steal and kill and destroy. I came that they may have life and have it abundantly. 11 I am the good shepherd. The good shepherd lays down his life for the sheep. 12 He who is a hired hand and not a shepherd, who does not own the sheep, sees the wolf coming and leaves the sheep and flees, and the wolf snatches them and scatters them. 13 He flees because he is a hired hand and cares nothing for the sheep. 14 I am the good shepherd. I know my own and my own know me, 15 just as the Father knows me and I know the Father; and I lay down my life for the sheep. 16 And I have other sheep that are not of this fold. I must bring them also, and they will listen to my voice. So there will be one flock, one shepherd. 17 For this reason the Father loves me, because I lay down my life that I may take it up again. 18 No one takes it from me, but I lay it down of my own accord. I have authority to lay it down, and I have authority to take it up again. This charge I have received from my Father."

(ONLY the One True God could make such a claim and Ever Lives to PROVE that claim! In other words, HE SAVES TO THE UTMOST ALL WHO TRUST IN HIM! -
https://www.biblegateway.com/passage/?search=Psalm%2023&version=KJV)

There is no doubt Jesus Christ REPEATEDLY AND OPENLY CLAIMED TO BE GOD! Those who heard Him and didn't believe, SAY SO!

John 10:32-36
King James Version
32   Jesus answered them, Many good works have I shewed you from my Father; for which of those works do ye stone me?
33   The Jews answered him, saying, For a good work we stone thee not; but for blasphemy; and because that thou, being a man, makest thyself God.
34   Jesus answered them, Is it not written in your law, I said, Ye are gods? 35 If he called them gods, unto whom the word of God came, and the scripture cannot be broken;
36 Say ye of him, whom the Father hath sanctified, and sent into the world, Thou blasphemest; because I said, I am the Son of God?

(This above quotation is proof that God made mankind in His Image just like He tells in Genesis 1:27 and so yes, God tells us all immediately that He is a Man and men are gods, just as He confirms in this passage!)

Bottom line, not one muslim sees, hears or knows God and that's due to the fact islam has been filling their heads with nothing but lies. All muslims must repent! If they don't stop ripping the Words of God, in the Holy Bible, out of context in a vain effort to deny the One True God, Jesus Christ, then they will perish in their sins as the liars and antichrists that they are showing themselves to be! (twisting His Words, is exactly what the devil did and still does) IF YOU DON'T KNOW THE ONE WHO IS TRUTH, IT'S BECAUSE YOU ARE FILLED WITH LIES!

ALL LIARS will be cast into the lake of fire! IF YOU DO NOT KNOW THE ONE WHO IS TRUTH, it's because you are believing and passing on lies, you are a liar!

Beware of Antichrists
...21I have not written to you because you lack knowledge of the truth, but because you have it, and because no lie comes from the truth. 22Who is the

liar, if it is not the one who denies that Jesus is the Christ? This is the antichrist, who denies the Father and the Son. 23Whoever denies the Son does not have the Father, but whoever confesses the Son has the Father as well.... https://biblehub.com/1_john/2-22.htm

REMEMBER! "CHRIST"/"MESSIAH" MEANS YOU ARE ACKNOWLEDGING JESUS CHRIST IS YHWH WHO CAME IN THE FLESH!

1 John 4:1-6
English Standard Version
Test the Spirits
4 Beloved, do not believe every spirit, but test the spirits to see whether they are from God, for many false prophets have gone out into the world. 2 By this you know the Spirit of God: every spirit that confesses that Jesus Christ has come in the flesh is from God, 3 and every spirit that does not confess Jesus is not from God. This is the spirit of the antichrist, which you heard was coming and now is in the world already. 4 Little children, you are from God and have overcome them, for he who is in you is greater than he who is in the world. 5 They are from the world; therefore they speak from the world, and the world listens to them. 6 We are from God. Whoever knows God listens to us; whoever is not from God does not listen to us. By this we know the Spirit of truth and the spirit of error.

King James Bible
And without controversy great is the mystery of godliness: God was manifest in the flesh, justified in the Spirit, seen of angels, preached unto the Gentiles, believed on in the world, received up into glory.
https://biblehub.com/kjv/1_timothy/3-16.htm

...19We know that we are of God, and that the whole world is under the power of the evil one. 20And we know that the Son of God has come and has given us understanding, so that we may know Him who is true; and we are in Him who is true— in His Son Jesus Christ. He is the TRUE God and eternal life. 21Little children, keep yourselves from idols....
https://biblehub.com/1_john/5-20.htm

If you don't know GOD, personally, it means you are still being deceived by the devil, because you are refusing to listen to and believe the One True God, Jesus Christ, and His Witnesses, true Christians, who know Him because He has given us His Holy Spirit of Truth.

6We are from God. Whoever knows God listens to us; whoever is not from God does not listen to us. That is how we know the Spirit of truth and the spirit of deception. https://biblehub.com/1_john/4-6.htm

John 8:47
Whoever belongs to God hears the words of God. The reason you do not hear is that you do not belong to God."

John 14:17
the Spirit of truth. The world cannot receive Him, because it neither sees Him nor knows Him. But you do know Him, for He abides with you and will be in you.

1 Corinthians 14:37
If anyone considers himself a prophet or spiritual person, let him acknowledge that what I am writing you is the Lord's command.

SO, ANYONE REJECTING ANY PART OF THE HOLY BIBLE IS NOT OF GOD! THEY ARE STILL BEING DECIEVED BY THE SPIRIT OF ERR, THE DEVIL! (Understand there is a difference between rejecting errant interpretations, false doctrines, and rejecting the Words of GOD, IN CONTEXT and PLAINLY STATED.) For just like the devil, there are those who handle the contents of the Holy Bible deceitfully! Anyone creating a doctrine by ripping words OUT OF CONTEXT in order TO DENY THE REST OF HOLY WRIT (like muslims who search for every location they can to DENY Jesus Christ claimed and proved He is God) are acting like the devil and children of devil, LIARS! who will all be cast into the lake of fire for attempting to lead people

AWAY FROM GOD, JESUS CHRIST! Instead of to Him and obeying Him and His Holy Commandments in the Holy Bible, like all true Disciples of Christ, Christians!

Again, True Christians, are ones who KNOW JESUS CHRIST, personally, because He has given them His Holy Spirit of Truth! So, if they cannot look you in the eyes and say they know Him, beyond all doubt, then they are someone still lost in their sins and still subject to being deceived by the spirit of err, just as lost in ignorance, lies, deceptions and self-delusions, as the rest of humanity. Yes, YOU CAN CALL ON JESUS CHRIST AND BE SAVED AND STILL NOT KNOW HIM, but if you are breathing and have strength and life to do so, you need to obey Him and Repent and Be Baptized in His Name, so He will then give you the promise of His Holy Spirit and turn you into a living, true, witness of His now and forever!

JESUS CHRIST IS THE TRUTH; SO, EVERYONE EVERYWHERE OBEY HIS COMMANDMENT TO REPENT AND BE BAPTIZED IN HIS NAME! BE FILLED WITH HIS HOLY SPIRIT OF TRUTH AND THEN TELL EVERYONE ELSE WHO STILL DOESN'T KNOW HIM THAT THEY MUST ALSO REPENT AND BELIEVE IN HIM AND HIS GOSPEL IN THE HOLY BIBLE! IF THEY CANNOT LOOK YOU IN THE EYE AND SAY TO YOUR FACE THAT THEY KNOW GOD, JESUS CHRIST, PERSONALLY, BECAUSE HE HAS GIVEN THEM HIS HOLY SPIRIT OF TRUTH, THEN FIND SOMEONE WHO CAN TO BAPTIZE YOU IN HIS NAME PROPERLY!

The Great Commission
...15And He said to them, "Go into all the world and preach the gospel to every creature. 16Whoever believes and is baptized will be saved, but whoever does not believe will be condemned.
https://biblehub.com/mark/16-16.htm

DON'T ARGUE WITH GOD! IF YOU HAVEN'T OBEYED HIM YET, YOU NEED TO DO SO FOR YOUR OWN GOOD AND THE GOOD OF ALL CREATION!!!!!!!!

Matthew 28:18-20
18 And Jesus came and said to them, "All authority in heaven and on earth has been given to me. 19 Go therefore and make disciples of all nations, baptizing them in[a] the name of the Father and of the Son and of the Holy Spirit, 20 teaching them to observe all that I have commanded you. And behold, I am with you always, to the end of the age."

"Brothers, what shall we do?" 38 Peter replied, "Repent and be baptized, every one of you, in the name of Jesus Christ for the forgiveness of your sins, and you will receive the gift of the Holy Spirit. 39This promise belongs to you and your children and to all who are far off—to all whom the Lord our God will call to Himself."... https://biblehub.com/acts/2-38.htm

John 14:20-26
English Standard Version
20 In that day you will know that I am in my Father, and you in me, and I in you. 21 Whoever has my commandments and keeps them, he it is who loves me. And he who loves me will be loved by my Father, and I will love him and manifest myself to him." 22 Judas (not Iscariot) said to him, "Lord, how is it that you will manifest yourself to us, and not to the world?" 23 Jesus answered him, "If anyone loves me, he will keep my word, and my Father will love him, and we will come to him and make our home with him. 24 Whoever does not love me does not keep my words. And the word that you hear is not mine but the Father's who sent me.
25 "These things I have spoken to you while I am still with you. 26 But the Helper, the Holy Spirit, whom the Father will send in my name, he will teach you all things and bring to your remembrance all that I have said to you.

The entire Holy Bible is about Jesus Christ revealing Himself to us that He is the One True God! It's why He says it's ALL ABOUT HIM!

John 5:39-40
39 You search the Scriptures because you think that in them you have eternal life; and it is they that bear witness about me, 40 yet you refuse to come to me that you may have life.

so muslims! STOP DENYING JESUS CHRIST IS THE ONE TRUE GOD, when you KNOW that you don't KNOW Him! Even His last book in the Holy Bible tells us that it is a Revelation of Jesus Christ!
https://biblehub.com/interlinear/revelation/1-1.htm

To know God requires knowing Jesus Christ, plain and simple; no ifs ands or buts. Jesus Christ then reveals HIMSELF as being the ONE TRUE GOD, because that is who He is and gives us a full understanding that He is much, much, much more than just His Humble Appearance as the Messiah who came in a flesh and bone body like our own, two thousand years ago. JESUS CHRIST EVER LIVES TO CONFIRM HE IS THE ONE TRUE GOD AND THAT SALVATION IS IN NO ONE AND NOTHING ELSE! YOU EITHER KNOW THE SAVIOR AND ARE REALLY SAVED OR YOU DON'T AND ARE STILL LOST IN YOUR SINS, LIES, DECEPTIONS AND SELF-DELUSIONS.

God's Grace Brings Salvation
...12It instructs us to renounce ungodliness and worldly passions, and to live sensible, upright, and godly lives in the present age, 13as we await the blessed hope and glorious appearance of our great God and Savior Jesus Christ. 14He gave Himself for us to redeem us from all lawlessness and to purify for Himself a people for His own possession, zealous for good deeds.... https://biblehub.com/titus/2-13.htm

Peter and John Before the Council
...11This Jesus is 'the stone you builders rejected, which has become the cornerstone.' 12 Salvation exists in no one else, for there is no other name under heaven given to men by which we must be saved."
https://biblehub.com/acts/4-12.htm

If you have BELIEVED the Gospel of Jesus Christ in the Holy Bible and have been baptized in water, in His Name, with the Baptism of Repentance, and still do not KNOW GOD, still do not HEAR Him speaking to you, still do not receive dreams and visions from Him teaching you Truth, then you need to find anyone nearby who can look you in the eyes and tell you they KNOW our Lord Jesus Christ because He has given them His Holy Spirit to lay hands on you and pray for you to receive His Holy Spirit and have your spiritual ears opened to hear His Voice and your spiritual eyes opened to perceive His dreams and visions, and your understanding opened to comprehend and remember what God teaches you. God can give His Holy Spirit to all who believe Him and all who are baptized in His Name, but sometimes He wants you to meet others and impart blessings to one another in that meeting. He has plans and purposes for all.

For example, I have FAITH that JESUS CHRIST can HEAL ANYONE OF ANYTHING and so I can say to you, BE HEALED IN JESUS MIGHTY NAME! It's just a matter of meeting Him and BELIEVING Him! Sometimes, it requires meeting someone in person. All things work together for good! Sometimes we bear an injury for what must seem a long-time asking God to heal us or even our whole lives. I know Him who I believe in, even if I die, I trust Him to one day make me all well! Never to suffer again!

KEY ELEMENTS OF PROPER BAPTISM: whoever is being baptized MUST BE TRULY REPENTANT! not just sorrowful for all their sins, but be ready to turn from every wicked, thought, word, way and deed, and to Love and Obey God, live righteously, by His Grace and Power! they have to stop imagining they know better than God how to run His Creation, including their own life! THEY MUST BE READY TO FOLLOW JESUS CHRIST AND OBEY HIS COMMANDMENTS IN THE HOLY BIBLE! If they are not truly repentant, they may as well just be going for a swim in water, baptism has no meaning, if the person isn't repentant and ready to Love and Obey the One True God, Jesus Christ!

Whoever is the one performing the baptism MUST ALREADY KNOW JESUS CHRIST BECAUSE HE HAS GIVEN THEM HIS HOLY SPIRIT OF TRUTH! It can be a man or woman, young or old, BUT THEY MUST KNOW JESUS CHRIST AND HAVE ALREADY RECEIVED HIS HOLY SPIRIT! otherwise, they are only an actor or actress doing their best to put on a performance, even though they really don't understand what they're doing or the reasons why.

There needs to be sufficient water for the one being baptized to be submerged completely under water! their body needs to go under water from the bottom of their feet to the top of their head! Ideally, this is a natural pool area in a gentle river or clean lake, not a stagnant pond, but a body of water that has inlets and outlets so that the water is moving and clean, but it can be a tub of water or pool, just as long as it's deep enough for the one being baptized to be completely submerged.

The one who is performing the baptism places their right hand upon the forehead of the one being baptized and says, "I baptize you in the Name of the Father, the Son, and the Holy Ghost/Spirit; which Name is (in English) Jesus Christ!" (Yahoshuah/Yeshua Ha Mashiach in Hebrew) and then the one being baptized goes completely under water and comes back up. No stress! they don't have to be under water for more than a second or two, they just need to go under completely and can come back up immediately for air. Again, ideally this is a pool area of gentle clean water at the side of a clean river or lake, in which both the baptizer and the one being baptized is safe from any dangerous currents and can stand firmly on the river or lake bed; so is in no danger whatsoever! OR it CAN be performed in a tub or pool; which is why I said "IDEALLY". In other words, try to follow the scriptures as closely as you can! John the Baptist baptized people in the Jordan River, a natural flowing river, and yet in safe locations where people weren't in danger of being swept away or drowning. So natural bodies of water are best! Gentle, safe locations in God's Creation, under His Watchful Eyes.

And the RIGHT HAND is preferable as opposed to the left because God uses the RIGHT HAND to indicate His Power and Authority in Scripture, but if someone is full of His Spirit and for some reason cannot use his or her right hand, they CAN USE their left one to baptize people! God knows our thoughts and intents of our hearts, so He knows who to Give His Holy Spirit of Truth to, and who has not yet fulfilled His Commandments, and as such, still does not have His HOLY SPIRIT upon and within them.

I repeat, IF YOU STILL DO NOT HEAR GOD SPEAKING WITH YOU, AND YOU HAVE TRULY REPENTED AND BEEN CORRECTLY BAPTIZED IN HIS NAME, THEN YOU NEED TO 1) PRAY WITH ALL SERIOUSNESS AND DESIRE FOR GOD TO GIVE YOU HIS HOLY SPIRIT OF TRUTH AND 2) SEEK ANYONE WHO CAN LOOK YOU IN THE EYES AND SAY THEY KNOW OUR LORD JESUS CHRIST, THE ONE TRUE GOD, BEYOND ALL DOUBT, TO LAY THEIR HANDS UPON YOU AND TO PRAY FOR YOU TO ALSO RECEIVE HIS HOLY SPIRIT OF TRUTH!

Acts 19
Paul in Ephesus
19 And it happened that while Apollos was at Corinth, Paul passed through the inland[a] country and came to Ephesus. There he found some disciples. 2 And he said to them, "Did you receive the Holy Spirit when you believed?" And they said, "No, we have not even heard that there is a Holy Spirit." 3 And he said, "Into what then were you baptized?" They said, "Into John's baptism." 4 And Paul said, "John baptized with the baptism of repentance, telling the people to believe in the one who was to come after him, that is, Jesus." 5 On hearing this, they were baptized in[b] the name of the Lord Jesus. 6 And when Paul had laid his hands on them, the Holy Spirit came on them, and they began speaking in tongues and prophesying. 7 There were about twelve men in all.

14 Now when the apostles at Jerusalem heard that Samaria had received the word of God, they sent to them Peter and John, 15 who came down and prayed for them that they might receive the Holy Spirit, 16 for he had not yet fallen on any of them, but they had only been baptized in the

name of the Lord Jesus. 17 Then they laid their hands on them and they received the Holy Spirit. -

https://www.biblegateway.com/passage/?search=Acts%208&version=ESV

Yes, God, Jesus Christ, CAN give you His Holy Spirit of Truth by just seeking Him and Asking Him, but the tried and true method, is following His Clear Instructions in the Holy Bible, instead of trying to ignore them! In other words, God includes each of us individually in His Plan of Salvation and Perfection of His Creation, because He is teaching us to not just Love and Appreciate Him but to Love and Appreciate one another, and that none of His Sons and Daughters are expendable. We each have a Divine Purpose to Glorify Him! (Heb 6:1-2, Matt 28:18-20, Acts 2:38-39, John 14:3-26 these foundational steps of the Christian Faith lead to knowing our Eternal Creator with all certainty; and then just keep walking with Him forever!)

So, spend time studying the Holy Bible and asking God to teach you personally, only then will you be certain that you know Truth; because YOU KNOW THE ONE WHO IS THE TRUTH!

John 14:6-9
New King James Version
6	Jesus said to him, "I am the way, the truth, and the life. No one comes to the Father except through Me.
The Father Revealed
7	"If you had known Me, you would have known My Father also; and from now on you know Him and have seen Him."
8	Philip said to Him, "Lord, show us the Father, and it is sufficient for us." 9 Jesus said to him, "Have I been with you so long, and yet you have not known Me, Philip? He who has seen Me has seen the Father; so how can you say, 'Show us the Father'?

John 8:32-36

King James Version
32 And ye shall know the truth, and the truth shall make you free.
33 They answered him, We be Abraham's seed, and were never in bondage to any man: how sayest thou, Ye shall be made free? 34 Jesus answered them, Verily, verily, I say unto you, Whosoever committeth sin is the servant of sin.
35 And the servant abideth not in the house for ever: but the Son abideth ever.
36 If the Son therefore shall make you free, ye shall be free indeed.

https://www.facebook.com/photo/?fbid=6800758120003089&set=a.115635768515391 - Jesus Christ tells us He is God from Genesis to Revelation many hundreds of times over. His very Name is the Name of God; describing God.

Jesus Christ Says He is God/YHWH HUNDREDS of Times in the Holy Bible

Jesus Christ says He is God repeatedly.

1) Jesus Christ ALWAYS RECEIVED WORSHIP AS GOD
https://www.openbible.info/topics/worshipping_jesus and even complains when people should have and didn't:

The Ten Lepers
...16He fell facedown at Jesus' feet in thanksgiving to Him—and he was a Samaritan. 17"Were not all ten cleansed?" Jesus asked. "Where then are the other nine? 18Was no one found except this foreigner to return and give glory to God?"... https://biblehub.com/luke/17-17.htm

2) Jesus Christ says the entire Holy Bible is all about Him, the One who has Eternal Life and that we must come to Him to have that life.

John 5:39-40
English Standard Version
39 You search the Scriptures because you think that in them you have eternal life; and it is they that bear witness about me, 40 yet you refuse to come to me that you may have life.

3) He says He is the One who has been telling us He is God from the Beginning and that if we don't believe Him, we will die in our sins!

…23Then He told them, "You are from below; I am from above. You are of this world; I am not of this world. 24That is why I told you that you would die in your sins. For unless you believe that I am He, you will die in your sins." 25"Who are You?" they asked. "Just what I have been telling you from the beginning," Jesus replied…. https://biblehub.com/john/8-24.htm

John 8:48-59
Before Abraham Was, I Am
48 The Jews answered him, "Are we not right in saying that you are a Samaritan and have a demon?" 49 Jesus answered, "I do not have a demon, but I honor my Father, and you dishonor me. 50 Yet I do not seek my own glory; there is One who seeks it, and he is the judge. 51 Truly, truly, I say to you, if anyone keeps my word, he will never see death." 52 The Jews said to him, "Now we know that you have a demon! Abraham died, as did the prophets, yet you say, 'If anyone keeps my word, he will never taste death.' 53 Are you greater than our father Abraham, who died? And the prophets died! Who do you make yourself out to be?" 54 Jesus answered, "If I glorify myself, my glory is nothing. It is my Father who glorifies me, of whom you say, 'He is our God.'[a] 55 But you have not known him. I know him. If I were to say that I do not know him, I would be

a liar like you, but I do know him and I keep his word. 56 Your father Abraham rejoiced that he would see my day. He saw it and was glad." 57 So the Jews said to him, "You are not yet fifty years old, and have you seen Abraham?"[b] 58 Jesus said to them, "Truly, truly, I say to you, before Abraham was, I am." 59 So they picked up stones to throw at him, but Jesus hid himself and went out of the temple.

(the people that heard and saw Him first hand understood He was claiming to be God, it's why those who didn't believe Him picked up stones to stone Him!)

5) He plainly acknowledged He is God:

Jesus Appears to Thomas
...27Then Jesus said to Thomas, "Put your finger here and look at My hands. Reach out your hand and put it into My side. Stop doubting and believe." 28Thomas replied, "My Lord and my God!" 29Jesus said to him, "Because you have seen Me, you have believed; blessed are those who have not seen and yet have believed."... https://biblehub.com/john/20-28.htm

6) He gives us His Holy Spirit of Truth to testify to the entire world that He is God:

The Ascension
...7Jesus replied, "It is not for you to know times or seasons that the Father has fixed by His own authority. 8But you will receive power when the Holy Spirit comes upon you, and you will be My witnesses in Jerusalem, and in all Judea and Samaria, and to the ends of the earth."
https://biblehub.com/acts/1-8.htm

7) He Begins the Holy Bible with telling us He is God and tells us His Name and how to identify He is God HUNDREDS OF TIMES OVER!

https://www.youtube.com/watch?v=0p2ZqRCipX4

https://www.accordingtothescriptures.org/prophecy/353prophecies.html

The Fulfillment of the Law
16In the same way, let your light shine before men, that they may see your good deeds and glorify your Father in heaven. 17Do not think that I have come to abolish the Law or the Prophets. I have not come to abolish them, but to fulfill them. 18For I tell you truly, until heaven and earth pass away, not a single jot, not a stroke of a pen, will disappear from the Law until everything is accomplished.... https://biblehub.com/matthew/5-17.htm

ONLY THE ONE TRUE GOD CAN FULFILL ALL HIS LAW AND PROPHECIES! JESUS CHRIST IS YHWH WHO CAME IN THE FLESH!

8 - He Ends the Holy Bible with telling us He is God and that His Rewards (and Consequences) are with Him when He returns!

Jesus is Coming
...12"Behold, I am coming soon, and My reward is with Me, to give to each one according to what he has done. 13I am the Alpha and the Omega, the First and the Last, the Beginning and the End." 14Blessed are those who wash their robes, so that they may have the right to the tree of life and may enter the city by its gates.... https://biblehub.com/revelation/22-13.htm

9) Even the stars He Created and Made tell us Jesus Christ is God!

https://www.youtube.com/watch?v=PHCftvj_Prw

https://www.youtube.com/watch?v=EUQEMqF5dL8

10) billions on earth from all over this world are telling everyone Jesus Christ is God because He has given them His Holy Spirit of Truth and they KNOW BEYOND ALL DOUBT HE IS THE ONE TRUE GOD!

20And we know that the Son of God has come and has given us understanding, so that we may know Him who is true; and we are in Him who is true— in His Son Jesus Christ. He is the TRUE God and eternal life. 21Little children, keep yourselves from idols....
https://biblehub.com/1_john/5-20.htm

Jesus Christ is the SAME YHWH who spoke with Moses and all the Prophets!

Moses at the Burning Bush
...13Then Moses asked God, "Suppose I go to the Israelites and say to them, 'The God of your fathers has sent me to you,' and they ask me, 'What is His name?' What should I tell them?" 14God said to Moses, "I AM WHO I AM. This is what you are to say to the Israelites: 'I AM has sent me to you.'" 15God also told Moses, "Say to the Israelites, 'The LORD, the God of your fathers—the God of Abraham, the God of Isaac, and the God of Jacob—has sent me to you.' This is My name forever, and this is how I am to be remembered in every generation.... https://biblehub.com/exodus/3-14.htm

John 8:58
"Truly, truly, I tell you," Jesus declared, "before Abraham was born, I am!"

Hebrews 13:8
Jesus Christ is the same yesterday and today and forever.

Revelation 1:8
"I am the Alpha and the Omega," says the Lord God, who is and was and is to come--the Almighty.

So, Jesus Christ is YHWH who came in the flesh and who tells us all to worship only Him and no one and nothing else!

https://www.youtube.com/watch?v=WtfjPSQhrGY - part 1 of 3 - the REAL Mt. Sinai still exists validating the historicity contained in the Holy Bible.

https://www.youtube.com/watch?v=gxBb4dDeTXA - part 2of 3

https://www.youtube.com/watch?v=ENiv5NMA0r0 - part 3 of 3

So those who DON'T KNOW GOD personally yet, should be listening to THE BILLIONS OF US WHO DO! JESUS CHRIST IS THE ONE TRUE GOD!

https://www.facebook.com/photo/?fbid=6471680786244159&set=a.115635768515391 - Jesus Christ told His Prophets hundreds of times that He would come in the flesh as the Messiah. READ THOSE PROPHECIES! - https://www.accordingtothescriptures.org/prophecy/353prophecies.html

And so, when God came in the flesh, He said so plainly:

John 5:39-40
39 You search the Scriptures because you think that in them you have eternal life; and it is they that bear witness about me, 40 yet you refuse to come to me that you may have life.

That the entire Holy Bible is all about Him, the One who has Eternal Life and the One everyone must come to in order to have that life!

Jesus Appears to Thomas
...25So the other disciples told him, "We have seen the Lord!" But he replied, "Unless I see the nail marks in His hands, and put my finger where the nails have been, and put my hand into His side, I will never believe." 26 Eight days later, His disciples were once again inside with the doors locked, and Thomas was with them. Jesus came and stood among them and said, "Peace be with you." 27Then Jesus said to Thomas, "Put your finger here and look at My hands. Reach out your hand and put it into My side. Stop doubting and believe." 28Thomas replied, "My Lord and my God!" 29Jesus said to him, "Because you have seen Me, you have believed; blessed are those who have not seen and yet have believed."...
https://biblehub.com/john/20-28.htm

This is about the first question a muslim has asked that actually made me somewhat hopeful inside, at least for that one. He was asking about the baptism of repentance.
Water Baptism is to be performed when a person truly repents of their wicked ways and is ready to obey our Lord and Savior, Jesus, the Christ, the One True God.

It symbolized laying down your old sinful self (dying to wickedness and evil) and being raised by God into your New Life with Him. (yes, it also has ties to ritual cleansing in the past, Mikvah, washing yourself from the top of your head to the bottom of your feet, cleansed entirely.)

Ephesians 2:1-10
And you were dead in the trespasses and sins in which you once walked, following the course of this world, following the prince of the power of the

air, the spirit that is now at work in the sons of disobedience— among whom we all once lived in the passions of our flesh, carrying out the desires of the body and the mind, and were by nature children of wrath, like the rest of mankind. But God, being rich in mercy, because of the great love with which he loved us, even when we were dead in our trespasses, made us alive together with Christ—by grace you have been saved— and raised us up with him and seated us with him in the heavenly places in Christ Jesus, so that in the coming ages he might show the immeasurable riches of his grace in kindness toward us in Christ Jesus. For by grace you have been saved through faith. And this is not your own doing; it is the gift of God, not a result of works, so that no one may boast. For we are his workmanship, created in Christ Jesus for good works, which God prepared beforehand, that we should walk in them.

Ambassadors for Christ
…16So from now on we regard no one according to the flesh. Although we once regarded Christ in this way, we do so no longer. 17Therefore if anyone is in Christ, he is a new creation. The old has passed away. Behold, the new has come! 18All this is from God, who reconciled us to Himself through Christ and gave us the ministry of reconciliation:…
https://biblehub.com/2_corinthians/5-17.htm

It absolutely is to be performed by total immersion, not sprinkling, and is to be done when a person is truly repentant of their sins and ready to obey and follow Jesus Christ, now and forever. Babes and little children are innocent. The Baptism of Repentance is to be done once someone realizes they have sinned against God and are ready to Repent of those sins and obey Him for the rest of their existence. (Christ was around 30 years of age, for example, when He went through it, not because He needed to repent of anything Himself, but was leading the way for us all to follow Him.)

The Great Commission
…18Then Jesus came to them and said, "All authority in heaven and on earth has been given to Me. 19Therefore go and make disciples of all

nations, baptizing them in the name of the Father, and of the Son, and of the Holy Spirit, 20and teaching them to obey all that I have commanded you. And surely I am with you always, even to the end of the age."...
https://biblehub.com/matthew/28-19.htm

37When the people heard this, they were cut to the heart and asked Peter and the other apostles, "Brothers, what shall we do?" 38 Peter replied, "Repent and be baptized, every one of you, in the name of Jesus Christ for the forgiveness of your sins, and you will receive the gift of the Holy Spirit. 39This promise belongs to you and your children and to all who are far off—to all whom the Lord our God will call to Himself."...
https://biblehub.com/acts/2-38.htm

It's your first outward act of obedience to God after hearing and understanding the Gospel of our Lord Jesus Christ and His Commandment to us all to Repent of our wicked ways, and return to Him, follow Him and obey Him now and forever.

Acts 8:36-38
And as they went on their way, they came unto a certain water: and the eunuch said, See, here is water; what doth hinder me to be baptized? And Philip said, If thou believest with all thine heart, thou mayest. And he answered and said, I believe that Jesus Christ is the Son of God. And he commanded the chariot to stand still: and they went down both into the water, both Philip and the eunuch; and he baptized him.

muslims sadly are unbelievably hung up on not understanding why God, Jesus Christ, would die for us on the cross. I say sadly, because the scriptures plainly tell us that the Message of the Cross is foolishness to those who are PERISHING! (headed for the lake of fire) but to those who are Saved it is the POWER of GOD! https://biblehub.com/1_corinthians/1-18.htm

There are MANY reasons God did what He did, not ONLY to Redeem/Save us, but to openly PROVE HE IS THE ONE TRUE GOD!

If God had not come into this world He created and made, and showed Himself to us, Proved He is God by all His Many Divine Miracles, and then Proved He is the One who has Eternal Life and is the Way to Heaven by ascending into Heaven in front of Eyewitnesses after publicly dying, being buried, raising His Body from the Grave and transfiguring it, then all of us would still be just as lost as muslims and the rest of humanity who are only IMAGINING their god, but do not KNOW the ONE TRUE REAL GOD!

Even though His Own Chosen Disciples had seen Him do all kinds of miracles, it wasn't until AFTER they saw Him scourged, crucified, dead and buried and then RAISED FROM THE DEAD, transfigured, Immortal and Glorious, that they knew beyond all doubt that He was indeed the One True God!

Jesus Appears to Thomas
...25So the other disciples told him, "We have seen the Lord!" But he replied, "Unless I see the nail marks in His hands, and put my finger where the nails have been, and put my hand into His side, I will never believe." 26 Eight days later, His disciples were once again inside with the doors locked, and Thomas was with them. Jesus came and stood among them and said, "Peace be with you." 27Then Jesus said to Thomas, "Put your finger here and look at My hands. Reach out your hand and put it into My side. Stop doubting and believe." 28Thomas replied, "My Lord and my God!" 29Jesus said to him, "Because you have seen Me, you have believed; blessed are those who have not seen and yet have believed."...
https://biblehub.com/john/20-28.htm

Even after He had proven He is the One who has Eternal Life and the Power to bring the dead back to life:

John 5:39-40
39 You search the Scriptures because you think that in them you have eternal life; and it is they that bear witness about me, 40 yet you refuse to come to me that you may have life.

Jesus Comforts Martha and Mary
…24Martha replied, "I know that he will rise again in the resurrection at the last day." 25 Jesus said to her, "I am the resurrection and the life. Whoever believes in Me will live, even though he dies. 26And everyone who lives and believes in Me will never die. Do you believe this?"…
https://biblehub.com/john/11-25.htm

Even after they had seen Jesus Christ perform miracles that no one else in the entire world had ever done:

The Hatred of the World
…23Whoever hates Me hates My Father as well. 24If I had not done among them the works that no one else did, they would not be guilty of sin; but now they have seen and hated both Me and My Father. 25But this is to fulfill what is written in their Law: 'They hated Me without reason.'…
https://biblehub.com/john/15-24.htm

some STILL doubted!

The Great Commission
…17When they saw Him, they worshiped Him, but some doubted.18Then Jesus came to them and said, "All authority in heaven and on earth has

been given to Me. 19Therefore go and make disciples of all nations, baptizing them in the name of the Father, and of the Son, and of the Holy Spirit, 20and teaching them to obey all that I have commanded you. And surely I am with you always, even to the end of the age."...
https://biblehub.com/matthew/28-19.htm

NEVER ONCE DID JESUS CHRIST REFUSE WORSHIP! AND HE IS THE ONE WHO OPENLY PREACHED TO WORSHIP ONLY GOD! SO, JESUS CHRIST MOST DEFINITELY CLAIMED TO BE GOD! (and proved it beyond reasonable doubt like no one else in the entire history of the world) -
https://www.openbible.info/topics/worshipping_jesus

So Divine Miracles, even publicly dying and raising His Body from the Grave, STILL was not enough for some! It wasn't until they WATCHED HIM ASCEND INTO HEAVEN and AFTER HE POURED OUT HIS HOLY SPIRIT OF TRUTH upon them, that the Apostles and Disciples began to Preach the Gospel (GOD SPEAKS!) to the world and is how Christianity began!

The Ascension
...7Jesus replied, "It is not for you to know times or seasons that the Father has fixed by His own authority. 8But you will receive power when the Holy Spirit comes upon you, and you will be My witnesses in Jerusalem, and in all Judea and Samaria, and to the ends of the earth." 9After He had said this, they watched as He was taken up, and a cloud hid Him from their sight.... https://biblehub.com/acts/1-8.htm

JESUS CHRIST IS GOD! HE IS LORD! HE IS THE ONLY SAVIOR! they preached even when those who had just crucified Him, threatened to kill them for doing so! THEY WENT ON PREACHING! JESUS CHRIST IS GOD! HE IS LORD! HE IS THE ONLY SAVIOR!

God, Jesus Christ, STILL gives His Holy Spirit of Truth to all who believe and obey Him.

Three Thousand Believe
37When the people heard this, they were cut to the heart and asked Peter and the other apostles, "Brothers, what shall we do?" 38 Peter replied, "Repent and be baptized, every one of you, in the name of Jesus Christ for the forgiveness of your sins, and you will receive the gift of the Holy Spirit. 39This promise belongs to you and your children and to all who are far off—to all whom the Lord our God will call to Himself."...
https://biblehub.com/acts/2-38.htm

Peter and John Before the Council
...11This Jesus is 'the stone you builders rejected, which has become the cornerstone.' 12 Salvation exists in no one else, for there is no other name under heaven given to men by which we must be saved."
https://biblehub.com/acts/4-12.htm

SALVATION is all about KNOWING THE SAVIOR, GOD! JESUS CHRIST! and that's why He showed Himself, proved Himself, said what He said and did what He did, including publicly dying on the cross in our behalf. (Just as He told us He would do in His Own Law and Prophecies given to mankind by Him centuries before He came in the flesh.)

https://www.accordingtothescriptures.org/prophecy/353prophecies.html

https://bible.knowing-jesus.com/topics/God,-As-Redeemer

https://www.preceptaustin.org/tetelestai-paid_in_full - yes, God paid the price in full, but if you reject Him, you are still under His death sentence for violating His Commandments (and is why everyone rejecting Jesus Christ and His Salvation, still is lost in their sins and still doesn't know Him!) SO, OBEY GOD AND REPENT AND BE BAPTIZED IN HIS NAME TODAY! AND PRAY TO RECEIVE HIS HOLY SPIRIT UNTIL YOU DO KNOW HIM!

Today another muslim was denying Jesus Christ is Immanuel (along with the hundreds of other prophecies telling us Jesus Christ is Immanuel - https://www.accordingtothescriptures.org/prophecy/353prophecies.html)

God uses hundreds of Names for Himself in the Scriptures "Immanuel" is just one of them. And yes, Jesus Christ is Immanuel, God with us.

https://urbanareas.net/info/100-biblical-names-god/ - the Names of God in the scriptures describe who God is.

When He came in the flesh, one of those Names was Immanuel, God with us, because God was indeed with us and walked among us.

The Birth of Jesus
...22All this took place to fulfill what the Lord had said through the prophet: 23"Behold, the virgin will be with child and will give birth to a son, and they will call Him Immanuel" (which means, "God with us"). 24When Joseph woke up, he did as the angel of the Lord had commanded him, and embraced Mary as his wife.... https://biblehub.com/matthew/1-23.htm

John 5:39-40

39 You search the Scriptures because you think that in them you have eternal life; and it is they that bear witness about me, 40 yet you refuse to come to me that you may have life.

Jesus Christ plainly stated the entire Holy Bible was all about Him, the One who has Eternal Life and the One to whom all must come to in order to have that life.

When you deny His Words in the Holy Bible, you are calling God Almighty a liar and are committing a very great sin of blasphemy. You are also calling all those who heard and saw Him liars as well. Face it, you weren't there to hear Him yourself, so the only way you can know for certain if Jesus Christ is God or not, is to have the sense to ask Him! He ever lives to answer any and all with enough sense to call upon Him. In addition, He told us exactly how anyone can receive His Own Holy Spirit of Truth; so, all who obey Him receive His Holy Spirit and thereby KNOW the ONE TRUE GOD.

The Great Commission
…18Then Jesus came to them and said, "All authority in heaven and on earth has been given to Me. 19Therefore go and make disciples of all nations, baptizing them in the name of the Father, and of the Son, and of the Holy Spirit, 20and teaching them to obey all that I have commanded you. And surely I am with you always, even to the end of the age."…
https://biblehub.com/matthew/28-19.htm

"Brothers, what shall we do?" 38 Peter replied, "Repent and be baptized, every one of you, in the name of Jesus Christ for the forgiveness of your sins, and you will receive the gift of the Holy Spirit. 39This promise belongs to you and your children and to all who are far off—to all whom the Lord our God will call to Himself."… https://biblehub.com/acts/2-38.htm

John 14:20-26

20 In that day you will know that I am in my Father, and you in me, and I in you. 21 Whoever has my commandments and keeps them, he it is who loves me. And he who loves me will be loved by my Father, and I will love him and manifest myself to him." 22 Judas (not Iscariot) said to him, "Lord, how is it that you will manifest yourself to us, and not to the world?" 23 Jesus answered him, "If anyone loves me, he will keep my word, and my Father will love him, and we will come to him and make our home with him. 24 Whoever does not love me does not keep my words. And the word that you hear is not mine but the Father's who sent me.

25 "These things I have spoken to you while I am still with you. 26 But the Helper, the Holy Spirit, whom the Father will send in my name, he will teach you all things and bring to your remembrance all that I have said to you.

a muslim was online today boasting about islam being some kind of "complete religion". Whenever I read something like that, I feel like regurgitating.

a muslim doesn't even know God, so no islam is not a "complete religion"; it's a demonic cult full of lies and obviously so.

1) muslims are all taught to chant that their allah (name of a pagan idol) has no Sons, no Daughters and no partners

The One True God, Jesus Christ, Created and Made an entire world full of billions of Children who all belong to Him and is why He told us to call Him, "Our Father".

God has included us all in His Plans and Purposes by specifically Commanding us all to Obey Him. So by definition everyone obeying God is a partner with God.

partner - https://www.merriam-webster.com/dictionary/partner
1 of 2 noun
part·ner ˈpärt-nər also ˈpärd-
Synonyms of partner
1 a
: one associated with another especially in an action : ASSOCIATE, COLLEAGUE
our military partners throughout the world b
: a person with whom one shares an intimate relationship : one member of a couple
Evan and his partner are going on a Caribbean cruise. c
: either of two persons who dance together d
: one of two or more persons who play together in a game against an opposing side partners in card games
2
: a member of a partnership especially in a business
partners in a law firm also : such membership
3
: one of the heavy timbers that strengthen a ship's deck to support a mast —usually used in plural
4 archaic : one that shares :
PARTAKER

so from the very foundation of the doctrines of islam, islam teaches muslims to believe lies about our Eternal Creator and such obvious lies that they are in denial of reality before our very eyes.

But throughout the entire quran, there are so many lies and evil instructions that, to those of us who know better, muslims look completely and thoroughly deceived, to the point of evil madness.

https://www.thereligionofpeace.com/pages/articles/jesusmuhammad.aspx - the quran openly advocates crimes against humanity, because islam came from the devil and lying, violent criminals; not God Almighty. (it's why the quran is polar opposite of the Truth in the Holy
Bible and teaches muslims to deny the One True God, Jesus Christ.)

2) throughout history and to this very day, islam has generated the most violent terrorist organizations of any worldview on earth.

God told us a tree is known by its fruit; so islam is obviously evil (from the devil).

https://www.google.com/search?client=opera&q=list+of+islamic+terrorist+groups&sourceid=opera&ie=UTF-8&oe=UTF-8 - people who mock google and the results of the google search engine don't understand that google and all Internet search engines function like a librarian in the world's largest library, it just points you to the accumulated knowledge of mankind and in that knowledge of islam, its history, its doctrines and practices to this day, islam is obviously a demonic cult and criminal organization and the furthest thing from anything true or "complete religion".

islam is so thoroughly evil that it has many unique evils like "acid throwing", whipping raped victims instead of punishing the rapists, beating women to death if they don't dress oppressively, killing anyone who tries to leave their cult, honor killings, suicide bombings, tortures and many other human rights violations still today. so no, islam is not a complete religion, instead it's completely unacceptable by anyone who has even a tiny amount of accurate knowledge about it.

http://www.annaqed.com/en/muslims-under-themicroscope/muhammad-and-his-crimes-against-humanity - the real muhammad was nothing to imitate and everything to loathe, a man so vile that his depraved notion of

paradise was to have a perpetual hard-on, just to molest virgins, and yes, his sick notions of virgins was little boys and girls. so muslims are in a demonic cult, that advocates child abuse openly as their highest aspiration, their idea of heaven. SICK! DEPRAVED! EVIL!
http://www.answeringmuslims.com/2014/03/muhammad-and-thighingof-aisha.html - the real muhammad was factually a child molester, among his many other crimes that he advocates in the vile quran.

Ann sheds some light on what qurans are good for (fuel for a fire) and reads straight from the contents as to just some of the many hundreds of reasons why they should all be burned -
https://www.youtube.com/watch?v=htshvld51UE - Ann is RIGHT! (despite any and all muslims that try in vain to refute her - the quran openly advocates crimes against humanity and cannot be legally practiced in any lawful nation; no ifs, ands or buts!)

https://www.youtube.com/watch?v=pu_YlJdwpao

All muslims need to comprehend that islam is an extremely evil demonic cult and criminal organization! The entire world needs to understand that fact! islam is NOTHING ACCEPTABLE IN ANY WAY! muslims are constantly online with their nonsense of, "you just don't understand islam." yes, yes I do! muslims pretending like islam is anything acceptable are the ones who don't!

No, no one in their right mind with true information is a muslim. all muslims are EXTREMELY deceived!

Every single muslim is on their way to the lake of fire for denying the One True God, Jesus Christ, and bowing to the lying devil, allah, and his lying criminal false prophet, muhammad, instead. muslims are so deceived they apparently can no longer tell truth from lies, right from wrong, good from evil or God Almighty from the devil, or they wouldn't be a muslim. islam is obviously evil, and obviously full of LIES!

https://www.google.com/search?client=opera&q=islamic+apostasy+death+penalty+nations&sourceid=opera&ie=UTF-8&oe=UTF-8 - any cult that threatens to murder you for trying to leave it is a CULT OF MURDERERS! so islam is EVIL. no ifs, ands or buts!

https://www.thereligionofpeace.com/pages/quran/index.aspx - the quran OPENLY ADVOCATES CRIMES AGAINST HUMANITY! and is why islam has founded the largest number of violent terrorist organizations in the history of the world!

https://www.google.com/search?client=opera&q=list+of+islamic+terrorist+groups&sourceid=opera&ie=UTF-8&oe=UTF-8 - so no! no one in their right mind with truthful information would choose to join islam UNLESS they have a very strange desire to end up in the lake of fire! under the Wrath of the One True God!

Beware of Antichrists
...21I have not written to you because you lack knowledge of the truth, but because you have it, and because no lie comes from the truth. 22Who is the liar, if it is not the one who denies that Jesus is the Christ? This is the antichrist, who denies the Father and the Son. 23Whoever denies the Son does not have the Father, but whoever confesses the Son has the Father as well.... https://biblehub.com/1_john/2-22.htm (all muslims are deceived by a lying antichrist, muhammad and his many, many lies in the vile quran!)

A New Heaven and a New Earth

...7The one who overcomes will inherit all things, and I will be his God, and he will be My son. 8But to the cowardly and unbelieving and abominable and murderers and sexually immoral and sorcerers and idolaters and all liars, their place will be in the lake that burns with fire and sulfur. This is the second death." https://biblehub.com/revelation/21-8.htm

All muslims who refuse to repent of following wicked muhammad and his many lies, will end up in the lake of fire! EVERYONE NEEDS TO FOLLOW JESUS CHRIST WHO IS THE ONLY ONE IN ALL HISTORY TO PROVE HE HAS ETERNAL LIFE AND IS THE WAY TO HEAVEN!

https://www.thereligionofpeace.com/pages/articles/jesusmuhammad.aspx

https://www.facebook.com/photo.php?fbid=6809546799124221&set=pb.100002069048072.-2207520000&type=3

Yet another muslim was trying to tell us that muhammad was the last prophet today after someone posted the truth that Jesus Christ said only He was the Way to Heaven and Eternal Life; whereas muhammad said he had no idea where he was going.

muhammad died by poisoning... the way he said he would die if he was false - https://youtu.be/KCTP6LJd620?t=1564

and the only place a criminal like muhammad guides anyone into, is the flames of damnation.
https://www.thereligionofpeace.com/pages/articles/jesusmuhammad.aspx

muslims need to let it sink in, muhammad died horribly and was buried.

Jesus Christ claimed to have Eternal Life and the Only Way to have that Life and Ascended into Heaven in front of eyewitnesses PROVING HE IS THE WAY TO ETERNAL LIFE AND HEAVEN! so you can follow muhammad to the rotting grave and the lake of fire (Rev 21:8), but the wise follow Jesus Christ into Heaven and Life Everlasting!

John 5:39-40
39 You search the Scriptures because you think that in them you have eternal life; and it is they that bear witness about me, 40 yet you refuse to come to me that you may have life.

The Ascension
...7Jesus replied, "It is not for you to know times or seasons that the Father has fixed by His own authority. 8But you will receive power when the Holy Spirit comes upon you, and you will be My witnesses in Jerusalem, and in all Judea and Samaria, and to the ends of the earth." 9After He had said this, they watched as He was taken up, and a cloud hid Him from their sight.10 They were looking intently into the sky as He was going, when suddenly two men dressed in white stood beside them. 11"Men of Galilee," they said, "why do you stand here looking into the sky? This same Jesus, who has been taken from you into heaven, will come back in the same way you have seen Him go into heaven."...
https://biblehub.com/acts/1-8.htm

Some muslim today was saying muslims never speak badly about God, Jesus Christ or the Holy Bible, but every muslim denies Jesus Christ is God when He said so and proved it and is alive to answer any with enough sense to call upon Him. How would you feel if you were king of your country and everyone denied you instead? so muslims are always SAYING they won't talk bad about Jesus Christ, God, the Holy Bible and yet just being a muslim does just that! All muslims are believing muhammad and his many lies in the quran over God Almighty, Jesus Christ, His Prophets and His Eyewitness Apostles in the Holy Bible. So muslims, just by being muslims, are calling God and All His Chosen Prophets and Apostles all liars. (Which is more likely? that the criminal muhammad who came along over 6 centuries after the facts he denied in the Holy Bible is telling the truth, or God and All His Prophets in the Holy Bible? muhammad was factually a rapist, robber, child molester, slaver and mass murderer! how can ANYONE believe muhammad over GOD? the quran over the HOLY BIBLE? only those most obviously deceived... muslims! - https://www.thereligionofpeace.com/pages/articles/jesusmuhammad.aspx sadly, far too many muslims have been so thoroughly brainwashed that when they find out the truth that muhammad was a criminal gang leader, who began the cult of islam, they just can't believe it.)

John 5:39-40
39 You search the Scriptures because you think that in them you have eternal life; and it is they that bear witness about me, 40 yet you refuse to come to me that you may have life.

Jesus Christ plainly said He is the One that the entire Holy Bible is all about, the One who has Eternal Life and the One whom all must come to in order to have that life!

so when muslims DENY Jesus Christ is God, they are openly calling GOD a liar! (blasphemy) instead God calls all muslims liars:

Beware of Antichrists
...21 I have not written to you because you lack knowledge of the truth, but because you have it, and because no lie comes from the truth. 22 Who is the liar, if it is not the one who denies that Jesus is the Christ? This is the antichrist, who denies the Father and the Son. 23 Whoever denies the Son does not have the Father, but whoever confesses the Son has the Father as well.... https://biblehub.com/1_john/2-22.htm

It should be obvious to muslims that they are making themselves the enemy of the One True God, Jesus Christ, by denying Him, because NONE of them KNOW Him! muslims do not see, hear or know God, because they are all DENYING Him instead!

If muslims don't repent of believing and passing on lies about God, they will all experience His Wrath.

36Whoever believes in the Son has eternal life. Whoever rejects the Son will not see life. Instead, the wrath of God remains on him."
https://biblehub.com/john/3-36.htm

2 Thessalonians 1:8-9

8   In flaming fire taking vengeance on them that know not God, and that obey not the gospel of our Lord Jesus Christ:

9   Who shall be punished with everlasting destruction from the presence of the Lord, and from the glory of his power;

Another muslim was denying the fact that Jesus Christ is God online today. (that is evidence of the spirit of antichrist to deny Jesus Christ is the One True God who came in the flesh! - 1Jn 4:1-6; 1Jn 2:22) all lying antichrists will be cast into the lake of fire! Rev 21:8 so all muslims MUST REPENT and become Christians, Disciples of Jesus Christ or they will all end up in the lake of fire!

muslims tend to focus only on that tiny portion of time when God came in the flesh, humbly as a Man, the Messiah, in order to deny Jesus Christ is the One True God.

Instead, Jesus Christ has always been God and always will be God. He told His Prophets hundreds of times He would come in the flesh:

https://www.accordingtothescriptures.org/prophecy/353prophecies.html

So, when He did so, Jesus Christ, said the entire Holy Bible was all about Him, the One who has Eternal Life and the One everyone must come to in order to have that Life.

John 5:39-40
39 You search the Scriptures because you think that in them you have eternal life; and it is they that bear witness about me, 40 yet you refuse to come to me that you may have life.

So, Jesus Christ plainly stated He is God and proved it by doing so many Divine Miracles that those who saw and heard Him said the whole world couldn't contain the books if they were all written down.

...24This is the disciple who testifies to these things and who has written them down. And we know that his testimony is true. 25 There are many more things that Jesus did. If all of them were written down, I suppose that not even the world itself would have space for the books that would be written. https://biblehub.com/john/21-25.htm

After Jesus Christ publicly claimed to be the One True God, the One who has Eternal Life and the Power to Raise the dead back to Life, He then publicly died, raised His Body from the Grave and ascended back into Heaven in front of eyewitnesses PROVING His Claims!

So yes, Jesus Christ is God, and proved it like no one else in the entire history of the world!

ANOTHER muslim was again denying that the Holy Bible plainly tells us all that Jesus Christ is the One True God. (even after I had already shown them plainly that the Holy Bible redundantly says so!)

I just showed you that the scriptures plainly state Jesus Christ is God and does so from Genesis to Revelation and you choose to argue? let this sink into your presently deceived mind! you don't see, hear or know God BECAUSE YOU ARE DENYING HIM INSTEAD!

https://www.facebook.com/photo.php?fbid=6471680786244159&set=pb.100002069048072.-2207520000&type=3 and
https://www.facebook.com/photo.php?fbid=6800758120003089&set=pb.100002069048072.-2207520000&type=3 and
https://www.facebook.com/photo.php?fbid=6809546799124221&set=pb.100002069048072.-2207520000&type=3

Jesus the Christ Said
24That is why I told you that you would die in your sins. For unless you believe that I am He, you will die in your sins." 25"Who are You?" they asked. "Just what I have been telling you from the beginning," Jesus replied....

Some still haven't understood the meaning of His Words or everyone, everywhere would know Jesus Christ is the One True God.

Only the One True God has been talking with mankind "from the beginning" and telling us that He is such. So does the contents of the Holy Bible tell us that Jesus Christ is the One True God "from the Beginning"?

YES! OVER AND OVER AND OVER AGAIN; THROUGHOUT THE ENTIRE CONTENTS OF THE HOLY BIBLE JESUS CHRIST IS THE ONE TRUE GOD!

JESUS CHRIST IS YHWH THE ONE TRUE GOD
Since the Beginning, Jesus Christ, the One True God, told the Prophets He would come into this world He created and made as the Humble Servant Messiah. READ THE HUNDREDS OF PROPHECIES and educate yourself!

https://www.accordingtothescriptures.org/prophecy/353prophecies.html

The scriptures make it CRYSTAL CLEAR that God emptied Himself to come into this world He created and made as the Messiah!

From the very first verse in the Holy Bible, Jesus Christ is plainly our Eternal Creator and reveals He is our Savior!
https://youtu.be/_3CQtIWnx7c?t=3225

The Attitude of Christ
...6Who, existing in the form of God, did not consider equality with God something to be grasped, 7but emptied Himself, taking the form of a servant, being made in human likeness. 8And being found in appearance as a man, He humbled Himself and became obedient to death—even death on a cross.... https://biblehub.com/philippians/2-7.htm

There were many reasons God did this; here are just a few:

1) to condemn sin in the flesh. that is, God PROVED His Commandments can be kept as a Man and are not impossible!

Living in the Spirit
...2For in Christ Jesus the law of the Spirit of life set you free from the law of sin and death. 3For what the law was powerless to do in that it was weakened by the flesh, God did by sending His own Son in the likeness of sinful man, as an offering for sin. He thus condemned sin in the flesh, 4so that the righteous standard of the law might be fulfilled in us, who do not walk according to the flesh but according to the Spirit....

2) to keep and fulfill His Law and Prophecies.

The Fulfillment of the Law
16In the same way, let your light shine before men, that they may see your good deeds and glorify your Father in heaven. 17Do not think that I have come to abolish the Law or the Prophets. I have not come to abolish them, but to fulfill them. 18For I tell you truly, until heaven and earth pass away, not a single jot, not a stroke of a pen, will disappear from the Law until everything is accomplished.... https://biblehub.com/matthew/5-17.htm

Ever since God has spoken with mankind, mankind has been debating what His Words even mean; so not only does mankind not obey God, they don't even understand His Instructions correctly. SO ONLY GOD CAN KEEP AND FULFILL ALL HIS LAW AND PROPHECIES! (JESUS CHRIST IS GOD!)

3) To Redeem mankind from our death sentences for breaking His Law! If God did not suffer and die for mankind then His Law and Prophecies WOULD NOT BE FULFILLED AND GOD WOULD HAVE LIED! So, our REDEEMER and SAVIOR IS GOD! JESUS CHRIST! who has fulfilled His Law, Kept His Word/Prophecies and has PROVEN His Divinity as He is Alive to answer any and all with enough sense to call upon Him!

Ambassadors for Christ
…18All this is from God, who reconciled us to Himself through Christ and gave us the ministry of reconciliation: 19 that God was reconciling the world to Himself in Christ, not counting men's trespasses against them. And He has committed to us the message of reconciliation. 20Therefore we are ambassadors for Christ, as though God were making His appeal through us. We implore you on behalf of Christ: Be reconciled to God.... https://biblehub.com/2_corinthians/5-19.htm

…10"You are My witnesses," declares YHWH, "and My servant whom I have chosen, so that you may consider and believe Me and understand that I am He. Before Me no god was formed, and after Me none will come. 11I, yes I, am YHWH, and there is no Savior but Me. 12I alone decreed and saved and proclaimed—I, and not some foreign god among you. So, you are My witnesses," declares YHWH, "that I am God....
https://biblehub.com/isaiah/43-11.htm

JESUS CHRIST IS YHWH!
https://www.youtube.com/watch?v=0p2ZqRCipX4&t=7s

The Witness of Scripture
…42but I know you, that you do not have the love of God within you. 43I have come in My Father's name, and you have not received Me; but if someone else comes in his own name, you will receive him. https://biblehub.com/john/5-43.htm (muslims, for example, reject the One True God, Jesus Christ, and accept the lying criminal muhammad)

John 14:6-9
6 Jesus said to him, "I am the way, and the truth, and the life. No one comes to the Father except through me. 7 If you had known me, you

would have known my Father also.[a] From now on you do know him and have seen him."

8 Philip said to him, "Lord, show us the Father, and it is enough for us." 9 Jesus said to him, "Have I been with you so long, and you still do not know me, Philip? Whoever has seen me has seen the Father. How can you say, 'Show us the Father'? (READ VERSE 9 UNTIL IT SINKS IN!)

THERE IS NO SAVIOR BUT YHWH/JESUS CHRIST!

…11This Jesus is 'the stone you builders rejected, which has become the cornerstone.' 12 Salvation exists in no one else, for there is no other name under heaven given to men by which we must be saved." 13When they saw the boldness of Peter and John and realized that they were unschooled, ordinary men, they marveled and took note that these men had been with Jesus.… https://biblehub.com/acts/4-12.htm

God's Grace Brings Salvation
…12It instructs us to renounce ungodliness and worldly passions, and to live sensible, upright, and godly lives in the present age, 13as we await the blessed hope and glorious appearance of our great God and Savior Jesus Christ. 14He gave Himself for us to redeem us from all lawlessness and to purify for Himself a people for His own possession, zealous for good deeds.… https://biblehub.com/titus/2-13.htm

Jesus Christ is the One True God.

Jesus Appears to Thomas
…27Then Jesus said to Thomas, "Put your finger here and look at My hands. Reach out your hand and put it into My side. Stop doubting and believe." 28Thomas replied, "My Lord and my God!" 29Jesus said to him,

"Because you have seen Me, you have believed; blessed are those who have not seen and yet have believed."... https://biblehub.com/john/20-28.htm

20And we know that the Son of God has come and has given us understanding, so that we may know Him who is true; and we are in Him who is true— in His Son Jesus Christ. He is the TRUE God and eternal life. 21Little children, keep yourselves from idols....
https://biblehub.com/1_john/5-20.htm

4) God said what He said on the cross in fulfillment of one of the many prophecies He told us! He also said what He said BECAUSE THE SINS OF MANKIND WERE UPON HIM IN THAT MOMENT! The Righteous suffering and dying for the unrighteous! The Innocent for the Guilty! in Fulfillment of His LAW and PROPHECIES! READ THEM AND EDUCATE YOURSELF!
https://www.accordingtothescriptures.org/prophecy/353prophecies.html

Abraham and Moses knew Jesus Christ the One True God:
https://www.facebook.com/photo/?fbid=6433644810047757&set=a.115635768515391

So, the One True God said, if you refuse to recognize Him as He has declared Himself to be - JESUS the Christ, then you will die in your sins! The reason for that truthful statement is forgiveness of sins is found ONLY IN HIM, THE ONE TRUE GOD, JESUS CHRIST!

Gentiles Hear the Good News
34 So Peter opened his mouth and said: "Truly I understand that God shows no partiality, 35 but in every nation anyone who fears him and does what is right is acceptable to him. 36 As for the word that he sent to Israel, preaching good news of peace through Jesus Christ (he is Lord of all), 37 you yourselves know what happened throughout all Judea, beginning from Galilee after the baptism that John proclaimed: 38 how God anointed

Jesus of Nazareth with the Holy Spirit and with power. He went about doing good and healing all who were oppressed by the devil, for God was with him. 39 And we are witnesses of all that he did both in the country of the Jews and in Jerusalem. They put him to death by hanging him on a tree, 40 but God raised him on the third day and made him to appear, 41 not to all the people but to us who had been chosen by God as witnesses, who ate and drank with him after he rose from the dead. 42 And he commanded us to preach to the people and to testify that he is the one appointed by God to be judge of the living and the dead. 43 To him all the prophets bear witness that everyone who believes in him receives forgiveness of sins through his name."

The Holy Spirit Falls on the Gentiles
44 While Peter was still saying these things, the Holy Spirit fell on all who heard the word. 45 And the believers from among the circumcised who had come with Peter were amazed, because the gift of the Holy Spirit was poured out even on the Gentiles. 46 For they were hearing them speaking in tongues and extolling God. Then Peter declared, 47 "Can anyone withhold water for baptizing these people, who have received the Holy Spirit just as we have?" 48 And he commanded them to be baptized in the name of Jesus Christ. Then they asked him to remain for some days.

verse 36 - JESUS CHRIST IS LORD OF ALL and verse 43 - all prophets bear witness of Jesus Christ and that forgiveness of sins is only through Him! verses 44-48 the Holy Spirit of God is given in the Name of Jesus Christ, the One True God for the purpose of testifying about Him who is the Truth, the One True God, to everyone, everywhere until everyone KNOWS HIM!

Acts 1:8
8But you will receive power when the Holy Spirit comes upon you, and you will be My witnesses in Jerusalem, and in all Judea and Samaria, and to the ends of the earth."

THE HOLY SPIRIT OF GOD IS GIVEN BY GOD TO TESTIFY ABOUT HIM TO EVERYONE, EVERYWHERE UNTIL EVERYONE KNOWS HE IS GOD! JESUS CHRIST IS GOD!!!!!!!!

SALVATION EXISTS ONLY IN JESUS CHRIST, BECAUSE ONLY THE ONE TRUE GOD CAN SAVE US!

Peter and John Before the Council
...11This Jesus is 'the stone you builders rejected, which has become the cornerstone.' 12 Salvation exists in no one else, for there is no other name under heaven given to men by which we must be saved." 13When they saw the boldness of Peter and John and realized that they were unschooled, ordinary men, they marveled and took note that these men had been with Jesus.... https://biblehub.com/acts/4-12.htm

Now why is it so important for each and every soul to personally know the One True God who created and made the heavens and earth and all therein?

1) He tells us that if we fail to recognize that He is God, believe in Him and obey His Commandments, that we will surely perish in our sins. So what does dying in our sins mean?

...35The Father loves the Son and has placed all things in His hands. 36Whoever believes in the Son has eternal life. Whoever rejects the Son will not see life. Instead, the wrath of God remains on him."

so, it means that instead of having eternal life, people that die in their sins will inherit the Wrath of GOD!

and what is the "Wrath of God"?

Do Not Harden Your Hearts

…10Therefore I was angry with that generation, and I said, 'Their hearts are always going astray, and they have not known My ways.' 11So I swore on oath in My anger, ' They shall never enter My rest.'" 12See to it, brothers, that none of you has a wicked heart of unbelief that turns away from the living God.… https://biblehub.com/hebrews/3-11.htm

The Three Angels and Babylon's Fall

…10he too will drink the wine of God's anger, poured undiluted into the cup of His wrath. And he will be tormented in fire and sulfur in the presence of the holy angels and of the Lamb. 11And the smoke of their torment rises forever and ever. Day and night there is no rest for those who worship the beast and its image, or for anyone who receives the mark of its name." 12Here is a call for the perseverance of the saints who keep the commandments of God and the faith of Jesus.… https://biblehub.com/revelation/14-11.htm

2And many who sleep in the dust of the earth will awake, some to everlasting life, but others to shame and everlasting contempt. https://biblehub.com/daniel/12-2.htm

Matthew 25:46
And they will go away into eternal punishment, but the righteous into eternal life."

John 5:28
Do not be amazed at this, for the hour is coming when all who are in their graves will hear His voice

John 5:29 and come out--those who have done good to the resurrection of life, and those who have done evil to the resurrection of judgment.

A New Heaven and a New Earth

...7The one who overcomes will inherit all things, and I will be his God, and he will be My son. 8But to the cowardly and unbelieving and abominable and murderers and sexually immoral and sorcerers and idolaters and all liars, their place will be in the lake that burns with fire and sulfur. This is the second death." https://biblehub.com/revelation/21-8.htm

SO, EVERYONE WHO FAILS TO ACKNOWLEDGE AND OBEY OUR LIVING LORD JESUS CHRIST AS THE ONE TRUE GOD THAT HE IS, IS DOOMING THEMSELVES TO SUFFERING, SHAME AND TORMENT IN THE LAKE OF FIRE! THE SMOKE OF THEIR TORMENT ASCENDS UP DAY AND NIGHT FOREVER AND EVER!

God's Message - Chose to LIVE RIGHTEOSLY, ALLOW HIM to PERFECT YOU! Do NOT choose to live wickedly - the Greatest Rewards and most horrible consequence hang in the balance! CHOOSE TO LIVE RIGHTEOUSLY WITH OUR LORD JESUS CHRIST, he will not always allow this time of learning - to choose to LOVE what is GOOD AND RIGHT and hate was it is evil and wrong. It's just your lifetime to decide! CHOOSE GOD! CHOOSE LOVE! CHOOSE JESUS CHRIST!

2) Conversely, everyone who does acknowledge and obey the Living Lord Jesus Christ, as the One True God that He is, will enter into Paradise, Creation Perfected, where they will be Comforted and Blessed with Every Good Gift forever and ever. Rev 21:7

The Witness of John
...11He came to His own, and His own did not receive Him. 12But to all who did receive Him, to those who believed in His name, He gave the right to become children of God— 13children born not of blood, nor of the desire or will of man, but born of God.... https://biblehub.com/john/1-12.htm

A New Heaven and a New Earth

...6And He told me, "It is done! I am the Alpha and the Omega, the Beginning and the End. To the thirsty I will give freely from the spring of the water of life. 7The one who overcomes will inherit all things, and I will be his God, and he will be My son.

Overcoming the World

...4because everyone born of God overcomes the world. And this is the victory that has overcome the world: our faith. 5Who then overcomes the world? Only he who believes that Jesus is the Son of God. 6This is the One who came by water and blood, Jesus Christ—not by water alone, but by water and blood. And it is the Spirit who testifies to this, because the Spirit is the truth.... https://biblehub.com/1_john/5-5.htm

"Son of God" means Visible Image of the Invisible God (still is GOD!):

Colossians 1:15-19

The Supremacy of the Son of God

15 The Son is the image of the invisible God, the firstborn over all creation. 16 For in him all things were created: things in heaven and on earth, visible and invisible, whether thrones or powers or rulers or authorities; all things have been created through him and for him. 17 He is before all things, and in him all things hold together. 18 And he is the head of the body, the church; he is the beginning and the firstborn from among the dead, so that in everything he might have the supremacy. 19 For God was pleased to have all his fullness dwell in him,

Good and Perfect Gifts

...16Do not be deceived, my beloved brothers. 17Every good and perfect gift is from above, coming down from the Father of the heavenly lights, with whom there is no change or shifting shadow. 18He chose to give us birth through the word of truth, that we would be a kind of firstfruits of His creation.... https://biblehub.com/james/1-17.htm

We are plainly told that anyone who refuses to acknowledge Jesus the Christ is the One True God, who came in the flesh, declared and proved Himself to us, IS AN ANTICHRIST! someone who is still dead to Him; lost in their sins and are making themselves to be one of His enemies who will inherit His Wrath!

https://www.facebook.com/photo/?fbid=6389305527815019&set=a.115635768515391 - SO YOU HAVE A CHOICE TO MAKE: DO YOU WANT TO BE A SON OR DAUGHTER OF THE MOST HIGH, ONE TRUE GOD, JESUS, THE CHRIST AND INHERIT EVERY GOOD THING FOREVER OR DO YOU WANT TO BE A CHILD OF THE DEVIL AND EXPERIENCE HIS WRATH FOR DELIBERATELY REJECTING THE ONE TRUE GOD AND WILLFULLY CHOOSING TO BE WICKED AND EVIL ALL YOUR DAYS WITHOUT REPENTANCE?

SO, GOD, JESUS CHRIST, OFFERS EACH OF US MAXIMUM REWARDS AND MAXIMUM CONSEQUENCES ALL BASED ON KNOWING HIM, ACKNOWLEDGING HIM, BELIEVING AND OBEYING HIM AS THE ONE TRUE GOD THAT HE IS! IT IS THEREFORE OF THE UTMOST, SUPREME IMPORTANCE FOR EVERYONE, EVERYWHERE TO KNOW, LOVE AND OBEY THE LIVING LORD JESUS CHRIST! NOT JUST YOUR PRESENT EXISTENCE BUT YOUR EVERLASTING DESTINY DEPENDS ON YOUR RELATIONSHIP WITH HIM!!!!!!!!

And so, if you ever come to your senses and obey Him and come to know the One True God personally, tell everyone else until everyone else knows Him also!

The Great Commission

…15And He said to them, "Go into all the world and preach the gospel to every creature. 16Whoever believes and is baptized will be saved, but whoever does not believe will be condemned.
https://biblehub.com/mark/16-16.htm

…18Then Jesus came to them and said, "All authority in heaven and on earth has been given to Me. 19Therefore go and make disciples of all nations, baptizing them in the name of the Father, and of the Son, and of the Holy Spirit, 20and teaching them to obey all that I have commanded you. And surely I am with you always, even to the end of the age."…
https://biblehub.com/matthew/28-19.htm

Three Thousand Believe - Jesus Christ is the Name of the Father, the Son, and the Holy Spirit, the One True God -

38 Peter replied, "Repent and be baptized, every one of you, in the name of Jesus Christ for the forgiveness of your sins, and you will receive the gift of the Holy Spirit. 39This promise belongs to you and your children and to all who are far off—to all whom the Lord our God will call to Himself."…
https://biblehub.com/acts/2-38.htm

Jesus Promises the Holy Spirit
…20On that day you will know that I am in My Father, and you are in Me, and I am in you. 21Whoever has My commandments and keeps them is the one who loves Me. The one who loves Me will be loved by My Father, and I will love him and reveal Myself to him."
https://biblehub.com/john/14-21.htm

READ IT AGAIN! THE ONE TRUE GOD, JESUS CHRIST, PROMISED TO REVEAL HIMSELF TO ALL WHO LOVE AND OBEY HIM!

EVERY LOCATION IN THE HOLY BIBLE THAT SAYS "GOD" or "LORD" is a direct reference to JESUS CHRIST! (so, all your citations that you just mentioned are all about Jesus Christ! JUST AS I HAD JUST SHOWED YOU!)

John 5:39-40
39 You search the Scriptures because you think that in them you have eternal life; and it is they that bear witness about me, 40 yet you refuse to come to me that you may have life.

THE ENTIRE HOLY BIBLE IS ALL ABOUT JESUS CHRIST, THE ONE TRUE GOD!

The Fulfillment of the Law
16In the same way, let your light shine before men, that they may see your good deeds and glorify your Father in heaven. 17Do not think that I have come to abolish the Law or the Prophets. I have not come to abolish them, but to fulfill them. 18For I tell you truly, until heaven and earth pass away, not a single jot, not a stroke of a pen, will disappear from the Law until everything is accomplished.... https://biblehub.com/matthew/5-17.htm

ONLY GOD CAN FULFILL ALL HIS LAW AND PROPHECIES!

Jesus Opens the Scriptures
...26Was it not necessary for the Christ to suffer these things and then to enter His glory?" 27And beginning with Moses and all the Prophets, He explained to them what was written in all the Scriptures about Himself.

ALL PROPHETS TESTIFY THAT JESUS CHRIST IS LORD OF ALL!

Acts 10:34-43

34 So Peter opened his mouth and said: "Truly I understand that God shows no partiality, 35 but in every nation anyone who fears him and does what is right is acceptable to him. 36 As for the word that he sent to Israel, preaching good news of peace through Jesus Christ (he is Lord of all), 37 you yourselves know what happened throughout all Judea, beginning from Galilee after the baptism that John proclaimed: 38 how God anointed Jesus of Nazareth with the Holy Spirit and with power. He went about doing good and healing all who were oppressed by the devil, for God was with him. 39 And we are witnesses of all that he did both in the country of the Jews and in Jerusalem. They put him to death by hanging him on a tree, 40 but God raised him on the third day and made him to appear, 41 not to all the people but to us who had been chosen by God as witnesses, who ate and drank with him after he rose from the dead. 42 And he commanded us to preach to the people and to testify that he is the one appointed by God to be judge of the living and the dead. 43 To him all the prophets bear witness that everyone who believes in him receives forgiveness of sins through his name."

verse 36 JESUS CHRIST IS LORD OF ALL verse 43 ALL PROPHETS BEAR WITNESS THAT JESUS CHRIST IS LORD OF ALL AND THAT FORGIVENESS OF SINS IS ONLY THROUGH HIM, BY NAME!

Peter and John Before the Council
...11This Jesus is 'the stone you builders rejected, which has become the cornerstone.' 12 Salvation exists in no one else, for there is no other name under heaven given to men by which we must be saved."
https://biblehub.com/acts/4-12.htm

SALVATION IS ONLY BY JESUS CHRIST, THE ONE TRUE GOD! (1Jn 5:20, John 20:24-29)

which is why Jesus Christ always receives worship:
https://www.openbible.info/topics/worshipping_jesus

Far too many muslims imagine they can ignore the entire Holy Bible if they find any verse anywhere in it that they can twist in order to deny the Divinity of Jesus Christ and one of the most twisted of all verses by them is Numbers 23:19.

Yes, Jesus Christ is God, He says so throughout the entire Holy Bible. So, ripping one verse from it in a vain effort to deny that fact is known as practicing deceit.

muslims tend to focus only on that tiny portion of time when God came in the flesh, humbly as a Man, the Messiah, in order to deny Jesus Christ is the One True God.

Instead, Jesus Christ has always been God and always will be God. He told His Prophets hundreds of times He would come in the flesh:

https://www.accordingtothescriptures.org/prophecy/353prophecies.html

So, when He did so, Jesus Christ, said the entire Holy Bible was all about Him, the One who has Eternal Life and the One everyone must come to in order to have that Life.

John 5:39-40

39 You search the Scriptures because you think that in them you have eternal life; and it is they that bear witness about me, 40 yet you refuse to come to me that you may have life.

So, Jesus Christ plainly stated He is God and proved it by doing so many Divine Miracles that those who saw and heard Him said the whole world couldn't contain the books if they were all written down.

...24This is the disciple who testifies to these things and who has written them down. And we know that his testimony is true. 25 There are many more things that Jesus did. If all of them were written down, I suppose that not even the world itself would have space for the books that would be written. https://biblehub.com/john/21-25.htm

After Jesus Christ publicly claimed to be the One True God, the One who has Eternal Life and the Power to Raise the dead back to Life, He then publicly died, raised His Body from the Grave and ascended back into Heaven in front of eyewitnesses PROVING His Claims!

So yes, Jesus Christ is God, and proved it like no one else in the entire history of the world!

And so, Numbers 23:19 is all about the contrast between sinful man and the Holy LORD, He doesn't LIE like sinful men do, and he doesn't even need to repent like the sons of Adam, HE IS HOLY, Perfect and Sinless!

ANOTHER muslim was again denying that the Holy Bible plainly tells us all that Jesus Christ is the One True God. (even after I had already shown them plainly that the Holy Bible redundantly says so!)

I just showed you that the scriptures plainly state Jesus Christ is God and does so from Genesis to Revelation and you choose to argue? let this sink into your presently deceived mind! you don't see, hear or know God BECAUSE YOU ARE DENYING HIM INSTEAD!

https://www.facebook.com/photo.php?fbid=6471680786244159&set=pb.100002069048072.-2207520000&type=3 and
https://www.facebook.com/photo.php?fbid=6800758120003089&set=pb.100002069048072.-2207520000&type=3 and
https://www.facebook.com/photo.php?fbid=6809546799124221&set=pb.100002069048072.-2207520000&type=3

EVERY LOCATION IN THE HOLY BIBLE THAT SAYS "GOD" or "LORD" is a direct reference to JESUS CHRIST! (so, all your citations that you just mentioned are all about Jesus Christ! JUST AS I HAD JUST SHOWED YOU!)

John 5:39-40
39 You search the Scriptures because you think that in them you have eternal life; and it is they that bear witness about me, 40 yet you refuse to come to me that you may have life.

THE ENTIRE HOLY BIBLE IS ALL ABOUT JESUS CHRIST, THE ONE TRUE GOD!

The Fulfillment of the Law
16In the same way, let your light shine before men, that they may see your good deeds and glorify your Father in heaven. 17Do not think that I have come to abolish the Law or the Prophets. I have not come to abolish them, but to fulfill them. 18For I tell you truly, until heaven and earth pass away,

not a single jot, not a stroke of a pen, will disappear from the Law until everything is accomplished.... https://biblehub.com/matthew/5-17.htm

ONLY GOD CAN FULFILL ALL HIS LAW AND PROPHECIES!

Jesus Opens the Scriptures
...26Was it not necessary for the Christ to suffer these things and then to enter His glory?" 27And beginning with Moses and all the Prophets, He explained to them what was written in all the Scriptures about Himself.

ALL PROPHETS TESTIFY THAT JESUS CHRIST IS LORD OF ALL!

Acts 10:34-43
34 So Peter opened his mouth and said: "Truly I understand that God shows no partiality, 35 but in every nation anyone who fears him and does what is right is acceptable to him. 36 As for the word that he sent to Israel, preaching good news of peace through Jesus Christ (he is Lord of all), 37 you yourselves know what happened throughout all Judea, beginning from Galilee after the baptism that John proclaimed: 38 how God anointed Jesus of Nazareth with the Holy Spirit and with power. He went about doing good and healing all who were oppressed by the devil, for God was with him. 39 And we are witnesses of all that he did both in the country of the Jews and in Jerusalem. They put him to death by hanging him on a tree, 40 but God raised him on the third day and made him to appear, 41 not to all the people but to us who had been chosen by God as witnesses, who ate and drank with him after he rose from the dead. 42 And he commanded us to preach to the people and to testify that he is the one appointed by God to be judge of the living and the dead. 43 To him all the prophets bear witness that everyone who believes in him receives forgiveness of sins through his name."

verse 36 JESUS CHRIST IS LORD OF ALL verse 43 ALL PROPHETS BEAR WITNESS THAT JESUS CHRIST IS LORD OF ALL AND THAT FORGIVENESS OF SINS IS ONLY THROUGH HIM, BY NAME!

Peter and John Before the Council
…11This Jesus is 'the stone you builders rejected, which has become the cornerstone.' 12 Salvation exists in no one else, for there is no other name under heaven given to men by which we must be saved."
https://biblehub.com/acts/4-12.htm

SALVATION IS ONLY BY JESUS CHRIST, THE ONE TRUE GOD! (1Jn 5:20, John 20:24-29)

which is why Jesus Christ always receives worship:
https://www.openbible.info/topics/worshipping_jesus

(numbers 23:19 does NOT say GOD IS NOT A MAN. (PERIOD) INSTEAD it says, God doesn't tell lies like sinful men do, and God doesn't even need to repent like the sons of Adam. (YOU HAVE TO STUDY! LOOK AT THE ORIGINAL WORDS!) https://biblehub.com/interlinear/numbers/23-19.htm in the original language there are no punctuation marks and so it uses the word "ish" for sinful men that tell lies and then it uses "sons of Adam" and then the context makes it very clear that it is talking about God's CHARACTER; not His Essence! when it follows up with "Does He speak and not act? Does He promise and not fulfill?" so the verse in no way is disagreeing with the rest of the entire Holy Bible that plainly tells us Jesus Christ is GOD! (This is one of the verses muslims use the most and is the reason I mention this REDUNDANTLY, they need to let it sink in!)

Another deceived muslim was wickedly falsely accusing Christianity and Christians of being accursed according to the Holy Bible because Jesus Christ was crucified.

no islam is accursed, according to the Holy Bible, not Christianity.

Galatians 1:6-9
No Other Gospel
6 I am astonished that you are so quickly deserting him who called you in the grace of Christ and are turning to a different gospel— 7 not that there is another one, but there are some who trouble you and want to distort the gospel of Christ. 8 But even if we or an angel from heaven should preach to you a gospel contrary to the one we preached to you, let him be accursed. 9 As we have said before, so now I say again: If anyone is preaching to you a gospel contrary to the one you received, let him be accursed.

the lying muhammad and his lies in the quran and islam as a whole are accursed for denying the Gospel of Jesus Christ in the Holy Bible and for proclaiming a different evil one and a different evil god.

The Holy Bible tells us Jesus Christ, the One True God, took the consequences of our sins upon Himself and nailed them to the cross. It's why He said, "It is Finished", when He had done what was necessary to Redeem and Save us. So, Jesus Christ bore our sins, and the curse of His Law upon Himself, when He was crucified in our place. If you refuse to accept Jesus Christ and His Loving Sacrifice for you, you must bear the Divine Consequences of your sins yourself and God says that will mean that He casts you into the lake of fire.

Christ's Example of Suffering
...23When they heaped abuse on Him, He did not retaliate; when He suffered, He made no threats, but entrusted Himself to Him who judges justly. **24**He Himself bore our sins in His body on the tree, so that we might

die to sin and live to righteousness. "By His stripes you are healed." **25**For "you were like sheep going astray," but now you have returned to the Shepherd and Overseer of your souls.... https://biblehub.com/1_peter/2-24.htm

Alive in Christ
...**13**When you were dead in your trespasses and in the uncircumcision of your sinful nature, God made you alive with Christ. He forgave us all our trespasses, **14**having canceled the debt ascribed to us in the decrees that stood against us. He took it away, nailing it to the cross! **15**And having disarmed the powers and authorities, He made a public spectacle of them, triumphing over them by the cross....
https://biblehub.com/colossians/2-14.htm https://bible.knowing-jesus.com/topics/God,-As-Redeemer AND https://www.preceptaustin.org/tetelestai-paid_in_full

Christ Redeemed Us
...**12**The law, however, is not based on faith; on the contrary, "The man who does these things will live by them." **13**Christ redeemed us from the curse of the law by becoming a curse for us. For it is written: "Cursed is everyone who is hung on a tree." **14**He redeemed us in order that the blessing promised to Abraham would come to the Gentiles in Christ Jesus, so that by faith we might receive the promise of the Spirit....
https://biblehub.com/galatians/3-13.htm

So, Christians are Redeemed by God, Saved from the Curse of His Law, because He bore our sins and the consequences for them when He was crucified in our behalf! BUT EVERYONE WHO IS REJECTING JESUS CHRIST AS THEIR LORD AND SAVIOR ARE STILL UNDER THE DIVINE CURSE FOR BREAKING HIS COMMANDMENTS. So, Christianity and Christians are Blessed; but everyone, including muslims, who are rejecting Jesus Christ as their Lord and Savior are cursed. Divine Consequences come upon all nations and people who are rejecting our Eternal Creator or ignoring Him and His Words given to us all in the contents of the Holy Bible.

ONLY THE ONE TRUE GOD, JESUS CHRIST, SAVES US! Acts 4:12; Isaiah 43:11

EVERYONE! ALL persons, including muslims! ARE COMMANDED BY THE ONE TRUE GOD TO REPENT OF THEIR SINS, INCLUDING THINKING THEY KNOW BETTER THAN HIM, AND GET BAPTIZED IN THE NAME OF JESUS CHRIST! EVERYONE! pray to receive His Holy Spirit of Truth, because if you rebel wickedly against this Divine Commandment, you will die in your sins! All who REFUSE to Obey Jesus Christ, the One True God, will be cast into the lake of fire! Jn 3:36, 2 Th 1:8-9; Rev 21:8

OBEY OUR LORD JESUS CHRIST NOW! or face His Wrath for deliberately rebelling against the One True God!

The Great Commission
...15And He said to them, "Go into all the world and preach the gospel to every creature. 16Whoever believes and is baptized will be saved, but whoever does not believe will be condemned.
https://biblehub.com/mark/16-16.htm

37When the people heard this, they were cut to the heart and asked Peter and the other apostles, "Brothers, what shall we do?" 38 Peter replied, "Repent and be baptized, every one of you, in the name of Jesus Christ for the forgiveness of your sins, and you will receive the gift of the Holy Spirit. 39This promise belongs to you and your children and to all who are far off—to all whom the Lord our God will call to Himself."...
https://biblehub.com/acts/2-38.htm

Peter and John Before the Council

...11This Jesus is 'the stone you builders rejected, which has become the cornerstone.' 12 Salvation exists in no one else, for there is no other name under heaven given to men by which we must be saved."
https://biblehub.com/acts/4-12.htm

Yet another muslim was committing great sin, by lying about the Words of God in the Holy Bible and falsely claiming a contradiction when there isn't any in any of his citations. His first citation was about the fact Jesus Christ suffered and died for our sins. His next citation (out of context) was Jesus Christ telling rebellious unbelievers that they would die in their sins for wickedly denying who He is. His third citation was about the fact that each person is held responsible by God for their own sins. (all verses taken out of context, far too many lying muslims do that habitually, showing the spirit of the deceiver is within them; so any time a muslim or anyone cites a verse out of the Holy Bible to claim a contradiction, PUT THE VERSE OR PASSAGE THEY ARE CITING BACK IN CONTEXT, virtually every time, it's deliberate deception on their part.)

When you rip the Words of God out of context to make false claims, it makes you look deliberately deceptive, very evil; like the devil. you need to repent.

The Resurrection of Christ
...2By this gospel you are saved, if you hold firmly to the word I preached to you. Otherwise, you have believed in vain. 3For what I received I passed on to you as of first importance: that Christ died for our sins according to the Scriptures, 4that He was buried, that He was raised on the third day according to the Scriptures,... https://biblehub.com/1_corinthians/15-3.htm

Gospel is archaic English for God-speaks or Good News because when God Speaks it is Good News for all who have ears to hear. So, the Gospel of Jesus Christ has been given us in the Holy Bible, anyone denying that God came in the flesh to Redeem and Save us according to His Own Law and Prophecies is still in their sins and will die in their sins (God tells us that is how to discern the spirit of antichrist from His Holy Spirit of Truth 1Jn 4:1-6, 1Jn 2:22-27; ALL of 1Jn chapters 1-5), IF THEY GO ON DENYING HIM; REFUSING TO OBEY HIS COMMANDMENT TO REPENT AND BE BAPTIZED IN HIS NAME AND FILLED WITH HIS HOLY SPIRIT OF TRUTH; which is what the next verse you cited is all about.

John 8:21-25
21 So he said to them again, "I am going away, and you will seek me, and you will die in your sin. Where I am going, you cannot come." 22 So the Jews said, "Will he kill himself, since he says, 'Where I am going, you cannot come'?" 23 He said to them, "You are from below; I am from above. You are of this world; I am not of this world. 24 I told you that you would die in your sins, for unless you believe that I am he you will die in your sins." 25 So they said to him, "Who are you?" Jesus said to them, "Just what I have been telling you from the beginning.

So, the ones who die in their sins are all those who refuse to believe Jesus Christ and that He is the One True God just as He has been telling us since the Beginning.

Salvation is ONLY in GOD Isaiah 43:11 and the Name given us by God, who He really is, IS JESUS CHIRST! Acts 4:12

Those who reject Jesus Christ and His Salvation, die in their sins!

and then we come to your third citation. Ezekiel 18:20
https://www.biblegateway.com/passage/?search=Ezekiel%2018&version=ESV - this passage is about the fact that God Judges each soul according to

their own ways, those who do wickedly will suffer for it and those who live righteously, will not.

20 The soul who sins shall die. The son shall not suffer for the iniquity of the father, nor the father suffer for the iniquity of the son. The righteousness of the righteous shall be upon himself, and the wickedness of the wicked shall be upon himself.

Each person bears individual responsibility for their own sins. The verse does not say "no one can die for anyone else" and it also does not say, GOD cannot suffer and die for the sins of mankind to Save and Redeem us. That would violate His Own Law of Redemption and Prophecies of Salvation if it did:

https://bible.knowing-jesus.com/topics/God,-As-Redeemer

https://www.preceptaustin.org/tetelestai-paid_in_full

So, repent of this great evil, of deliberately misrepresenting what God tells us in the Holy Bible.

By the way, there is NONE righteous according to God, but all have sinned WITH THE EXCEPTION of Jesus Christ!

9What then? Are we any better? Not at all. For we have already made the charge that Jews and Greeks alike are all under sin. 10As it is written: "There is no one righteous, not even one. 11There is no one who understands, no one who seeks God.... https://biblehub.com/romans/3-

10.htm

BUT GOD DIED FOR US IN ORDER TO BE FORGIVEN UNDER HIS LAW AND PROPHECIES! HE REDEEMED US!

Christ's Sacrifice for the Ungodly
...**7**Very rarely will anyone die for a righteous man, though for a good man someone might possibly dare to die. **8**But God proves His love for us in this: While we were still sinners, Christ died for us. **9**Therefore, since we have now been justified by His blood, how much more shall we be saved from wrath through Him!... https://biblehub.com/romans/5-8.htm

Wow, I have seen muslims constantly misunderstanding the Holy Bible but this is by far the most serious and common misunderstanding. Some muslims obviously think the Father and the Son are two different beings when Jesus Christ plainly said the Father and the Son are ONE. (John 10:30) (to hate Him is to hate the Father, etc. etc - John 15:22-25) people then ask well why didn't He just say, "Me" and I reply, HE DID! verse 25! God, Jesus Christ, talks about "the Father" and "the Son" just so we understand He is much more than just His Humble Appearance as a Man, MUCH MORE!

John 14:6-9
6 Jesus said to him, "I am the way, the truth, and the life. No one comes to the Father except through Me.

The Father Revealed
7 "If you had known Me, you would have known My Father also; and from now on you know Him and have seen Him."

8 Philip said to Him, "Lord, show us the Father, and it is sufficient for us."

9 Jesus said to him, "Have I been with you so long, and yet you have not known Me, Philip? He who has seen Me has seen the Father; so how can you say, 'Show us the Father'?

READ VERSE 9! JESUS CHRIST SAID, "HE WHO HAS SEEN ME HAS SEEN THE FATHER..."

Some people are like: wait, is the Holy Bible telling us that Jesus Christ is the Father and the Son? YES! GOD IS SUPREME IN EVERYTHING!

Colossians 1:15-19
The Supremacy of the Son of God
15 The Son is the image of the invisible God, the firstborn over all creation. 16 For in him all things were created: things in heaven and on earth, visible and invisible, whether thrones or powers or rulers or authorities; all things have been created through him and for him. 17 He is before all things, and in him all things hold together. 18 And he is the head of the body, the church; he is the beginning and the firstborn from among the dead, so that in everything he might have the supremacy. 19 For God was pleased to have all his fullness dwell in him,

So, Jesus Christ is the: God of gods, Man of men, Spirit of spirits, Angel of angels, Father of fathers, Son of sons, Servant of servants, Prophet of prophets, King of kings, Lord of lords, First and Last, Beginning and End, etc. etc. etc. which is why the Holy Bible refers to Him in all these ways and more!

(It's the reason Jesus Christ is the ONE NAME of "the Father", "the Son" and "the Holy Spirit".)

The Great Commission

…**18**Then Jesus came to them and said, "All authority in heaven and on earth has been given to Me. **19**Therefore go and make disciples of all nations, baptizing them in the name of the Father, and of the Son, and of the Holy Spirit, **20**and teaching them to obey all that I have commanded you. And surely I am with you always, even to the end of the age."…
https://biblehub.com/matthew/28-19.htm

37When the people heard this, they were cut to the heart and asked Peter and the other apostles, "Brothers, what shall we do?" **38** Peter replied, "Repent and be baptized, every one of you, in the name of Jesus Christ for the forgiveness of your sins, and you will receive the gift of the Holy Spirit. **39**This promise belongs to you and your children and to all who are far off—to all whom the Lord our God will call to Himself."…
https://biblehub.com/acts/2-38.htm

(And the reason God sends His Holy Spirit in HIS NAME - JESUS CHRIST- to TESTIFY that HE IS GOD to the entire world! Acts 1:8; 4:12)

37When the people heard this, they were cut to the heart and asked Peter and the other apostles, "Brothers, what shall we do?" 38 Peter replied, "Repent and be baptized, every one of you, in the name of Jesus Christ for the forgiveness of your sins, and you will receive the gift of the Holy Spirit. 39This promise belongs to you and your children and to all who are far off—to all whom the Lord our God will call to Himself."… https://biblehub.com/acts/2-38.htm

Peter and John Before the Council

…**11**This Jesus is 'the stone you builders rejected, which has become the cornerstone.' 12 Salvation exists in no one else, for there is no other name under heaven given to men by which we must be saved."
https://biblehub.com/acts/4-12.htm

Another muslim was denying the Crucifixion, Death and Resurrection of Jesus Christ, because that is a common lie that islam and their vile quran teaches them.

Yes, Jesus Christ was crucified, dead and buried, resurrected and glorified; just like the Holy Bible says very clearly many times over.

https://youtu.be/LLnClp3OVmE?t=1884 - the most studied book on earth plainly tells us of the life, crucifixion, death, resurrection and ascension of Jesus Christ and the most studied artifact, His Burial Cloth, is evidence of that fact. All muslims are believing lies and obviously so.

Another muslim was publicly lying saying that Jesus Christ wasn't God and wasn't worshiped as such in the Holy Bible.

Everywhere Jesus Christ quotes the Words in the Holy Bible about worshiping God, HE IS REFERRING TO HIMSELF! (not anyone or anything else)

John 5:39-40
39 You search the Scriptures because you think that in them you have eternal life; and it is they that bear witness about me, 40 yet you refuse to come to me that you may have life.

Jesus Christ plainly stated the entire Holy Bible is about HIM, THE ONE WHO HAS ETERNAL LIFE, and the One whom everyone must come to in order to have that life.

Jesus Christ ALWAYS receives worship because He is GOD!

https://www.openbible.info/topics/worshipping_jesus

He expressed displeasure when people that should have worshiped and thanked Him, didn't!

The Ten Lepers
…16He fell facedown at Jesus' feet in thanksgiving to Him—and he was a Samaritan. 17"Were not all ten cleansed?" Jesus asked. "Where then are the other nine? 18Was no one found except this foreigner to return and give glory to God?"… https://biblehub.com/luke/17-17.htm

ALL places in the Holy Bible that say "GOD" or "LORD" are referring to JESUS CHRIST!

Jesus Appears to Thomas
…27Then Jesus said to Thomas, "Put your finger here and look at My hands. Reach out your hand and put it into My side. Stop doubting and believe." 28Thomas replied, "My Lord and my God!" 29Jesus said to him, "Because you have seen Me, you have believed; blessed are those who have not seen and yet have believed."… https://biblehub.com/john/20-28.htm

So, another muslim was pointing out that Jesus can't be God because He was praying to God in the Garden of Gethsemane and was dangerously calling a Christian, "a fool". No one who acknowledges that Jesus Christ is Lord, the One True God, just as the scriptures redundantly state is a fool. muslims misunderstand such passages because they ignore all the many times Jesus Christ plainly states He is God, in order to look for any verse or passage that seems to imply He isn't.

Do your best not to call anyone a fool, especially not anyone who acknowledges the Truth that Jesus Christ is the One True God who came in the flesh. When "the Son" prays to "the Father" and says things like "not my will but Yours" He is not referring to someone other than Himself. He is teaching us about the battle between the mortal desires of the flesh and those proper desires of His Spirit.

It's the same battle discussed in Romans Chapters 7-8.

The Son means Visible Image of God:

John 14:6-9
6 Jesus said to him, "I am the way, the truth, and the life. No one comes to the Father except through Me.

The Father Revealed
7 "If you had known Me, you would have known My Father also; and from now on you know Him and have seen Him."

8 Philip said to Him, "Lord, show us the Father, and it is sufficient for us."

9 Jesus said to him, "Have I been with you so long, and yet you have not known Me, Philip? He who has seen Me has seen the Father; so how can you say, 'Show us the Father'?

Colossians 1:15-19
The Supremacy of the Son of God
15 The Son is the image of the invisible God, the firstborn over all creation.
16 For in him all things were created: things in heaven and on earth, visible and invisible, whether thrones or powers or rulers or authorities; all

things have been created through him and for him. 17 He is before all things, and in him all things hold together. 18 And he is the head of the body, the church; he is the beginning and the firstborn from among the dead, so that in everything he might have the supremacy. 19 For God was pleased to have all his fullness dwell in him,

and the Father refers to His Eternal, Invisible, Pervasive and Transcendent Existence - Eph 4:6

So, when the Son was praying to the Father, He was not praying to someone other than Himself, His Spirit, to find the Strength necessary to force His Body to obey His Will and go through the suffering and death He had come into this world to do.

The scriptures tell us God deliberately emptied Himself to walk among us as one of us, a Man, one who was tested in all ways like us, but without sin.

The Attitude of Christ
...6Who, existing in the form of God, did not consider equality with God something to be grasped, 7but emptied Himself, taking the form of a servant, being made in human likeness. 8And being found in appearance as a man, He humbled Himself and became obedient to death—even death on a cross.... https://biblehub.com/philippians/2-7.htm

Jesus the Great High Priest
14Therefore, since we have a great high priest who has passed through the heavens, Jesus the Son of God, let us hold firmly to what we profess. 15For we do not have a high priest who is unable to sympathize with our weaknesses, but we have one who was tempted in every way that we are, yet was without sin. 16Let us then approach the throne of grace with

confidence, so that we may receive mercy and find grace to help us in our time of need.... https://biblehub.com/hebrews/4-15.htm

When God walked in the flesh as the Messiah, humbly as a Man, He proved His Commandments can be kept as one of us and thereby condemned sin in the flesh.

Living in the Spirit
...2For in Christ Jesus the law of the Spirit of life set you free from the law of sin and death. 3For what the law was powerless to do in that it was weakened by the flesh, God did by sending His own Son in the likeness of sinful man, as an offering for sin. He thus condemned sin in the flesh, 4so that the righteous standard of the law might be fulfilled in us, who do not walk according to the flesh but according to the Spirit....
https://biblehub.com/romans/8-3.htm

And so, His Prayers in Gethsemane were telling us all that when we follow God, when we follow Jesus Christ, we will face things difficult and unpleasant for our flesh, even suffering and death, but we will also pray and receive strength from God to go through whatever He calls us to. Those who know Him follow Him not just when people are shouting Hosannah and Praising God, but when people are reviling Him, persecuting and maltreating Him. We follow Him in life and in His suffering and death; knowing we are also following Him into Heaven and Life Everlasting just as He demonstrated by rising from the dead and ascending into Heaven as PROOF, HE IS THE WAY, THE TRUTH AND THE LIFE just as He stated.

Today a muslim surprised me with a question I hadn't heard from any of them in all these years. Asking about where in the Holy Bible does it say that it was written by the Prophets and Eyewitnesses of God, Jesus Christ?

Eyewitnesses of His Majesty

16For we did not follow cleverly devised fables when we made known to you the power and coming of our Lord Jesus Christ, but we were eyewitnesses of His majesty. **17**For He received honor and glory from God the Father when the voice came to Him from the Majestic Glory, saying, "This is My beloved Son, in whom I am well pleased."...20Above all, you must understand that no prophecy of Scripture comes from one's own interpretation. 21For no such prophecy was ever brought forth by the will of man, but men spoke from God as they were carried along by the Holy Spirit. https://biblehub.com/2_peter/1-21.htm

2 Samuel 23:2
The Spirit of the LORD spoke through me; His word was on my tongue.

Habakkuk 2:2-3 Amplified Bible (AMP)
Then the LORD answered me and said, "Write the vision And engrave it plainly on [clay] tablets So that the one who reads it will run. For the vision is yet for the appointed [future] time It hurries toward the goal [of fulfillment]; it will not fail. Even though it delays, wait [patiently] for it, Because it will certainly come; it will not delay.

Most people don't ask such a question because the Names of the Prophets appears on/within their respective books.

John 5:39-40
39 You search the Scriptures because you think that in them you have eternal life; and it is they that bear witness about me, 40 yet you refuse to come to me that you may have life.

Jesus Opens the Scriptures

...26Was it not necessary for the Christ to suffer these things and then to enter His glory?" 27And beginning with Moses and all the Prophets, He explained to them what was written in all the Scriptures about Himself.
https://biblehub.com/luke/24-27.htm

Hebrews 1:1-6
God, who at sundry times and in divers manners spake in time past unto the fathers by the prophets, hath in these last days spoken unto us by his Son, whom he hath appointed heir of all things, by whom also he made the worlds; who being the brightness of his glory, and the express image of his person, and upholding all things by the word of his power, when he had by himself purged our sins, sat down on the right hand of the Majesty on high; being made so much better than the angels, as he hath by inheritance obtained a more excellent name than they. For unto which of the angels said he at any time, Thou art my Son, This day have I begotten thee? And again, I will be to him a Father, And he shall be to me a Son? And again, when he bringeth in the firstbegotten into the world, he saith, And let all the angels of God worship him.

All Scripture is God-Breathed
...15From infancy you have known the Holy Scriptures, which are able to make you wise for salvation through faith in Christ Jesus. 16All Scripture is God-breathed and is useful for instruction, for conviction, for correction, and for training in righteousness, 17so that the man of God may be complete, fully equipped for every good work....
https://biblehub.com/2_timothy/3-16.htm

muslims constantly tell others that muhammad was the last prophet and that islam is the correct religion; ignoring everything true in the process. God ever lives and because God ever lives, there is no such thing as a "last prophet". Only God Himself is the First and the Last, none of His creatures.

Have you muslims ever really thought about who makes someone to be a Prophet? That's right, the Holy Spirit of God Almighty is what causes anyone to hear the Words of God and is empowered to write them down and/or speak them to others. (The reason I don't think muslims have really thought very hard about who makes a person into a Prophet, is that they are following a lying criminal muhammad in their lying quran, instead of God, Jesus Christ, and His Prophets in the Holy Bible.)

Since the Spirit of God, Jesus Christ, is what causes anyone to be a prophet and is the reason why all true prophets testify that Jesus Christ is the One True God (since muhammad didn't HE IS A FALSE PROPHET!):

Eyewitnesses of His Majesty
…20Above all, you must understand that no prophecy of Scripture comes from one's own interpretation. 21For no such prophecy was ever brought forth by the will of man, but men spoke from God as they were carried along by the Holy Spirit. https://biblehub.com/2_peter/1-21.htm

I Will Pour Out My Spirit
28And afterward, I will pour out My Spirit on all people. Your sons and daughters will prophesy, your old men will dream dreams, your young men will see visions. 29Even on My menservants and maidservants, I will pour out My Spirit in those days.… https://biblehub.com/joel/2-28.htm

Acts 2:17
In the last days, God says, I will pour out My Spirit on all people. Your sons and daughters will prophesy, your young men will see visions, your old men will dream dreams.

… For the testimony of Jesus is the spirit of prophecy."
https://biblehub.com/revelation/19-10.htm

Living in the Spirit
8Those controlled by the flesh cannot please God. 9You, however, are controlled not by the flesh, but by the Spirit, if the Spirit of God lives in you. And if anyone does not have the Spirit of Christ, he does not belong to Christ. 10But if Christ is in you, your body is dead because of sin, yet your spirit is alive because of righteousness....
https://biblehub.com/romans/8-9.htm

8But you will receive power when the Holy Spirit comes upon you, and you will be My witnesses in Jerusalem, and in all Judea and Samaria, and to the ends of the earth." https://biblehub.com/acts/1-8.htm

37When the people heard this, they were cut to the heart and asked Peter and the other apostles, "Brothers, what shall we do?" 38 Peter replied, "Repent and be baptized, every one of you, in the name of Jesus Christ for the forgiveness of your sins, and you will receive the gift of the Holy Spirit. 39This promise belongs to you and your children and to all who are far off—to all whom the Lord our God will call to Himself."...
https://biblehub.com/acts/2-38.htm

Acts10

36

As for the word that he sent to Israel, preaching good news of peace through **Jesus Christ (he is Lord of all),** ...

43

To him **all the prophets** bear witness that everyone who believes in him receives forgiveness of sins through his name."

NOTE: This means all true prophets were CHRISTIANS even before they were identified as such after JESUS CHRIST came in the flesh! not one of them were antichristian muslims!

So, everyone who testifies that Jesus Christ is the One True God is giving evidence that God has given them His Holy Spirit of Truth. (Acts 10:34-43) because ALL Prophets testify of Jesus Christ and that forgiveness of sins is only through Him, by Name.

Jesus Opens the Scriptures
…26Was it not necessary for the Christ to suffer these things and then to enter His glory?" 27And beginning with Moses and all the Prophets, He explained to them what was written in all the Scriptures about Himself.
https://biblehub.com/luke/24-27.htm

John 5:39-40
39 You search the Scriptures because you think that in them you have eternal life; and it is they that bear witness about me, 40 yet you refuse to come to me that you may have life.

So, God, Jesus Christ, sends His Holy Spirit of Truth upon all who repent and are baptized in His Name, in order to empower them to speak and write His Words, telling everyone He is the One True God. This means it is God, by His Holy Spirit of Truth, who makes anyone a prophet or prophetess and so all who receive Jesus Christ, by His Holy Spirit of Truth, into their lives are such.

In other words, all true Christians are prophets and prophetesses because the Holy Spirit of Jesus Christ is with them, just like He was with all the Prophets in the Holy Bible. Yes, not all Christians are called to the office of a Prophet, but all Christians are prophets and prophetesses to a greater or lesser extent. Every time they hear the Voice of His Holy Spirit telling them to speak His Words, they are doing exactly what the Prophets of old did in their generations.

The Promise of the Holy Spirit
...12I still have much to tell you, but you cannot yet bear to hear it. 13However, when the Spirit of truth comes, He will guide you into all truth. For He will not speak on His own, but He will speak what He hears, and He will declare to you what is to come. 14He will glorify Me by taking from what is Mine and disclosing it to you....
https://biblehub.com/john/16-13.htm

It's why everyone needs to obey God, Jesus Christ, and Repent and Be Baptized in His Name so that they KNOW GOD PERSONALLY BEYOND ALL DOUBT, and then go and tell everyone, everywhere until everyone does!

KNOW THE LORD! KNOW THE LORD! - https://biblehub.com/jeremiah/31-34.htm

Another common lie from muslims is that they wrongly claim the Holy Bible is corrupt and so much so that they believe the evil, lying quran instead that openly teaches to break the Commandments of God in the Holy Bible and to deny the One True God, JESUS CHRIST. (muslims are deceived and so much so, that they lie about the Words of God in the Holy Bible.) so one of them was ripping Jeremiah 8:8 out of context to falsely claim that the Holy Bible calls itself corrupt when it absolutely doesn't. ANYTIME a lying muslim rips a verse OUT OF CONTEXT, just put it back in!

No, it doesn't; the Holy Bible contains the Words of God which He said will never pass away.

33 Heaven and earth will pass away, but My words will never pass away.
https://biblehub.com/luke/21-33.htm

so what does your cited passage actually say? -

Sin and Treachery

4 "You shall say to them, Thus says the Lord: When men fall, do they not rise again? If one turns away, does he not return? 5 Why then has this people turned away in perpetual backsliding? They hold fast to deceit; they refuse to return. 6 I have paid attention and listened, but they have not spoken rightly; no man relents of his evil, saying, 'What have I done?' Everyone turns to his own course, like a horse plunging headlong into battle.7 Even the stork in the heavens knows her times, and the turtledove, swallow, and crane keep the time of their coming, but my people know not the rules of the Lord.8 "How can you say, 'We are wise, and the law of the Lord is with us'? But behold, the lying pen of the scribes has made it into a lie.9 The wise men shall be put to shame; they shall be dismayed and taken; behold, they have rejected the word of the Lord, so what wisdom is in them?10 Therefore I will give their wives to others and their fields to conquerors, because from the least to the greatest everyone is greedy for unjust gain; from prophet to priest, everyone deals falsely.11 They have healed the wound of my people lightly, saying, 'Peace, peace,' when there is no peace.12 Were they ashamed when they committed abomination? No, they were not at all ashamed; they did not know how to blush. Therefore, they shall fall among the fallen; when I punish them, they shall be overthrown, says the Lord.13 When I would gather them, declares the Lord, there are no grapes on the vine, nor figs on the fig tree; even the leaves are withered, and what I gave them has passed away from them."14 Why do we sit still? Gather together; let us go into the fortified cities and perish there, for the Lord our God has doomed us to perish and has given us poisoned water to drink, because we have sinned against the Lord.15 We looked for peace, but no good came; for a time of healing, but behold, terror.

So God is speaking (He doesn't lie and forbids His Words to be altered or changed in meaning) So who is He calling lying scribes? (false prophets and false teachers, not the true!)

https://www.esv.org/Isaiah+29:13;Matthew+15:8–9;Mark+7:6–7;Ezekiel+33:31/

Isaiah 29:13

13 And the Lord said:"Because this people draw near with their mouth and honor me with their lips, while their hearts are far from me, and their fear of me is a commandment taught by men,

Matthew 15:8–9

8"'This people honors me with their lips, but their heart is far from me;9 in vain do they worship me, teaching as doctrines the commandments of men.'"

Mark 7:6–7

6   And he said to them, "Well did Isaiah prophesy of you hypocrites, as it is written, "'This people honors me with their lips, but their heart is far from me;

7   in vain do they worship me, teaching as doctrines the commandments of men.'

Ezekiel 33:31

31And they come to you as people come, and they sit before you as my people, and they hear what you say but they will not do it; for with lustful talk in their mouths they act; their heart is set on their gain.

and also:

The Tradition of the Elders

(Matthew 15:1–9)

1Then the Pharisees and some of the scribes who had come from Jerusalem gathered around Jesus, 2and they saw some of His disciples eating with hands that were defiled—that is, unwashed.3Now in holding to the tradition of the elders, the Pharisees and all the Jews do not eat until they wash their hands ceremonially. 4And on returning from the market, they do not eat unless they wash. And there are many other traditions for them to observe, including the washing of cups, pitchers, kettles, and couches for dining.5So the Pharisees and scribes questioned

Jesus: "Why do Your disciples not walk according to the tradition of the elders? Instead, they eat with defiled hands."6Jesus answered them, "Isaiah prophesied correctly about you hypocrites, as it is written: 'These people honor Me with their lips, but their hearts are far from Me.7They worship Me in vain; they teach as doctrine the precepts of men.'8You have disregarded the commandment of God to keep the tradition of men."9He went on to say, "You neatly set aside the command of God to maintain your own tradition. 10For Moses said, 'Honor your father and your mother' and 'Anyone who curses his father or mother must be put to death.' 11But you say that if a man says to his father or mother, 'Whatever you would have received from me is Corban' (that is, a gift devoted to God), 12he is no longer permitted to do anything for his father or mother. 13Thus you nullify the word of God by the tradition you have handed down. And you do so in many such matters."

What Defiles a Man

(Matthew 15:10–20)

14Once again Jesus called the crowd to Him and said, "All of you, listen to Me and understand: 15Nothing that enters a man from the outside can defile him; but the things that come out of a man, these are what defile him."17After Jesus had left the crowd and gone into the house, His disciples inquired about the parable.18"Are you still so dull?" He asked. "Do you not understand? Nothing that enters a man from the outside can defile him, 19because it does not enter his heart, but it goes into the stomach and then is eliminated." (Thus all foods are clean.)20He continued: "What comes out of a man, that is what defiles him. 21For from within the hearts of men come evil thoughts, sexual immorality, theft, murder, adultery, 22greed, wickedness, deceit, debauchery, envy, slander, arrogance, and foolishness. 23All these evils come from within, and these are what defile a man."

So, God was telling us about people who twist His Words, ignore them, misinterpret them, for their own vain traditions and evil purposes. (like the

Babylonian talmud and quran or many bad commentaries on the Sacred Scriptures) not the Holy Bible which is Divinely Inspired throughout.

All Scripture is God-Breathed

...15From infancy you have known the Holy Scriptures, which are able to make you wise for salvation through faith in Christ Jesus. 16All Scripture is God-breathed and is useful for instruction, for conviction, for correction, and for training in righteousness, 17so that the man of God may be complete, fully equipped for every good work....
https://biblehub.com/2_timothy/3-16.htm

17Sanctify them by the truth; Your word is truth.

https://biblehub.com/john/17-17.htm So the Holy Bible contains the Words of God and is Truth, whereas what some people say or write about His Words are lies. In other words, it's bad interpretations of His Words that are corrupt, not the Words of God. The Holy Bible is the standard of Truth in all the world, otherwise there would be none and everyone would be lost in their own vain imaginations.

Today a muslim was online, lying to himself and the world, falsely claiming that islam was the only way to Heaven. He, like virtually all muslims online, was arrogantly posting lying memes and telling people to read their Holy Bibles (implying falsely that muslims understand the Holy Bible while the billions of Christians in the world don't).

So, I told him, like I tell any and all muslims: No, islam is most definitely NOT the way to Heaven and is instead a sure way to end up in the lake of fire. (damnation) Only Jesus Christ is the way to Heaven. (Salvation - Acts 4:12, John 14:6-9, Acts 1:7-11) If you had practiced what you preach and read the Holy Bible, you would know that.

John 5:39-40

39 You search the Scriptures because you think that in them you have eternal life; and it is they that bear witness about me, 40 yet you refuse to come to me that you may have life.

Jesus Christ plainly stated that the entire Holy Bible is all about Him, the One who has Eternal Life and the One everyone must come to in order to have that life. He also stated He has the Power to Raise the dead back to life.

Jesus Comforts Martha and Mary

...24Martha replied, "I know that he will rise again in the resurrection at the last day." 25 Jesus said to her, "I am the resurrection and the life. Whoever believes in Me will live, even though he dies. 26And everyone who lives and believes in Me will never die. Do you believe this?"...
https://biblehub.com/john/11-25.htm

Then He proved it by publicly dying, raising His Body from the Grave, transfiguring it, making it Immortal and Glorious and Ascending into Heaven in front of eyewitnesses. PROVING HE IS THE WAY TO HEAVEN! NO ONE ELSE!

John 14:6-9

6
  Jesus said to him, "I am the way, the truth, and the life. No one comes to the Father except through Me.

The Father Revealed

7
  "If you had known Me, you would have known My Father also; and from now on you know Him and have seen Him."

8
  Philip said to Him, "Lord, show us the Father, and it is sufficient for us."

9

Jesus said to him, "Have I been with you so long, and yet you have not known Me, Philip? He who has seen Me has seen the Father; so how can you say, 'Show us the Father'?

Who is the Way? JESUS CHRIST! Who is the Truth? JESUS CHRIST! Who is the Life? JESUS CHRIST!

Jesus Appears to Thomas
...27Then Jesus said to Thomas, "Put your finger here and look at My hands. Reach out your hand and put it into My side. Stop doubting and believe." 28Thomas replied, "My Lord and my God!" 29Jesus said to him, "Because you have seen Me, you have believed; blessed are those who have not seen and yet have believed."... https://biblehub.com/john/20-28.htm

The Ascension
...7Jesus replied, "It is not for you to know times or seasons that the Father has fixed by His own authority. 8But you will receive power when the Holy Spirit comes upon you, and you will be My witnesses in Jerusalem, and in all Judea and Samaria, and to the ends of the earth."
https://biblehub.com/acts/1-8.htm

Anyone not testifying that Jesus Christ is the Only Way to Heaven is lying and He tells us all liars will be cast into the lake of fire. Since islam teaches muslims to deny Jesus Christ as the One True God, the Only Savior to Mankind, the Only Way to Eternal Life and Heaven, it means islam is the way to the flames of damnation, not Heaven.

Peter and John Before the Council
...11This Jesus is 'the stone you builders rejected, which has become the cornerstone.' 12 Salvation exists in no one else, for there is no other name

under heaven given to men by which we must be saved."
https://biblehub.com/acts/4-12.htm

Beware of Antichrists
...21I have not written to you because you lack knowledge of the truth, but because you have it, and because no lie comes from the truth. 22Who is the liar, if it is not the one who denies that Jesus is the Christ? This is the antichrist, who denies the Father and the Son. 23Whoever denies the Son does not have the Father, but whoever confesses the Son has the Father as well.... https://biblehub.com/1_john/2-22.htm

All muslims are lying about God, Jesus Christ, because they are believing the lies of islam and the quran, instead of God and His True Words in the Holy Bible.

A New Heaven and a New Earth
...7The one who overcomes will inherit all things, and I will be his God, and he will be My son. 8But to the cowardly and unbelieving and abominable and murderers and sexually immoral and sorcerers and idolaters and all liars, their place will be in the lake that burns with fire and sulfur. This is the second death." https://biblehub.com/revelation/21-8.htm

So, unless muslims Repent and Get Baptized in the Name of our Lord and Savior JESUS CHRIST, praying to receive His Holy Spirit, whereby they become true Christians, they will all end up in the lake of fire.

"Brothers, what shall we do?" 38 Peter replied, "Repent and be baptized, every one of you, in the name of Jesus Christ for the forgiveness of your sins, and you will receive the gift of the Holy Spirit. 39This promise belongs to you and your children and to all who are far off—to all whom the Lord our God will call to Himself."... https://biblehub.com/acts/2-38.htm

So then yet another muslim was lying to herself and the world, by clearly misinterpreting the Words of God in the Holy Bible and telling everyone that "Son of Man" in Daniel didn't refer to Jesus Christ, but to all holy people (plural). (The spirit of err is real and deceives people so that they don't understand what's true, especially about the Words of God in the Holy Bible. 1Jn 5:19, Jn 8:43-45) EVERYONE MUST OBEY GOD AND REPENT AND GET BAPTIZED IN HIS NAME AND PRAY TO RECEIVE HIS HOLY SPIRIT OF TRUTH. When the One True God, Jesus Christ, enters your life by His Holy Spirit of Truth, He kicks the lying spirit of err out! So, to KNOW TRUTH with absolute certainty and to prevent yourself from continuing to be deceived by the lying devil, you MUST obey Jesus Christ, the One True God!

When people lie publicly about God and His Words in the Holy Bible, those who know better must correct them! So, I responded: you imagine you can say "Son of Man" refers to many even though it is clearly singular. You are deluding yourself and attempting to deceive others with your delusions.

Jesus Christ plainly stated He is the "Son of Man" and "the Son of God"; both of these phrases refer to Him as the Messiah, God in the flesh.

The Unbelief of the Jews
...32But Jesus responded, "I have shown you many good works from the Father. For which of these do you stone Me?" 33" We are not stoning You for any good work," said the Jews, "but for blasphemy, because You, who are a man, declare Yourself to be God." 34Jesus replied, "Is it not written in your Law: 'I have said you are gods'?35If he called them gods to whom the word of God came— and the Scripture cannot be broken— 36then what about the One whom the Father sanctified and sent into the world? How then can you accuse Me of blasphemy for stating that I am the Son of God?... https://biblehub.com/john/10-33.htm

The Jews who heard Him understood that "Son of God" was a reference to the Messiah, God in the flesh, which is why they accused Him of blasphemy for openly claiming to be God.

25The woman said, "I know that Messiah" (called Christ) "is coming. When He comes, He will explain everything to us." 26Jesus answered, "I who speak to you am He."... https://biblehub.com/john/4-25.htm

https://hebrew4christians.com/Names_of_G-d/Messiah/messiah.html - Messiah/Christ refers to GOD who came in the flesh!

Many Disciples Turn Back
...61Aware that His disciples were grumbling about this teaching, Jesus asked them, "Does this offend you? 62Then what will happen if you see the Son of Man ascend to where He was before? 63The Spirit gives life; the flesh profits nothing. The words I have spoken to you are spirit and they are life.... https://biblehub.com/john/6-62.htm

The reason God, Jesus Christ, refers to Himself as both the "Son of Man" and the "Son of God" is that both of these phrases are what He said about Himself in the Scriptures REFERRING TO GOD the Messiah and that He would come in the flesh!

https://www.desiringgod.org/messages/son-of-god-son-of-man-king-ofisrael

Learn what is true, by obeying God and Repenting and Getting Baptized in the Name of our Lord Jesus Christ and pray to receive His Holy Spirit of

Truth as He Commands. Once God gives you His Holy Spirit of Truth, then He will teach you how to understand His Words in the Holy Bible properly.

The Great Commission
...15And He said to them, "Go into all the world and preach the gospel to every creature. 16Whoever believes and is baptized will be saved, but whoever does not believe will be condemned.
https://biblehub.com/mark/16-16.htm

"Brothers, what shall we do?" 38 Peter replied, "Repent and be baptized, every one of you, in the name of Jesus Christ for the forgiveness of your sins, and you will receive the gift of the Holy Spirit. 39This promise belongs to you and your children and to all who are far off—to all whom the Lord our God will call to Himself."... https://biblehub.com/acts/2-38.htm

John 14:20-26
20 In that day you will know that I am in my Father, and you in me, and I in you. 21 Whoever has my commandments and keeps them, he it is who loves me. And he who loves me will be loved by my Father, and I will love him and manifest myself to him." 22 Judas (not Iscariot) said to him, "Lord, how is it that you will manifest yourself to us, and not to the world?" 23 Jesus answered him, "If anyone loves me, he will keep my word, and my Father will love him, and we will come to him and make our home with him. 24 Whoever does not love me does not keep my words. And the word that you hear is not mine but the Father's who sent me.

25 "These things I have spoken to you while I am still with you. 26 But the Helper, the Holy Spirit, whom the Father will send in my name, he will teach you all things and bring to your remembrance all that I have said to you.

So, then a muslim was falsely accusing Christians of lying, which is something they do because they are currently deceived by lies themselves; so, when Christians tell them the Truth, their brainwashing causes them to refuse to believe that truth and instead falsely accuse Christians rather habitually online.

Christians don't lie; especially about God and His Words in the Holy Bible. but muslims constantly do and that is due to the fact they have filled their heads full of lies from the quran and islam, instead of the True Words of God in the Holy Bible.

A New Heaven and a New Earth
...7The one who overcomes will inherit all things, and I will be his God, and he will be My son. 8But to the cowardly and unbelieving and abominable and murderers and sexually immoral and sorcerers and idolaters and all liars, their place will be in the lake that burns with fire and sulfur. This is the second death." https://biblehub.com/revelation/21-8.htm

Christians know that the Lord Jesus Christ tells us He will cast all liars into the lake of fire; so no, Christians are not lying about God and His Words in the Holy Bible. instead, it's muslims.

Beware of Antichrists
...21I have not written to you because you lack knowledge of the truth, but because you have it, and because no lie comes from the truth. 22Who is the liar, if it is not the one who denies that Jesus is the Christ? This is the antichrist, who denies the Father and the Son. 23Whoever denies the Son does not have the Father, but whoever confesses the Son has the Father as well.... https://biblehub.com/1_john/2-22.htm

And the reason for that is due to the fact that until someone obeys Jesus Christ, the One True God, Repents and Gets Baptized in His Name; filled with His Holy Spirit of Truth, the evil devil, by his spirit of err is deceiving them.

...19We know that we are of God, and that the whole world is under the power of the evil one. 20And we know that the Son of God has come and has given us understanding, so that we may know Him who is true; and we are in Him who is true— in His Son Jesus Christ. He is the TRUE God and eternal life. https://biblehub.com/1_john/5-20.htm

1 John 4:1-6
Test the Spirits
4 Beloved, do not believe every spirit, but test the spirits to see whether they are from God, for many false prophets have gone out into the world. 2 By this you know the Spirit of God: every spirit that confesses that Jesus Christ has come in the flesh is from God, 3 and every spirit that does not confess Jesus is not from God. This is the spirit of the antichrist, which you heard was coming and now is in the world already. 4 Little children, you are from God and have overcome them, for he who is in you is greater than he who is in the world. 5 They are from the world; therefore they speak from the world, and the world listens to them. 6 We are from God. Whoever knows God listens to us; whoever is not from God does not listen to us. By this we know the Spirit of truth and the spirit of error.

The way anyone can tell you are being deceived by the devil, is your post falsely accuses Christians. (the devil is the false accuser of Christians)

The War in Heaven
...9And the great dragon was hurled down—that ancient serpent called the devil and Satan, the deceiver of the whole world. He was hurled to the earth, and his angels with him. 10And I heard a loud voice in heaven saying: "Now have come the salvation and the power and the kingdom of our God, and the authority of His Christ. For the accuser of our brothers has been thrown down— he who accuses them day and night before our

God. 11They have conquered him by the blood of the Lamb and by the word of their testimony. And they did not love their lives so as to shy away from death.... https://biblehub.com/revelation/12-10.htm

So, you need to obey God, Repent and Get Baptized in His Name so that the devil can no longer deceive you.

The Great Commission
...15And He said to them, "Go into all the world and preach the gospel to every creature. 16Whoever believes and is baptized will be saved, but whoever does not believe will be condemned.
https://biblehub.com/mark/16-16.htm

37When the people heard this, they were cut to the heart and asked Peter and the other apostles, "Brothers, what shall we do?" 38 Peter replied, "Repent and be baptized, every one of you, in the name of Jesus Christ for the forgiveness of your sins, and you will receive the gift of the Holy Spirit. 39This promise belongs to you and your children and to all who are far off—to all whom the Lord our God will call to Himself."...
https://biblehub.com/acts/2-38.htm

Peter and John Before the Council
...11This Jesus is 'the stone you builders rejected, which has become the cornerstone.' 12 Salvation exists in no one else, for there is no other name under heaven given to men by which we must be saved."
https://biblehub.com/acts/4-12.htm

muslims are constantly online arrogantly boasting about how only they are the ones doing what God wants; praying in the way God wants, when that isn't the case at all.

No, muslims do not pray like any of the prophets in the Holy Bible.

All Prophets in the Holy Bible tell us Jesus Christ is God, LORD OF ALL. To pray like a prophet in the Holy Bible isn't about some kind of ritual or position of the Body, it's about KNOWING GOD AND WORSHIPPING HIM IN SPIRIT AND TRUTH.

muslims instead are doing everything God tells us NOT to do.

The Lord's Prayer
4so that your giving may be in secret. And your Father, who sees what is done in secret, will reward you. 5And when you pray, do not be like the hypocrites. For they love to pray standing in the synagogues and on the street corners to be seen by men. Truly I tell you, they already have their full reward.6But when you pray, go into your inner room, shut your door, and pray to your Father, who is unseen. And your Father, who sees what is done in secret, will reward you. 7And when you pray, do not babble on like pagans, for they think that by their many words they will be heard. 8Do not be like them, for your Father knows what you need before you ask Him. 9So then, this is how you should pray: 'Our Father in heaven, hallowed be Your name. 10Your kingdom come, Your will be done, on earth as it is in heaven.11Give us this day our daily bread. 12And forgive us our debts, as we also have forgiven our debtors. 13And lead us not into temptation, but deliver us from the evil one.'14For if you forgive men their trespasses, your heavenly Father will also forgive you. 15But if you do not forgive men their trespasses, neither will your Father forgive yours....
https://biblehub.com/matthew/6-9.htm

So, dressing in robes, and bowing down in the direction of a stone (committing open idolatry - kaaba) at set times in set methods ritualistically, and boasting that you are doing what the prophets did, (when that isn't the case) is doing exactly what God told us all NOT to do.

muslims are not praying like God or His Prophets in the Holy Bible, they don't even know God.

https://www.thereligionofpeace.com/pages/articles/jesusmuhammad.aspx

Then a muslim was complaining that when he cites something like John 14:9 Christians will say it's not a parable but when he cites John 6:54, they will say it is. (Obviously, his reading comprehension is challenged to the point that he doesn't even understand the meaning of the words he is using like "parable".)

that's because the context is very clear which is a metaphor and which isn't.

Obviously, God was not telling people to become cannibals and vampires (the whole world cannot physically eat just one small body; so it's impossible and obviously not something literal but spiritual in meaning), so the words of John 6:54 are a metaphor which He explained means He is the Source of Eternal Life and everything we need to have that Life.

The Words of Eternal Life
60 When many of his disciples heard it, they said, "This is a hard saying; who can listen to it?" 61 But Jesus, knowing in himself that his disciples were grumbling about this, said to them, "Do you take offense at this? 62 Then what if you were to see the Son of Man ascending to where he was before? 63 It is the Spirit who gives life; the flesh is no help at all. The words that I have spoken to you are spirit and life. 64 But there are some of you who do not believe." (For Jesus knew from the beginning who those were who did not believe, and who it was who would betray him.) 65 And he said, "This is why I told you that no one can come to me unless it is granted him by the Father."

66 After this many of his disciples turned back and no longer walked with him. 67 So Jesus said to the twelve, "Do you want to go away as well?" 68 Simon Peter answered him, "Lord, to whom shall we go? You have the words of eternal life, 69 and we have believed, and have come to know, that you are the Holy One of God."

So, in context God clearly explained He was NOT talking about his flesh body, but about His Spirit; that He is the One who has Eternal Life and that without Him and His Words none of us have that life!

John 5:39-40
39 You search the Scriptures because you think that in them you have eternal life; and it is they that bear witness about me, 40 yet you refuse to come to me that you may have life.

So yes, Christians will tell you which is which because obviously you're so deceived you can't tell yourself. (Obey God Repent and Get Baptized in the Name of our Lord Jesus Christ and pray to receive His Holy Spirit of Truth; that way the devil will stop deceiving you with his unholy spirit of err.)

Some muslim was ranting nonsense by saying gibberish like, if you can show me pink elephants can fly, I still won't believe Jesus Christ is the God who Created the sun, moon and stars. (a display of irrational skepticism)

Jesus Christ is alive, so it's not like you can't ask Him to let you know if He's the One True God. muslims and atheists act like God, Jesus Christ, just wants people to blindly believe in Him with no justification whatsoever, when that absolutely isn't the case.

Jesus Christ is STILL doing miracles TODAY as proof He is God; like no one else in the entire history of the world! Jesus Christ has been doing miracles throughout all history as proof He is the One True God. So yes, Jesus Christ is God, and obviously so.

https://www.youtube.com/watch?v=rn73J9A0SnU - Jesus Christ is still doing miracles today all over the world; proving He is God.

https://www.youtube.com/watch?v=X3wGdjYnWRI - modern miracles today often come with evidence like medical records.

In addition, God, Jesus Christ, told everyone how to know Him personally; so, no one has any excuse:

The Great Commission

...18Then Jesus came to them and said, "All authority in heaven and on earth has been given to Me. 19Therefore go and make disciples of all nations, baptizing them in the name of the Father, and of the Son, and of the Holy Spirit, 20and teaching them to obey all that I have commanded you. And surely I am with you always, even to the end of the age."... https://biblehub.com/matthew/28-19.htm

"Brothers, what shall we do?" 38 Peter replied, "Repent and be baptized, every one of you, in the name of Jesus Christ for the forgiveness of your sins, and you will receive the gift of the Holy Spirit. 39This promise belongs to you and your children and to all who are far off—to all whom the Lord our God will call to Himself."... https://biblehub.com/acts/2-38.htm

John 14:20-26

20 In that day you will know that I am in my Father, and you in me, and I in you. 21 Whoever has my commandments and keeps them, he it is who loves me. And he who loves me will be loved by my Father, and I will love him and manifest myself to him." 22 Judas (not Iscariot) said to him, "Lord, how is it that you will manifest yourself to us, and not to the world?" 23 Jesus answered him, "If anyone loves me, he will keep my word, and my Father will love him, and we will come to him and make our home with him. 24 Whoever does not love me does not keep my words. And the word that you hear is not mine but the Father's who sent me.

25 "These things I have spoken to you while I am still with you. 26 But the Helper, the Holy Spirit, whom the Father will send in my name, he will teach you all things and bring to your remembrance all that I have said to you.

One of the more common scriptures muslims twist in a vain attempt to deny the Divinity of Jesus Christ is John 17:3. muslims tend to completely disregard the context whenever they make their many false claims about the Words of God in the Holy Bible.

muslims have the very bad habit of ignoring context in the Holy Bible.

John 14:6-9
6 Jesus said to him, "I am the way, the truth, and the life. No one comes to the Father except through Me.

The Father Revealed
7 "If you had known Me, you would have known My Father also; and from now on you know Him and have seen Him."

8 Philip said to Him, "Lord, show us the Father, and it is sufficient for us."

9 Jesus said to him, "Have I been with you so long, and yet you have not known Me, Philip? He who has seen Me has seen the Father; so how can you say, 'Show us the Father'?

Jesus Christ had already plainly stated to see Him is to see the Father.

John 5:39-40
39 You search the Scriptures because you think that in them you have eternal life; and it is they that bear witness about me, 40 yet you refuse to come to me that you may have life.

Jesus Christ had already stated that the entire Holy Bible is about Him, the One who has Eternal Life and the One everyone must come to in order to have that life.

https://biblehub.com/interlinear/john/17-3.htm - notice in the original language there are no punctuation marks and that the word "kai" is used to CONNECT "only true God" and "Jesus Christ". kai means AND, EVEN, ALSO, NAMELY; so, the verse reads ...only true God AND Jesus Christ or ...only true God EVEN Jesus Christ or ... only true God ALSO Jesus Christ or ...only true God NAMELY Jesus Christ.

Since we see the phrase "only true God" elsewhere referring to Jesus Christ (1Jn 5:20), it's wrong of muslims to imagine that this verse is saying anything different. (YOU CANNOT SEPARATE "GOD" FROM "JESUS CHRIST" BECAUSE THAT IS WHO HE IS!)

He uses the words "the Father" to refer to His Invisible, Eternal, Pervasive and Transcendent Existence (Ephesians 4:6) and "the Son" to refer to His Visible Image (John 14:6-9 and Col 1:15-19) and is why the Father and the Son are ONE (Jn 10:30) similar to how your own body and your own invisible spirit are one.

So no, John 17:3 isn't suddenly telling us God and Eternal Life is anyone else other than Jesus Christ. muslims are just desperately trying in vain to deny Him.

Jesus Appears to Thomas
...27Then Jesus said to Thomas, "Put your finger here and look at My hands. Reach out your hand and put it into My side. Stop doubting and believe." 28Thomas replied, "My Lord and my God!" 29Jesus said to him, "Because you have seen Me, you have believed; blessed are those who have not seen and yet have believed."... https://biblehub.com/john/20-28.htm

Jesus Christ says He is God hundreds of times over in the Holy Bible, He just explains that we need to understand that He is much more than just His Appearance as a Man in the flesh. Which is why He would say things like the Father is Greater than the Son and yet also say that to hate the Son is to hate the Father and that the Father and the Son are One. (because the body dies without the spirit, so the spirit is greater than the body and the body does nothing without the spirit)

so, Jesus Christ isn't confused by telling us hundreds of times He is God and receiving worship and then presumably, suddenly denying it anywhere in the Holy Bible; muslims are just not understanding His Words. Jesus Christ repeatedly said and proved He is God, it's just people who are presently denying Him don't understand His Words because they are all still being deceived by the devil. Everyone must repent and be baptized in the Name of Jesus Christ and pray to receive His Holy Spirit of Truth, only when God comes into your life will you begin to understand His Words in the Holy Bible correctly. (Matt 28:18-20; Acts 2:38-39; John 14:20-26)

a muslim was just hammering on and on about how God ALLOWED polygamy even in the Holy Bible (as a vain attempt to justify their own sexually immoral cult of islam) and so I responded:

you muslims are still practicing polygamy, even though God advises against it, because you are perpetuating immorality and barbarism in your evil cult.

In the Christian nations, we read in the Holy Bible that God calls us to a higher moral standard and plainly states that His intention from the Beginning for Holy Matrimony is to be between one man and one woman. Those who stray from His Commandments, even a little, stray into consequences, as plainly shown in that men who marry more than one wife have inevitable jealousies, rivalries, and sometimes even more serious hostilities between the wives and children of different wives. The man who strays from God and His Righteous Commandments in that regard has to deal constantly with the women and children who want to know that he loves them all the same and treats them all fairly, rather than having favorites. In the Holy Bible, there are numerous accounts of serious rivalries between wives and siblings from polygamous relations. God, our Creator intends His Creation to be One with Him, Husband and Bride, SINGULAR, as the scriptures state. Men who are simply thinking with their penis, instead of their minds and spirits, look for any way to sexually gratify their flesh, and so polygamy is advocated in your vile cult; instead of obeying God and His Example of One Man and One Woman in Holy Matrimony lifelong.

Because western civilization fought off raping, robbing, murdering, slaving muslims, we looked upon islam as a criminal organization and so reject your sexually immoral practices and your delusions of perpetual hard-ons just to molest virgins in your depraved notions of paradise. muslims are sexually immoral wicked persons, who imagine they are right with God, even though none of them see, hear or know Him. They are all headed to the lake of fire (Rev 21:8) for bowing to a false god, and his many evil lies in the quran, for sowing to their base desires of these bodies of death, instead of the high standards of truly righteous living the One True God, Jesus Christ, calls us all to. muslims, YOU ARE COMMANDED TO REPENT as are EVERYONE! You will know you are right with GOD, when Jesus Christ, gives you His Holy Spirit and you KNOW Him!

So, in Christian nations after fighting off rapists, who murdered innocent men, and stole their wives and children (muslims) they passed laws against any such overt wickedness and made polygamy illegal. God still ALLOWS it, but it still has many consequences even today.

https://www.youtube.com/watch?v=I_To-cV94Bo

https://www.google.com/search?client=opera&q=inbreeding+among+muslims+causing+birth+defects+and+low+IQs&sourceid=opera&ie=UTF8&oe=UTF-8 - because muslims are in a sexually immoral cult, it has resulted in inbreeding as men marry even children, cousins, sisters to gratify the lusts of their flesh. So islamic nations have the highest incidence of birth defects in the world and low IQs.

Christian nations flee immorality, because even though God ALLOWS it, it causes such consequences.

Even in the New Testament, God tells us His Standard over and over is for marriage to be between one man and one woman.

Qualifications for Overseers
1This is a trustworthy saying: If anyone aspires to be an overseer, he desires a noble task. 2An overseer, then, must be above reproach, the husband of but one wife, temperate, self-controlled, respectable,

hospitable, able to teach, 3not dependent on wine, not violent but gentle, peaceable, and free of the love of money....
https://biblehub.com/1_timothy/3-2.htm

God didn't want sexually immoral people, who had already married more than one wife, to be teaching generations of people, He was calling to repentance (to cease being sexually immoral) so even though polygamists could and did convert to Christianity, they were not allowed to teach or become in positions of authority within the Church, instead they were told to labor honorably and support their wives and children.

So, you are just not grasping that God ALLOWS mankind to make mistakes, even to sin and commit crimes, but COMMANDS us to REPENT and stop doing those things.

I was surprised to find someone wrongly arguing today that the last prophet was John the Baptist and that all prophets were only Israelites. Surprised because they were arguing that in an islamic forum. muslims all practically shout that muhammad, an Arab, was the last prophet of God. So, I think this person was trying to argue against muslims but was making a statement that isn't true.

Have you ever thought about who makes someone to be a Prophet? That's right, the Holy Spirit of God Almighty is what causes anyone to hear the Words of God and is empowered to write them down and/or speak them to others.

Since the Holy Spirit of God, Jesus Christ, is what causes anyone to be a prophet:

Eyewitnesses of His Majesty
...20Above all, you must understand that no prophecy of Scripture comes from one's own interpretation. 21For no such prophecy was ever brought forth by the will of man, but men spoke from God as they were carried along by the Holy Spirit. https://biblehub.com/2_peter/1-21.htm

I Will Pour Out My Spirit
28And afterward, I will pour out My Spirit on all people. Your sons and daughters will prophesy, your old men will dream dreams, your young men will see visions. 29Even on My menservants and maidservants, I will pour out My Spirit in those days.... https://biblehub.com/joel/2-28.htm

Acts 2:17
In the last days, God says, I will pour out My Spirit on all people. Your sons and daughters will prophesy, your young men will see visions, your old men will dream dreams.

... For the testimony of Jesus is the spirit of prophecy."
https://biblehub.com/revelation/19-10.htm

Living in the Spirit
8Those controlled by the flesh cannot please God. 9You, however, are controlled not by the flesh, but by the Spirit, if the Spirit of God lives in you. And if anyone does not have the Spirit of Christ, he does not belong to Christ. 10But if Christ is in you, your body is dead because of sin, yet your spirit is alive because of righteousness....
https://biblehub.com/romans/8-9.htm

8But you will receive power when the Holy Spirit comes upon you, and you will be My witnesses in Jerusalem, and in all Judea and Samaria, and to the ends of the earth." https://biblehub.com/acts/1-8.htm

37When the people heard this, they were cut to the heart and asked Peter and the other apostles, "Brothers, what shall we do?" 38 Peter replied, "Repent and be baptized, every one of you, in the name of Jesus Christ for the forgiveness of your sins, and you will receive the gift of the Holy Spirit. 39This promise belongs to you and your children and to all who are far off—to all whom the Lord our God will call to Himself."...
https://biblehub.com/acts/2-38.htm

So, everyone who testifies that Jesus Christ is the One True God is giving evidence that God has given them His Holy Spirit of Truth. (Acts 10:34-43) because ALL Prophets testify of Jesus Christ and that forgiveness of sins is only through Him, by Name.

Jesus Opens the Scriptures
...26Was it not necessary for the Christ to suffer these things and then to enter His glory?" 27And beginning with Moses and all the Prophets, He explained to them what was written in all the Scriptures about Himself.
https://biblehub.com/luke/24-27.htm

John 5:39-40
39 You search the Scriptures because you think that in them you have eternal life; and it is they that bear witness about me, 40 yet you refuse to come to me that you may have life.

So, God, Jesus Christ, sends His Holy Spirit of Truth upon all who repent and are baptized in His Name, in order to empower them to speak and write His Words, telling everyone He is the One True God. This means it is God, by His Holy Spirit of Truth, who makes anyone a prophet or prophetess and so all who receive Jesus Christ, by His Holy Spirit of Truth, into their lives are such.

In other words, all true Christians are prophets and prophetesses because the Holy Spirit of Jesus Christ is with them, just like He was with all the Prophets in the Holy Bible. Yes, not all Christians are called to the office of a Prophet, but all Christians are prophets and prophetesses to a greater or lesser extent. Every time they hear the Voice of His Holy Spirit telling them to speak His Words, they are doing exactly what the Prophets of old did in their generations.

The Promise of the Holy Spirit
...12I still have much to tell you, but you cannot yet bear to hear it. 13However, when the Spirit of truth comes, He will guide you into all truth. For He will not speak on His own, but He will speak what He hears, and He will declare to you what is to come. 14He will glorify Me by taking from what is Mine and disclosing it to you....
https://biblehub.com/john/16-13.htm

It's why everyone needs to obey God, Jesus Christ, and Repent and Be Baptized in His Name so that they KNOW GOD PERSONALLY BEYOND ALL DOUBT, and then go and tell everyone, everywhere until everyone does!

KNOW THE LORD! KNOW THE LORD! - https://biblehub.com/jeremiah/31-34.htm

So, then he argued that all prophets are Israelites and asked about whether or not there were prophets outside of the Holy Bible (as if he completely failed to comprehend what I had just stated.)

Acts 10:43 ALL PROPHETS BEAR WITNESS OF JESUS CHRIST, the WITNESSES OF JESUS CHRIST are CHRISTIANS Acts 11:26 THEREFORE ALL PROPHETS ARE CHRISTIANS! God gives us His Holy Spirit to bear witness of Him! Acts 1:8, The Holy Spirit of Jesus Christ is within the Prophets, His Disciples,

Christians; God is bearing witness of Himself to the world, through everyone who has received Him! Rom 8:9-15

My comment plainly states that all true prophets are only prophets because of the One True God, YHWH/JESUS CHRIST, who gives them His Holy Spirit of Truth, whereby they hear His Voice and learn from Him also by dreams, visions and revelations He teaches them.

In other words, a prophet is not a prophet just because they were born from one of the twelve tribes (I challenge anyone today to prove with historic documentation that they are directly descended from the real man, Israel, or His Twelve Sons.)

Israelites have been scattered throughout the entire world. (Diaspora) So there is no way for people living today to know with all certainty whether or not they are physical descendants of the Patriarchs. They would have to have had generations of family history all the way to Israel and his twelve sons. Maybe some do have those records, I'm just not aware of any.

Regardless, just being born in the flesh to one of the twelve tribes, doesn't make anyone a prophet. Prophets, as I already plainly showed you, are such because of the Holy Spirit of God, the Truth, Jesus Christ. "Jesus Christ" is merely the English for YHWH, who came in the flesh as Yahoshuah Ha Mashiach (Yeshua).
https://www.facebook.com/photo.php?fbid=6800758120003089&set=pb.100002069048072.-2207520000&type=3

So, all prophets testify of YHWH/JESUS CHRIST, the One True God, who came in the flesh and showed and proved Himself. Acts 1:8, Acts 10:34-43 https://www.facebook.com/photo.php?fbid=6471680786244159&set=pb.100002069048072.-2207520000&type=3

Even Abraham knew Jesus Christ, the One True God:

https://www.facebook.com/photo.php?fbid=6433644810047757&set=pb.100002069048072.-2207520000&type=3

Which is why all prophets testify of Him (because God, Jesus Christ, gave them His Holy Spirit to do so - Acts 1:8; 2:17, 2:38-39; 4:12; 10:34-48; 2Pet 2:21; 1Jn 2:20-27; 2Tim 3:16)

Since it is the Holy Spirit of God Himself who makes anyone to be a prophet, it means that everyone who has the Holy Spirit of Jesus Christ, is a prophet or prophetess to a greater or lesser extent. In other words, God no longer speaks to just one or two people, but speaks with any and all who love and obey Him. THIS IS GREAT NEWS! EVERYONE CAN KNOW GOD! AND EVERYONE SHOULD!

I Will Pour Out My Spirit
28And afterward, I will pour out My Spirit on all people. Your sons and daughters will prophesy, your old men will dream dreams, your young men will see visions. 29Even on My menservants and maidservants, I will pour out My Spirit in those days.... https://biblehub.com/joel/2-28.htm

Orderly Worship

...30And if a revelation comes to someone who is seated, the first speaker should stop. 31For you can all prophesy in turn so that everyone may be instructed and encouraged. 32The spirits of prophets are subject to prophets.... https://biblehub.com/1_corinthians/14-31.htm

It is the presence of God alone, by His Holy Spirit, that enables anyone to hear Him and thereby prophesy. Those who attempt to speak or write in behalf of God without His Presence in their life, are false prophets.

The way we tell if someone has His Holy Spirit or not is given to us plainly enough:

1 John 4:1-6

Test the Spirits

4 Beloved, do not believe every spirit, but test the spirits to see whether they are from God, for many false prophets have gone out into the world. 2 By this you know the Spirit of God: every spirit that confesses that Jesus Christ has come in the flesh is from God, 3 and every spirit that does not confess Jesus is not from God. This is the spirit of the antichrist, which you heard was coming and now is in the world already. 4 Little children, you are from God and have overcome them, for he who is in you is greater than he who is in the world. 5 They are from the world; therefore they speak from the world, and the world listens to them. 6 We are from God. Whoever knows God listens to us; whoever is not from God does not listen to us. By this we know the Spirit of truth and the spirit of error.

You seem to be ignoring all these things I have shown you, which isn't a good sign about you. (Dealing with the one not recognizing that CHRISTIANS are prophets and prophetesses. Acts 2:17,18)

6We are from God. Whoever knows God listens to us; whoever is not from God does not listen to us. That is how we know the Spirit of truth and the spirit of deception. https://biblehub.com/1_john/4-6.htm

Those who know God, Jesus Christ, by the presence of His Holy Spirit of Truth, are prophets or prophetesses because God Himself is the Prophet of prophets. (Col 1:15-19 - God, Jesus Christ, is Supreme in Everything)

Peter Preaches to the Crowd

...16No, this is what was spoken by the prophet Joel: 17' In the last days, God says, I will pour out My Spirit on all people. Your sons and daughters will prophesy, your young men will see visions, your old men will dream dreams. 18Even on My menservants and maidservants I will pour out My Spirit in those days, and they will prophesy....
https://biblehub.com/acts/2-17.htm

Some statistics claim that there are approximately 3 billion people who call themselves Christians on earth today. I find that difficult to believe, because only the presence of Jesus Christ by His Holy Spirit makes anyone to be a Christian -Romans 8:7-11) But if even half that number were true Christians, it would mean we have over a billion true prophets and prophetesses today on earth.

Anyone who tells others that they must KNOW the LORD JESUS CHRIST and obey His Commandments in the Holy Bible are fulfilling prophesy from God:

https://biblehub.com/jeremiah/31-34.htm - those persons are all prophets and prophetesses to a greater or lesser extent because they have the Prophet of prophets, Jesus Christ, living inside of them by His Holy Spirit of Truth.

John 14:20-26

English Standard Version

20 In that day you will know that I am in my Father, and you in me, and I in you. 21 Whoever has my commandments and keeps them, he it is who loves me. And he who loves me will be loved by my Father, and I will love him and manifest myself to him." 22 Judas (not Iscariot) said to him, "Lord, how is it that you will manifest yourself to us, and not to the world?" 23 Jesus answered him, "If anyone loves me, he will keep my word, and my Father will love him, and we will come to him and make our home with him. 24 Whoever does not love me does not keep my words. And the word that you hear is not mine but the Father's who sent me.

25 "These things I have spoken to you while I am still with you. 26 But the Helper, the Holy Spirit, whom the Father will send in my name, he will teach you all things and bring to your remembrance all that I have said to you.

Yes, while not all Christians are called to the same High Calling of Prophets in the scriptures, it is clear that that prophesy by; 17' In the last days, God says, I will pour out My Spirit on all people. Your sons and daughters will prophesy, your young men will see visions, your old men will dream dreams. 18Even on My menservants and maidservants I will pour out My Spirit in those days, and they will prophesy.... Acts 2:17, 18

One of the very worst lies muslims believe is that Jesus Christ wasn't crucified and rip words out of context while ignoring the rest of the Holy Bible to make other false claims like saying His Disciples didn't witness the facts they testify about in the Holy Bible.

Eyewitnesses of His Majesty
15And I will make every effort to ensure that after my departure, you will be able to recall these things at all times. 16For we did not follow cleverly devised fables when we made known to you the power and coming of our Lord Jesus Christ, but we were eyewitnesses of His majesty. 17For He received honor and glory from God the Father when the voice came to Him from the Majestic Glory, saying, "This is My beloved Son, in whom I am well pleased."... https://biblehub.com/2_peter/1-16.htm

When muslims deny the crucifixion of Jesus Christ they are denying the most certain facts of all ancient history and calling God Almighty, His Prophets and Eyewitnesses all liars. The crucifixion of Jesus Christ is not just attested to in the Holy Bible, but by numerous external sources.

https://coldcasechristianity.com/writings/is-there-any-evidence-for-jesusoutside-the-bible/

https://youtu.be/LLnClp3OVmE?t=1886 - we have the burial cloth of Jesus Christ as external evidence for the historicity of the Sacred Text in the Holy Bible! So muslims are believing lies, and when muslims believe lies, it turns them into liars (and worse, liars about God!) As such, muslims are headed to the lake of fire, unless they repent and learn to trust Jesus Christ and His Words in the Holy Bible instead of the lying criminal muhammad and his lies in the quran.
https://www.thereligionofpeace.com/pages/articles/jesusmuhammad.aspx

Yes, the Disciples witnessed it.

Jesus Appears to Thomas
...25So the other disciples told him, "We have seen the Lord!" But he replied, "Unless I see the nail marks in His hands, and put my finger where the nails have been, and put my hand into His side, I will never believe." 26 Eight days later, His disciples were once again inside with the doors locked, and Thomas was with them. Jesus came and stood among them and said, "Peace be with you." 27Then Jesus said to Thomas, "Put your finger here and look at My hands. Reach out your hand and put it into My side. Stop doubting and believe." 28Thomas replied, "My Lord and my God!" 29Jesus said to him, "Because you have seen Me, you have believed; blessed are those who have not seen and yet have believed."...
https://biblehub.com/john/20-27.htm

It's what convinced them (on top of all the other miracles and statements) that Jesus Christ was indeed God as He had claimed.

It's why they gave their lives to telling the world about Him and why the Holy Bible even exists.

https://tile.loc.gov/storageservices/public/gdcmassbookdig/foxesbookofmart00fo/foxesbookofmart0 0fo.pdf

muslims shouldn't rip words out of the Holy Bible to make false claims, but I see them doing it daily. Like how they wrongly claim Jesus Christ was only sent to the house of Israel.

When your Mommy and Daddy sent you to grade school as a little kid, did it mean you were only sent to grade school forever? NO? then try not to interpret a passage that says at one moment in time on a certain day, the Messiah, Jesus Christ was sent to " the lost sheep of the house of Israel".

Even if that was the case, the tribes of Israel have been scattered worldwide, so no one knows today whether or not they are of "the lost sheep of the house of Israel". Unless throughout their family tree from generation to generation, they kept records.

But we know simply by taking time to read a little more of the Holy Bible that the Messiah, Jesus Christ, is for all nations, worldwide.

The Great Commission

...18Then Jesus came to them and said, "All authority in heaven and on earth has been given to Me. 19Therefore go and make disciples of all nations, baptizing them in the name of the Father, and of the Son, and of the Holy Spirit, 20and teaching them to obey all that I have commanded you. And surely I am with you always, even to the end of the age."...
https://biblehub.com/matthew/28-19.htm

9After this I looked and saw a multitude too large to count, from every nation and tribe and people and tongue, standing before the throne and before the Lamb. They were wearing white robes and holding palm branches in their hands. 10And they cried out in a loud voice: "Salvation to our God, who sits on the throne, and to the Lamb!"...
https://biblehub.com/revelation/7-9.htm

Today a muslim was telling us how wonderful his imaginary allah is who forgives sins without blood sacrifice. So I responded:

When muslims say their god forgives sin without blood, it's yet another reason islam is teaching muslims lies.

Redemption through His Blood
...21In the same way, he sprinkled with blood the tabernacle and all the vessels used in worship. 22According to the law, in fact, nearly everything must be purified with blood, and without the shedding of blood there is no forgiveness. 23So it was necessary for the copies of the heavenly things to be purified with these sacrifices, but the heavenly things themselves with better sacrifices than these.... https://biblehub.com/hebrews/9-22.htm

The One True God, who declares Himself in the Holy Bible (not the lying quran) plainly tells us that He designed life to be in the blood and that's the fact!

11For the life of the flesh is in the blood, and I have given it to you to make atonement for your souls upon the altar; for it is the blood that makes atonement for the soul. https://biblehub.com/leviticus/17-11.htm

If you lose your blood in your body, you die! Furthermore, the blood brings nutrients and inspiration to each cell in the body and cleanses each cell in the body, so the REAL GOD PLAINLY SHOWS WE NEED HIS BLOOD TO LIVE AND BE CLEANSED just like the blood in our bodies brings life to and cleanses every cell! This is why the Law of God in the Holy Bible has blood sacrifices for purification and God tells us is necessary for Atonement/Redemption/Salvation.

https://bible.knowing-jesus.com/topics/God,-As-Redeemer - so without the Holy Blood of Jesus Christ, spiritually applied by God to your life, you are dead to God still lost in your sins, covered in filth, unclean! It's why everyone denying the Gospel of Jesus Christ in the Holy Bible; rejecting Him and His Holy Blood shed for them, still doesn't know God, because they are still dead to God; lost in their sins! The Holy God will not enter into a person by His Holy Spirit until they REPENT and are cleansed by Him, spiritually, through the Holy Blood of Jesus Christ! (Eph 2:1-10; Isaiah 59:2; Matt 26:28; Luke 22:20)

https://www.preceptaustin.org/tetelestai-paid_in_full

And should you go on rejecting Jesus Christ and His Holy Blood, shed for you, you will perish in your sins and be cast into the lake of fire!

Walking in the Light

...6If we say we have fellowship with Him yet walk in the darkness, we lie and do not practice the truth. 7But if we walk in the light as He is in the light, we have fellowship with one another, and the blood of Jesus His Son cleanses us from all sin. 8If we say we have no sin, we deceive ourselves, and the truth is not in us.... https://biblehub.com/1_john/1-7.htm

So, the One True God Jesus Christ, designed visible creation to demonstrate spiritual truth, without His Holy Blood, you will DIE IN YOUR SINS!

24That is why I told you that you would die in your sins. For unless you believe that I am He, you will die in your sins." 25"Who are You?" they asked. "Just what I have been telling you from the beginning," Jesus replied.... https://biblehub.com/john/8-24.htm

A New Heaven and a New Earth
...7The one who overcomes will inherit all things, and I will be his God, and he will be My son. 8But to the cowardly and unbelieving and abominable and murderers and sexually immoral and sorcerers and idolaters and all liars, their place will be in the lake that burns with fire and sulfur. This is the second death." https://biblehub.com/revelation/21-8.htm

What's more is that the scriptures plainly state:

The War in Heaven
...10And I heard a loud voice in heaven saying: "Now have come the salvation and the power and the kingdom of our God, and the authority of His Christ. For the accuser of our brothers has been thrown down—he who accuses them day and night before our God. 11 They have conquered him by the blood of the Lamb and by the word of their testimony. And they did not love their lives so as to shy away from death. https://biblehub.com/revelation/12-11.htm

That we overcome the devil, death, and accusations, BY THE BLOOD OF THE LAMB and the Word of our Testimonies. JESUS CHRIST IS LORD! My Lord and My Savior! So, the scriptures are very specific about Salvation that is MOST DEFINITELY through His Atoning Sacrifice, His Blood shed for us on the Cross!

Today, as typical of muslims, they were mocking Jesus Christ on dying on the cross, completely missing the reasons He did so. Jesus Christ had openly stated He is God, the One who has Eternal Life, the One who has Power to raise all the dead back to life, the One who will Judge all souls, etc. etc. He then PROVED IT, by publicly dying and raising His Body from the Grave, transfiguring it, making it immortal and glorious, and ascending back into Heaven in front of eyewitnesses. It's why the Apostles were bowing at His feet, like Thomas and saying, "My LORD and My GOD!" to which Jesus Christ confirmed that He is. (John 20:25-29)

Everyone, including muslims, need to comprehend that the Holy Bible plainly tells us the Truth about our Eternal Creator, the One True God, Jesus, the Christ.

https://www.accordingtothescriptures.org/prophecy/353prophecies.html - HUNDREDS of prophecies fulfilled just during His lifetime on earth! He has been fulfilling more ever since! These hundreds of prophecies make knowing the One True God a mathematic certainty!

God came in the flesh just as He told His Prophets.

John 5:39-40

39 You search the Scriptures because you think that in them you have eternal life; and it is they that bear witness about me, 40 yet you refuse to come to me that you may have life.

Jesus Christ by words and miracles stated and proved He is the One True God, like no one else in all of history. As His final proof before He returned to Heaven ascending there in front of eyewitnesses, He publicly died, raised His Body from the Grave and transfigured it making it Immortal and Glorious. After He Ascended into Heaven He poured out His Holy Spirit upon His Chosen Apostles and Disciples who then proclaimed the Gospel of Jesus Christ and wrote the New Testament. Christianity began on earth because God Almighty came to earth, showed Himself and Proved Himself and told us all how to know Him personally, so no one has any excuse.

The Apostles and Disciples were so convinced that they had seen and heard God Almighty, Jesus Christ, personally that they suffered torturous deaths rather than recant of one word of the Holy Bible and their testimonies!

Acts 5:29-32

29
But Peter and the apostles answered, "We must obey God rather than men. 30 The God of our fathers raised Jesus, whom you killed by hanging him on a tree. 31 God exalted him at his right hand as Leader and Savior, to give repentance to Israel and forgiveness of sins. 32 And we are witnesses to these things, and so is the Holy Spirit, whom God has given to those who obey him."

https://tile.loc.gov/storageservices/public/gdcmassbookdig/foxesbookofmart00fo/foxesbookofmart00fo.pdf

If the One True God, Jesus Christ, hadn't done so then everyone would not know God, and would only be imagining who their god is (like everyone still does who doesn't know Jesus Christ, the One True God.)

So you will either obey the REAL God, Jesus Christ, and repent and get baptized in His Name (Matt 28:18-20; Acts 2:38-39; 4:12) and come to know Him by receiving His Holy Spirit (Jn 14:20-26; 8:32-36) or you will perish in your sins and be cast into the lake of fire for wickedly rebelling against our Eternal Creator, Lord and Savior. Rev 21:8, Jn 3:36, Jn 8:24,25 A muslim was falsely claiming that no prophet read the New Testament; so, I responded:

The Marriage of the Lamb
…9Then the angel told me to write, "Blessed are those who are invited to the marriage supper of the Lamb." And he said to me, "These are the true words of God." 10So I fell at his feet to worship him. But he told me, "Do not do that! I am a fellow servant with you and your brothers who rely on the testimony of Jesus. Worship God! For the testimony of Jesus is the spirit of prophecy." https://biblehub.com/revelation/19-10.htm

"…THE TESTIMONY OF JESUS IS THE SPIRIT OF PROPHECY." (ALL Prophets testify of Jesus Christ, LORD of All.) So not only did the Words of God in the Holy Bible come from God to mankind through the Prophets, the Prophets have been reading and proclaiming those Words of God (in both the Old and New Testaments) throughout history; to this very day.

Eyewitnesses of His Majesty
…20Above all, you must understand that no prophecy of Scripture comes from one's own interpretation. 21For no such prophecy was ever brought forth by the will of man, but men spoke from God as they were carried along by the Holy Spirit. https://biblehub.com/2_peter/1-21.htm

Acts 1:7-11

7 And he said unto them, It is not for you to know the times or the seasons, which the Father hath put in his own power.

8 But ye shall receive power, after that the Holy Ghost is come upon you: and ye shall be witnesses unto me both in Jerusalem, and in all Judaea, and in Samaria, and unto the uttermost part of the earth.

9 And when he had spoken these things, while they beheld, he was taken up; and a cloud received him out of their sight.

10 And while they looked stedfastly toward heaven as he went up, behold, two men stood by them in white apparel;

11 Which also said, Ye men of Galilee, why stand ye gazing up into heaven? this same Jesus, which is taken up from you into heaven, shall so come in like manner as ye have seen him go into heaven.

So, the Holy Spirit of God is given by God, Jesus Christ, to empower people to testify about Him, which is why the Prophets all do so:

Acts 10:34-43
Gentiles Hear the Good News
34 So Peter opened his mouth and said: "Truly I understand that God shows no partiality, 35 but in every nation anyone who fears him and does what is right is acceptable to him. 36 As for the word that he sent to Israel, preaching good news of peace through Jesus Christ (he is Lord of all), 37 you yourselves know what happened throughout all Judea, beginning from Galilee after the baptism that John proclaimed: 38 how God anointed Jesus of Nazareth with the Holy Spirit and with power. He went about doing good and healing all who were oppressed by the devil, for God was with him. 39 And we are witnesses of all that he did both in the country of the Jews and in Jerusalem. They put him to death by hanging him on a tree, 40 but God raised him on the third day and made him to appear, 41 not to all the people but to us who had been chosen by God as witnesses,

who ate and drank with him after he rose from the dead. 42 And he commanded us to preach to the people and to testify that he is the one appointed by God to be judge of the living and the dead. 43 To him all the prophets bear witness that everyone who believes in him receives forgiveness of sins through his name."

verse 36 - Jesus Christ is Lord of All verse 43 ALL prophets bear witness of Jesus Christ, that forgiveness of sins is only through Him, by Name.

Jesus Opens the Scriptures
…26Was it not necessary for the Christ to suffer these things and then to enter His glory?" 27And beginning with Moses and all the Prophets, He explained to them what was written in all the Scriptures about Himself. https://biblehub.com/luke/24-27.htm (ALL PROPHETS KNEW JESUS CHRIST AS THE ONE TRUE GOD AND TESTIFIED ABOUT HIM!)

https://www.accordingtothescriptures.org/prophecy/353prophecies.html

Which is why Jesus Christ, the One True God, tells us the entire Holy Bible is all about Him:

John 5:39-40
39 You search the Scriptures because you think that in them you have eternal life; and it is they that bear witness about me, 40 yet you refuse to come to me that you may have life.

In other words, the entire Holy Bible came from the Prophets of God, because true Prophets of God, have the Holy Spirit of God, of Jesus Christ. To further clarify, all true Christians are prophets to a greater or lesser extent, because all Christians testify of Jesus Christ, by the presence of the Holy Spirit of Truth, Jesus Christ, in and upon their lives. (Romans 8:8-11)

Again, a muslim was asking about how can the Father be Greater and yet, "trinitarians" say the Father and Son are equal.

People often talk about "the Father" and "the Son" without even understanding what God has taught us those terms mean.

John 14:6-9

6 Jesus said to him, "I am the way, the truth, and the life. No one comes to the Father except through Me.

The Father Revealed

7 "If you had known Me, you would have known My Father also; and from now on you know Him and have seen Him."

8 Philip said to Him, "Lord, show us the Father, and it is sufficient for us."

9 Jesus said to him, "Have I been with you so long, and yet you have not known Me, Philip? He who has seen Me has seen the Father; so how can you say, 'Show us the Father'?

So, Jesus Christ plainly stated that anyone who has seen Him has seen "the Father", GOD!

He also said:

...29My Father who has given them to Me is greater than all. No one can snatch them out of My Father's hand. 30I and the Father are one."
https://biblehub.com/john/10-30.htm

So, we have to ask ourselves how can these statements be true?

How can the Father and the Son be One? How can looking at the Son cause us to see the Father? and how can the Father be Greater than the Son if they are One?

So, we read further:

6one God and Father of all, who is over all and through all and in all.
https://biblehub.com/ephesians/4-6.htm

So "the Father" refers to the aspect of God that is over all, through all and in all.

Colossians 1:15-19
The Supremacy of the Son of God
15 The Son is the image of the invisible God, the firstborn over all creation. 16 For in him all things were created: things in heaven and on earth, visible and invisible, whether thrones or powers or rulers or authorities; all things have been created through him and for him. 17 He is before all things, and in him all things hold together. 18 And he is the head of the body, the church; he is the beginning and the firstborn from among the dead, so that in everything he might have the supremacy. 19 For God was pleased to have all his fullness dwell in him,

and "the Son" refers to the "image of the invisible God" (in all, through all and above all)

So, then we can understand that to look at Jesus Christ is to see God, but not ALL that God is, because God is "in all, through all, and above all." And again, we read:

26 As the body without the spirit is dead, so faith without deeds is dead.
https://biblehub.com/james/2-26.htm

That our bodies don't even live without our spirits. So that is why the Son said He does nothing without the Father and that is why the Son said the Father is Greater, because when God walked among us in the flesh, looking just like another Man, as one of us, He was merely saying the same thing using the phrases: "the Father" and "the Son", that the Visible Image of God does nothing without the Invisible Spirit of God, and so His Spirit is Greater than His Body (especially when it was then a flesh and bone body like our own.) But do you understand that these phrases in no way mean that "the Father" is someone other than Jesus Christ?

Just like your own spirit isn't someone different from who you are while your spirit is one with your own body.

In other words, NO ONE CAN SEE ALL THAT GOD IS because He has an aspect that is INVISIBLE, PERMEATES AND TRANSCENDS ALL CREATION (called "the Father" Eph 4:6)! BUT we CAN see God when we look at our Lord Jesus Christ, the Visible Image of God (called "the Son" Col 1:15-19)! As God plainly told us also in John 1:1-14, John 14:6-9.

Even though the scriptures tell us "the fullness of God" indwelled Jesus Christ (Col 1:19), they also tell us God "emptied Himself" to come in the flesh as a Man, the Messiah:

The Attitude of Christ
...**6**Who, existing in the form of God, did not consider equality with God something to be grasped, **7**but emptied Himself, taking the form of a servant, being made in human likeness. **8**And being found in appearance as a man, He humbled Himself and became obedient to death—even death on a cross.... https://biblehub.com/philippians/2-7.htm

I understand these various contexts to tell us that when God Almighty came in the flesh, His Eternal Existence, His Invisible, Pervasive, Transcendent Self, remained as such, even though God was walking among us humbly. BUT in that humble form, God experienced pain, hunger, thirst, everything we all endure while we are in these weak mortal bodies. Which is why I look at the scriptures as telling us Jesus Christ has always been the SAME GOD who Created the Heavens and earth, spoke with Moses and the Prophets, but ONLY DURING HIS BRIEF INCARNATION in the flesh as the Messiah, does He ever seem to defer to His Eternal Existence as "the Father". And that when He departed this world He Created and Made, He transfigured that formerly weak, mortal body, and made it Immortal and Glorious. (end of the four Gospels, Acts Ch. 1, 1Cor 15) And as such was no longer a weak mortal like all of us in these flesh and bone bodies, but is now Immortal and Glorious, the Visible Image of Almighty God. (which is why there is no conflict or contradiction, just lack of understanding and comprehension that the Words Jesus Christ spoke FROM THE BEGINNING have to ALL be taken IN CONTEXT to be understood correctly.)

And so BEFORE Jesus Christ came in the flesh He is the Eternal God and during His Incarnation He was still the Eternal God, but His then mortal body was weak like our own (emptied Himself and took on the form of a Servant, God walking humbly with us and showing us how to live not just by His Words but by His Deeds; His Example) and then when He raised His Body from the Grave, transfigured it, made it Immortal and Glorious, and ascended back into Heaven from where He had come from into this world. NOTE: that the scriptures MAKE IT VERY CLEAR that the ETERNAL EXISTENCE OF JESUS CHRIST NEVER STOPPED BEING SUCH WHICH IS WHY HE IS CALLED THE EVERLASTING FATHER! So just because GOD chose to INCARNATE and WALK AMONG US, didn't mean HE CEASED BEING GOD, ALL-PERVASIVE, ALL-TRANSCENDANT, and ETERNAL. Which is why Christ centered on the fact that this brief mortality of Himself was NOT ALL THAT HE IS, it's why He tells us the FLESH IS TEMPORAL, but the spirit is everlasting! So, try to realize that you must be at peace with Jesus Christ, or you will die in your sins and it won't go well with your soul.

…**61**Aware that His disciples were grumbling about this teaching, Jesus asked them, "Does this offend you? **62**Then what will happen if you see the Son of Man ascend to where He was before? **63**The Spirit gives life; the flesh profits nothing. The words I have spoken to you are spirit and they are life…. https://biblehub.com/john/6-62.htm

23Then He told them, "You are from below; I am from above. You are of this world; I am not of this world. **24**That is why I told you that you would die in your sins. For unless you believe that I am He, you will die in your sins." **25**"Who are You?" they asked. "Just what I have been telling you from the beginning," Jesus replied…. https://biblehub.com/john/8-24.htm

So Jesus Christ has been telling mankind He is God from the Beginning and is why He tells us that anyone who doesn't believe Him will die in their sins, because He came in the flesh and proved He is God not just by doing miracles that no one else had done, but by publicly dying, raising His Body from the Grave, transfiguring it and making it Immortal and Glorious and then Ascended back into Heaven in front of eyewitnesses. It's why the Apostles and Disciples immediately began preaching about Him to everyone, even when their own lives were threatened for doing so.

Jesus Appears to Thomas
…**27**Then Jesus said to Thomas, "Put your finger here and look at My hands. Reach out your hand and put it into My side. Stop doubting and believe." **28**Thomas replied, "My Lord and my God!" **29**Jesus said to him,

"Because you have seen Me, you have believed; blessed are those who have not seen and yet have believed."... https://biblehub.com/john/20-28.htm

The Apostles Before the Council
...**28**"We gave you strict orders not to teach in this name," he said. "Yet you have filled Jerusalem with your teaching and are determined to make us responsible for this man's blood." **29**But Peter and the other apostles replied, "We must obey God rather than men. **30**The God of our fathers raised up Jesus, whom you had killed by hanging Him on a tree.... https://biblehub.com/acts/5-29.htm

So, do you understand this common problem muslims have now? muslims are looking ONLY at the Words of Jesus Christ, WHEN HE CAME IN THE FLESH, and are ignoring the Words of Jesus Christ SINCE THE BEGINNING and AFTER HE ASCENDED (in both the Old and New Testaments). The ENTIRE HOLY BIBLE IS ALL ABOUT JESUS CHRIST AS THE ONE TRUE GOD AND HIS WORDS ARE FROM GENESIS TO REVELATION (not just during His earthly ministry in a flesh and bone body; in the Four Gospels). So "Trinitarians" ARE looking at the Words of Jesus Christ, THROUGHOUT THE ENTIRE HOLY BIBLE, whereas muslims are focusing only on His Words while He was in a flesh and bone body and hence are not perceiving Jesus Christ for who He really is - the One True God.

Concluding Remarks
...**19**We know that we are of God, and that the whole world is under the power of the evil one. **20**And we know that the Son of God has come and has given us understanding, so that we may know Him who is true; and we are in Him who is true— in His Son Jesus Christ. He is the TRUE God and eternal life. **21**Little children, keep yourselves from idols.... https://biblehub.com/1_john/5-20.htm

John 5:39-40

39 You search the Scriptures because you think that in them you have eternal life; and it is they that bear witness about me, 40 yet you refuse to come to me that you may have life.

So your invisible spirit is one with your visible body of flesh and bone and your spirit is greater than your body of flesh and bone, because without the spirit the body is dead and can do nothing; when we die our spirit departs from our body that returns to the dust of the earth from which it was created and made. So "the Father" is not a different God than "the Son" any more than your own body is different person from your own spirit. When you read the Words of God, you need to let God define His Own Terms.

Rather typically, another muslim was sneering at "pork eaters" today so I replied:

You are in a cult of people who do not see, hear or know God and is why none of you understand what you read in the Holy Bible.

https://www.facebook.com/photo.php?fbid=6454153697996868&set=pb.100002069048072.-2207520000&type=3 - God was plain enough when He said that food doesn't defile us because it enters our mouths, passes through our digestive system and is eliminated; rather, He said it is our evil words and evil deeds that defile us.

Furthermore, muslims are in a cult that promotes eating other unclean creatures and so when they condemn others in that regard, they are doing so hypocritically:

https://sunnah.com/bukhari:5686 and "Are Muslims allowed to eat camel?

The list of animals forbidden by kashrut is more restrictive, as kashrut requires that to be kosher, mammals must chew cud and must have cloven hooves. Thus, some animals such as camels and rabbits are halal, but not kosher. Kashrut requires strict separation of dairy and meat products, even when they are kosher." -
https://en.wikipedia.org/wiki/Comparison_of_Islamic_and_Jewish_dietary_laws#:~:text=The%20list%20of%20animals%20forbidden,even%20when%20they%20are%20kosher.

So, there are religious people who imagine some creatures and food combinations are forbidden to eat, whereas other religious people disagree, but let's consider what that means long term, over the generations. When religious people imagine God will punish them for eating something that returns to the dust of the earth instead of another thing that returns to the dust of the earth, they are under deceptions and delusions. Those deceptions and delusions actually cause "unclean creatures" to overpopulate and become nuisances:

https://www.google.com/search?client=opera&q=wild+pigs+spreading+and+becoming+a+problem&sourceid=opera&ie=UTF-8&oe=UTF-8 and https://www.nature.com/articles/s41598-021-92691-1

It's the creatures that mankind doesn't put on the menu that are often becoming infestations that are doing much damage. So, deceptions and delusions factually cause problems all over this world, which is why I wish people would come to their senses and FIRST OBEY GOD SO THAT YOU KNOW HIM PERSONALLY, THEN you will all begin to understand His Words correctly and many of these problems will vanish away with the Knowledge of Truth.

Read
https://www.facebook.com/photo.php?fbid=6454153697996868&set=pb.

100002069048072.-2207520000&type=3 for more information on this topic.

A muslim was rhetorically asking today why Jesus Christ said He is the Truth in Jn 14:6 but then said the Spirit of Truth would guide us into Truth. (muslims wrongly imagine the lying criminal muhammad is the Holy Spirit, when a perverted rapist, robber, slaver and murderer is Unholy and has nothing whatsoever to do with the Holy Living God!)

A rapist, robber, liar, murderer and child molester like muhammad is from the devil, muslims! you are following an evil man into the flames of damnation! REPENT! follow JESUS CHRIST and His Words in the Holy Bible! - https://www.thereligionofpeace.com/pages/articles/jesusmuhammad.aspx

The reason Jesus Christ said that HE is the Way, the Truth and the Life and that to see Him is to see God, is due to the fact that is who He is! (Jn 14:69) And the reason why He said the Spirit of Truth also guides into all Truth is due to the fact that the Holy Spirit of Truth IS the Spirit of Jesus Christ, the One True God, and is how the prophets KNEW Him and spoke His Words. (The Spirit of God was with all true prophets causing them to all testify that JESUS CHRIST is LORD, the ONE TRUE GOD. Which is why anyone who does NOT testify that Jesus Christ is Lord, the One True God, does NOT have His Holy Spirit of Truth!)

Acts 1:7-11, Acts 10:34-43, 1Jn 4:1-6, 1Jn 2:22-27; 1Jn 5:20

His SPIRIT of TRUTH is given ONLY IN HIS NAME! Acts 2:38-39; 4:12, Matt 28:18-20, Jn 14:20-26 and when the Spirit of Truth, the Spirit of Jesus Christ, the Holy Spirit of the One True God, comes upon and within us, HE THEN REVEALS HIMSELF TO US (is how we KNOW the Living God personally and hear Him speaking to us, just like He spoke with all the prophets!) Acts 2:17,18, Jn 16:13, Jn 8:32-26

A muslim was online pretending as if they have anything to say to Christians... all we muslims are asking you to do is worship and pray to the same God, Jesus Christ did. (the muslim has not one clue who God is, because they all wickedly deny Him instead)

I know it's difficult for you to comprehend but EVERY WORD, EVERY PRAYER of Jesus Christ is GOD speaking!

Belief and Unbelief

...48There is a judge for the one who rejects Me and does not receive My words: The word that I have spoken will judge him on the last day. 49 I have not spoken on My own, but the Father who sent Me has commanded Me what to say and how to say it. 50And I know that His command leads to eternal life. So I speak exactly what the Father has told Me to say."...
https://biblehub.com/john/12-49.htm

When God came in the flesh as a Man, humbly, and walked among us, He didn't cease being God!

ONLY GOD ALWAYS SPEAKS HIS WORDS IN THE EXACT WAY, HE WANTS THEM SPOKEN!

John 5:39-40

39 You search the Scriptures because you think that in them you have eternal life; and it is they that bear witness about me, 40 yet you refuse to come to me that you may have life.

Our Heavenly Father is GOD, JESUS CHRIST! (muslims just refuse to comprehend that God has an Eternal, Invisible, Pervasive and Transcendent Existence -Eph 4:6 AND He has a Visible Image! JESUS CHRIST! Col 1:14-19 now we know God in His entirety ONLY BECAUSE HE REVEALS HIMSELF TO US THROUGH JESUS CHRIST! John 14:20-26) so anyone denying Jesus Christ is God, does not know God! and instead is committing idolatry by worshipping an imaginary one of their own makings. It would be the same as someone walking up to you in the presence of your physical body and denying you to your face and claiming their imagination of you is the real you. RIDICULOUS!

JESUS CHRIST IS GOD! and until the muslim obeys His Commandment to Repent and Be Baptized in His Name and becomes a Christian, they are a wicked antichrist, and idolater, openly denying the One True God and putting an imaginary false one in His Place.

John 14:6-9

6 Jesus said to him, "I am the way, the truth, and the life. No one comes to the Father except through Me.

The Father Revealed

7 "If you had known Me, you would have known My Father also; and from now on you know Him and have seen Him."

8 Philip said to Him, "Lord, show us the Father, and it is sufficient for us."

9 Jesus said to him, "Have I been with you so long, and yet you have not known Me, Philip? He who has seen Me has seen the Father; so how can you say, 'Show us the Father'?

read verse 9 as many times as it takes!

JESUS CHRIST IS THE ONE TRUE GOD WHO IS WORSHIPPED AS SUCH; NO ONE ELSE!

Jesus Appears to Thomas

...27Then Jesus said to Thomas, "Put your finger here and look at My hands. Reach out your hand and put it into My side. Stop doubting and believe." 28Thomas replied, "My Lord and my God!" 29Jesus said to him, "Because you have seen Me, you have believed; blessed are those who have not seen and yet have believed."... https://biblehub.com/john/20-28.htm

https://www.openbible.info/topics/worshipping_jesus

The muslim has NO IDEA who God is because they overtly DENY Him instead! The ONLY WAY TO KNOW GOD IS TO KNOW JESUS CHRIST! So Christians are worshiping the One True God because we KNOW Him.

A common saying of muslims is that they believe Jesus Christ to be a prophet (just another prophet, like the rest even though the Holy Bible plainly tells us all prophets testify that Jesus Christ is LORD, the One True God. - Acts 10:34-43; Luke 24:27; Jn 5:39-40)

muslims are always making this claim and yet none of them believe His Words or Obey His Commandments.

John 5:39-40
39 You search the Scriptures because you think that in them you have eternal life; and it is they that bear witness about me, 40 yet you refuse to come to me that you may have life.

The Great Commission
...15And He said to them, "Go into all the world and preach the gospel to every creature. 16Whoever believes and is baptized will be saved, but whoever does not believe will be condemned.
https://biblehub.com/mark/16-16.htm

muslims don't believe the Words of Jesus Christ or obey His Commandments. They only SAY they believe He is a Prophet, yet by their own beliefs call Him and His Eyewitness Apostles in the Holy Bible all liars.

Jesus Appears to Thomas
...27Then Jesus said to Thomas, "Put your finger here and look at My hands. Reach out your hand and put it into My side. Stop doubting and believe." 28Thomas replied, "My Lord and my God!" 29Jesus said to him, "Because you have seen Me, you have believed; blessed are those who have not seen and yet have believed."... https://biblehub.com/john/20-28.htm

Jesus Christ claimed to be the One who has and gives Eternal Life, He died publicly and then raised His Body from the Grave, transfigured it making it Immortal and Glorious and then Ascended into Heaven; thereby PROVING He is the One True God and the Way to Heaven which is why the scriptures tell us plainly that SALVATION IS FOUND IN NO ONE ELSE BUT JESUS CHRIST, THE ONE TRUE GOD!

Peter and John Before the Council
...11This Jesus is 'the stone you builders rejected, which has become the cornerstone.' 12 Salvation exists in no one else, for there is no other name under heaven given to men by which we must be saved."
https://biblehub.com/acts/4-12.htm

A muslim asked about how do we have the words of the conversation between Jesus Christ and Pilate (wrongly imagining their conversation was entirely private.)

The entire Holy Bible is inspired by God, Jesus Christ, which is why it's all about Him. (God, Jesus Christ, told the Prophets and His Eyewitness Apostles, what to say and write down therein.)

All Scripture is God-Breathed
...15From infancy you have known the Holy Scriptures, which are able to make you wise for salvation through faith in Christ Jesus. 16All Scripture is God-breathed and is useful for instruction, for conviction, for correction, and for training in righteousness, 17so that the man of God may be complete, fully equipped for every good work....
https://biblehub.com/2_timothy/3-16.htm

Eyewitnesses of His Majesty
...20Above all, you must understand that no prophecy of Scripture comes from one's own interpretation. 21For no such prophecy was ever brought forth by the will of man, but men spoke from God as they were carried along by the Holy Spirit. https://biblehub.com/2_peter/1-21.htm

So the Words of God, Jesus Christ, in the Holy Bible are all about Him, because the scriptures all come from Him.

John 5:39-40
39 You search the Scriptures because you think that in them you have eternal life; and it is they that bear witness about me, 40 yet you refuse to come to me that you may have life.

The Fulfillment of the Law
17Do not think that I have come to abolish the Law or the Prophets. I have not come to abolish them, but to fulfill them. 18For I tell you truly, until heaven and earth pass away, not a single jot, not a stroke of a pen, will disappear from the Law until everything is accomplished....
https://biblehub.com/matthew/5-17.htm

Jesus Opens the Scriptures
...26Was it not necessary for the Christ to suffer these things and then to enter His glory?" 27And beginning with Moses and all the Prophets, He explained to them what was written in all the Scriptures about Himself.
https://biblehub.com/luke/24-27.htm

A common problem with muslims is that they cannot seem to grasp why Jesus Christ deliberately accepted His Crucifixion and Death (in our behalf):

Suffering and death came as a consequence for our sins, crimes, disobedience to God, Jesus Christ. When He came in the flesh and suffered and died on the cross, He was showing us that:

1) all sin, all disobedience to Him, leads to suffering and death and God HATES sin that much!

2) in that He was willing to suffer and die to Redeem us back to Himself, God, Jesus Christ, shows that He LOVES us that much!

This is why the Saved perceive the Love of God and the Power of God by what He did on the cross for us.

The Message of the Cross
17For Christ did not send me to baptize, but to preach the gospel, not with words of wisdom, lest the cross of Christ be emptied of its power. 18For the message of the cross is foolishness to those who are perishing, but to us who are being saved it is the power of God. 19For it is written: "I will destroy the wisdom of the wise; the intelligence of the intelligent I will frustrate."…
https://biblehub.com/1_corinthians/1-18.htm

God, Jesus Christ, is our Redeemer/Savior:
https://bible.knowingjesus.com/topics/God,-As-Redeemer who Himself Paid the Price for our sins in full:
https://www.preceptaustin.org/tetelestai-paid_in_full not to go on sinning, but to see sin as He does and hate it as He does and by His Grace and Power cease from it:

Children of God
…8The one who practices sin is of the devil, because the devil has been sinning from the very start. This is why the Son of God was revealed, to destroy the works of the devil. 9Anyone born of God refuses to practice sin, because God's seed abides in him; he cannot go on sinning, because he has been born of God. 10By this the children of God are distinguished from the children of the devil: Anyone who does not practice righteousness is not of God, nor is anyone who does not love his brother.…
https://biblehub.com/1_john/3-9.htm

12But to all who did receive Him, to those who believed in His name, He gave the right to become children of God— 13children born not of blood, nor of the desire or will of man, but born of God.…
https://biblehub.com/john/1-12.htm

It is the realization that our own sins put God, Jesus Christ, on the cross in our behalf that causes the truly repentant Christian to fervently pray for the Presence of His Holy Spirit in our lives and to keep us from sinning, but to give us spirits that LOVE and OBEY Him and His Righteous Commandments Now and Forever! It is seeing the Love of God in such display that inspires us to follow Him, even if others hate and maltreat us, like they did Him. It is knowing God that creates in us the desire to please Him, to choose to be Faithful and True, like Himself, to choose to submit to Him and trust in Him to make us to be Good and Righteous like He is, to believe that He is going to Perfect us according to His Words (1Cor 15 and throughout the scriptures in the Holy Bible.)

Sadly rather typically, a muslim was online boasting about their imaginary allah and denying Jesus Christ as the One True God.

I hate to say that muslims are acting like boneheads, but it needs to be said. Not one muslim sees, hears or knows God and that is evident because like this post all muslims are denying Him instead. JESUS CHRIST IS REAL! (allah is just the name of a pagan idol) JESUS CHRIST PROVED HE IS GOD LIKE NO ONE ELSE IN ALL HISTORY! He is ALIVE to answer any with enough sense to call upon Him! So NO! your imaginary allah is NOT! JESUS CHRIST IS GOD AND VERIFIABLY SO!

Peter and John Before the Council

...11This Jesus is 'the stone you builders rejected, which has become the cornerstone.' 12 Salvation exists in no one else, for there is no other name under heaven given to men by which we must be saved."
https://biblehub.com/acts/4-12.htm

20And we know that the Son of God has come and has given us understanding, so that we may know Him who is true; and we are in Him who is true— in His Son Jesus Christ. He is the TRUE God and eternal life.
https://biblehub.com/1_john/5-20.htm

Jesus Appears to Thomas

...27Then Jesus said to Thomas, "Put your finger here and look at My hands. Reach out your hand and put it into My side. Stop doubting and believe." 28Thomas replied, "My Lord and my God!" 29Jesus said to him, "Because you have seen Me, you have believed; blessed are those who have not seen and yet have believed."... https://biblehub.com/john/20-28.htm

John 5:39-40

39 You search the Scriptures because you think that in them you have eternal life; and it is they that bear witness about me, 40 yet you refuse to come to me that you may have life.

One of the things that really makes me feel like puking is when muslims arrogantly portray themselves as if they are so much better than the rest of mankind and that their lying cult is the truth. How they offer "PBUH" lipservice as they deny the Living God and tell those of us who know Him that He is just another one of many prophets. (their nauseating arrogance is tangible, while they post such horrific lies about the One True God!)

When muslims denigrate the Lord Jesus Christ, by denying He is the One True God, they are making themselves to be His enemies/antichrists just like the devil!

Beware of Antichrists
...21I have not written to you because you lack knowledge of the truth, but because you have it, and because no lie comes from the truth. 22Who is the liar, if it is not the one who denies that Jesus is the Christ? This is the antichrist, who denies the Father and the Son. 23Whoever denies the Son

does not have the Father, but whoever confesses the Son has the Father as well.... https://biblehub.com/1_john/2-22.htm

The scriptures are crystal clear that ANYONE who denies Jesus is the Christ/Messiah (GOD IN THE FLESH) is an antichrist!

1 John 4:1-6
Test the Spirits
4 Beloved, do not believe every spirit, but test the spirits to see whether they are from God, for many false prophets have gone out into the world. 2 By this you know the Spirit of God: every spirit that confesses that Jesus Christ has come in the flesh is from God, 3 and every spirit that does not confess Jesus is not from God. This is the spirit of the antichrist, which you heard was coming and now is in the world already. 4 Little children, you are from God and have overcome them, for he who is in you is greater than he who is in the world. 5 They are from the world; therefore they speak from the world, and the world listens to them. 6 We are from God. Whoever knows God listens to us; whoever is not from God does not listen to us. By this we know the Spirit of truth and the spirit of error.

JESUS CHRIST PLAINLY STATED HE IS GOD, THE MESSIAH!

Jesus and the Samaritan Woman
...25The woman said, "I know that Messiah" (called Christ) "is coming. When He comes, He will explain everything to us." 26 Jesus answered, "I who speak to you am He." https://biblehub.com/john/4-26.htm

https://hebrew4christians.com/Names_of_G-d/Messiah/messiah.html - Messiah/Christ is GOD IN THE FLESH!

John 5:39-40
39 You search the Scriptures because you think that in them you have eternal life; and it is they that bear witness about me, 40 yet you refuse to come to me that you may have life.

SALVATION IS IN NO ONE ELSE BUT THE ONE TRUE GOD JESUS CHRIST!

…10"You are My witnesses," declares the LORD, "and My servant whom I have chosen, so that you may consider and believe Me and understand that I am He. Before Me no god was formed, and after Me none will come. 11I, yes I, am the LORD, and there is no Savior but Me. 12I alone decreed and saved and proclaimed—I, and not some foreign god among you. So you are My witnesses," declares the LORD, "that I am God….
https://biblehub.com/isaiah/43-11.htm

Peter and John Before the Council
…11This Jesus is 'the stone you builders rejected, which has become the cornerstone.' 12 Salvation exists in no one else, for there is no other name under heaven given to men by which we must be saved."
https://biblehub.com/acts/4-12.htm

Jesus Christ plainly stated that anyone who doesn't believe He is God just as He has been telling mankind from the Beginning will die in their sins!

24That is why I told you that you would die in your sins. For unless you believe that I am He, you will die in your sins." 25"Who are You?" they asked. "Just what I have been telling you from the beginning," Jesus replied…. https://biblehub.com/john/8-24.htm

So unless muslims repent and become Christians, they will die in their sins and end up in the lake of fire!

A New Heaven and a New Earth
...7The one who overcomes will inherit all things, and I will be his God, and he will be My son. 8But to the cowardly and unbelieving and abominable and murderers and sexually immoral and sorcerers and idolaters and all liars, their place will be in the lake that burns with fire and sulfur. This is the second death." https://biblehub.com/revelation/21-8.htm

The Great Commission
...15And He said to them, "Go into all the world and preach the gospel to every creature. 16Whoever believes and is baptized will be saved, but whoever does not believe will be condemned.
https://biblehub.com/mark/16-16.htm

37When the people heard this, they were cut to the heart and asked Peter and the other apostles, "Brothers, what shall we do?" 38 Peter replied, "Repent and be baptized, every one of you, in the name of Jesus Christ for the forgiveness of your sins, and you will receive the gift of the Holy Spirit. 39This promise belongs to you and your children and to all who are far off—to all whom the Lord our God will call to Himself."...
https://biblehub.com/acts/2-38.htm

Get it Straight, muslims! Jesus Christ is NOT just another prophet, HE IS THE ONE about whom all prophets testify!

Jesus Opens the Scriptures
...**26**Was it not necessary for the Christ to suffer these things and then to enter His glory?" **27**And beginning with Moses and all the Prophets, He

explained to them what was written in all the Scriptures about Himself.
https://biblehub.com/luke/24-27.htm

...**42**And He commanded us to preach to the people and to testify that He is the One appointed by God to judge the living and the dead. **43**All the prophets testify about Him that everyone who believes in Him receives forgiveness of
sins through His name." **44**While Peter was still speaking these words, the Holy Spirit fell upon all who heard his message....
https://biblehub.com/acts/10-43.htm

Don't Argue! READ AND UNDERSTAND THE CONTEXT!

Acts 10:34-43

English Standard Version

Gentiles Hear the Good News

34
 So Peter opened his mouth and said: "Truly I understand that God shows no partiality, **35** but in every nation anyone who fears him and does what is right is acceptable to him. **36** As for the word that he sent to Israel, preaching good news of peace through Jesus Christ (he is Lord of all), **37** you yourselves know what happened throughout all Judea, beginning from Galilee after the baptism that John proclaimed: **38** how God anointed Jesus of Nazareth with the Holy Spirit and with power. He went about doing good and healing all who were oppressed by the devil, for God was with him. **39** And we are witnesses of all that he did both in the country of the Jews and in Jerusalem. They put him to death by hanging him on a tree, **40** but God raised him on the third day and made him to appear, **41** not to all the people but to us who had been chosen by God as witnesses, who ate and drank with him after he rose from the dead. **42** And he commanded us to preach to the people and to testify that he is the one appointed by God to be judge of the living and the dead. **43** To him all the prophets bear witness that everyone who believes in him receives forgiveness of sins through his name."

verse 36 - JESUS CHRIST IS LORD OF ALL! verse 43 - ALL prophets testify of JESUS CHRIST, LORD OF ALL, and that forgiveness of sins is ONLY through HIM, by NAME!

Acts 4:12 SALVATION IS ONLY IN JESUS CHRIST!

islam isn't what muslims seem to imagine it is. The lies of islam, muhammad and the quran, are the reason not one muslim sees, hears or knows God. (which means muslims are all still dead to Him, lost in their sins.)

Sin Separates Us from God

1Surely the arm of the LORD is not too short to save, nor His ear too dull to hear. 2But your iniquities have built barriers between you and your God, and your sins have hidden His face from you, so that He does not hear. 3For your hands are stained with blood, and your fingers with iniquity; your lips have spoken lies, and your tongue mutters injustice....
https://biblehub.com/isaiah/59-2.htm

The only way for anyone to be Saved is through Jesus Christ (Acts 4:12) everyone MUST repent and be baptized in His Name and pray to receive His Holy Spirit. (Mark 16:15-16, Matt 28:18-20, Acts 2:38-39; John 14:20-26; Luke 11:13)

islam, the lies of muhammad in the quran and hadiths, are deceiving muslims away from the One True God, Jesus Christ, and His True Words in the Holy Bible. islam isn't anything good or commendable, if muslims fail to repent, and receive our Lord and Savior, Jesus, the Christ, they will die in their sins and be cast into the lake of fire. muslims need to leave the demonic, lying cult of islam and become True Christians, who KNOW the

Living God, and are no longer practicing religion, the doctrines of lying men, like wicked muhammad, in vain.

https://www.thereligionofpeace.com/pages/articles/jesusmuhammad.aspx - whenever you confront muslims they SAY it's not in their text, but these verses are in there text. muslims are guilty of lying about the Holy Text in the Scriptures and they also lie about their own text as well! I have never found an honest muslim about both of these matters! We have to DEPROGRAM them from their cult for the sake of the world!

When muslims choose to follow muhammad instead of Jesus Christ, it makes them look as if they have a strange desire to burn in the lake of fire (it makes them all look deceived to the point of self-destructive stupidity and insanity!)

https://www.thereligionofpeace.com/pages/articles/jesusmuhammad.aspx - muslims are following a rapist, robber, slaver, child molester and murderer and yet act like we all should join them on their way to the flames of damnation.

Jesus Christ publicly died, raised His Body from the Grave and Ascended into Heaven in front of eyewitnesses, proving He is the One True God who has Eternal Life and is the Way to Heaven; no one else. Acts 1:7-11; 4:12; Jn 5:39-40

Far too many muslims are constantly ripping words out of context in the Holy Bible, in a vain effort to deny the Divinity of Jesus Christ. (that is an extremely evil thing to do and means such muslims are determined to make themselves to be the enemy of God!) How would you feel if you were the leader of your nation but everyone in your nation REFUSED to acknowledge you and instead INSISTED you weren't? Now imagine denying the One who came in the flesh, plainly said He is God and Proved it like no one else in the entire history of the world! This is why God, Jesus

Christ, plainly tells us anyone denying He is God will die in their sins and be cast into the lake of fire (John 8:24,25; Rev 21:8) and furthermore calls all such wicked persons liars and antichrists (His enemies) 1Jn 2:21-23. so ALL muslims MUST repent and become Christians or they will end up in the lake of fire!

Jesus Christ also said to see Him is to see the Father John 14:9 and that He and the Father are One. Jn 10:30.

So how can that be true and still say the Father is Greater? answer: similar to the fact your own body and spirit are one and yet your spirit is greater because when you die, your body returns to the dust while your spirit still exists to give an account to God, Jesus Christ.

If you imagine that isn't the case the scriptures make it crystal clear that it is.

Colossians 1:15-19

The Supremacy of the Son of God

15 The Son is the image of the invisible God, the firstborn over all creation. 16 For in him all things were created: things in heaven and on earth, visible and invisible, whether thrones or powers or rulers or authorities; all things have been created through him and for him. 17 He is before all things, and in him all things hold together. 18 And he is the head of the body, the church; he is the beginning and the firstborn from among the dead, so that in everything he might have the supremacy. 19 For God was pleased to have all his fullness dwell in him,

To see Jesus Christ is to see God. Jesus Christ is Lord. He plainly says so from Genesis through Revelation in the Holy Bible. Only when He came in a flesh and bone body does "the Son" say "the Father" is greater. (again, just as your own spirit is greater than your own body)

Jesus Appears to Thomas

...27Then Jesus said to Thomas, "Put your finger here and look at My hands. Reach out your hand and put it into My side. Stop doubting and believe." 28Thomas replied, "My Lord and my God!" 29Jesus said to him, "Because you have seen Me, you have believed; blessed are those who have not seen and yet have believed."... https://biblehub.com/john/20-28.htm

The Law of Liberty

...10Why, then, do you judge your brother? Or why do you belittle your brother? For we will all stand before God's judgment seat. 11 It is written: "As surely as I live, says the Lord, every knee will bow before Me; every tongue will confess to God." 12So then, each of us will give an account of himself to God.... https://biblehub.com/romans/14-11.htm

Isaiah 45:23

By Myself I have sworn; truth has gone out from My mouth, a word that will not be revoked: Every knee will bow before Me, every tongue will swear allegiance.

Philippians 2:10

that at the name of Jesus every knee should bow, in heaven and on earth and under the earth,

Another muslim was asking how can Jesus Christ save us when He couldn't save Himself.

I always wonder why muslims say such a thing. No one else in the entire history of the world claimed to be God, the One who has Eternal Life, and then proved it like Jesus Christ! NO ONE!

He spoke and transformed reality just by speaking, He did so many miracles that those who witnessed them said if all that He did had been written not even the whole world could contain the books! He then publicly died and raised His own Body from the grave, transfigured it, made it Immortal and Glorious and Ascended up into Heaven in front of eyewitnesses!

Those Apostles and Disciples that heard and saw Him were so convinced that Jesus Christ is the One True God, they began telling the whole world! When those who had crucified Him commanded them to stop, they went on and accepted torturous demises rather than recant of one word in the Holy Bible!

So what do you mean "save Himself"? Everything Jesus Christ said and did was to Save us!

Peter and John Before the Council
...11This Jesus is 'the stone you builders rejected, which has become the cornerstone.' 12 Salvation exists in no one else, for there is no other name under heaven given to men by which we must be saved."
https://biblehub.com/acts/4-12.htm

37When the people heard this, they were cut to the heart and asked Peter and the other apostles, "Brothers, what shall we do?" 38 Peter replied, "Repent and be baptized, every one of you, in the name of Jesus Christ for

the forgiveness of your sins, and you will receive the gift of the Holy Spirit. 39This promise belongs to you and your children and to all who are far off—to all whom the Lord our God will call to Himself."...
https://biblehub.com/acts/2-38.htm

The Great Commission
...15And He said to them, "Go into all the world and preach the gospel to every creature. 16Whoever believes and is baptized will be saved, but whoever does not believe will be condemned.
https://biblehub.com/mark/16-16.htm

Sadly; rather typically, some muslim was saying yet another lie taught them by islam that Jesus was only for Israel and that Jesus served their imaginary evil, "allah". So I replied (as usual) - muslims NEED to be DEPROGRAMMED from their evil, lying cult! They've all been brainwashed/deceived with nothing but lies!

No, Jesus Christ never mentioned "allah" even once in the Holy Bible. allah is the name of a pagan idol that was popularized by the criminal conman, muhammad, and his gang, who began the cult of islam over six centuries after the Holy Bible was completed.

Jesus Christ is the One True God; allah is purely imaginary. It's why not one muslim, sees, hears or knows God.

Jesus Christ is the GOD of EVERYONE! (Acts 10:34-43 v 36 Jesus Christ is LORD of ALL and v 43 ALL prophets testify of JESUS CHRIST, LORD OF ALL, and that forgiveness of sins is only through Him, by Name! and Matt 28:18-20 teach ALL nations My Commandments... and Rev 7:9 a vast multitude from ALL nations, languages and tribes Redeemed/Saved by Jesus Christ, the One True God.

https://www.thereligionofpeace.com/pages/articles/jesusmuhammad.aspx

EVERYONE is Commanded by the REAL GOD to Repent and Be Baptized in His Name.

Everywhere God says He is God from Genesis to Revelation is Jesus Christ speaking:

John 5:39-40
39 You search the Scriptures because you think that in them you have eternal life; and it is they that bear witness about me, 40 yet you refuse to come to me that you may have life.

In case your reading comprehension is challenged, when Jesus Christ said the scriptures are all about Him, the One who has Eternal Life and the One everyone must come to in order to have that Life, He was saying He is God.

...24That is why I told you that you would die in your sins. For unless you believe that I am He, you will die in your sins." 25"Who are You?" they asked. "Just what I have been telling you from the beginning," Jesus replied. https://biblehub.com/john/8-25.htm

For those lacking reading comprehension, when Jesus Christ said if you don't believe He is One who has been telling mankind He is God from the Beginning that you will die in your sins, that was again Jesus Christ telling us that the entire Holy Bible is telling us plainly He is God.

If you still don't understand that Jesus Christ said and proved He is God, then you should at least have the sense to ASK HIM! He ever lives to answer any and all with enough sense to call upon Him.

Jesus Christ always receives worship as the One True God that He is: https://www.openbible.info/topics/worshipping_jesus

You're not understanding what the Holy Bible teaches us if you don't understand that Jesus Christ is the One True God.

Yet another muslim was asking how can Jesus Christ save us when He couldn't save Himself.

I always wonder why muslims say such a thing. No one else in the entire history of the world claimed to be God, the One who has Eternal Life, and then proved it like Jesus Christ! NO ONE!

He said He is the Way to Heaven, the One who has Eternal Life, and that we all must come to Him to have that Life AND THEN HE PROVED IT BY PUBLICLY DYING, RAISING HIS BODY UP FROM THE GRAVE, TRANSFIGURED IT MAKING IT IMMORTAL AND THEN ROSE INTO HEAVEN IN FRONT OF EYEWITNESSES! JESUS CHRIST PROVED IT! HE IS GOD!

He spoke and transformed reality just by speaking, He did so many miracles that those who witnessed them said if all that He did had been written not even the whole world could contain the books! He then publicly died and raised His own Body from the grave, transfigured it, made it Immortal and Glorious and Ascended up into Heaven in front of eyewitnesses!

Those Apostles and Disciples that heard and saw Him were so convinced that Jesus Christ is the One True God, they began telling the whole world! When those who had crucified Him commanded them to stop, they went on and accepted torturous demises rather than recant of one word in the Holy Bible! So what do you mean "save Himself"? Everything Jesus Christ said and did was to Save us!

Peter and John Before the Council
…11This Jesus is 'the stone you builders rejected, which has become the cornerstone.' 12 Salvation exists in no one else, for there is no other name under heaven given to men by which we must be saved."
https://biblehub.com/acts/4-12.htm

37When the people heard this, they were cut to the heart and asked Peter and the other apostles, "Brothers, what shall we do?" 38 Peter replied, "Repent and be baptized, every one of you, in the name of Jesus Christ for the forgiveness of your sins, and you will receive the gift of the Holy Spirit. 39This promise belongs to you and your children and to all who are far off—to all whom the Lord our God will call to Himself."…
https://biblehub.com/acts/2-38.htm

The Great Commission
…15And He said to them, "Go into all the world and preach the gospel to every creature. 16Whoever believes and is baptized will be saved, but whoever does not believe will be condemned.
https://biblehub.com/mark/16-16.htm

Every man on earth with children is a father, and yet that same man is also a son, and when that same man dies his spirit departs from his body that returns to the dust of the earth; so every man with children is a father, son and spirit and still just one man, but muslims act as if this is a difficult concept to grasp; even though we know GOD IS GREATER THAN ALL and so refers to Himself as The Father, The Son and The Holy Spirit and is still ONE GOD!

The Great Commission
…18Then Jesus came to them and said, "All authority in heaven and on earth has been given to Me. 19Therefore go and make disciples of all nations, baptizing them in the name of the Father, and of the Son, and of the Holy Spirit, 20and teaching them to obey all that I have commanded you. And surely I am with you always, even to the end of the age."…
https://biblehub.com/matthew/28-19.htm

ONE NAME FOR ONE GOD!

"Brothers, what shall we do?" 38 Peter replied, "Repent and be baptized, every one of you, in the name of Jesus Christ for the forgiveness of your sins, and you will receive the gift of the Holy Spirit. 39This promise belongs to you and your children and to all who are far off—to all whom the Lord our God will call to Himself."… https://biblehub.com/acts/2-38.htm

Peter and John Before the Council
…11This Jesus is 'the stone you builders rejected, which has become the cornerstone.' 12 Salvation exists in no one else, for there is no other name under heaven given to men by which we must be saved."
https://biblehub.com/acts/4-12.htm

THE ONE NAME OF THE ONE GOD WHO IS THE FATHER, THE SON AND THE HOLY SPIRIT IS JESUS CHRIST! (english)

Then another muslim was hypocritically disdaining the Holy Bible by claiming it was written by sinners. I say hypocritically because their quran came from one of the worst criminals in the history of the world! - https://www.thereligionofpeace.com/pages/articles/jesusmuhammad.aspx - muhammad was a rapist, child molester, robber, slaver and mass murderer; besides one of the most evil liars about God that ever walked the planet! (teaching muslims to bow to an evil imaginary god they call "allah" which was just the name of a pagan idol, and instead deny the One True God, Jesus Christ.)

So I replied:

No, the Holy Bible was written by Prophets who heard God Almighty speaking to them and telling them what to write down:

Eyewitnesses of His Majesty

...20Above all, you must understand that no prophecy of Scripture comes from one's own interpretation. 21For no such prophecy was ever brought forth by the will of man, but men spoke from God as they were carried along by the Holy Spirit. https://biblehub.com/2_peter/1-21.htm

The Call of Jeremiah

...8Do not be afraid of them, for I am with you to deliver you," declares the LORD. 9Then the LORD reached out His hand, touched my mouth, and said to me: "Behold, I have put My words in your mouth. 10See, I have appointed you today over nations and kingdoms to uproot and tear down,

to destroy and overthrow, to build and plant."...
https://biblehub.com/jeremiah/1-9.htm

All Scripture is God-Breathed

...15From infancy you have known the Holy Scriptures, which are able to make you wise for salvation through faith in Christ Jesus. 16All Scripture is God-breathed and is useful for instruction, for conviction, for correction, and for training in righteousness, 17so that the man of God may be complete, fully equipped for every good work....
https://biblehub.com/2_timothy/3-16.htm

So even though all have sinned and fallen short, the Prophets, who recorded His Words in the contents of the Holy Bible, were called by God to hear Him and speak and write down His Words. (they were sinners who REPENTED of their sins and walked with God by the presences of His Holy Spirit in their lives; and while not perfect compared to the common connotations of "sinners" were righteous men and women.)

16Whoever listens to you listens to Me; whoever rejects you rejects Me; and whoever rejects Me rejects the One who sent Me."
https://biblehub.com/luke/10-16.htm

33 Heaven and earth will pass away, but My words will never pass away.
https://biblehub.com/luke/21-33.htm

The GOOD NEWS of GOD (Gospel of Jesus Christ) to mankind is that now He is willing to SPEAK WITH EVERYONE, everyone who will Obey His Commandment to REPENT and BE BAPTIZED in His Name and He will give them His SAME Holy Spirit that He gave the Prophets! In other words, ANYONE can KNOW GOD ALMIGHTY PERSONALLY! and EVERYONE SHOULD!

The Great Commission

...15And He said to them, "Go into all the world and preach the gospel to every creature. 16Whoever believes and is baptized will be saved, but whoever does not believe will be condemned.
https://biblehub.com/mark/16-16.htm

"Brothers, what shall we do?" 38 Peter replied, "Repent and be baptized, every one of you, in the name of Jesus Christ for the forgiveness of your sins, and you will receive the gift of the Holy Spirit. 39This promise belongs to you and your children and to all who are far off—to all whom the Lord our God will call to Himself."... https://biblehub.com/acts/2-38.htm

Ask, Seek, Knock

...12Or if he asks for an egg, will give him a scorpion? 13So if you who are evil know how to give good gifts to your children, how much more will your Father in heaven give the Holy Spirit to those who ask Him!"
https://biblehub.com/luke/11-13.htm

Yet another muslim today was asking who sent Jesus Christ? (it's their common way of denying Jesus Christ is God)

God (the Father) sent Himself the same way you and us all send our bodies (God - the Son) to do things all the time.

https://www.facebook.com/photo.php?fbid=6384981581580747&set=pb.100002069048072.-2207520000&type=3 - read and learn. you, like every deceived muslim, I have ever encountered are not letting God define His Own Terms and instead are applying your own imaginations to what you read in the Holy Bible.

God tells us that our spirits are what gives our bodies life, He uses analogies like horse and rider. In other words, our spirits are supposed to control our bodies (not the other way around). So our bodies do nothing without our spirits (are dead and return to dust) when our spirits leave our body. James 2:26; Eccl 12:7 so our spirits are one with our bodies as long as we walk in the flesh on earth, but upon death our spirits return to our Eternal Creator to give account to Him. The is why "the Son" said He does nothing without "the Father" but also said that He and the Father are ONE. (John 10:30) and that to see Him is to see the Father (John 14:9) So Jesus Christ is God who sent His Visible Image into His Creation to Show Himself, Declare Himself and Make Himself Clearly Known to us, His Creation. (John 5:39-40, John 1:1-14; Col 1:15-19; John 14:6-**20,21-26**, 1Tim 3:16) The Eternal, Invisible, Pervasive and Transcendent Aspect of God He calls "the Father" (Ephesians 4:6) and His Visible Image, He calls "the Son" and He is the Truth (John 14:6; 8:32-36) so He calls His Spirit the Holy Spirit of Truth. ONE GOD who is DEFINING HIS OWN TERMS to us! Jesus Christ is GOD, who is the Father, the Son and the Holy Spirit of Truth and is why there is only ONE NAME for the Father, the Son and the Holy Spirit of Truth - JESUS CHRIST (english). YAHOSHUAH HA MASCHIACH (as close as I know to spell out the sounds of His Name in Hebrew) But God, Jesus Christ, speaks all languages, so whatever His Name has been declared to you in your translation of the Holy Bible, He recognizes! He knows those who are seeking to know, love and obey Him from those who don't. Again, Matt 28:18-20 tells us there is ONE NAME for ONE GOD who calls Himself "the Father, the Son, and the Holy Spirit (of Truth)" and that ONE NAME in English is given us clearly in Acts 2:38,39 when the Apostle Peter speaking by the Power of the Holy Spirit of Truth upon him, commanded everyone to be baptized in the Name of Jesus Christ and subsequently stated NO OTHER NAME than that of the ONE TRUE GOD, JESUS CHRIST, is given us (Acts 4:12) AGAIN, EVEN THE NAME OF GOD HAS BEEN TRANSLATED INTO OVER 5000 LANGUAGES TO DATE! Jesus Christ, the One True God understands them ALL! He KNOWS who is seeking Him, the Truth, from those who are not! You simply need to be referring to the One True God who has plainly declared Himself in the contents of the Holy Bible! And obey His Commandment to Repent of thinking you know better than Him and of every evil thought, word, way and deed and Get Baptized in His Name and pray to receive His Holy Spirit and then study His Words in the Holy Bible and apply them to your life now and forever! IF YOU LOVE AND OBEY JESUS CHRIST, HE WILL GIVE YOU HIS OWN HOLY SPIRIT OF TRUTH AND YOU WILL KNOW GOD PERSONALLY BEYOND ALL DOUBT!!!!!!!! The Spirit of God is who He is without His Body, just like your spirit is who you are without your body!

One thing is FOR SURE, God is not "allah"! JESUS CHRIST/YHWH is not "allah"; when you look at the commands of allah, with all his murdering ways, raping ways, slaving ways, etc "allah" is another name for the devil! https://www.thereligionofpeace.com/pages/quran/index.aspx

https://www.facebook.com/photo.php?fbid=6554933757918861&set=pb.100002069048072.-2207520000&type=3 - all muslims I have ever encountered wrongly imagine "the Father" is someone else other than Jesus Christ, when that just isn't the case.

The Book of Revelation is the REVELATION OF JESUS CHRIST. (first chapter and verse)

When we OBEY Jesus Christ HE REVEALS HIMSELF to us (John 14:20,21) so why would just another prophet reveal himself to us, when it is the duty of all prophets to reveal God to us?

That's because ALL prophets TESTIFY that JESUS CHRIST IS GOD! (Acts 10:36,43; 4:12; Isaiah 43:11)

When God came in the flesh He said all the scriptures are about HIM, the ONE who has Eternal Life and the ONE all must come to in order to have that life!

John 5:39-40
39 You search the Scriptures because you think that in them you have eternal life; and it is they that bear witness about me, 40 yet you refuse to come to me that you may have life.

Which is why all the prophets testify that Jesus Christ is God.

https://www.accordingtothescriptures.org/prophecy/353prophecies.html

Jesus Opens the Scriptures
...26Was it not necessary for the Christ to suffer these things and then to enter His glory?" 27And beginning with Moses and all the Prophets, He explained to them what was written in all the Scriptures about Himself.
https://biblehub.com/luke/24-27.htm

Jesus Christ said He is God from Genesis to Revelation and when He came in the flesh He proved He is God beyond all reasonable doubt, publicly dying and raising His Body from the Grave and then Made it Immortal and Glorious and Ascended into Heaven in front of eyewitnesses. Those who saw Him were so convinced He is God they fell at His feet saying so and HE ACKNOWLEDGED IT!

Jesus Appears to Thomas
...27Then Jesus said to Thomas, "Put your finger here and look at My hands. Reach out your hand and put it into My side. Stop doubting and believe." 28Thomas replied, "My Lord and my God!" 29Jesus said to him, "Because you have seen Me, you have believed; blessed are those who have not seen and yet have believed."... https://biblehub.com/john/20-28.htm

God then sent His Holy Spirit upon them to empower them to tell the entire world about Him, which they immediately did! (why the Holy Bible exists)

Acts 1-2:28-39 EVERYONE HEAR THE AWESOME NEWS! THE GOSPEL OF JESUS CHRIST! GOD CAME INTO THIS WORLD HE CREATED AND MADE, SHOWED HIMSELF, PROVED HIMSELF BY DOING MIRACLES NO ONE ELSE HAS EVER DONE, INCLUDING PUBLICLY DYING, BURIED THREE DAYS AND NIGHTS, AND RAISED HIS BODY FROM THE GRAVE TRANSFIGURED IT, MAKING IT IMMORTAL AND GLORIOUS AND ASCENDED RIGHT INTO HEAVEN IN FRONT OF EYEWITNESSES! HE COMMANDS EVERYONE TO REPENT AND BE BAPTIZED IN HIS NAME AND BE FILLED WITH HIS HOLY SPIRIT SO THAT YOU ALSO CAN KNOW THE ONE TRUE GOD, JESUS CHRIST!

And those who had just crucified the Living God, commanded His Apostles and Disciples to stop telling everyone that AWESOME TRUTH AND GREAT NEWS! but one by one the Apostles and Disciples said it was more important to OBEY GOD and accepted torturous deaths rather than recant of one word in the Holy Bible!

https://tile.loc.gov/storageservices/public/gdcmassbookdig/foxesbookofmart00fo/foxesbookofmart00fo.pdf

I've encountered far too many of you muslims sneering at Christians as if we're the misguided ones, when it's YOU! following the lies of muhammad who came along over six centuries later and so had no knowledge whatsoever of the facts he denied in the Holy Bible! THE FACTS OF THE PROPHETS, HIS EYEWITNESS APOSTELS AND DISCIPLES, AND GOD ALMIGHTY PLAINLY TELLS US! JESUS CHRIST IS THE ONE TRUE GOD! and so the reason not one muslim sees, hears or knows God is that all of you have been deceived into denying Him instead! Repent! muslims! REPENT! Obey God! Get Baptized in the Name of our Lord Jesus Christ and pray to receive

His Holy Spirit of Truth, then study His Words in the Holy Bible and apply them to your living!

muslims and the entire world needs to comprehend that the Father, the Son and the Holy Spirit are NOT three different entities! no more than your own spirit and own body are two different persons!

Jesus Christ told His Prophets He would come in the flesh as the Messiah/Christ.

https://www.accordingtothescriptures.org/prophecy/353prophecies.html

Jesus and the Samaritan Woman
…25The woman said, "I know that Messiah" (called Christ) "is coming. When He comes, He will explain everything to us." 26 Jesus answered, "I who speak to you am He." https://biblehub.com/john/4-26.htm

God refers to the Visible Image of Himself as "the Son" and He refers to His Invisible, Eternal, Pervasive, Transcendent Existence as "the Father". But there is One Name for One God, Jesus Christ, they are not two different beings, no more than your own spirit and body are two different persons.

John 14:6-9
6 Jesus said to him, "I am the way, the truth, and the life. No one comes to the Father except through Me.

The Father Revealed
7 "If you had known Me, you would have known My Father also; and from now on you know Him and have seen Him."

8 Philip said to Him, "Lord, show us the Father, and it is sufficient for us."

9 Jesus said to him, "Have I been with you so long, and yet you have not known Me, Philip? He who has seen Me has seen the Father; so how can you say, 'Show us the Father'?

God, Jesus Christ, has ALL Honorable Titles: Father of fathers, Son of sons, Servant of servants, God of gods, Man of men, Angel of angels, Spirit of spirits, etc. etc.

Colossians 1:15-19
The Supremacy of the Son of God
15 The Son is the image of the invisible God, the firstborn over all creation. 16 For in him all things were created: things in heaven and on earth, visible and invisible, whether thrones or powers or rulers or authorities; all things have been created through him and for him. 17 He is before all things, and in him all things hold together. 18 And he is the head of the body, the church; he is the beginning and the firstborn from among the dead, so that in everything he might have the supremacy. 19 For God was pleased to have all his fullness dwell in him,

So "the Son" is the Visible Image of God and "the Father" is His Invisible, Eternal, Pervasive and Transcendent Existence:

Unity in the Body
...5one Lord, one faith, one baptism; 6one God and Father of all, who is over all and through all and in all. https://biblehub.com/ephesians/4-6.htm

One Name for God who is the Father, the Son and the Holy Spirit (and has ALL Honorable Titles).

The Great Commission
...18Then Jesus came to them and said, "All authority in heaven and on earth has been given to Me. 19Therefore go and make disciples of all nations, baptizing them in the name of the Father, and of the Son, and of the Holy Spirit, 20and teaching them to obey all that I have commanded you. And surely I am with you always, even to the end of the age."...
https://biblehub.com/matthew/28-19.htm

The ONE Name of the ONE GOD in English is Jesus, the Christ.

37When the people heard this, they were cut to the heart and asked Peter and the other apostles, "Brothers, what shall we do?" 38 Peter replied, "Repent and be baptized, every one of you, in the name of Jesus Christ for the forgiveness of your sins, and you will receive the gift of the Holy Spirit. 39This promise belongs to you and your children and to all who are far off—to all whom the Lord our God will call to Himself."...
https://biblehub.com/acts/2-38.htm

Peter and John Before the Council
...11This Jesus is 'the stone you builders rejected, which has become the cornerstone.' 12 Salvation exists in no one else, for there is no other name under heaven given to men by which we must be saved."
https://biblehub.com/acts/4-12.htm

A muslim was asking Christians why do we dislike islam (the reasons are so many, even a very large book is insufficient) But as succinctly as possible:

islam, by definition from God Himself, is an accursed, demonic, antichristian cult. islam causes muslims to maltreat others that they call insulting names like kafir and infidel, because their cult is ruled by satan and teaches them to hate others. At the worst their cult cause muslims to murder not only each other but non-muslims.

Galatians 1:6-9

No Other Gospel

6 I am astonished that you are so quickly deserting him who called you in the grace of Christ and are turning to a different gospel— 7 not that there is another one, but there are some who trouble you and want to distort the gospel of Christ. 8 But even if we or an angel from heaven should preach to you a gospel contrary to the one we preached to you, let him be accursed. 9 As we have said before, so now I say again: If anyone is preaching to you a gospel contrary to the one you received, let him be accursed.

Gospel is archaic English for God-Speaks so the quran not only denies the Gospel of Jesus Christ, the Holy Bible, but proclaims an entirely different one; a god so different that he is more like the devil in the Holy Bible, than Jesus Christ.

https://www.thereligionofpeace.com/pages/articles/jesusmuhammad.aspx

So islam is an accursed, demonic cult because it is proclaiming lies and causing muslims to deny the One True God, Jesus Christ.

lies are from the devil:

John 8:43-45

43 Why do you not understand what I say? It is because you cannot bear to hear my word. 44 You are of your father the devil, and your will is to do your father's desires. He was a murderer from the beginning, and does not stand in the truth, because there is no truth in him. When he lies, he speaks out of his own character, for he is a liar and the father of lies. 45 But because I tell the truth, you do not believe me.

Furthermore, muslims openly proclaim their imaginary allah has no sons and no partners, that makes all muslims antichrists who are obviously deceived and deluded.

Beware of Antichrists
...21I have not written to you because you lack knowledge of the truth, but because you have it, and because no lie comes from the truth. 22Who is the liar, if it is not the one who denies that Jesus is the Christ? This is the antichrist, who denies the Father and the Son. 23Whoever denies the Son does not have the Father, but whoever confesses the Son has the Father as well.... https://biblehub.com/1_john/2-22.htm

muslims are deceived and deluded antichrists, not just because God says so plainly in the Holy Bible, but because with their own words it's plain to see!

The REAL GOD Created and Made an entire world full of billions of children who all belong to Him! (plain to see right before our eyes, so if a muslim is bowing down to a god that has no sons, no children, no partners, then it's obvious their god is not the REAL GOD!)

Furthermore muslims are deluded by definition when they say their god has no partners and yet try their hardest to do whatever their imaginary allah tells them to (which makes them all partners by definition).

So islam is an accursed, demonic, antichristian cult that deceives people into denying the One True God and reality before their own eyes. islam is evil and obviously so.

when you compare the real muhammad with Jesus Christ, muhammad seems to be like the devil in the flesh an obvious antichrist.

https://www.thereligionofpeace.com/pages/articles/jesusmuhammad.aspx

And when you examine all the lies and evil instructions in the quran against the provably and verifiably Divinely Inspired Holy Bible, it's obvious the quran is evil and from the devil.

https://www.thereligionofpeace.com/pages/quran/index.aspx

islam has generated more violent terrorists organizations than any in all the history of the world. It threatens to murder anyone who tries to leave it! THE REST OF HUMANITY NEEDS TO DECLARE islam AN OVERT CRIMINAL ORGANIZATIONS IN DOCTRINE AND PRACTICE TO LEAVE THE islamic WORLD FREE TO COME OUT FROM UNDER ITS EVIL! The vast majority of muslims are not extremists and most of them do not practice islam per se, they just are OPPRESSED by its evil it take the rest of humanity to release them! Only then we will be able to contain the islamic extremism.

Yet another woefully deceived muslim was citing verses out of the Holy Bible that refer to Jesus Christ as a Man, as if that automatically disqualifies Him as God. (in their deceived minds, God cannot be a Man like us, even though God tells us all quite plainly in the very first Chapter of the Holy Bible men are made in His Image. Gen 1:27) and He was citing other passages that say Jesus Christ is God and then cited the passage that says confusion is not of God. And rather than realize the Truth that God is Supreme in EVERYTHING (Col 1:14-19) meaning Jesus Christ is the God of gods, AND Man of men, AND Spirit of spirits AND Angel of angels, Father of fathers, Son of sons, Teacher of teachers, Prophet of prophets, etc. etc. the muslim was arguing that his confusion meant the Holy Bible isn't from God. (Rather than realizing the problem isn't with the Words of God in the Holy Bible, but with him.)

None of those verses he cited say "Jesus is not God" instead the entire Holy Bible plainly states many hundreds of times over that He is. In fact, there is not one location in the entire Holy Bible that denies Jesus Christ is God, but just the opposite from Genesis to Revelation the entire Holy Bible redundantly tells us over and over that He is the One True God. John 5:39-40

39 You search the Scriptures because you think that in them you have eternal life; and it is they that bear witness about me, 40 yet you refuse to come to me that you may have life.

Jesus Christ plainly stated the entire Holy Bible is about Him, the One who has Eternal Life and the One everyone must come to in order to have that life.

Jesus Appears to Thomas

…27Then Jesus said to Thomas, "Put your finger here and look at My hands. Reach out your hand and put it into My side. Stop doubting and believe." 28Thomas replied, "My Lord and my God!" 29Jesus said to him, "Because you have seen Me, you have believed; blessed are those who have not seen and yet have believed."… https://biblehub.com/john/20-28.htm

Jesus Christ not only states hundreds of times in the Holy Bible (every mention of God is referring to Him) that He is God, but clearly acknowledges it to His Own Disciples bowing down and worshipping Him.

https://www.openbible.info/topics/worshipping_jesus - never once did Jesus Christ tell anyone to stop worshipping Him as the One True God.

So, if you're confused, don't blame Him or His Words in the Holy Bible, it's due to the fact you still haven't obeyed Him and Repented of your sins and been Baptized in His Name, so the devil is still deceiving you.

The Great Commission
...18Then Jesus came to them and said, "All authority in heaven and on earth has been given to Me. 19Therefore go and make disciples of all nations, baptizing them in the name of the Father, and of the Son, and of the Holy Spirit, 20and teaching them to obey all that I have commanded you. And surely I am with you always, even to the end of the age."...
https://biblehub.com/matthew/28-19.htm

37When the people heard this, they were cut to the heart and asked Peter and the other apostles, "Brothers, what shall we do?" 38 Peter replied, "Repent and be baptized, every one of you, in the name of Jesus Christ for the forgiveness of your sins, and you will receive the gift of the Holy Spirit. 39This promise belongs to you and your children and to all who are far off—to all whom the Lord our God will call to Himself."... https://biblehub.com/acts/2-38.htm

Peter and John Before the Council

...11This Jesus is 'the stone you builders rejected, which has become the cornerstone.' 12 Salvation exists in no one else, for there is no other name under heaven given to men by which we must be saved."
https://biblehub.com/acts/4-12.htm

The reason ONLY Jesus Christ Saves us, is due to the fact HE IS GOD!

...19We know that we are of God, and that the whole world is under the power of the evil one. 20And we know that the Son of God has come and has given us understanding, so that we may know Him who is true; and we are in Him who is true— in His Son Jesus Christ. He is the TRUE God and eternal life. https://biblehub.com/1_john/5-20.htm

If you don't know God, Jesus Christ, personally, it means He hasn't given you His Holy Spirit of Truth (Acts 1:7-9; Jn 14:20-26) because you still haven't obeyed Him and as such are still being deceived by the devil, just as verse 1Jn 5:19 plainly states.

ONLY JESUS CHRIST THE ONE TRUE GOD CAN SET YOU FREE! Jn 8:32-36 from the devil who has ALREADY deceived the world.
https://www.biblegateway.com/verse/en/2%20Timothy%202%3A26

Call on JESUS CHRIST, THE ONE TRUE GOD! Obey Him! REPENT AND GET BAPTIZED IN HIS NAME! PRAY TO RECEIVE HIS HOLY SPIRIT OF TRUTH! Luke 11:13

Look Jesus Christ PLAINLY SAID that satanil is the Father of all LIES and I've shown you herein how islam in LYING to muslims and getting them to do great evil LIKE MURDER! satanil is a liar and murderer! Hence islam is an accursed demonic cult just as God plainly tells us in His Words, the Holy Bible! Gal 1:6-12, Jn 8:43-45, 1Jn 4:1-6, Jn 3:36, Rev 21:8

John 8:43-45

English Standard Version

43
Why do you not understand what I say? It is because you cannot bear to hear my word. **44** You are of your father the devil, and your will is to do your father's desires. He was a murderer from the beginning, and does not stand in the truth, because there is no truth in him. When he lies, he

speaks out of his own character, for he is a liar and the father of lies. ⁴⁵ But because I tell the truth, you do not believe me.

HERE ARE JUST SOME OF THE WAYS islam in plainly of the devil and is in fact a criminal organization! https://www.thereligionofpeace.com/pages/quran/index.aspx - read all of these instruction none of which are abrogated to see islam is indeed a violent criminal organization in DOCTRINE and when muslim do as it says - IN PRACTICE! islam must be internationally banned! or we're all allowing a NOTORIOUS criminal organization to exist among us!

These and all the lies of islam points out that allah is just another name for the devil!

QUOTE from thereligionofpeace.com

"**Quran**

Quran (2:244) - *"Then fight in the cause of Allah, and know that Allah Heareth and knoweth all things."* (See also: Response to Apologists)

Quran (2:216) - **"Fighting is prescribed for you,** *and ye dislike it. But it is possible that ye dislike a thing which is good for you, and that ye love a thing which is bad for you. But Allah knoweth, and ye know not."* Not only does this verse establish that violence can be virtuous, but it also contradicts the myth that fighting is intended only in self-defense, since the audience was obviously not under attack at the time. From the Hadith, we know that this verse was narrated at a time that Muhammad was actually trying to motivate his people into raiding merchant caravans for loot. (See also: Response to Apologists)

Quran (3:56) - *"As to those who reject faith, I will punish them with terrible agony in this world and in the Hereafter, nor will they have anyone to help."* (See also: Response to Apologists)

Quran (3:151) - *"Soon shall We cast terror into the hearts of the Unbelievers, for that they joined companions with Allah, for which He had sent no authority".* This speaks directly of polytheists, yet it also includes

Christians, since they believe in the Trinity (ie. what Muhammad incorrectly believed to be 'joining companions to Allah'). (See also: Response to Apologists)

Quran (4:74) - *"Let those fight in the way of Allah who sell the life of this world for the other. Whoso fighteth in the way of Allah, be he slain or be he victorious, on him We shall bestow a vast reward."* The martyrs of Islam are unlike the early Christians, who were led meekly to the slaughter. These Muslims are killed in battle as they attempt to inflict death and destruction for the cause of Allah. This is the theological basis for today's suicide bombers. (See also: Response to Apologists)

Quran (4:76) - *"Those who believe fight in the cause of Allah, and those who disbelieve, fight in the cause of Taghut (Satan, etc.). So fight you against the friends of Shaitan (Satan)"* The Arabic for the word "fight" is from *qital*, meaning physical combat.

Quran (4:89) - *"They but wish that ye should reject Faith, as they do, and thus be on the same footing (as they): But take not friends from their ranks until they flee in the way of Allah (From what is forbidden). But if they turn renegades, seize them and slay them wherever ye find them; and (in any case) take no friends or helpers from their ranks."* (See also: Response to Apologists)

Quran (4:95) - *"Not equal are those of the believers who sit (at home), except those who are disabled (by injury or are blind or lame, etc.), and those who strive hard and fight in the Cause of Allah with their wealth and their lives. Allah has preferred in grades those who strive hard and fight with their wealth and their lives above those who sit (at home).Unto each, Allah has promised good (Paradise), but Allah has preferred those who strive hard and fight, above those who sit (at home) by a huge reward "* This passage criticizes "peaceful" Muslims who do not join in the violence, letting them know that they are less worthy in Allah's eyes. It also demolishes the modern myth that "Jihad" doesn't mean holy war in the Quran, but rather a spiritual struggle. Not only is this Arabic word (mujahiduna) used in this passage, but it is clearly *not* referring to anything spiritual, since the physically disabled are given exemption. (The Hadith reveals the context of the passage to be in response to a blind man's protest that he is unable to engage in Jihad, which would not make sense if it meant an internal struggle). (See also: Response to Apologists)

Quran (4:101) - *"And when you (Muslims) travel in the land, there is no sin on you if you shorten your Salat (prayer) if you fear that the disbelievers may attack you, verily, **the disbelievers are ever unto you open enemies.**"* Mere disbelief makes one an "open" enemy of Muslims.

Quran (4:104) - *"And be not weak hearted in pursuit of the enemy; if you suffer pain, then surely they (too) suffer pain as you suffer pain..."* Is pursuing an injured and retreating enemy really an act of self-defense? (See also: Response to Apologists)

Quran (5:33) - *"The punishment of those who wage war against Allah and His messenger and strive to make mischief in the land is only this, that they should be murdered or crucified or their hands and their feet should be cut off on opposite sides or they should be imprisoned; this shall be as a disgrace for them in this world, and in the hereafter they shall have a grievous chastisement"* (See also: Response to Apologists)

Quran (8:12) - *"(Remember) when your Lord inspired the angels... "I will cast terror into the hearts of those who disbelieve. Therefore strike off their heads and strike off every fingertip of them"* No reasonable person would interpret this to mean a spiritual struggle, given that it both followed and preceded confrontations in which non-Muslims were killed by Muslims. The targets of violence are "*those who disbelieve*" - further defined in the next verse (13) as those who "*defy and disobey Allah.*" Nothing is said about self-defense. In fact, the verses in sura 8 were narrated shortly after a battle provoked by Muhammad, who had been trying to attack a lightly-armed caravan to steal goods belonging to other people. (See also: Response to Apologists)

Quran (8:15) - *"O ye who believe! When ye meet those who disbelieve in battle, turn not your backs to them. (16)Whoso on that day turneth his back to them, unless maneuvering for battle or intent to join a company, he truly hath incurred wrath from Allah, and his habitation will be hell, a hapless journey's end."*

Quran (8:39) - *"And fight with them until there is no more fitna* (disorder, unbelief) *and religion is all for Allah"* Some translations interpret "fitna" as "persecution", but the traditional understanding of this word is not supported by the historical context (See notes for 2:193). The Meccans were simply refusing Muhammad access to their city during the pilgrimage. Other Muslims were allowed to travel there - but not as an armed group, since Muhammad had declared war on Mecca prior to his eviction. The Meccans were also acting in defense of their religion, as it was Muhammad's intention to destroy their idols and establish Islam by force (which he later did). Hence the critical part of this verse is to fight until *"religion is only for Allah"*, meaning that the true justification of violence was the unbelief of the opposition. According to the Sira (Ibn Ishaq/Hisham 324) Muhammad further explains that *"Allah must have no rivals."* (See also: Response to Apologists)

Quran (8:57) - *"If thou comest on them in the war, deal with them so as to strike fear in those who are behind them, that haply they may remember."*

Quran (8:67) - *"It is not for a Prophet that he should have prisoners of war until he had made a great slaughter in the land..."*

Quran (8:59-60) - *"And let not those who disbelieve suppose that they can outstrip (Allah's Purpose). Lo! they cannot escape. Make ready for them all thou canst of (armed) force and of horses tethered, that thereby ye may dismay the enemy of Allah and your enemy."* As Ibn Kathir puts it in his tafsir on this passage, "Allah commands Muslims to prepare for war against disbelievers, as much as possible, according to affordability and availability." (See also: Response to Apologists)

Quran (8:65) - *"O Prophet, exhort the believers to fight..."*

Quran (9:5) - *"So when the sacred months have passed away, then slay the idolaters wherever you find them, and take them captive and besiege them and lie in wait for them in every ambush, then if they repent and keep up prayer and pay the poor-rate, leave their way free to them."* According to this verse, the best way of staying safe from Muslim violence at the time of Muhammad was to convert to Islam: prayer (*salat*) and the poor tax (*zakat*) are among the religion's Five Pillars. The popular claim that the Quran only inspires violence within the context of self-defense is seriously challenged by this passage as well, since the Muslims to whom it was written were obviously not under attack. Had they been, then there would have been no waiting period (earlier verses make it a duty for Muslims to fight in self-defense, even during the sacred months). The historical context is Mecca *after* the idolaters were subjugated by Muhammad and posed no threat. Once the Muslims had power, they violently evicted those unbelievers who would not convert. (See also: Response to Apologists)

[Note: The verse says to fight unbelievers "*wherever you find them*". Even if the context is a time of battle (which it was not) the reading appears to sanction attacks against those "unbelievers" who are not on the battlefield. In 2016, the Islamic State referred to this verse in urging the faithful to commit terror attacks: *Allah did not only command the 'fighting' of disbelievers, as if to say He only wants us to conduct frontline operations against them. Rather, He has also ordered that they be slain wherever they may be – on or off the battlefield.* (source)]

Quran (9:14) - "*Fight against them so that Allah will punish them by your hands and disgrace them and give you victory over them and heal the breasts of a believing people.*" Humiliating and hurting non-believers not only has the blessing of Allah, but it is ordered as a means of carrying out his punishment and even "heals" the hearts of Muslims.

Quran (9:20) - "*Those who believe, and have left their homes and striven with their wealth and their lives in Allah's way are of much greater worth in Allah's sight. These are they who are triumphant.*" The Arabic word interpreted as "striving" in this verse is the same root as "Jihad". The context is obviously holy war.

Quran (9:29) - "*Fight those who believe not in Allah nor the Last Day, nor hold that forbidden which hath been forbidden by Allah and His Messenger, nor acknowledge the religion of Truth, (even if they are) of the People of the Book, until they pay the Jizya with willing submission, and feel themselves subdued.*" "People of the Book" refers to Christians and Jews. According to this verse, they are to be violently subjugated, with the sole justification being their religious status. Verse 9:33 tells Muslims that Allah has instructed them to make Islam "superior over all religions." This chapter was one of the final "revelations" from Allah and it set in motion the tenacious military expansion, in which Muhammad's companions managed to conquer two-thirds of the Christian world in the next 100 years. Islam is intended to dominate all other people and faiths. (See also: Response to Apologists)

Quran (9:30) - *"And the Jews say: Ezra is the son of Allah; and the Christians say: The Messiah is the son of Allah; these are the words of their mouths; they imitate the saying of those who disbelieved before; may Allah destroy them; how they are turned away!"* (See also: Response to Apologists)

Quran (9:38-39) - *"O ye who believe! what is the matter with you, that, when ye are asked to go forth in the cause of Allah, ye cling heavily to the earth? Do ye prefer the life of this world to the Hereafter? But little is the comfort of this life, as compared with the Hereafter. Unless ye go forth, He will punish you with a grievous penalty, and put others in your place."* This is a warning to those who refuse to fight, that they will be punished with Hell. The verse also links physical fighting to the "cause of Allah" (or "way of Allah"). (See also: Response to Apologists)

Quran (9:41) - *"Go forth, light or heavy* (some translations read "armed") *and strive with your wealth and your lives in the way of Allah! That is best for you if ye but knew."* See also the verse that follows (9:42) - *"If there had been immediate gain (in sight), and the journey easy, they would (all) without doubt have followed thee, but the distance was long, (and weighed) on them"* This contradicts the myth that Muslims are to fight only in self-defense, since the wording implies that battle will be waged a long distance from home (in another country and - in this case - on Christian soil, according to the historians). (See also: Response to Apologists)

Quran (9:73) - *"O Prophet! strive hard against the unbelievers and the hypocrites and be unyielding to them; and their abode is hell, and evil is the destination."* Dehumanizing those who reject Islam, by reminding Muslims that unbelievers are merely firewood for Hell, makes it easier to justify slaughter. It explains why today's devout Muslims generally have little regard for those outside the faith. The inclusion of "hypocrites" (non-practicing) within the verse also contradicts the apologist's defense that the targets of hate and hostility are wartime foes, since there was never an opposing army made up of non-religious Muslims in Muhammad's time. (See also Games Muslims Play: Terrorists Can't Be Muslim Because They Kill Muslims for the role this verse plays in Islam's perpetual internal conflicts). (See also: Response to Apologists)

Quran (9:88) - *"But the Messenger, and those who believe with him, strive and fight with their wealth and their persons: for them are (all) good things: and it is they who will prosper."* (See also: Response to Apologists)

Quran (9:111) - *"Allah hath purchased of the believers their persons and their goods; for theirs (in return) is the garden (of Paradise): they fight in His cause, and slay and are slain: a promise binding on Him in truth, through the Law, the Gospel, and the Quran: and who is more faithful to his covenant than Allah? then rejoice in the bargain which ye have concluded: that is the achievement supreme."* How does the Quran define a true believer? (See also: Response to Apologists)

Quran (9:123) - *"O you who believe! fight those of the unbelievers who are near to you and let them find in you hardness."* (See also: Response to Apologists)

Quran (17:16) - *"And when We wish to destroy a town, We send Our commandment to the people of it who lead easy lives, but they transgress therein; thus the word proves true against it, so We destroy it with utter destruction."* Note that the crime is moral transgression, and the punishment is "utter destruction." (Before ordering the 9/11 attacks, Osama bin Laden first issued Americans an invitation to Islam).

Quran (18:65-81) - This parable lays the theological groundwork for honor killings, in which a family member is murdered because they brought shame to the family, either through apostasy or perceived moral indiscretion. The story (which is not found in any Jewish or Christian source) tells of Moses encountering a man with "special knowledge" who does things which don't seem to make sense on the surface, but are then justified according to later explanation. One such action is to murder a youth for no apparent reason (v.74). However, the wise man later explains that it was feared that the boy would "grieve" his parents by "disobedience and ingratitude." He was killed so that Allah could provide them a 'better' son. [Note: This parable along with verse 58:22 is a major reason that honor killing is sanctioned by Sharia. Reliance of the Traveler (Umdat al-Saliq) says that punishment for murder is not applicable when a parent or grandparent kills their offspring (o.1.12).] (See also: Response to Apologists)

Quran (21:44) - "...*See they not that We gradually reduce the land (in their control) from its outlying borders? Is it then they who will win?*"

Quran (25:52) - "*Therefore listen not to the Unbelievers, but strive against them with the utmost strenuousness with it.*" - The root for Jihad is used twice in this verse - although it may not have been referring to Holy War when narrated, since it was prior to the hijra at Mecca. The "it" at the end is thought to mean the Quran. Thus the verse may have originally meant a non-violent resistance to the 'unbelievers.' Obviously, this changed with the hijra. 'Jihad' after this is almost exclusively within a violent context. The enemy is always defined as people, rather than ideas.

Quran (33:60-62) - "*If the hypocrites, and those in whose hearts is a disease (evil desire for adultery, etc.), and those who spread false news among the people in Al-Madinah, cease not, We shall certainly let you overpower them, then they will not be able to stay in it as your neighbors but a little while Accursed, wherever found, they shall be seized and killed with a (terrible) slaughter.*" This passage sanctions slaughter (rendered as "merciless" and "horrible murder" in other translations) against three groups: hypocrites (Muslims who refuse to "fight in the way of Allah" (3:167) and hence don't act as Muslims should), those with "diseased hearts" (which include Jews and Christians 5:51-52), and "alarmists" or "agitators - those who speak out against Islam. It is worth noting that the victims are to be *sought out,* which is what today's terrorists do.

Quran (47:3-4) - "*Those who disbelieve follow falsehood, while those who believe follow the truth from their Lord... So, when you meet (fighting Jihad in Allah's Cause), those who disbelieve smite at their necks till when you have killed and wounded many of them, then bind a bond firmly (on them, i.e. take them as captives)... If it had been Allah's Will, He Himself could certainly have punished them (without you). But (He lets you fight), in order to test you, some with others. But those who are killed in the Way of Allah, He will never let their deeds be lost.*" Holy war is to be pursued against those who reject Allah. The unbelievers are to be killed and wounded. Survivors are to be held captive for ransom. The only reason Allah doesn't do the dirty work himself is to to test the faithfulness of Muslims. Those who kill pass the test. (See also: 47:4 for more context) (See also: Response to Apologists)

Quran (47:35) - *"Be not weary and faint-hearted, crying for peace, when ye should be uppermost* (Shakir: "have the upper hand") *for Allah is with you,"* (See also: Response to Apologists)

Quran (48:17) - *"There is no blame for the blind, nor is there blame for the lame, nor is there blame for the sick (that they go not forth to war). And whoso obeyeth Allah and His messenger, He will make him enter Gardens underneath which rivers flow; and whoso turneth back, him will He punish with a painful doom."* Contemporary apologists sometimes claim that Jihad means 'spiritual struggle.' If so, then why are the blind, lame and sick exempted? This verse also says that those who do not fight will suffer torment in hell.

Quran (48:29) - *"Muhammad is the messenger of Allah. And those with him are hard (ruthless) against the disbelievers and merciful among themselves"* Islam is **not** about treating everyone equally. This verse tells Muslims that two very distinct standards are applied based on religious status. Also the word used for 'hard' or 'ruthless' in this verse shares the same root as the word translated as 'painful' or severe' to describe Hell in over 25 other verses including 65:10, 40:46 and 50:26..

Quran (61:4) - *"Surely Allah loves those who fight in His cause"* Religion of Peace, indeed! The verse explicitly refers to "rows" or "battle array," meaning that it is speaking of physical conflict. This is followed by (61:9), which defines the "cause": *"He it is who has sent His Messenger (Mohammed) with guidance and the religion of truth (Islam) to make it* **victorious over all religions even though the infidels may resist.***"* (See next verse, below). Infidels who resist Islamic rule are to be fought. (See also: Response to Apologists)

Quran (61:10-12) - *"O You who believe! Shall I guide you to a commerce that will save you from a painful torment. That you believe in Allah and His Messenger (Muhammad), and that you strive hard and fight in the Cause of Allah with your wealth and your lives, that will be better for you, if you but know! (If you do so) He will forgive you your sins, and admit you into Gardens under which rivers flow, and pleasant dwelling in Gardens of'Adn-Eternity ['Adn(Edn) Paradise], that is indeed the great success."* This verse refers to physical battle waged to make Islam victorious over other religions (see verse 9). It uses the Arabic root for the word Jihad.

Quran (66:9) - *"O Prophet! Strive against the disbelievers and the hypocrites, and be stern with them. Hell will be their home, a hapless journey's end."* The root word of "Jihad" is used again here. The context is clearly holy war, and the scope of violence is broadened to include "hypocrites" - those who call themselves Muslims but do not act as such. (See also: Response to Apologists)

Quran (2:191-193) - *"And kill them wherever you find them, and turn them out from where they have turned you out. And Al-Fitnah [disbelief or unrest] is worse than killing... but if they desist, then lo! Allah is forgiving and merciful. And fight them until there is no more Fitnah [disbelief and worshipping of others along with Allah] and worship is for Allah alone. But if they cease, let there be no transgression except against Az-Zalimun(the polytheists, and wrong-doers, etc.)"* (Translation is from the Noble Quran) The verse prior to this (190) refers to *"fighting for the cause of Allah those who fight you"* leading some to claim that the entire passage refers to a defensive war in which Muslims are defending their homes and families. The historical context of this passage is **not** defensive warfare, however, since Muhammad and his Muslims had just relocated to Medina and were *not* under attack by their Meccan adversaries. In fact, the verses urge *offensive* warfare, in that Muslims are to drive Meccans out of their own city (which they later did). Verse 190 thus means to fight those who offer resistance to Allah's rule (ie. Muslim conquest). The use of the word "persecution" by some Muslim translators is disingenuous - the actual Arabic words for persecution (*idtihad*) - and oppression are not used instead of *fitna*. Fitna can mean disbelief, or the disorder that results from unbelief or temptation. A strict translation is 'sedition,' meaning rebellion against authority (the authority being Allah). This is certainly what is meant in this context since the violence is explicitly commissioned *"until religion is for Allah"* - ie. unbelievers desist in their unbelief. [Editor's note: these notes have been modified slightly after a critic misinterpreted our language. Verse 193 plainly says that 'fighting' is sanctioned even if the *fitna* 'ceases'. This is about religious order, not real persecution.] (See also: Response to Apologists)

Hadith and Sira

Sahih Bukhari (52:177) - *Allah's Apostle said, "The Hour will not be established until you fight with the Jews, and the stone behind which a Jew will be hiding will say. "O Muslim! There is a Jew hiding behind me, so kill him."*

Sahih Bukhari (52:256) - *The Prophet... was asked whether it was permissible to attack the pagan warriors at night with the probability of exposing their women and children to danger. The Prophet replied, "They (i.e. women and children) are from them (i.e. pagans)."* In this command, Muhammad establishes that it is permissible to kill non-combatants in the process of killing a perceived enemy. This provides justification for the many Islamic terror bombings.

Sahih Bukhari (52:65) - *The Prophet said, 'He who fights that Allah's Word (Islam) should be superior, fights in Allah's Cause.* Muhammad's words are the basis for offensive Jihad - spreading Islam by force. This is how it was understood by his companions, and by the terrorists of today. (See also Sahih Bukhari 3:125)

Sahih Bukhari (52:220) - *Allah's Apostle said... 'I have been made victorious with terror'*

Sahih Bukhari (52:44) - *A man came to Allah's Apostle and said, "Instruct me as to such a deed as equals Jihad (in reward)." He replied, "I do not find such a deed."*

Abu Dawud (14:2526) (considered daif) - *The Prophet said, Three things are the roots of faith: to refrain from (killing) a person who utters, "There is no god but Allah" and not to declare him unbeliever whatever sin he commits, and not to excommunicate him from Islam for his any action; and jihad will be performed continuously since the day Allah sent me as a prophet...*

Abu Dawud (14:2527) (considered daif) - *The Prophet said: Striving in the path of Allah (jihad) is incumbent on you along with every ruler, whether he is pious or impious*

Sahih Muslim (1:33) - *the Messenger of Allah said: I have been commanded to fight against people till they testify that there is no god but Allah, that Muhammad is the messenger of Allah*

Sahih Bukhari (8:387) - *Allah's Apostle said, "I have been ordered to fight the people till they say: 'None has the right to be worshipped but Allah'. And if they say so, pray like our prayers, face our Qibla and slaughter as we slaughter, then their blood and property will be sacred to us and we will not interfere with them except legally."*

Sahih Muslim (1:30) - *"The Messenger of Allah said: I have been commanded to fight against people so long as they do not declare that there is no god but Allah."*

Sahih Bukhari (52:73) - *"Allah's Apostle said, 'Know that Paradise is under the shades of swords'."*

Sahih Bukhari (11:626) - [Muhammad said:] *"I decided to order a man to lead the prayer and then take a flame to burn all those, who had not left their houses for the prayer, burning them alive inside their homes."*

Sahih Muslim (1:149) - *"Abu Dharr reported: I said: Messenger of Allah, which of the deeds is the best? He (the Holy Prophet) replied: Belief in Allah and Jihad in His cause..."*

Sahih Muslim (20:4645) - *"...He (the Messenger of Allah) did that and said: There is another act which elevates the position of a man in Paradise to a grade one hundred (higher), and the elevation between one grade and the other is equal to the height of the heaven from the earth. He (Abu Sa'id) said: What is that act? He replied: Jihad in the way of Allah! Jihad in the way of Allah!"*

Sahih Muslim (20:4696) - *"the Messenger of Allah (may peace be upon him) said: 'One who died but did not fight in the way of Allah nor did he express any desire (or determination) for Jihad died the death of a hypocrite.'"*

Sahih Muslim (19:4321-4323) - Three hadith verses in which Muhammad shrugs over the news that innocent children were killed in a raid by his men against unbelievers. His response: *"They are of them* (meaning the enemy)."

Sahih Muslim (19:4294) - *"Fight against those who disbelieve in Allah. Make a holy war... When you meet your enemies who are polytheists, invite them to three courses of action. If they respond to any one of these, you also accept it and withhold yourself from doing them any harm. Invite them to (accept) Islam; if they respond to you, accept it from them and desist from fighting against them... If they refuse to accept Islam, demand from them the Jizya. If they agree to pay, accept it from them and hold off your hands. If they refuse to pay the tax, seek Allah's help and fight them."*

Sahih Muslim (31:5917) - *"Ali went a bit and then halted and did not look about and then said in a loud voice: 'Allah's Messenger, on what issue should I fight with the people?' Thereupon he (the Prophet) said: 'Fight with them until they bear testimony to the fact that there is no god but Allah and Muhammad is his Messenger'."* The pretext for attacking the peaceful farming community of Khaybar was not obvious to the Muslims. Muhammad's son-in-law Ali asked the prophet of Islam to clarify the reason for their mission to kill, loot and enslave. Muhammad's reply was straightforward. The people should be fought because they are not Muslim.

Sahih Muslim (31:5918) - *"I will fight them until they are like us."* Ali's reply to Muhammad, after receiving clarification that the pretext for attacking Khaybar was to convert the people (see above verse).

Sahih Bukhari 2:35 *"The person who participates in (Holy Battles) in Allah's cause and nothing compels him do so except belief in Allah and His Apostle, will be recompensed by Allah either with a reward, or booty (if he survives) or will be admitted to Paradise (if he is killed)."*

Sunan an-Nasa'i (Sahih) *"Whoever dies without having fought or thought of fighting, he dies on one of the branches of hypocrisy"*

Sunan Ibn Majah 24:2794 (Sahih) - *"I came to the Prophet and said: 'O Messenger of Allah, which Jihad is best?' He said: '(That of a man) whose blood is shed and his horse is wounded.'"* Unlike the oft-quoted "Greater/Lesser" verse pertaining to Jihad, this is judged to be authentic, and clearly establishes that the 'best' Jihad involves physical violence.

Tabari 7:97 *The morning after the murder of Ashraf, the Prophet declared,*

"Kill any Jew who falls under your power." Ashraf was a poet, killed by Muhammad's men because he insulted Islam. Here, Muhammad widens the scope of his orders to kill. An innocent Jewish businessman was then slain by his Muslim partner, merely for being non-Muslim.

Tabari 9:69 *"Killing Unbelievers is a small matter to us"* The words of Muhammad, prophet of Islam.

Tabari 17:187 *"'By God, our religion (din) from which we have departed is better and more correct than that which these people follow. Their religion does not stop them from shedding blood, terrifying the roads, and seizing properties.' And they returned to their former religion."* The words of a group of Christians who had converted to Islam, but realized their error after being shocked by the violence and looting committed in the name of Allah. The price of their decision to return to a religion of peace was that the men were beheaded and the woman and children enslaved by the caliph Ali.

Ibn Ishaq/Hisham 484: - *"Allah said, 'A prophet must slaughter before collecting captives. A slaughtered enemy is driven from the land. Muhammad, you craved the desires of this world, its goods and the ransom captives would bring. But Allah desires killing them to manifest the religion.'"*

Ibn Ishaq/Hisham 990: Cutting off someone's head while shouting 'Allahu Akbar' is not a 'perversion of Islam', but a tradition of Islam that began with Muhammad. In this passage, a companion recounts an episode in which he staged a surprise ambush on a settlement: *"I leapt upon him and cut off his head and ran in the direction of the camp shouting 'Allah akbar' and my two companions did likewise".*

Ibn Ishaq/Hisham 992: - *"Fight everyone in the way of Allah and kill those who disbelieve in Allah."* Muhammad's instructions to his men prior to a military raid.

Ibn Kathir (Commentary on verses 2:190-193 - *Since Jihad involves killing and shedding the blood of men, Allah indicated that these men are committing disbelief in Allah, associating with Him (in the worship) and hindering from His path, and this is a much greater evil and more disastrous than killing.* One of Islam's most respected scholars clearly believed that Jihad means physical warfare.

Saifur Rahman, The Sealed Nectar p.227-228 - *"Embrace Islam... If you two accept Islam, you will remain in command of your country; but if your refuse my Call, you've got to remember that all of your possessions are perishable. My horsemen will appropriate your land, and my Prophethood will assume preponderance over your kingship."* One of several letters from Muhammad to rulers of other countries. The significance is that the recipients were not making war or threatening Muslims. Their subsequent defeat and subjugation by Muhammad's armies was justified merely on the basis of their unbelief."
END QUOTE

These are quotes taken from the Verses of Violence on www.thereligionofpeace.com. The so called religion of peace is the one advocating the most violence of all the major worldviews. It cannot be allowed under a free and moral society.

Unbelievable after how many have suffered and died that islam hasn't been recognized as a criminal organization and banned worldwide. https://www.politicalislam.com/tears-of-jihad/ those who do evil as muslims are only obeying the evil dictates of their evil imaginary god https://www.thereligionofpeace.com/pages/quran/index.aspx so not just throughout history but to this day, islam in doctrine and practice is a criminal organization.

islam is a cult so evil it threatens to MURDER ANYONE WHO TRIES TO LEAVE IT! islam is a cult of MURDERERS! look up the apostasy death penalty nations! islam is openly a cult of MURDERERS! it cannot be allowed by the sane people of this world to be practiced! muhammad is someone so evil, muslims are forbidden to discuss it! Instead, they insist that muhammad was a white man who had black slaves and yet black Africans call themselves muslims on pain of death. muhammad was a pedophile and instead of deploring him for being such, muslims are taught to venerate him. muhammad came along 6 centuries after the well establish facts of Christ Crucified and taught people to disbelieve those facts OVER THE PROPHETS AND EYEWITNESSES who saw Christ Crucified and OVER HIS BURIAL CLOTH, the Shroud of Turin! muhammad was an overt liar and criminal who taught muslims to lie and commit crimes!

When I see muslims routinely deny facts in front of their own eyes, I think to myself save the world from islam, especially muslims! muslims are held in a cult that they can't escape from except by taking their life into their own hands. Anyone who is not a muslim faces persecution in islamic dominate regions and yet people don't understand ITS FROM THE DEVIL! muslims have been BRAINWASHED by their evil cult that badly, some of them appear that they can't tell right from wrong, good from evil, or God Almighty from the damn devil! The rest of mankind HAS GOT TO TELL MUSLIMS that they are no longer allowed to practice their wicked cult, IT IS EVIL! It is a CRIMINAL ORGANIZATION, no matter how you describe it! If muslims only knew that muhammad was a lying criminal, not anything to imitate at all!
https://www.thereligionofpeace.com/pages/articles/jesusmuhammad.aspx

Some of the evil things: acid throwers, honor killings, childhood marriages, pedophilia, slavery, murder, suicide bombings, misogyny, tortures, amputations, and more ALL LEGAL IN islam. THERE IS NO WAY WE SHOULD BE PERMITTING ANY OF THESE PEOPLE FROM ACCESSING OUR NATIONS, not until they agree to NEVER, EVER, EVER practice islam again!

SAVE THE WORLD FROM islam, ESPECIALLY MUSLIMS! Never again have children brainwashed from birth to follow the devil.

The entire Holy Bible plainly tells us Jesus Christ is the One True God, but muslims DESPERATELY try to deny Him instead. The harp on the same verses over and over as if those verses say what they imagine, rather than what they really say. John 17:3 is one of those common verses muslims use to deny Jesus Christ is God, even though that's exactly who He is and is why not one muslim knows Him.

In the minds of far too many muslims, they search the entire Holy Bible and ignore the many hundreds of times over that Jesus Christ says and proves He is God and receives worship as God to find any of His Words that they can twist the meaning of to deny Him. (that's how evil those muslims are and why God calls muslims antichrists.)

Beware of Antichrists

...21I have not written to you because you lack knowledge of the truth, but because you have it, and because no lie comes from the truth. 22Who is the liar, if it is not the one who denies that Jesus is the Christ? This is the antichrist, who denies the Father and the Son. 23Whoever denies the Son does not have the Father, but whoever confesses the Son has the Father as well.... https://biblehub.com/1_john/2-22.htm

...29My Father who has given them to Me is greater than all. No one can snatch them out of My Father's hand. 30I and the Father are one." 31At this, the Jews again picked up stones to stone Him.... https://biblehub.com/john/10-30.htm

John 14:6-9

6 Jesus said to him, "I am the way, the truth, and the life. No one comes to the Father except through Me.

The Father Revealed

7 "If you had known Me, you would have known My Father also; and from now on you know Him and have seen Him."

8 Philip said to Him, "Lord, show us the Father, and it is sufficient for us."

9 Jesus said to him, "Have I been with you so long, and yet you have not known Me, Philip? He who has seen Me has seen the Father; so how can you say, 'Show us the Father'?

So how can "the Father" be greater than "the Son" and yet also be One? and how can looking at the Son cause us to see the Father?

The same way your own invisible spirit is one with your visible body, but when you die your body returns to the dust while your spirit goes to give an account to God, JESUS CHRIST! (so, the invisible spirit is greater than the visible body even though spirit and body are one.) Has this fact sunk in yet, muslims?

So, Jesus Christ plainly stated the ENTIRE HOLY BIBLE IS ALL ABOUT HIM THE ONE WHO HAS ETERNAL LIFE AND THE ONE ALL MUST COME TO IN ORDER TO HAVE THAT LIFE.

John 5:39-40

39 You search the Scriptures because you think that in them you have eternal life; and it is they that bear witness about me, 40 yet you refuse to come to me that you may have life.

So, John 17:3 is just rephrasing all the above! God is not just "the Son" which refers to His Visible Image, but is Eternal, Invisible, Pervasive and Transcendent over all His Creation (Eph 4:6) but to see the Son is to see God! because JESUS CHRIST IS THE VISIBLE IMAGE OF THE INVISBLE GOD! Col 1:14-19 And yes, the Eternal God sent Himself into His Creation to show and declare unto us who He is!

This is Eternal Life to know YOU the ONLY TRUE GOD **AND** JESUS CHRIST whom You have sent! KNOWING GOD **AND** JESUS CHRIST = Eternal Life BECAUSE Jesus Christ is the VISIBLE IMAGE of GOD! Col 1:14-19, 1Jn 5:20, Jn 14:6-9 (muslims are always trying to separate Jesus Christ from God when that isn't possible! no more than we can separate you from yourself! (all that you are, spirit and body, living soul)) While God emptied Himself to walk among us humbly as a Man, it is only at that time does He make such statements https://biblehub.com/philippians/2-7.htm that tells us God is experiencing what it's like to be one of us, a man in a flesh and bone body. But AGAIN, you cannot deny that the entire Holy Bible plainly tells us Jesus Christ is God over not comprehending these few verses correctly. (Not understanding how the Eternal Creator can send a then temporal (flesh and bone mortal body) Image of Himself into His Creation and yet still remain also Invisible, Eternal, Pervasive and Transcendent simultaneously. Eph 4:6, 2Cor 5:19)

Unity in the Body

…**5**one Lord, one faith, one baptism; **6**one God and Father of all, who is over all and through all and in all. https://biblehub.com/ephesians/4-6.htm

Ambassadors for Christ

…**18**All this is from God, who reconciled us to Himself through Christ and gave us the ministry of reconciliation: **19** that God was reconciling the world to Himself in Christ, not counting men's trespasses against them. And He has committed to us the message of reconciliation. **20**Therefore we are ambassadors for Christ, as though God were making His appeal through us. We implore you on behalf of Christ: Be reconciled to God…. https://biblehub.com/2_corinthians/5-19.htm

The fact you (muslim who posted his wicked denial of the One True God) don't comprehend that is due to your willful denial of Him! WICKED! you must repent! and you must get baptized in His Name or you will know His Wrath! Jn 3:36; 2Th 1:8,9, Rev. 21:8 you must pray to receive His Holy

Spirit of Truth and STOP DENYING THE ONE TRUE GOD! or you will surely perish in your sins! Jn 8:24-25; Acts 4:12; Mark 16:15-16; Acts 2:38-39; Jn 14:20-26; Luke 11:13

muslims NEED to comprehend that Jesus Christ is the One who will Judge their souls! If you deny He is the One True God, you will die in your sins!

John 8:24-25

24 I told you that you would die in your sins, for unless you believe that I am he you will die in your sins." **25** So they said to him, "Who are you?" Jesus said to them, "Just what I have been telling you from the beginning.

Dying in your sins means being cast into the lake of fire!

A New Heaven and a New Earth
...**7**The one who overcomes will inherit all things, and I will be his God, and he will be My son. **8**But to the cowardly and unbelieving and abominable and murderers and sexually immoral and sorcerers and idolaters and all liars, their place will be in the lake that burns with fire and sulfur. This is the second death." https://biblehub.com/revelation/21-8.htm

If you spend your entire life, lying to yourself and everyone, DENYING the ONLY ONE who can SAVE you, you will perish in your sins!

Peter and John Before the Council
...**11**This Jesus is 'the stone you builders rejected, which has become the cornerstone.' **12** Salvation exists in no one else, for there is no other name under heaven given to men by which we must be saved."
https://biblehub.com/acts/4-12.htm

muslims, you need to realize that to those of us who know the Almighty personally, when you denigrate Him to being just another sinner like yourselves, it makes you all look like demonic scum! You are letting the devil deceive you into imagining the One who spoke and changed reality instantly just by speaking was someone as mortal as yourself, when that isn't the case! Show anyone else in the entire history of the world that claimed to be God and proved it like Jesus Christ or shut your blasphemous mouths!

In other words, yet another muslim was quoting the passage that says no man can die for another man, when the context is quite clear it is talking about guilty sinners, people already under their own Divine death penalty cannot die for anyone else because they are already sentenced to death by God! BUT GOD CAN AND DID SUFFER AND DIE TO SAVE US! So, any fool rejecting His Salvation DESERVES His Damnation!

The reason Jesus Christ is the ONLY SAVIOR (Acts 4:12) is because He is the ONLY TRUE GOD! 1 Jn 5:20 and as such is the ONLY ONE who could satisfy His Own Law of Redemption and Prophecies of Redemption and Salvation regarding the souls He Created and Made.

https://bible.knowing-jesus.com/topics/God,-As-Redeemer

So, when muslims falsely accuse Jesus Christ of being just another sinner like them, they are acting as if they want to die in their sins and burn in the flames of damnation. Jn 3:36; 8:24-25; Rev 21:8; 2Th 1:8-9

So muslims need to stop denigrating the One True God, Jesus Christ, and instead Repent and Obey Him! Mark 16:15-16; Acts 2:38-39; 4:12

Yet another muslim was smugly asking if any Christian could tell them what page Jesus Christ tells us He is God in the Holy Bible (he was acting like it can't be found). When God tells us people are spiritually blind, the evidence is due to the fact that billions still don't know Him! and apparently can read the Holy Bible and not have one clue of what the Words of God in it are actually telling us.

Jesus Christ says He is God from the very first page of the Holy Bible in Genesis to the last page in the Book of Revelation.

John 5:39-40
39 You search the Scriptures because you think that in them you have eternal life; and it is they that bear witness about me, 40 yet you refuse to come to me that you may have life.

Jesus Christ plainly states that the entire Holy Bible is about Him the One who has Eternal Life and the One everyone must come to in order to have that life.

The first verse in the Holy Bible refers to God as the Aleph-Tav (Hebrew for the Alpha and the Omega, the First and the Last):

https://biblehub.com/interlinear/genesis/1-1.htm - notice the fourth word in the original language of the Holy Bible is the Aleph-Tav

https://www.hebrew4christians.com/Grammar/Unit_One/Jesus_and_the_Aleph-Bet/jesus_and_the_aleph-bet.html - there are many commentaries that correctly identify Jesus Christ as the Aleph-Tav -

https://www.google.com/search?client=opera&q=aleph+tav+jesus%27+signature&sourceid=opera&ie=UTF-8&oe=UTF-8#ip=1

How do we know Jesus Christ is the Aleph-Tav because He says so quite plainly (and ever exists to confirm that Truth):

John 8:24-25
24 I told you that you would die in your sins, for unless you believe that I am he you will die in your sins." 25 So they said to him, "Who are you?" Jesus said to them, "Just what I have been telling you from the beginning.

Jesus Christ states that the entire Holy Bible is about Him the One who has Eternal Life and the One all must come to in order to have that life AND He states He is the One who has been telling us He is God since the Beginning! AND states that anyone who doesn't believe He is God, will die in their sins!

Jesus Appears to Thomas
...27Then Jesus said to Thomas, "Put your finger here and look at My hands. Reach out your hand and put it into My side. Stop doubting and believe." 28Thomas replied, "My Lord and my God!" 29Jesus said to him, "Because you have seen Me, you have believed; blessed are those who have not seen and yet have believed."... https://biblehub.com/john/20-28.htm

When His Disciples bowed down at His Feet and Worshiped Him saying plainly, He is Lord and God, He CONFIRMS that TRUTH!

https://www.openbible.info/topics/worshipping_jesus - Jesus Christ ALWAYS receives worship as the One True God, BECAUSE THAT IS WHO HE

IS!

Jesus is Coming
...12"Behold, I am coming soon, and My reward is with Me, to give to each one according to what he has done. 13I am the Alpha and the Omega, the First and the Last, the Beginning and the End."
https://biblehub.com/revelation/22-13.htm

So, from the first page to the last in the Holy Bible, Jesus Christ plainly tells us He is God!

A muslim was online committing blasphemy by falsely accusing Jesus Christ of being a muslim.

When you repeat a lie, it makes you a liar. When you lie about God, it makes you a blasphemer.

Jesus Christ never was and never will be a muslim. He calls muslims antichrists, His enemies because they are all wickedly denying He is the One True God. 1Jn 2:22, 1Jn 4:1-6

Furthermore, the lying, evil, darkness of islam didn't emerge on earth until over 600 years AFTER God, Jesus Christ, came in the flesh and walked through this world He Created and Made. So, anyone falsely accusing Jesus Christ of being a muslim, is lying to themselves and the entire world and is committing very grave blasphemy!

muslims you're all doing the VERY THINGS GOD HATES! looking down your noses because people don't belong to your vile cult of islam! to the point of MURDERING THOSE PEOPLE. God made everyone! Do you REALLY THINK HE WANTS YOU TO MURDER OTHERS HE'S MADE! You muslims, have ALL BEEN DECIEVED by the lying devil and his lying false prophet, muhammad!

Jesus Christ Founded Christianity

Jesus Christ clearly founded Christianity! so yes, Jesus Christ is Christian by definition.

The recorded and verified facts of history tell us in no uncertain terms Jesus Christ founded Christianity:

https://www.youtube.com/watch?v=ay_Db4RwZ_M - the New Testament was written by the Eyewitness Apostles and Disciples of Jesus Christ.

In addition, there are external sources; other historians that verify not only did Jesus Christ exist at the time indicated in the Holy Bible, but that there were indeed eyewitnesses, His Apostles and Disciples, that began Preaching the Gospel of Jesus Christ immediately following His Resurrection (Pentecost as noted in the Book of Acts): https://coldcasechristianity.com/writings/is-there-any-evidence-for-jesusoutside-the-bible/ and https://biblearchaeologyreport.com/2022/11/18/top-ten-historicalreferences-to-jesus-outside-of-the-bible/

Peter's Confession of Christ

...15"But what about you?" Jesus asked. "Who do you say I am?" 16 Simon Peter answered, "You are the Christ, the Son of the living God."17Jesus replied, "Blessed are you, Simon son of Jonah! For this was not revealed to you by flesh and blood, but by My Father in heaven. 18And I tell you that

you are Peter, and on this rock I will build My church, and the gates of Hades will not prevail against it. 19I will give you the keys of the kingdom of heaven. Whatever you bind on earth will be bound in heaven, and whatever you loose on earth will be loosed in heaven."...
https://biblehub.com/matthew/16-18.htm

Jesus and the Samaritan Woman

...25The woman said, "I know that Messiah" (called Christ) "is coming. When He comes, He will explain everything to us." 26 Jesus answered, "I who speak to you am He." https://biblehub.com/john/4-26.htm

Peter and John Before the Council

...11This Jesus is 'the stone you builders rejected, which has become the cornerstone.' 12 Salvation exists in no one else, for there is no other name under heaven given to men by which we must be saved." 13When they saw the boldness of Peter and John and realized that they were unschooled, ordinary men, they marveled and took note that these men had been with Jesus.... https://biblehub.com/acts/4-12.htm

11For no one can lay a foundation other than the one already laid, which is Jesus Christ. https://biblehub.com/1_corinthians/3-11.htm

https://www.cgg.org/index.cfm/library/verses/id/3202/jesus-christ-ascornerstone-verses.htm God laid Jesus Christ as the Chief Cornerstone of His Church.

The Ascension

...7Jesus replied, "It is not for you to know times or seasons that the Father has fixed by His own authority. 8But you will receive power when the Holy Spirit comes upon you, and you will be My witnesses in Jerusalem, and in

all Judea and Samaria, and to the ends of the earth."
https://biblehub.com/acts/1-8.htm

(So, Jesus Christ sends His Holy Spirit of Truth to testify He is the One True God and HIS SPIRIT OF CHRIST is what makes a person a Christian!)

Living in the Spirit

8Those controlled by the flesh cannot please God. 9You, however, are controlled not by the flesh, but by the Spirit, if the Spirit of God lives in you. And if anyone does not have the Spirit of Christ, he does not belong to Christ. 10But if Christ is in you, your body is dead because of sin, yet your spirit is alive because of righteousness....

...15For you did not receive a spirit of slavery that returns you to fear, but you received the Spirit of sonship, by whom we cry, "Abba! Father!" 16The Spirit Himself testifies with our spirit that we are God's children. 17And if we are children, then we are heirs: heirs of God and co-heirs with Christ— if indeed we suffer with Him, so that we may also be glorified with Him....
https://biblehub.com/romans/8-9.htm

Before Jesus Christ, no Christians; After Jesus Christ, Christians! so Jesus Christ OBVIOUSLY founded Christianity and is a Christian!

https://www.biblegateway.com/passage/?search=Acts%209&version=KJV
- Saul who was persecuting Christians was confronted for doing so by the Lord Jesus Christ Himself! (and subsequently became the Apostle Paul)

Get it through your thick, brainwashed and deceived skulls muslims! Saul was persecuting Christians! meaning Christianity existed BEFORE He became the Apostle Paul! So, our Lord Jesus Christ clearly founded

Christianity and even defended His Disciples by directly confronting the zealot Saul who was persecuting them!

...The disciples were first called Christians at Antioch. https://biblehub.com/acts/11-26.htm muslims are lying to themselves and thinking that this was an insult, even though the scriptures are rife with mentioning that Christians were called such because they preached Christ and acted like Him. https://biblescan.com/search.php?q=christian Christian is always complimentary in the Holy Bible.

Christian means "Christ-like" and no one is more like Jesus Christ than Himself! So yes, Jesus Christ is a Christian. And it is His Presence in our lives by His Holy Spirit of Truth that makes us to be like Him, a Disciple of His, a Christian!

Jesus Christ is God. He is Supreme in everything.

John 14:6-9

6 Jesus said to him, "I am the way, the truth, and the life. No one comes to the Father except through Me.

The Father Revealed

7 "If you had known Me, you would have known My Father also; and from now on you know Him and have seen Him."

8 Philip said to Him, "Lord, show us the Father, and it is sufficient for us."

9 Jesus said to him, "Have I been with you so long, and yet you have not known Me, Philip? He who has seen Me has seen the Father; so how can you say, 'Show us the Father'?
Jesus Christ plainly said whoever has seen Him has seen the Father. (Jesus Christ is Visible Image of the Father.)

Colossians 1:15-19

The Supremacy of the Son of God

15 The Son is the image of the invisible God, the firstborn over all creation. 16 For in him all things were created: things in heaven and on earth, visible and invisible, whether thrones or powers or rulers or authorities; all things have been created through him and for him. 17 He is before all things, and in him all things hold together. 18 And he is the head of the body, the church; he is the beginning and the firstborn from among the dead, so that in everything he might have the supremacy. 19 For God was pleased to have all his fullness dwell in him,

This passage means that Jesus Christ is the: God of gods, Man of men, Spirit of spirits, Angel of angels, King of kings, Lord of lords, Father of fathers, Son of sons, Servant of servants, First and Last, Beginning and End, etc. etc. which is why the scriptures refer to Him in all these ways and more.

JESUS CHRIST, THE ONE TRUE GOD, IS SUPREME IN EVERYTHING!

another muslim today was lying to himself and the world with a story about a father and son and why didn't the father save his son, as their lame effort in denigrating Jesus Christ and wrongly imagining God will just wave away their sins, when they neglect the Savior and His Loving Act of Redemption on the Cross for them. So I replied and this reply is to everyone wrongly thinking their own beliefs will somehow trump God's Word, God's Will and God's Judgment!
God Himself came in the flesh as the Messiah. "Son of God" means "visible image of God" Jn 14:6-9; Col 1:14-19

John 14:6-9

6 Jesus said to him, "I am the way, the truth, and the life. No one comes to the Father except through Me.

The Father Revealed
7 "If you had known Me, you would have known My Father also; and from now on you know Him and have seen Him."

8 Philip said to Him, "Lord, show us the Father, and it is sufficient for us."

9 Jesus said to him, "Have I been with you so long, and yet you have not known Me, Philip? He who has seen Me has seen the Father; so how can you say, 'Show us the Father'?

Colossians 1:15-19
The Supremacy of the Son of God
15 The Son is the image of the invisible God, the firstborn over all creation. 16 For in him all things were created: things in heaven and on earth, visible and invisible, whether thrones or powers or rulers or authorities; all things have been created through him and for him. 17 He is before all things, and in him all things hold together. 18 And he is the head of the body, the church; he is the beginning and the firstborn from among the dead, so that in everything he might have the supremacy. 19 For God was pleased to have all his fullness dwell in him,

So, God Himself is our Redeemer and Savior; His Name in English is Jesus Christ. God came in the flesh to fulfill His Own Law and Prophecies; including His Law of Redemption and Salvation. (Matt 5:17-18; Jn 5:39-40) God's Law had already sentenced us all to death, only God Himself, the Holy One, was worthy to Redeem ALL mankind! (no one else) and that's what He did, He came and fulfilled His Own Law and Prophecies to Save us. So no, God doesn't wipe away sin, just because you wish Him to. (He doesn't violate His Own Words, His Own Law and Prophecies.) He did it with His Own Holy Blood and is why He said if you or anyone doesn't believe Him, you will die in your sins. (In other words, it's what GOD, JESUS CHRIST, says; NOT YOU or anyone else!) God, Jesus Christ, is the Judge of all souls, NOT YOU or anyone else! so NO! God doesn't just wave away your sins or anyone else's, HE PAID THE PRICE IN FULL! and if you or anyone isn't grateful to Him for doing so YOU WILL DIE IN YOUR SINS! Acts 4:12; 10:34-43 SALVATION in NO ONE ELSE BUT JESUS CHRIST! Forgiveness of sins in no other Name under Heaven than our LORD JESUS CHRIST! (English language for God Almighty, but whatever His Name is in your language of the Holy Bible; THE BIBLICAL GOD WHO CAME IN THE FLESH AND REDEEMED US is THE ONE TRUE GOD! Our Eternal Creator understands all languages, He knows the thoughts and intents of the heart for everyone, past, present and future)

https://bible.knowing-jesus.com/topics/God,-As-Redeemer

https://www.preceptaustin.org/tetelestai-paid_in_full

John 8:24-25
24 I told you that you would die in your sins, for unless you believe that I am he you will die in your sins." 25 So they said to him, "Who are you?" Jesus said to them, "Just what I have been telling you from the beginning.

So, stop blaspheming GOD! and stop IGNORING WHAT HE DID TO SAVE YOU!

A New Heaven and a New Earth
...7The one who overcomes will inherit all things, and I will be his God, and he will be My son. 8But to the cowardly and unbelieving and abominable and murderers and sexually immoral and sorcerers and idolaters and all liars, their place will be in the lake that burns with fire and sulfur. This is the second death." https://biblehub.com/revelation/21-8.htm

12But to all who did receive Him, to those who believed in His name, He gave the right to become children of God— 13children born not of blood, nor of the desire or will of man, but born of God....
https://biblehub.com/john/1-12.htm

The Great Commission
...15And He said to them, "Go into all the world and preach the gospel to every creature. 16Whoever believes and is baptized will be saved, but whoever does not believe will be condemned.
https://biblehub.com/mark/16-16.htm

37When the people heard this, they were cut to the heart and asked Peter and the other apostles, "Brothers, what shall we do?" 38 Peter replied, "Repent and be baptized, every one of you, in the name of Jesus Christ for the forgiveness of your sins, and you will receive the gift of the Holy Spirit. 39This promise belongs to you and your children and to all who are far off—to all whom the Lord our God will call to Himself."...
https://biblehub.com/acts/2-38.htm

Peter and John Before the Council
...11This Jesus is 'the stone you builders rejected, which has become the cornerstone.' 12 Salvation exists in no one else, for there is no other name under heaven given to men by which we must be saved."
https://biblehub.com/acts/4-12.htm

EVERYONE MUST RECOGNIZE THAT JESUS CHRIST IS THE ONE TRUE GOD AND THAT HE HAD ALREADY SENTENCED US ALL TO DEATH BECAUSE WE HAD ALL BROKEN HIS LAW, HIS COMMANDMENTS! THE ONLY WAY GOD COULD SAVE US IS BY FULFILLING HIS OWN LAW OF REDEMPTION! SO HE CAME IN THE FLESH AND REDEEMED US! WE ARE ALL NOT ONLY CREATED AND MADE BY HIM, BUT BOUGHT WITH THE PRICE OF HIS OWN HOLY BLOOD SHED FOR US! (and STOP THINKING why did God do this and why did God do that and Just REALIZE GOD DOESN'T LIE so the moment He said the soul that sins shall die, is the moment that's the way it is)! HE IS HOLY! NO SIN ALLOWED! NONE! so sinful mankind had died to Him, became separated from Him, and He came in the flesh and REDEEMED US ACCORDING TO HIS OWN LAW OF REDEMPTION AND HIS OWN PROPHECIES IN THAT REGARD! SO, THERE IS ABSOLUTELY NO FORGIVENESS OF SINS ANY OTHER WAY THAN THE WAY THE ONE TRUE GOD MADE! It's not your imagination! it's not your personal beliefs! IT'S THE WAY GOD MADE OR YOU ARE GOING TO DIE IN YOUR SINS AND BE CAST INTO THE LAKE OF FIRE! NO IFS, ANDS OR BUTS!

So, if everyone doesn't get with the Divine Program, so to speak, you're not going to like what happens to you for wickedly rebelling against Him and imagining you know better than the Almighty. OBEY GOD AND STOP ARGUING! You all need to seriously imagine a pit of hellish flames and smoke right next to you that you're about to be thrown into for refusing to obey the Living God and repent of your wicked ways, including thinking you know better than Him! It's Heaven with Jesus Christ or the flames of damnation without Him. OBEY HIM and stop arguing or acting like it's a difficult decision! I guarantee if you're one of the sadly far too many fools that will indeed be cast into the lake of fire, YOU'RE GOING TO WISH YOU HAD THE GOOD SENSE TO JUST SAY, YES, LORD! and REPENT and Get Baptized in His Name and DO IT NOW! Pray to receive His Holy Spirit of Truth! NOW! Don't procrastinate! you could die at any moment! don't put it off!

I encounter wicked, ignorant, deceived and self-deluded unbelievers laughing at these statements and if they don't come to their senses, they sure won't be when the find out the lake of fire is very real and God means what He says! In a dream or vision from God I saw part of the Judgment and people were wailing because they knew they had been told the plain truth over and over and over again and yet always just laughed at it or ignored it! TAKE GOD SERIOUSLY! TAKE WHAT HE TELLS US IN THE HOLY BIBLE VERY SERIOUSLY! Or you won't like where you end up, when He Judges you by His Words, just like He tells us.

Belief and Unbelief

...**47**As for anyone who hears My words and does not keep them, I do not judge him. For I have not come to judge the world, but to save the world. **48**There is a judge for the one who rejects Me and does not receive My words: The word that I have spoken will judge him on the last day. **49**I have not spoken on My own, but the Father who sent Me has commanded Me what to say and how to say it. **50**And I know that His command leads to eternal life. So I speak exactly what the Father has told Me to say." https://biblehub.com/john/12-48.htm

The Father and the Son

...**21**For just as the Father raises the dead and gives them life, so also the Son gives life to whom He wishes. **22**Furthermore, the Father judges no one, but has assigned all judgment to the Son, **23**so that all may honor the Son just as they honor the Father. Whoever does not honor the Son does not honor the Father who sent Him.... https://biblehub.com/john/5-22.htm

So, God came in the flesh to show Himself to us and tell us quite plainly that He came to Save us BUT ANYONE who rejects Him and His Words will be Judged by Him in the end! He will pour out His Wrath upon all unrepentant, wicked persons!

2 Thessalonians 1:8-9

8
   In flaming fire taking vengeance on them that know not God, and that obey not the gospel of our Lord Jesus Christ:

9
   Who shall be punished with everlasting destruction from the presence of the Lord, and from the glory of his power;

The Final Judgment

...**14**Then Death and Hades were thrown into the lake of fire. This is the second death—the lake of fire. **15**And if anyone was found whose name

was not written in the Book of Life, he was thrown into the lake of fire.
https://biblehub.com/revelation/20-15.htm

so muslims and all unbelievers wickedly refusing to obey God and His Commandments in the Holy Bible are headed for suffering! DON'T be so foolish as to ignore God and His Words in the Holy Bible!

Satan Cast into the Lake of Fire
...**9**And they marched across the broad expanse of the earth and surrounded the camp of the saints and the beloved city. But fire came down from heaven and consumed them. **10**And the devil who had deceived them was thrown into the lake of fire and sulfur, into which the beast and the false prophet had already been thrown. There they will be tormented day and night forever and ever. **11**Then I saw a great white throne and the One seated on it. Earth and heaven fled from His presence, and no place was found for them.... https://biblehub.com/revelation/20-10.htm

PEOPLE EVERYWHERE! GOD HAS MADE IT VERY CLEAR HE OFFERS ALL THOSE WHO WILL LEARN TO LOVE HIM AND EACH OTHER LIFE EVERLASTING IN HEAVEN/PARADISE WITH HIM BUT ALL WHO REFUSE TO REPENT AND REMAIN WICKED IN THEIR SINS WILL BE CAST INTO THE LAKE OF FIRE WITH THE DEVIL!

If you need further evidence of the evil of islam and the quran, then just read https://www.blastthetrumpet.org/PublicLetters/AAAUpdatedPublicAlertsMattersofLifeandDeath/MoreUpdates041215/Holy%20Bible%20versus%20the%20quran.pdf and the many citations in it.

Heaven and everything good, or cast away into the flames of damnation and everything evil! PEOPLE! STOP ACTING LIKE THIS IS A DIFFICULT

DECISION! OBEY GOD! REPENT AND GET BAPTIZED IN THE NAME OF JESUS CHRIST AND PRAY TO RECEIVE HIS HOLY SPIRIT OF TRUTH! DO IT RIGHT NOW IF YOU HAVE NEVER DONE IT YET!

Then study the Words of God in the Holy Bible and apply them to your living every day! Ask God to make you to be good like He is! Trust in Him no matter what to perfect you! GOD WILL KEEP HIS PROMISES TO US! HE DOESN'T LIE!

Some might look at all the martyrs down through history and ask themselves why did God allow His Own Sons and Daughters to be so maltreated? For a long time, I struggled with the book of Job but there is the answer. God has every right to test and try those He Created and Made to determine who will spend Eternity with Him! He suffered and died for us, is it too much of Him to ask us to follow Him not only when things are good, but when things are not? Is it too much for God to expect us to love Him in life and in death? FOLLOW JESUS CHRIST, HE ASCENDED INTO HEAVEN PROVING HE IS THE WAY THERE! Acts 1:8-11 do NOT follow those who end up in the lake of fire for wickedly denying Him and for refusing to obey His Righteous Commandments to Love Him and each other in the Holy Bible.

Some might imagine that I'm somehow hating on muslims and unbelievers to tell them that presently by denying Christ as the One True God that He is, they are wicked antichrists, but if I really hated unbelievers I wouldn't tell them the Truth, I would just let them all die in their sins and find out the very hard way that they should have accepted Jesus Christ and His Offer of Salvation and Forgiveness of their sins while He still gave them life and breath to do so. So, TELLING YOU ALL THE TRUTH is my way of loving you; praying and hoping you DO NOT END UP IN THE LAKE OF FIRE BUT INSTEAD SMILE FOREVER IN HEAVEN! OBEY GOD! OBEY JESUS CHRIST AND HIS COMMANDMENTS IN THE HOLY BIBLE!

muslims, I know this book is hard on your cult but it needs to be! you must realize islam is not from GOD, it's from the devil and leave it! or you will die in your sins just as our Lord Jesus Christ says. I'm loving you to tell you this truth. YOU MUST OBEY GOD, JESUS CHRIST, AND REPENT AND GET BAPTIZED IN HIS NAME!

See islam is of the devil and has created the greatest number of murderous terrorist organizations on earth https://www.google.com/search?client=opera&q=list+of+islamic+terrorist+groups&sourceid=opera&ie=UTF-8&oe=UTF-8 But Christianity has created the largest number of humanitarian charities in the history of the world, proving it comes from the GOOD LORD, JESUS CHRIST!

That is due to the fact that the One True God who gave us commandments like:

The Ten Commandments

20 And God spoke all these words, saying,

2 "I am the Lord your God, who brought you out of the land of Egypt, out of the house of slavery.

3 "You shall have no other gods before [a] me.

4 "You shall not make for yourself a carved image, or any likeness of anything that is in heaven above, or that is in the earth beneath, or that is in the water under the earth. **5** You shall not bow down to them or serve them, for I the Lord your God am a jealous God, visiting the iniquity of the fathers on the children to the third and the fourth generation of those who hate me, **6** but showing steadfast love to thousands[b] of those who love me and keep my commandments.

7 "You shall not take the name of the Lord your God in vain, for the Lord will not hold him guiltless who takes his name in vain.

8 **9**

"Remember the Sabbath day, to keep it holy. Six days you shall labor, and do all your work, **10** but the seventh day is a Sabbath to the Lord your God. On it you shall not do any work, you, or your son, or your daughter, your male servant, or your female servant, or your livestock, or the sojourner who is within your gates. **11** For in six days the Lord made heaven and earth, the sea, and all that is in them, and rested on the seventh day. Therefore, the Lord blessed the Sabbath day and made it holy.

12
"Honor your father and your mother, that your days may be long in the land that the Lord your God is giving you.

13 [c]
"You shall not murder.

14
"You shall not commit adultery.

15
"You shall not steal.

16
"You shall not bear false witness against your neighbor.

17
"You shall not covet your neighbor's house; you shall not covet your neighbor's wife, or his male servant, or his female servant, or his ox, or his donkey, or anything that is your neighbor's."

Told us that all these sins begin in our thoughts and to not even think on them!

Adultery

27You have heard that it was said, 'Do not commit adultery.' **28**But I tell you that anyone who looks at a woman to lust after her has already committed adultery with her in his heart. **29**If your right eye causes you to sin, gouge it out and throw it away. It is better for you to lose one part of your body than for your whole body to be thrown into hell....
https://biblehub.com/matthew/5-28.htm

Murder Begins in the Heart Matthew 5

21   [d]

"You have heard that it was said to those of old, 'You shall not murder, and whoever murders will be in danger of the judgment.' ²² But I say to you that whoever is angry with his brother [e]without a cause shall be in danger of the judgment. And whoever says to his brother, 'Raca!'[f] shall be in danger of the council. But whoever says, [g]'You fool!' shall be in danger of [h]hell fire. ²³ Therefore if you bring your gift to the altar, and there remember that your brother has something against you, ²⁴ leave your gift there before the altar, and go your way. First be reconciled to your brother, and then come and offer your gift.

Love One Another
...**14**We know that we have passed from death to life, because we love our brothers. The one who does not love remains in death. **15**Everyone who hates his brother is a murderer, and you know that eternal life does not reside in a murderer. **16**By this we know what love is: Jesus laid down His life for us, and we ought to lay down our lives for our brothers. **17**If anyone with earthly possessions sees his brother in need, but withholds his compassion from him, how can the love of God abide in him?...
https://biblehub.com/1_john/3-15.htm

So, in islam the devil tasks muslims with doing wickedly all while imagining they are doing righteously. And so muslims learn to despise non-muslims calling them names like kafir or infidel. But with Christianity we all realize we are all sinners and that we NEED GOD, JESUS CHRIST, to come into our lives and purify our hearts and minds. So, when we desire to be righteous and holy and turn from all wickedness and sins, then He comes into our lives by His Holy Spirit and begins transforming us so that we really do LOVE Him and others and learn to live righteously. This is why the commandment is TO REPENT of thinking you know better than God and of thinking you can perfect yourself! LEARN TO TRUST IN GOD, JESUS CHRIST, to perfect you!

islam is resistant to the One True God in that in all my conversations with muslims, they chiefly DENY JESUS CHRIST and His Divinity! and replace him with the evil, allah instead. Serving the devil, not realizing it perhaps, maybe some of them do. They just can't seem to grasp that GOD SHOWED HIMSELF so we all CAN KNOW HIM!

Ambassadors for Christ

...**18**All this is from God, who reconciled us to Himself through Christ and gave us the ministry of reconciliation: **19** that God was reconciling the world to Himself in Christ, not counting men's trespasses against them. And He has committed to us the message of reconciliation. **20**Therefore we are ambassadors for Christ, as though God were making His appeal through us. We implore you on behalf of Christ: Be reconciled to God....
https://biblehub.com/2_corinthians/5-19.htm

Read this in all the versions - GOD, WAS IN CHRIST, RECONCILING THE WORLD UNTO HIMSELF!

https://biblehub.com/kjv/2_corinthians/5-19.htm

God is still reconciling the world to Himself. He does it by saving someone who then spends the rest of their life trying to encourage others to repent and receive Him. Some who are not great orators or writers, still make the effort because God in them motivates them so strongly. This book may seem harsh, but its due to very real LOVE for God and everyone, even muslims! To recognize JESUS CHRIST and obey Him to their Salvation! Learn to LOVE GOD and each other!

I PRAY GOD, JESUS CHRIST, GIVES US ALL TRUE REPENTANCE FROM EVERY WICKED WAY! AMEN! He is the ONLY ONE who can SAVE US! (Acts 4:12)

The Great Commission

...**15**And He said to them, "Go into all the world and preach the gospel to every creature. **16**Whoever believes and is baptized will be saved, but whoever does not believe will be condemned.
https://biblehub.com/mark/16-16.htm

Matthew 28:18-20

18
And Jesus came and said to them, "All authority in heaven and on earth has been given to me. **19** Go therefore and make disciples of all nations, baptizing them in the name of the Father and of the Son and of the Holy Spirit, **20** teaching them to observe all that I have commanded you. And behold, I am with you always, to the end of the age."

37 When the people heard this, they were cut to the heart and asked Peter and the other apostles, "Brothers, what shall we do?" **38** Peter replied, "Repent and be baptized, every one of you, in the name of Jesus Christ for the forgiveness of your sins, and you will receive the gift of the Holy Spirit. **39** This promise belongs to you and your children and to all who are far off—to all whom the Lord our God will call to Himself."...
https://biblehub.com/acts/2-38.htm

Matthew 22:36-40
English Standard Version
36 "Teacher, which is the great commandment in the Law?" **37** And he said to him, "You shall love the Lord your God with all your heart and with all your soul and with all your mind. **38** This is the great and first commandment. **39** And a second is like it: You shall love your neighbor as yourself. **40** On these two commandments depend all the Law and the Prophets."

So, everything in the Holy Bible is about LOVING OUR ETERNAL CREATOR AND EACH OTHER! I have to ask myself, why would anyone object to that? That's simply the TRUTH; the only way to live peacefully together with each other, is for us to obey Our Eternal Creator's Commandments! LOVE HIM AND EACH OTHER!

Peace to all who Love and Obey God, Jesus Christ; His Wrath is upon all who refuse. Jn 3:36

Copyright 2024

www.ingramcontent.com/pod-product-compliance
Lightning Source LLC
Chambersburg PA
CBHW060102170426
43198CB00010B/736